Developing User Interfaces

Ensuring Usability Through Product & Process

DEBORAH HIX

H. REX HARTSON

John Wiley & Sons, Inc.

New York • Chichester • Brisbane • Toronto • Singapore

Permission to reprint the excerpts from the *OST/Motif® Style Guide, Revision1.0*
appearing in this book has been granted by Open Software Foundation, Inc.

In recognition of the importance of preserving what has been written, it is a policy of
John Wiley & Sons, Inc., to have books of enduring value published in the United
States printed on acid-free paper, and we exert our best efforts to that end.

Designations used by companies to distinguish their products are often claimed as
trademarks. In all instances where John Wiley & Sons, Inc., is aware of a claim, the
product names appear in initial capital or all capital letters. Readers, however,
should contact the appropriate companies for more complete information regarding
trademarks and registration.

This publication is designed to provide accurate and authoritative information in
regard to the subject matter covered. It is sold with the understanding that the
publisher is not engaged in rendering legal, accounting, or other professional
service. If legal advice or other expert assistance is required, the services of a
competent professional person should be sought. FROM A DECLARATION OF
PRINCIPLES JOINTLY ADOPTED BY A COMMITTEE OF THE AMERICAN BAR
ASSOCIATION AND A COMMITTEE OF PUBLISHERS.

Hix Deborah, 1950–
    Developing user interfaces : ensuring usability through product &
process / Deborah Hix, H. Rex Hartson.
        p.   cm.
    Includes bibliographical references and indexes.
    ISBN 0-471-57813-4
    1. User interfaces (Computer systems)   2. Computer software—
Development.   I. Hartson, H. Rex.   II. Title.
QA76.9.U83H59   1993
005.1'2—dc20   92-37685
                                                               CIP

Printed in the United States of America, Inc.
    10 9

 # Dedication

We dedicate this book fondly to Robert C. and Beverly H. Williges. Bob and Bev have been loving friends, dedicated colleagues, accomplished human factors and HCI researchers, and—most of all—courageous examples few could match in living with a positive attitude.

Foreword

This is a book whose time has come. Indeed, it is a book that is overdue. Why is that?

Usability of interactive computer systems is at the very core of the computer, communications, and information revolution, which is moving our society into the post-industrial era.

The means of production is less and less the sweat of our brow, or the leveraging of our muscle power with steam or water or electric power, or mindless repetition of work on the assembly line. Rather, the means of production increasingly is the leveraging of our intellectual power with computers.

This on-going revolution has two important technological directions, each representing an important and exciting frontier.

The first frontier, the *struggle for affordable hardware*, is well underway. Today's $1000 home computer exceeds the power of last decade's $100,000 computer. Future portable personal organizers, costing several hundred dollars, will nevertheless be even more powerful in order to recognize our speech and handwriting. By the year 2000, if not before, we'll be carrying wallet-size computers running at many hundreds of MIPS, rather than at today's tens of MIPS. Our home computers will be integrated with our HDTV sets, will run one GIPS or more, and will have perhaps a hundred megabytes of memory.

The second frontier, which to me represents the greater challenge, is at the core of what this book is all about: the challenge of *creating usable interactive systems* that provide effective communications with their users, so that the power of computers can be available to every person for meaningful and enjoyable use in their work lives, in their play lives, and in their home lives. This frontier is at the very heart of the new revolution, and is the frontier on which the revolution will continue to progress, or will falter and fail.

Why is this user-computer interface frontier the greater challenge? Well, hardware *is* successfully mass-produced, and we understand the physical laws that govern chip density, speed, and power dissipation. Every 15 months or so, price/ performance doubles.

Now look at the user interface. We don't yet have a comprehensive set of psychological laws that allow us to predict human performance, and we certainly don't double user productivity every 15 months! We can't quickly produce new user interface designs, and doing so involves much trial and error. Hence we are on much shakier ground. While important research is underway, the ground will not quickly stabilize. Yet for the promise and potential of computers to be realized, we must continue to make them more and more usable.

Our victory with today's "user friendly" interfaces is only a partial victory. Things are better than they used to be, but they are still pretty bad. The problem is that it is easy to take on the hostage syndrome, in which we begin to identify with those who imprison us, and look at things from their perspective. The complication is that in this case we who are computer scientists are both the hostages and the prison keepers. We're our own worst enemies, because we know the technology, have come to accept things as they are, and often allow ourselves to be limited by that knowledge.

The National Research Council's Computer Science and Telecommunications Board, in their recent report, Computing the Future (Hartmanis & Lin, 1992) says "New computing technology will have to be fitted to customer needs more precisely, thus placing a premium on knowledge of the customer's application." There are many reasons for this. First and foremost, it is the role of computers to serve people, not vice versa. The saying, "we must adapt the computer to the user, not the user to the computer" is as true now as ever.

Additionally, for the computer industry to continue to grow, more and more computers have to be sold (unit costs and profit margins are decreasing, so volume has to increase). And the computer industry *will* continue to grow. The only question is which of the current or emerging economic powers will most benefit from this growth. Thus national competitiveness becomes an essential part of the argument: Countries that want to maximize their opportunities for economic growth driven by the computer *must* consider usability as a key element of their strategy.

Is there a way out? The key is to focus on our users, something Hansen (1971) told us to do more than 20 years ago, when he said "Know thy User." Despite this entreaty and the work of many user interface researchers, it took computer science a good 15 years more to begin embracing the notion that user interface design is a legitimate part of an undergraduate computer science education! It was not until the late eighties that the ACM/IEEE Computer Science curriculum recommendations included user interface design (Denning et al., 1989). Now, fortunately, we see more undergraduate and graduate curriculum development, as evidenced by the recent ACM SIGCHI's Curricula for Human-Computer Interaction (Hewett, 1992).

What we do have presently, and what we know works, is a process called *design for usability*, which has in fact been practiced by most of today's successful purveyors of interactive computer software, originally Apple and their cadre of software vendors, and later Microsoft Corporation. It is this *process* on which this book focuses.

This book is an important milestone in our progress toward embracing user-centered design. A number of fine books on user interface design have been written by our colleagues, but they typically treat the process of user-centered design in a chapter or two, making it secondary to dialogue styles, interaction devices and technologies, psychological issues and models, screen design issues, and help strategies. This is one of the first books to emphasize *process*, and it fits brief discussions of the other issues into the process framework. Similarly, it is one of the first books to elaborate on the important theme that user interface development must be an integral part of the overall software engineering process, not an add-on or afterthought. This is a theme with which I particularly resonate, as it is a key motivation for much of our User Interface Design Environment research project.

It is for these reasons that this book is particularly appropriate for practitioners involved in developing interactive computer systems. Most of these practitioners are working in an environment structured by a well-developed software engineering process. But rarely is there a complementary well-developed user interface development process. The appropriate user interface development process is critical to ensuring usability in interactive systems, but is still poorly understood by many and actually used by even fewer practitioners. This book details a pragmatic approach to the interface development process in a way that is immediately useful to practitioners struggling to produce usable interfaces. It is a cohesive collection of practical techniques, advice, and hints on establishing an effective and efficient user interface development process in a real world development environment.

It is also for these reasons that I will be using this book in our own second-level graduate computer science course on the user interface development process. In this course, our students actually perform usability testing in our Center's usability lab. I want each of our student to have what I think of as a religious conversion experience, of watching helplessly through a half-silvered mirror as a perfectly competent user falters in doing something really simple with the student's carefully-designed user interface. This experience is the one sure way I know of convincing students that designing for usability is different than designing for themselves!

Thank you, Debby and Rex, for giving your colleagues this innovative and useful book.

Dr. James D. Foley
Director of the Graphics, Visualization & Usability Center
Georgia Tech
Atlanta, Georgia

Computing the Future: A Broader Agenda for Computer Science and Engineering. Hartmanis, J., and H. Lin, eds. National Academy Press, Washington, D.C., 1992.

Denning, P. J., D.E. Comer, D. Gries, M. C. Mulder, A. Tucker, A. J. Turner, & P. R.Young. Computing as a Discipline. *Communications of the ACM, 32,* 1, pp. 9–23.

Hansen, W. User Engineering Principles for Interactive Systems. *Proceedings 1971 Fall Joint Computer Conference,* AFIPS Press, Montvale, NJ, 1971, pp. 523–532.

Hewett, T., R. Baecker, S. Card, T. Carey, J. Gasen, M. Mantei, G. Perlman, G. Strong, & W. Verplank. *ACM SIGCHI Curricula for Human-Computer Interaction.* ACM, New York, NY 1992.

Contents

 Introduction

WHAT IS THIS BOOK ABOUT?

People who develop user interfaces don't intentionally set out to produce poor ones. However, as anyone who has ever used an interactive computer system knows, many interfaces are very hard to use. *Ensuring Usability* in an interface requires attention to two main components:

- The product
- The process by which the product is developed

The *product* in this case is the user interface itself: its content, plus the human factors issues, design guidelines, and interaction styles represented in the content. Many people think that knowing the guidelines or having a style guide is all that is needed to ensure a usable interface. Unfortunately, this is not the case.

Equally important, but generally less well-understood, is the *process*, which involves the life cycle, methods, techniques, and tools that are used in developing a user interface. A poor understanding of the user interface development process accounts for many of the usability problems found in interactive systems.

This book presents state-of-the-art material on both of these topics—user interface product and process—in a single volume, with a very practical orientation. Each major topic related to process contains exercises that let you apply the material just presented, with sample solutions for each, to help you track your progress and understanding. The exercises are carefully designed to help you learn to use the concepts, ideas, methods, and techniques immediately in your user interface development environment, thereby ensuring interface usability.

WHO SHOULD READ THIS BOOK?

Anyone who is involved in the development of user interfaces, or who wishes to learn more about their developments, will benefit from this book. It is appropriate for a very broad audience, including all kinds of *practitioners*—user interface designers, graphics designers, user interface evaluators, software engineers, programmers, systems analysts, software quality-assurance specialists, human factors engineers, cognitive psychologists, trainers, technical writers, documentation specialists, marketing personnel, and managers. Practitioners in any of these areas will find the hands-on approach of this book to be valuable. *Researchers* in human-computer interaction will also find useful information about the current state of user interfaces and their development.

This book is also appropriate for a college course at the senior or master's level. As such, it is useful to *teachers* and to *students* of user interface development. The exercises lend themselves especially well to classroom adaptation for an ongoing, semester-long project to design, prototype, and evaluate a user interface.

WHY IS THIS BOOK DIFFERENT?

This book provides "one-stop shopping" for user interface development information, by including both *product* and *process* in one volume. It addresses product in less detail and process in more detail. Because so many other sources exist for information on the *product* (content and human factors), this book presents all extraction of the most important aspects of user interface content and human factors. Material was chosen for inclusion based on commonality among the numerous existing sources and on our years of experience in the field. Various parts of the development *process* are also discussed in many different publications—books, journals, and conference proceedings—but no other source has brought them together into a cohesive methodology that is being used successfully in the real world for the process of user interface development.

WHAT ARE THE OBJECTIVES OF THIS BOOK?

Our goal for this book is simple: *to have readers learn how to develop an interface with high usability.* Toward this end, this book presents how to

- Write a customized style guide and apply human factors guidelines to your interface designs (Chapter 2)
- Understand and know when to use currently available interaction styles in your interface designs (Chapter 3)

- Understand and apply the concept of an iterative life cycle for user interface development (Chapter 4)
- Use systems analysis, conceptual design, and scenario design in early interface development activities (Chapter 5)
- Use behavioral, user-centered representation techniques for capturing your interface designs (Chapters 6 and 7)
- Establish usability specifications to measure quantitatively the usability of your interfaces (Chapter 8)
- Build effective rapid prototypes of your user interface designs (Chapter 9)
- Carry out formative evaluation as your interface evolves and perform cost/benefit analyses to determine which changes to the interface will have the biggest effect on its usability (Chapter 10)
- Develop a general understanding of user interface development tools and of a quantitative method to evaluate them (Chapter 11)
- Apply this material in your own user interface development environment (Chapter 12)

A good user interface is like a phone or an electric light; when it works, nobody notices it. A good user interface seems obvious, but what is not obvious is how to develop an interface so that it has high usability. Thus, our objectives address both what constitutes a usable product and the process by which usability of that product is ensured.

WHAT ARE THE ORGANIZATION AND CONTENT OF THIS BOOK?

Introduction and Part I: The Product

Following this introduction to the content of this book, Chapter 1 introduces the key concepts and terminology of the book. It establishes the need for a behavioral approach and appropriate supporting roles for user interface development, in order to ensure usability. The *product* is described in Part I, which consists of Chapters 2 and 3. Specifically, Chapter 2 discusses the differences among design guidelines, standards, commercial style guides, and customized style guides, and it explains why and how to write a style guide for your own organization or product. It also presents some well-established design guidelines, organized around basic principles such as consistency and user-centered design.

This moves quite naturally to a discussion of some specific interaction styles, such as windows, menus, form filling, graphical and direct manipulation interfaces, and some guidelines for their use, in Chapter 3. Chapters 2 and 3 include *representative*, rather than exhaustive, information, because the product is discussed in great detail in many other books, journal articles, style guides, and conference proceedings.

Part II: The Process

The *process is* described in Part II, the remainder of the book. Here, the coverage and explanation are more thorough than in Part I because no other single source addresses all activities of the user interface development process in a cohesive, integrated manner. Specifically, in Chapter 4, an iterative, evaluation-centered life cycle provides the setting for discussing interface development activities. This discussion raises the management issue of controlling the seemingly endless iterative development process, a problem that is answered in later chapters. Early development life cycle activities are the subject of Chapter 5, which presents an overview of systems (i.e., goals, needs, user, and task) analysis and design.

Chapter 6 introduces techniques for representing—writing down—user interface designs and focuses on a user-task-oriented behavioral approach called the User Action Notation. Chapter 7 continues as a practical how-to-use-it guide for the User Action Notation. The pivotal topic of measurable usability specifications is addressed in Chapter 8, which describes setting metrics for usability. Chapter 9 shows how rapid prototyping fits into the life cycle, supporting early interface evaluation, before the system itself has been completely constructed. The real payoff follows in Chapter 10, which presents formative evaluation—usability testing with users—as a key part of the development process. It also gives some pointers on how to set up your own usability lab when resources such as time, money, or personnel are scarce.

Chapter 11 describes user interface development tools in general and provides a quantitative method for selecting a tool that is best for your specific user interface development environment. It is not an objective of this book to report the latest in human-computer interaction research, or to disseminate up-to-the-minute but unproven techniques and technology. Despite the fast pace of changes in the user interface field, we want this book to remain relatively stable, offering information and techniques with longer-term value to the practitioner—techniques that won't be out-of-date in a year or two. As a result, a survey of types of user interface development tools, rather than an in-depth presentation, is presented here.

Good things, like months in the year and brownies from the bakery, come in dozens, and this book happens to have a dozen chapters. Chapter 12 wraps up by sharing some ideas about the practical matters of making the techniques in this book work in real-world user interface development environments. This is important because of such pragmatic realities as limited budgets and personnel, project schedules, and management.

To summarize, the chapters and their topics are as follows:

Chapter	Topic
1	Introduction, including definitions and roles
2	Style guides and interface design guidelines
3	Interaction styles
4	An iterative, evaluation-centered life cycle for user interface development
5	Systems analysis and design
6	Behavioral representation techniques for user interfaces, including the User Action Notation
7	More on the User Action Notation
8	Quantifiable usability specifications
9	Rapid prototyping
10	Formative evaluation and usability testing
11	Tools for user interface development
12	How to make this all work in your world

HOW DO YOU USE THE EXERCISES?

Don't Ignore Them

A Calendar Management System provides a running user interface development example for the application of material throughout the book. Indeed, the book is somewhat like a workbook in its use of *hands-on exercises* based on the Calendar Management System. Because this book is intended to convey practical techniques, this learning-by-doing approach helps you put the concepts to work in your environment. After each main topic, an exercise allows you to apply the new material immediately to the Calendar Management System interface. Although it would be easy to let yourself skip the exercises, we urge you to do as much on each of them as your time permits.

Find a Friend or Two

Developing a user interface is typically a collaborative effort, not performed in a vacuum by a single individual. To this end, working through the exercises with at least one other interested person will greatly enhance your understanding and learning of the materials. The exercises, which start in Chapter 5 and continue through Chapter 10, are most effective when performed in teams of three to five people, if possible, to help understand the kinds of communication, interaction, and negotiation that take place in developing a user interface. If you cannot put together a small group of suitable people to simulate a user interface development team, try to find at least one other person with whom you can work. Even if you cannot find a partner, you will benefit greatly by working through the exercises yourself. Performing the exercises, either singly or with a small team, will greatly contribute to your understanding of both the product and especially the process.

Work through Them Sequentially

You (and your team, if you are working with one) will obtain maximum benefit by reading the book sequentially and becoming comfortable with the material from one chapter, including the exercises, before you proceed to the next chapter. Most of the exercises build on results from previous exercises—just as in the real world. Sample solutions and explanations for the exercises are included, to compare with your own answers, so you can check your progress and understanding. The exercises provide a realistic exposure to the techniques presented in Part II of this book. You will, for example, learn a great deal from spending a few hours with a user interface prototype made with transparent plastic overheads and colored marking pens, using real human users as participants (subjects), for empirical evaluation of your designs.

Note the Format of the Exercises

Each exercise begins with a statement of its goal, followed by the activities you are to perform, and, where applicable, deliverables you are to produce. Each exercise also indicates the minimum amount of time you should spend on it to accomplish its goal. However, for some exercises, such as the rapid prototyping one (Chapter 9), you may want to spend a couple of days developing the prototype, rather than the couple of hours indicated. Obviously, the more time you spend working on the exercises, the more you will understand and appreciate the techniques they are designed to teach.

Convince Your Boss (for Practitioners Using the Exercises)

A development team that is already working together, or that expects to work together, on a real project could progress through this book, doing the exercises together over a period of about two weeks, working an average of half a day each day. This team might use a computer-based prototype and volunteer coworkers as participants to evaluate their design.

You're probably already wondering how to convince your boss that you should be given time to work through this book, either alone or with a small team. To help you answer this, go back to the objectives stated previously. Those objectives address the activities that are *critical for ensuring usability* in user interfaces. Those critical activities are what you will learn to do by working through this book.

You may already know how to do some of those activities or may even already be doing them in your development environment. For example, many development teams use rapid prototyping. Nonetheless, many teams don't know what to do with a rapid prototype once they've got it; they especially don't know how to use it as an effective vehicle for evaluating the usability of an interface. Many teams bring in users and have them try out the interface, but teams often don't know what data are most important to collect during user sessions, and they don't know the most effective analyses to perform once they've collected those data. Very few developers know about measurable usability specifications—what they are, how to establish them, and how to use them to help improve the usability of an interface.

An interface development team, in order to ensure usability in their interfaces, must know all the appropriate activities and must know how those activities interact. That is exactly what this book presents—a comprehensive, integrated approach to developing user interfaces. Following through the series of exercises is the best way to understand how this approach works and why it is effective. This book has been structured so that when you finish it, you are ready to apply all that you have learned to ensuring the usability of interfaces developed in your own interface development environment.

Convince Your Students (for Instructors Using the Exercises)

Instructors who are using this book as a text can present the material to their classes in the order presented here, and can assign the exercises as appropriate. In a classroom setting, however, students should spend a great deal more than the minimum indicated time for each exercise. We recommend that an instructor divide the class into teams of about five students each and use the Calendar Management System exercises as homework throughout the term, to give the teams an initial exposure to the material.

We strongly suggest that each team also choose an application other than the Calendar Management System to develop much more completely, as a larger scale, full-term project. The sky's the limit here; we have had students develop interfaces for all kinds of applications: electronic mail, an interactive Monopoly game, a personnel records system, interactive Yellow Pages™, a process control system, a circuit design package, a bar-tending aid, an interactive shopping guide, a videocassette recorder (VCR) programming system, and so on. Let the teams choose whatever they think will be fun and/or useful for them. This larger-scale term project, applying all the materials, is the most important part of a human-computer interaction course.

Again, for either real world or classroom use, go through the material, especially in Part II, in the order presented, as it is largely cumulative. Each topic builds on knowledge from previous topics, and each exercise builds on what was accomplished and learned in one or more of the previous exercises.

WHERE DID THIS BOOK COME FROM?

Real-World Experiences

Although we are researchers in human-computer interaction, we are also practitioners who have successfully used the techniques described in this book for real-world development projects, and we know of dozens of organizations that are applying this material. We have taught this material to hundreds of practitioners in business, industry, government, and military organizations. Much of the material in this book is taken, in fact, from short courses we have been teaching about user interface development for the past several years. It has become increasingly apparent that a much broader audience can be reached by a book than can be taught in person—that is the reason this book has come into existence. Because the book is rooted in the courses, the material has been iteratively evaluated and carefully refined through numerous presentations in short courses and through exposure to interactive system developers.

Research and Literature

Given that the book came from the short courses, where did we get the material in the courses? This is less easy to pinpoint, but there are several important sources. The largest single source for the material on the interface development process is our own research and applied work, as well as collaborations with the real world that we have established in an effort to keep our research efforts focused and pragmatic. In the Department of Computer Science at Virginia Tech, we established one of the pioneering research projects in human-computer interaction in 1979. Over the years, our project has had two general themes:

1. Human-computer interaction must be addressed as an integral part of software engineering.
2. Research in this field should be balanced with practical application.

The first theme means that human-computer interaction and user interface development have strong connections to software engineering, and interactive system development embraces them both. Difficulties arise if human-computer interaction is treated only as a behavioral problem or only as a computer science problem. Many people who enter the human-computer interaction area from computer science do not bring to the job an appreciation of human factors problems and the user. Many people who work in the behavioral world, such as human factors engineers, cognitive psychologists, and empiricists, do not have an appreciation for problems of the software engineering world. The development of high-quality user interfaces depends on cooperation between these two roles. The goal of much of our work in the past decade has been to help bridge the gap between the behavioral world and the computer science world, and to help forge the necessary connections between user interface development and software engineering. This theme also comes through strongly in our short courses and, now, in this book.

The second defining theme of our work over the past years has been technology exchange between academia and the real world—getting new concepts out into the real world; putting them into practice; and testing and refining them in the face of real needs, constraints, and limitations of a working environment. This includes helping software groups of all sizes to establish a workable user interface development component in their system development process. The short courses and this book are, of course, natural extensions of this kind of activity.

As researchers, we find that much of what we do is influenced by the human-computer interaction literature, and this book is no exception. Because this book is primarily for practitioners, however, it is not highly formal and academic. As a result, it contains fewer references to the literature than would a research-oriented book. Nonetheless, essential references have been included; after all, practitioners like to read the literature, too. The work of others is acknowledged through the reference citations at the end of each chapter and in the following acknowledgments.

ACKNOWLEDGMENTS

There are three people whose work has especially influenced the content of this book: Dr. Ben Shneiderman of the University of Maryland, Dr. Jim Foley of

Georgia Tech, and Dr. John Whiteside who was with Digital Equipment Corporation for many years.

We have had a long, happy, and supportive working relationship with Ben Shneiderman. Few individuals have contributed more broadly to the field of human-computer interaction. We have used his book, *Designing the User Interface: Strategies for Effective Human-Computer Interaction*, for our introductory courses in human-computer interaction. Rather than cite his book every time it is appropriate, let it be generally known that it was a significant influence on Part I of this book. We certainly do not claim to have originated the principles and guidelines in Part I, but we hope we have added value in the way they are distilled, organized, and presented.

We also want to acknowledge a long friendship and professional association with Jim Foley. The work that he and his group did in the early 1980s at the George Washington University (GWU) had a strong influence on us and on our own work in the formative years of our human-computer interaction (HCI) research project. Interactions among students from GWU and Virginia Tech in those early years were particularly rewarding. The Georgia Tech Graphics, Visualization, and Usability Center, which he founded and leads, is a unique facility that is producing ground-breaking results. We are indeed flattered that he agreed to write the Foreword to this book.

For many years, we have also enjoyed the collegiality of John Whiteside, whose work we hold in high regard. In our classes, we have used many of the ideas that he and his colleagues have developed in the area of usability engineering. Again, we hope we have added value in adapting this material and integrating it with our own in Part II of this book.

As with any project such as this book, there are numerous people who have contributed in many ways, both directly and indirectly. Dr. Roger Ehrich of Virginia Tech, our friend, colleague, and traveling companion, has participated in the HCI world in various ways over many years. Dr. George Casaday of Digital Equipment Corporation can take credit (or blame) for many of the funny remarks that appear throughout the book; we especially appreciate his encouragement when we were trying to decide whether to write this book. The Calendar Management System that serves as the running example throughout the book has been adapted from an idea by Dr. Marilyn Mantei of the University of Toronto. Dr. Kent Norman of the University of Maryland provided us with a copy of the Questionnaire for User Interface Satisfaction (QUIS).

Many people read all or parts of the manuscript for us. Jon Meads of Bell Northern Research (BNR) and Marc Rettig with the Association for Computing Machinery (ACM) made particularly detailed comments; in some cases, we used their words verbatim in our final revisions. Other reviewers (in alphabetical order) were Jeff Brandenburg of Virginia Tech; Joe Chase of Virginia Tech; Susan Keenan of Virginia Tech; Stuart Laughton of Schlumberger-Doll and Virginia Tech; Marshall McClintock of Microsoft; Karl Melder of Microsoft; Lucy Nowell of Virginia Tech; Mark Simpson of Microsoft; Dr. Anton Siochi of Christopher Newport University; Kent Sullivan of Microsoft; and Andrea Ting of Digital Equipment Corporation. Several anonymous reviewers also made very helpful comments.

Our editors, Diane Cerra and Terri Hudson, and others at John Wiley were extremely pleasant, supportive, and easy to work with throughout this entire project. Jamie Temple, of Pageworks, was also very cooperative in helping bring this together in a timely fashion. Karen Bowen, our trusty secretary, gave invaluable assistance at various stages, especially in tracking down permissions for reprinting material from other sources and in production of the index.

Over the years, the superior students, too numerous to name, that have participated in our HCI project here at Virginia Tech, and the many excellent students in our short courses, have forced us to seek detailed and reasonable answers for the most obscure questions. Ultimately, this has contributed to our fuller understanding of how all the material in this book fits together.

Our mates, Bob and Rieky, endured our sometimes prolonged absences with (mostly) good humor while we completed this book. Pumpkin and Tiger were also always there, but generally unaware.

Finally, the most difficult thing we had to do throughout this entire project was decide on order of authorship. We feel that the contributions by each of us were so evenly balanced that we wished we did not have to specify an order of authors. The actual order of authors' names ultimately was decided by a coin toss. And after all this, plus more than a decade of working together, we're still friends!

DEBBY HIX & REX HARTSON
Blacksburg, Virginia, USA

FURTHER INFORMATION

Either author can be contacted for further information about any of the topics covered in this book.

Deborah Hix
Department of Computer Science
Virginia Tech
562 McBryde Hall
Blacksburg, VA 24061 USA
hix @ cs. vt. edu

H. Rex Hartson
Department of Computer Science
Virginia Tech
562 McBryde Hall
Blacksburg, VA 24061 USA
hartson @ cs. vt. edu

About the Authors

DEBORAH HIX, PhD, is a Research Computer Scientist at Virginia Tech in Blacksburg, Virginia. She has done extensive consulting and training in the area of human-computer interaction for a broad variety of organizations from business, industry, and government. At Virginia Tech, she is a principal investigator on one of the nation's pioneering projects in human-computer interaction, investigating how to improve the usability of user interfaces through development of specialized methodologies, techniques, and tools. Hix's degrees are from Emory University and Virginia Tech.

H. REX HARTSON, PhD, is Professor of Computer Science at Virginia Tech in Blacksburg, Virginia. Since 1964, he has consulted and taught training courses for many organizations in business, industry, and government. He has worked as an engineer and researcher for the Xerox Corporation. He is the founder and principal investigator of the Human-Computer Interaction Project at Virginia Tech, one of the nation's pioneering university research projects in user interfaces. He did early research and development in user interface management systems, and currently is investigating the user interface development process, including design representation techniques, prototyping, and evaluation. Hartson's degrees are from the University of Michigan and Ohio State University.

1

Ensuring Usability in Human–Computer Interaction

1.1   THE UBIQUITOUS USER INTERFACE

"Do you want buttons or menus?" "Wow, this thing sure is user friendly!" Dozens, no thousands, of colors; three-dimensional (3-D) graphics; spreadsheets; word processors; realistic and engaging computer games. In the past decade, the area of human–computer interaction has blossomed from being a gleam in the eye of a few researchers to becoming an integral part of many people's daily lives. Today, the user interface is the first thing many people ask about when discussing a new software application. *To users, the interface is the system.* For today's users, communication with the system has become at least as important as computation by the system.

Now that these new graphics and interaction styles are here, have the problems of those old hard-to-use computers disappeared? Not a chance. On the way to one of our short course presentations, we stopped at an airline ticket counter so that one of us could purchase a ticket for a trip to Europe. After a half-hour struggle, the ticket agent, hands raised to the sky, asked "Why do computers have to make it so much harder than it really is?"

Later, arriving at the car-rental desk, we were given keys and cheerfully told we would find our blue Toyota sedan in slot B-14. After winding our way toward slot B-14, we discovered a gray Dodge van. Back to the rental desk. "I'm sorry, but the computer says that the Toyota is in B-14, and the van doesn't even seem to have a slot."

"Is it OK if we go by what's in the parking lot rather than what's in the computer?"

"Oh, wait a minute; I've misread the screen. That was for our rental lot across the street. I'm having trouble finding the information for this lot."

After driving away in a red Honda, we marveled as we made it through check-in at the hotel desk without a computer snafu of some sort. That evening, at the end of our dinner in the restaurant, we asked for separate checks, when came the horrified reply, "But it's already in the computer as one check, and I'll never figure out how to change it." By the time we were in the classroom the next morning, we were certainly motivated for the start of our short course on user interface development!

All these computers were undoubtedly computing quite well, but were they communicating? People are less and less willing to accept the kind of ridiculous situations described in the preceding scenarios. Once spoiled by a natural, easy-to-learn, easy-to-use, direct manipulation interface, many users cannot be cajoled or bribed to return to the old way. When users find they can, in fact, change something after it's "in the computer," they are unwilling to accept those old arguments.

One of our favorite motivational comments was made in reference to a 70-year-old-plus attorney and author, buying her first computer (a Macintosh™), to be used for writing books. Her son remarked, "She's been ready for a computer for years; computers just haven't been ready for her!" From the user's perspective, usability has become a key issue.

From the interactive system developer's perspective, ensuring usability has become an overwhelmingly important issue. Anywhere from an average of 48% to a maximum of nearly 100% of the code for an interactive system is now used to support the user interface (Myers & Rosson, 1992). From the viewpoint of many software engineers, however, the user interface is not really an integral part of the interactive system, but rather just a box that gets stuck somewhere between the stick figure and the important stuff such as the system functions. The emerging emphasis on usability is changing this perspective, so that the user interface is becoming a critical part of the whole interactive system, and user interface development is an integral part of the overall software engineering process.

Ensuring usability is also a pressing issue for companies that buy software. At one time, the cost of hardware was the principal cost of owning and using a computing system. As hardware costs dropped, they were eclipsed by software costs, especially the costs to develop new software. Today, the cost of *personware* is a primary consideration in acquiring interactive systems; this includes both training and daily usage costs for users. The initial cost of the system is paid only once, but the cost of each person's time for using the system—including lost productivity in fighting with the system and recovering from errors—is paid every day.

1.2   WHAT IS USABILITY?

The need for user friendliness is often heard. Do users really look for a friend in their computers, though, or is it just hassle-free productivity they seek? To us, the real issue is *usability*. One of our favorite definitions of usability comes from a colleague who asks, "If your computer were a person, how long 'til you punch it in the nose?" (Tom Carey, c. 1989). To begin with, usability—from a slightly more technical viewpoint—is a combination of the following user-oriented characteristics (Shneiderman, 1992):

- Ease of learning
- High speed of user task performance
- Low user error rate
- Subjective user satisfaction
- User retention over time

That is, usability is related to the effectiveness and efficiency of the user interface and to the user's reaction to that interface. The naturalness of the interface for the user is also an important aspect of usability. This serves as a simple starting point for this book, in the hope that you will have a much deeper understanding of usability after reading the whole book.

1.3   EVERYONE IS AN EXPERT

Talk with many programmers about user interfaces, and you'll hear about widgets, interaction styles, callbacks, and everything you'll need to build a user interface. You may sense a feeling of confidence—a feeling that powerful new interface software programming tools have transformed this programmer into a real interface expert. Anyone, in fact, *can* design a user interface. How often have you heard (or said), "This can't be hard; it's just common sense"? However, just because you are a programmer who knows how to use an interface toolkit doesn't mean that you can design a highly usable interface. Just because you use a Mac doesn't mean that you necessarily know a good user interface when you see one, and it certainly doesn't mean that you can develop one.

One of the reasons it has been difficult to convince interactive system developers of the need for high usability is that software engineers and managers have not always believed that there was, or is, a problem. Product planners and marketing people, too, sometimes see the user interface as a low-importance issue—something to provide "sales sizzle" (thanks to Jon Meads for this appropriate phrase), but with no real effect on either the purchase or the acceptance of a product.

It is easy to mistake various other positive signs as indicators that the interface is good or even adequate. Managers often say, "This system has to be good; it's selling like hotcakes." "The marketplace is showing a great deal of interest in our product." "We aren't hearing any complaints about the user interface." On closer inspection, it appears that a system might be selling well because it is the only one of its kind, or its marketing department or advertising is much more effective than that of the others. Sometimes, development managers are the only ones in town who don't hear the usability complaints.

Also, despite our preceding comments about users being less and less willing to endure poor-quality interfaces, some users simply won't complain. Donald Norman, in his eye-opening book, *The Psychology of Everyday Things,* recounts an incident in which evaluation of a new keyboard layout showed that the Save and Delete keys were so close together that users often hit the wrong one (Norman, 1988). The obvious result was that there were many (catastrophic) user errors. When the keyboard designers were told about the problem, their reply was that a pool of secretaries had already been using this keyboard for six months with no complaints. On interviewing the secretaries, Norman found that, in fact, they frequently had problems with the close proximity of the two keys, and they were often losing work. Every one of them said they hadn't complained because they thought they were making stupid mistakes, not that the keyboard design was bad!

Sometimes, managers require cost/benefit analyses to be convinced of anything. In the case of usability, however, because the customer (the person with authority to purchase an application or sign a development contract) is *not* always the final user, the distance between cost and benefit can be great. Nevertheless, a case can be made to management that the cost of low usability can be measured in terms of training costs and lost productivity.

If you wonder about the usability of your own product, here are some indicators to watch for. Interfaces with these characteristics are prime candidates for having problems with usability:

- It was designed by software people, not human–computer interaction specialists.
- It was developed by strict top-down, functional decomposition.
- It was not developed to meet written, measurable usability specifications.
- It was not prototyped as it was being developed.
- It was not developed by means of an iterative refinement process.
- It was not empirically evaluated.

This book can help you change these factors in your development process. This book is designed for those who have been struck by the importance of a good user interface and who want to find out more about what good usability means, how to ensure it, and how to know when you have it. This book is especially aimed toward practitioners—people who put theory into practice in a real-world interface development environment. The methods and techniques described here can be used by anyone who is involved in any part of the development of a user interface.

1.4   DEVELOPING HUMAN–COMPUTER INTERACTION

Human–computer interaction, often referred to as HCI, is what happens when a human user and a computer system get together to perform tasks. The study of human–computer interaction is a new and exciting field of endeavor devoted to answering the question of how best to make this interaction work. As a field, human–computer interaction includes user interface hardware and software, user and system modeling, cognitive and behavioral science, human factors, empirical studies, methodology, techniques, and tools. The goal of most of the work in human–computer interaction is, in one way or another, to provide the user with a high degree of usability.

How is developing the interaction design different from developing the user interface? As shown simplistically in Figure 1.1, interaction development is one of two parts of the user interface development process. The first part, shown on the bottom left, is interaction development, and the second part, shown on the bottom right, is interface software development. The *interaction component* is how a user interface works, its "look and feel" and behavior in response to what a user sees and hears and does while interacting with the computer. The *interface software* is the means for implementing the code that instantiates the interaction component. Both are necessary. However, *this book focuses on interaction development* and says very little about interface software development.

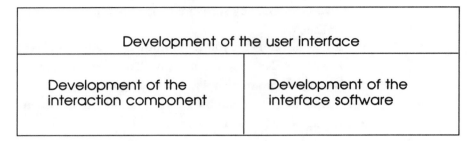

Figure 1.1. The parts of user interface development.

This book takes a practical approach, based on the application of principles and methods, to ensure high usability in interfaces for interactive systems. The process involves both art and science, yet it also draws on the engineering idea of making things good enough, but not necessarily perfect. Development of the interaction component begins with getting the right content in the product (Part I), but it especially has to do with the life cycle, methods, techniques, and tools that make up and support the interaction development process (Part II).

1.5   BEHAVIORAL AND CONSTRUCTIONAL DOMAINS

Because of the important difference between *development of the interaction component of an interface* and *development of the user interface software* that implements that interaction, the two kinds of development occur in different domains. Interaction design has special requirements that are not shared by software design. However, both historically and practically, interactive systems have not always been designed and developed with this distinction between the interaction component and the interface software. The interaction component has often been designed by software engineers and programmers, along with the software of an interactive system. The result has been interfaces of varying quality and usability. Considerable work in the field of human–computer interaction has been directed toward new approaches to user interface development, in hopes of improving quality and usability. Much of this book is about many of those new development ideas.

To emphasize the distinction being made here, the terms behavioral domain and constructional domain refer, respectively, to the working worlds of the people who design and develop the interaction component of user interfaces and the people who design and develop the user interface software.

In the *behavioral domain*, interaction is described abstractly (i.e., independently of software) in terms of the behavior of the user and the interface as they interact with each other. Development in the behavioral domain involves human factors guidelines and rules, human cognitive limitations, graphic design, interaction styles, scenarios, usability specifications, rapid prototyping, and evaluation with human users.

In the *constructional domain*, software engineers develop the software that implements the behavioral design. Constructional development involves widgets, algorithms, programming, procedure libraries, control and data flow, state transition diagrams, event handlers, callbacks, object-oriented representations, and some kinds of user interface description languages. A comparison of characteristics of the behavioral and constructional domains is given in Table 1.1.

Approaching user interface development in the *behavioral domain, from a user and task view*, should result in *higher usability* than approaching it from the constructional, or programmer's, view, where software is the primary focus. Part of the problem stems from an inherent, unavoidable conflict in developing user interfaces: What is best for a user is rarely easiest for a programmer.

Both behavioral and constructional development are necessary; a behavioral design must always be translated into a constructional design so that it can be implemented. Behavioral development does not replace constructional development; each serves different purposes. In the final product, of course, it is the merged results of both behavioral and constructional designs that determines usability. For example, when a good behavioral design runs intolerably slow, due to constructional tools, this can adversely influence usability.

In dealing with people's understanding of these issues and different domains, the last item in Table 1.1 is the most useful—a way to determine the domain about which you are talking or in which you are working at any given time. If a procedure is performed by the user (e.g., "move the cursor to icon X"), then it is

TABLE 1.1.   COMPARING THE BEHAVIORAL AND CONSTRUCTIONAL DOMAINS

	Behavioral	Constructional
What is being developed	**Interaction component** of interface	**Interface software** (to support interaction)
What view is adopted	View of the user	View of the system
What is described	User actions, perceptions, and tasks	System actions in response to what the user does
What is involved	Human factors, scenarios, detailed representations, usability specifications, evaluation	Algorithms, callbacks, data structures, widgets, programming
The locale	Where interaction designers and evaluators do their work	Where interface software implementers do their work
The test	Procedures performed by the user	Procedures performed by the system

behavioral. If a procedure is performed by the system (e.g., "when the cursor is moved to icon X, call this routine"), then it is constructional. Even this simple example shows that these are indeed two different views, albeit of the same thing.

1.6   ROLES IN USER INTERFACE DEVELOPMENT

Human factors people have not always had a cooperating role in user interface development. For years, many people working in the constructional domain believed that they could design interactive systems without help from behavioral domain people. There was also often a significant disinterest in interactive systems by some human factors people. Because managers ordered it, or because there were vague rumors that they should, constructional developers began grudgingly to let human factors engineers look at their designs. This resulted in decidedly secondary roles for human factors people. It led to the application of "human factors as peanut butter," spreading human factors over the design after it is otherwise finished (thanks to Clayton Lewis for this colorful description).

It also led to the "priest with a parachute" paradigm: The human factors engineer jumped into the middle of a project and stayed just long enough to give it a blessing. Anything more than a few minor changes and a blessing was, of course, unacceptable at this point, because the design had progressed too far for significant changes. If the human factors engineer did have enough authority to enforce some changes, then the role was viewed as that of the "building inspector," who might find "violations" that might have to be fixed. Human factors engineers are often described as the "watch dog," "bean counter," "token," "UI police," and other similar disparaging appellations. Fortunately, things are now changing, and many development projects feature teams that are comprised of people from both the behavioral and the constructional domains.

Despite recent changes, the roles still are not always clear. For example, when people say to us, "Oh, you do human factors work," we answer, "Not really." We are computer scientists who happen to have adopted the view of the human user, rather than the view of the system—somewhat unusual for computer scientists. We hope that this book may help to clear up misunderstandings about the various roles in interface development and their responsibilities and particularly their activities.

To that end, we state the assumptions on which we base our approach to the development process, that also set the tone and philosophy of the whole book. Our major focus is on two kinds of roles that logically correspond both to the two domains of user interface development and to the involvement of human factors with computer science during user interface development.

The first domain, the behavioral domain, is the human side of things. As discussed in the previous section, this broadly includes the areas of human factors, behavioral science, and cognitive psychology, and roles such as users, interaction designers and evaluators, and documentation specialists. The main role in the behavioral domain is that of the *user interaction developer*, which broadly includes people who carry out activities such as user class definition, interaction design, usability evaluation, and human factors engineering. It is the responsibility of people in this role to produce the product—to develop the content, behavior, and appearance of the interaction design. People in this role are directly responsible for ensuring usability, including user performance and satisfaction. They are concerned with critical design issues such as functionality, sequencing, content, and information access, as well as such details as what menus should look like, how forms should be formatted, whether to use a mouse or trackball, and how to ensure consistency across an interface. A major part of the developer's job is also concerned with setting measurable usability specifications, evaluating interaction designs with users, and redesigning based on analysis of users' evaluations of an interface.

The second domain, the constructional domain, is the computer side of things. This broadly includes areas involving machines, computer science, and software engineering, and roles such as software designers, software engineers, and programmers. The primary role in the constructional domain is that of the *user interface software developer*. People in this role are responsible for translating the interaction design into an interface software design and implementing it. They are responsible for producing the software—the algorithms, data structures, procedure calls, modules, and program code—to implement the user interface, to make the appearance and behavior of the interaction happen. These are the people who work with user interface software toolkits, widgets, and other programmed interface objects.

Beyond these two roles on which we focus in this book, a third distinct and important kind of role is that of the *problem domain expert*, a person who has in-depth knowledge of the area that an interactive application is being built to support. For example, this person is a civil engineer if the interactive system is an engineering aid for designing bridges, or a physician if the system is a medical one. While this role typically falls into the behavioral domain, it is important enough to single out for mention here.

People in these three kinds of roles must work together and share in the design and development not just of the user interface, but of the whole interactive system, as depicted in Figure 1.2. While these roles correspond to distinguishable activities, they are mutually dependent aspects of the same effort. These three roles represent essential ingredients in the development process, and trade-offs con-

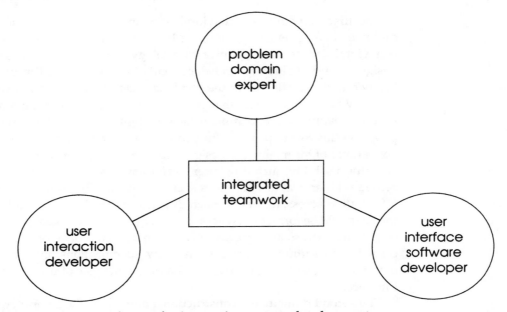

Figure 1.2. Roles in an integrated team for interactive system development.

cerning any one of them must be considered with regard to its impact on the other roles.

In the past, people from the behavioral and constructional worlds have not always worked together much, and indeed these worlds don't always seem compatible. People in these different worlds have different goals, attitudes, skills, perspectives, philosophies, needs, techniques, and tools. Ever since we started working in this field, we have believed that *cooperating and complementary roles, coming from both of these worlds, are essential to the development of high-quality user interfaces.*

The interaction developer and the interface software developer act as partners, together with the problem domain expert, in producing a user interface. They require a lot of communication during interface design and development as they work across the behavioral, constructional, and problem domain boundaries within a team of closely coordinated peers. For example, the interface software developer communicates with the interaction developer about software constraints that affect the interaction design. As an illustration, if a decision has been made to use the Open Software Foundation (OSF) Motif™ software toolkit, then the interaction design is limited to what can be done by Motif™ widgets. The interface software developer may also act as liaison between the interaction developer and the interface software implementer, as well as the people who develop and implement noninterface software, mediating the interaction designs in response to their constraints.

Although people in each of the roles work together as a closely integrated team, each of the roles must remain distinct within that team, so that people in each role can clearly identify their own responsibilities and activities. An analogous case in software engineering is the distinction between specification and implementation. Although these activities are inevitably intertwined via mutual dependencies (Swartout & Balzer, 1982), it is an important principle in the discipline of software engineering to maintain conceptual distinction and to know which development activities fall within the scope of each role. So it is also in the user interface world, especially with respect to the two roles of interaction developer and interface software developer. Confusion about these roles could result in interaction design being *driven by software concerns* (e.g., widgets or toolkits) rather than by tasks and user needs.

In practice, especially in small projects, the design and programming of a user interface (and perhaps all the other activities in its development, as well, such as evaluation) are often done in one person's head, but each activity should be done under a different hat! While you are reading this book, you should be wearing your *interaction developer* hat. This is the main role for which this book is intended. There are plenty of other books that are constructionally oriented (e.g., how to use the X Window System™ or Motif ™, or how to write user interface software) for the interface software developer role.

Recognition of the two different domains, the different activities in each domain, and the need for different roles to carry out those activities can help an individual person who is trying to serve both domains to go back and forth between them more easily. You will not have to do much domain or role switching while reading this book, however, because it is focused on the behavioral domain. The one exception is Chapter 11, which gives an overview of the topic of user interface development tools. These tools generally support implementation of the user interface software and are therefore in the constructional domain. As work in this field advances, some tools are also becoming available to support work by nonprogrammer roles in the behavioral domain.

1.7   DESIGN VERSUS DEVELOPMENT

You may have noticed our frequent use of the words *design* and *development* so far. It is important to understand our distinction between these two words. Throughout this book, the term *design* applies somewhat narrowly to the creative human activity by which tasks, objects, and features are synthesized and put together to make up a user interface. The term *development* refers to the broader activities of producing a user interface, *including design*, and also analysis, prototyping, evaluation, and iterative modification. Even as narrowly as it has been defined here, design is a major activity in the interaction development process; it is where the substance and appearance of the interface are synthesized. Because of its intimate relationship to other development activities, it is usually difficult to say when a developer is doing pure design.

1.8   THE VALUE OF USABILITY

As you go through this book, you may feel that you simply do not have the time and/or other resources to use all the different techniques being presented. At first, they will seem time-consuming and perhaps even daunting. You may be thinking, "We just don't have time to work much on the user interface." Well, in reality, *you don't have time not to*, although this may be hard for you to believe now.

What often happens is that most of the development dollars for an interactive system are poured into programming a great deal of functionality that never gets to the user, because too little time was spent developing an interface that would make that functionality accessible. Would it not have been better to reallocate some of those dollars and person-hours to developing an interface with high usability, even if it meant somewhat lower functionality in the system? Those dollars—and it is usually *lots* of them—spent on programming inaccessible functionality are essentially thrown away. Don't forget: To the user of an interactive system, *communication is at least as important as computation*.

REFERENCES

Myers, B. A., & Rosson, M. B. (1992). Survey on User Interface Programming. *Proceedings of CHI Conference on Human Factors in Computing Systems*, New York: ACM, 195–202.

Norman, D. A. (1988). *The Psychology of Everyday Things*. New York: Basic Books.

Shneiderman, B. (1992). *Designing the User Interface: Strategies for Effective Human-Computer Interaction*. Reading, MA: Addison-Wesley.

Swartout, W., & Balzer, R. (1982). On the Inevitable Intertwining of Specification and Implementation. *Communications of the ACM*, 25(7), 438–445.

Part I

The Product

≡2

User Interaction Design Guidance: Standards, Guidelines, and Style Guides

2.1 WHAT IS HUMAN FACTORS?

Our discussion of the product—the user interface itself—begins with a survey of various kinds of user interaction design guidance. In particular, the following discussion presents several kinds of human factors information that compose the vast body of work aimed at improving user interaction design. Part I of this book (Chapters 2 and 3) is an *introductory overview* that barely scratches the surface on user interaction design guidance and interaction styles. This material is not intended to be an in-depth presentation; it was neither our mandate nor our mission to write yet another book on design guidelines; neither was it our goal to deal with psychological underpinnings of the guidelines. Numerous other references go into far more detail on guidelines than is provided here.

This overview is included because extensive feedback from years of presentations of this material indicates that presenting just the process is not adequate. Interaction developers also want *human factors material about the product, to set the context* and to serve as important background information for the process of ensuring usability in interfaces. This is in accordance with the "one-stop shopping" philosophy for this book.

The lack of detail in Chapters 2 and 3 should not give the false impression that there really is not much to human factors that relates to developing human–computer interaction. On the contrary: It is an extremely complex and difficult aspect of producing a usable interface, filled with conflicts, trade-offs, and situational interpretations. Some of the more recent volumes that have been written on guidelines and rules for interaction design include *Designing User Interfaces* (Powell, 1990), *Graphic Design for Electronic Documents and User Interfaces* (Marcus, 1992), *Principles and Guidelines in Software User Interface Design* (Mayhew, 1992), and *Designing the User Interface: Strategies for Effective Human–Computer Interaction* (Shneiderman, 1992). These books offer details on guidelines and other aspects of human factors in interaction design, as well as copious examples. They give you much more specific information about particular design situations than is presented in this and the next chapter.

Because of the very nature of this material, you will find disconcerting conflicts and even inconsistencies in these books (and perhaps in our overview in Chapters 2 and 3 as well). This is not a shortcoming of the authors; rather, it indicates the difficulty of supplying one right answer to a specific user interaction design question. The difficulty of applying appropriate human factors guidance in interaction design is aptly expressed by Jim Foley, who bluntly claims that there is but one answer to any question about user interaction design: "It depends!"

Our overview begins by briefly examining what human factors is, especially as it relates to user interaction development. First and foremost, the study of *human factors is a science*. It includes the derivation of principles of human behavior, typically based on empirical testing using *human participants* (the term now being applied to what used to be called "subjects"). A fundamental goal of human factors work is to optimize human performance, including error reduction, increased throughput, user satisfaction, and user comfort. Obviously, then, in the world of user interaction development, human factors plays a major role because a main focus of usability is to improve user performance of tasks with an interactive computer system.

Human behavior is observable; human performance is measurable. Measuring the performance of a human, using an interactive system, for example, requires empirical testing. This involves several phases, including formation of a hypothesis, design of a study with appropriate human participants, collection of performance data based on observations of those participants performing tasks, analysis of data (usually via statistical methods), and, finally, confirmation or refutation of the hypothesis. These phases of empirical testing are well-known, for example, to human factors engineers, cognitive scientists, and statisticians, and have been applied for decades to the study of human performance. It is only rather recently that some of these same techniques have been adapted for use in evaluation of user performance with interactive systems. These adaptations are presented in detail in subsequent chapters, especially Chapter 10, on formative evaluation.

The formalized discipline of human factors took hold during World War II. There are many stories. In one, aircraft pilots, for no apparent reason, began unintentionally bailing out of their planes. An investigation into this situation revealed that the aircraft engineers had made a small design change in the cockpit. In the redesign, the release handle for the ejection seat had been switched with the throttle for the plane. This minor design modification had been the cause of the unexplained increase in number of ejections! The pilots yelled about the change; the engineers were indignant, saying that they had good reasons for their change. And besides, aren't pilots intelligent? Can't they learn this new design with a little training? Can't they adapt? Well, of course, pilots are smart and can be trained to adapt. Unfortunately, though, training may be effective only until a stressful situation arises. Then, under duress, a human reverts to the actions that are most natural, in many cases regardless of the amount of training. So the pilots who had learned to fly in the original cockpit were fine until they got into a stressful combat situation, at which time, they often reverted to their original long-known actions, with continued disastrous results.

All this gives a familiar ring to similar comments about users of interactive systems, especially from their designers. It can be a most enlightening exercise to watch an interaction designer, or a programmer who contributed to the interaction design, who is observing a user attempting to perform tasks with that interface. The observer's comments often used to include such remarks as "Why don't they understand?" "What are they trying to do?" "They figured out how to do that earlier; why can't they adapt?" and the favorite, "What a stupid user!"

However, user interaction designers are now realizing that *the user should not have to adapt to the interface*, but rather that the interface should be designed so that it is intuitive and natural for the user to learn and to use. With this realization, most designers now are very interested in users' reactions to their designs and are appreciative and responsive to those users' problems and suggestions.

2.2 KINDS OF HUMAN FACTORS INFORMATION

At least four kinds of human factors information heavily influence the product:

- User interaction standards
- User interaction design guidelines
- Commercial style guides
- Customized style guides

2.2.1 Standards

Standards for user interfaces are often mentioned in discussions about interaction design. *Standards* are official, publicly available documents that give requirements for user interaction design. Standards must be followed when designing the user interaction; they are enforceable by contract or by law. They have very general wording—so general, in fact, that it is often hard to determine whether the standards are being followed.

An example of a standards document for user interaction is MIL-STD-1472C, revised (1990), often used by the military. Entitled "User-Computer Interface," this 22-page subsection of a larger document is packed with both general descriptions and specific details about what the interface *shall* be like. An excerpt from this document is the following standard on "standardization" of display contents:

5.15.3.2.1. *Standardization.* The content of displays within a system shall be presented in a consistent, standardized manner.

Another example is the very first standard in this document:

5.15.1 *General.* Computer programs and equipment interfaces shall provide a functional interface between the system for which they are designed and users (operators/maintainers) of that system. This interface shall optimize compatibility with personnel and shall minimize conditions which can degrade human performance or contribute to human error.

At first reading, these sound like completely reasonable, and in fact even desirable, standards. However, a moment's reflection immediately raises some obvious questions: Who is going to decide exactly what these mean, and how? How will these requirements be checked and enforced, and by whom? The very vagueness that is characteristic of standards makes them extremely difficult to interpret and enforce, despite their requirement to be specifically and contractually monitored.

In all fairness, not all standards from the MIL-STD-1472C document are so vague. For example,

---

5.15.3.3.2 *Flash.* Flash coding shall be employed to call the user's attention to mission critical events only. No more than 2 flash rates shall be used. Where one rate is used, the rate shall be between 3 and 5 flashes per second. Where two rates are used, the second rate shall be less than 2 per second.

In sum, standards are very general and simple, perhaps even overly simple. They require much interpretation and tailoring to be very useful in user interaction design. Their main advantage is that they do indeed draw attention to the user interface, but they may be too vague and generic to offer effective guidance.

Approach standards documents with caution, expecting them to need massive interpretation in order to provide much concrete direction in the design of user interaction.

2.2.2   Guidelines

User interaction guidelines are what many people think of when they hear the phrase "human factors for user interfaces." Guidelines are often called the common sense part of user interaction design. Although this is true in the abstract, real-world designers often seem to misplace their common sense when working on user interaction. If guidelines are common sense, then why is this kind of sense so uncommon in many user interfaces? The answer is that *guidelines are not just common sense*, and, in particular, *applying them to specific situations is much more than just common sense*. Guidelines are often contradictory; determining which to apply, and how, in a particular design, requires a deeper and more expert knowledge and experience than many user interaction designers have. Yet, guidelines provide much of the foundation for producing both a style guide (as Sections 2.2.3 and 2.2.4 show) and, of course, the interaction design.

Guidelines are published in books, reports, and articles that are publicly available. They are not specific to a single organization, but rather apply across the broad spectrum of user interaction design. Even though they may be generally worded, a clear understanding of them can give invaluable design guidance. Guidelines are sometimes empirically derived and/or validated; often, they simply are educated opinion based on experience. A main difference between standards and guidelines is that standards are (at least theoretically) enforceable in a user interface, while guidelines serve more as suggestions for how to produce a good interface.

One of the best-known examples of a collection of guidelines is the compilation by Smith and Mosier at the MITRE Corporation (Smith & Mosier, 1986). This collection of 944 guidelines has evolved over more than a decade and is extensive in its coverage. It is organized around several major headings, such as Data Entry, Data Display, Sequence Control, User Guidance, Data Transmission, and Data Protection. Each guideline is carefully stated, then followed by an example, any notable exceptions, any appropriate comments on specific application of the guideline, and finally, a list of other references, such as MIL-STDs, books, articles, and other sections in the Smith and Mosier document itself. A specific excerpt from this document gives guidance on how to develop the display format for an interface:

2.5-1 *Consistent format.* Adopt a consistent organization for the location of various display features from one display to another.

— *Example*: One location might be used consistently for a display title, another area might be reserved for data output by the computer, and other areas dedicated to display of control options, instructions, error messages, and user command entry.

— *Exception*: It might be desirable to change display formats in some distinctive way to help a user distinguish one task or activity from another, but the displays of any particular type should still be formatted consistently among themselves.

— *Comment*: The objective is to develop display formats that are consistent with accepted usage and existing user habits. Consistent display formats will help establish and preserve user orientation. There is no fixed display format that is optimum for all data handling applications, since applications will vary in their requirements. However, once a suitable format has been devised, it should be maintained as a pattern to ensure consistent design of other displays.

— *Reference*: BB 1.1, 1.8.5, EG 2.2.5, 2.3, 2.3.3, MS 5.15.3.2.1, 5.15.3.3.4; Foley and Van Dam, 1982; Stewart, 1980; Taylor, McCan and Tuori, 1984. See also 4.0-6. (Smith & Mosier, 1986, p. 170)

Despite the thoroughness, examples, explanations, and cross-references of the Smith and Mosier document, it has some limitations. Most of the guidelines are strongly oriented toward nonwindowed, alphanumeric terminal interaction, without much attention given to graphical windowing interfaces. Even if an appropriate guideline applicable to a specific design situation is available, it can still be very difficult to find. The sheer volume of the document leads to this difficulty. Several PC-based interactive software packages are available for the

Smith and Mosier guidelines; these packages facilitate searching through this wealth of information.

In sum, guidelines are general in their applicability and require a fair amount of interpretation to be useful. Their main advantage is to offer flexible guidance and to help establish design goals and decisions, but they must be tailored in order to produce specific design rules.

Because guidelines are such an important foundation for user interaction design, an entire section (Section 2.3) is devoted to them. Stay tuned for many more guidelines and examples of their use.

> **Educate designers in the guidelines for user interaction. Apply these guidelines when producing a customized style guide (see Section 2.2.4) and throughout all aspects of the user interaction design.**

2.2.3   Commercial Style Guides

Commercial style guides are documents that are typically produced by one organization or vendor and are made commercially available. A style guide provides a much more concrete and useful framework for design than does a standards document. A style guide typically includes the following:

- Description of a specific interaction style or object, including both its "look" (appearance) and "feel" (behavior)
- Guidance on when and how to use a particular interaction style or object

A style guide can provide the basic conventions for a specific product or for a family of products. User interfaces can—in some cases, must—be certified for compliance with a specific style guide. Some organizations that provide these style guides as a target for vendors developing interactive systems in accordance with the style guide have an inventive approach to checking compliance of a user interface: Organization representatives travel to the vendor's site to evaluate compliance of a particular interactive application developed by the vendor. If the application interface is certifiably compliant, then the organization pays the travel expenses of its own representatives. If the application interface does not comply with the style guide, then the vendor must pay the representatives' travel expenses.

Most commercial style guides contain sections with *descriptions of particular interaction components*, such as windows, menus, controls, and dialogue boxes; keyboard and mouse usage; and message and help design. In addition to the textual descriptions, they contain *illustrations* of examples of the interaction components, and perhaps even *screen templates*, showing how sample screens might look. Several examples of commercial style guides currently are very popular, including

- User Interface Guidelines from Apple
- Common User Access (CUA™) from IBM
- OpenLook™ from AT&T/Xerox/Sun
- Motif™ from OSF

Many commercial style guides are associated with a commercially available toolkit. In this case, the toolkit supports the style defined in the corresponding guide. Such toolkits (discussed in more detail in Chapter 11) typically contain precoded interaction *objects* (often, especially in the X Windows world, called *widgets*) that can be used in implementing a user interface. The look and feel of a specific interaction object is encapsulated in a corresponding toolkit widget. The related style guide describes each object's default appearance and behavior.

Behavior and appearance of precoded objects can be severely constrained by a toolkit, giving an interaction designer little flexibility for modifications to those objects. However, many toolkits support changes to the precoded objects they contain, allowing a wide range of variation in an object's description, which can result in a very different appearance and/or behavior. Some style guides permit such changes within the bounds of maintaining style compliance, while others consider even relatively minor changes to object defaults as noncompliance.

An example from the OSF Motif™ style guide discusses pop-up menus:

4.3.2. *Pop-up menus*. Pop-up menus . . . usually contain push buttons, radio buttons, or check buttons, and can have selections that lead to dialog boxes or other controls. . . . Pop-up menus are always presented as a vertical column. Pop-up menus are associated with a particular area of the screen. The advantage of pop-up menus is that they require no mouse travel; they simply pop up at the current mouse location (provided that location has a menu associated with it). While pop-up menus take up no screen space until they are displayed, they provide no visual cue to their existence. (OSF, 1990, p. 4-10)

Commercial style guides can be used as the basis for producing a customized style guide (see Section 2.2.4) for individual interface development projects. They are especially useful if the interface is to be developed, for example, on one of the platforms and/or using one of the toolkits supported by the various vendors, as mentioned previously.

Some words of caution about style guides, however. First, *many commercially available style guides (and their corresponding toolkits) have not had a great deal of professional human factors input or evaluation.* In some cases, this lack of expertise is glaringly obvious. On the other hand, much of what is in many commercial style guides has at least reasonable usability and thereby provides a decent starting point for objects to be used in an interaction design.

Second, *a style guide alone is not enough to ensure usability of an interface.* A style guide can remove some of the constant decision making inherent in interaction design, by providing a specific look and feel for various interaction objects and styles. If interaction designers want to know what a pull-down menu should look like and how it should behave, they have only to refer to the style guide, rather than making the decision themselves.

A third point about style guides: They tend to give quite specific guidance on *what* a particular interaction object should look like, and even *how* it should behave. However, *they do not always state when to use that particular interaction object—* which is, of course, one of the hardest design decisions. Note that this is true in the foregoing statement about pop-up menus. There is, in fairness, an attempt later in the Motif™ style guide to help designers decide when to use a pop-up menu, specifically on deciding between a pop-up menu and push buttons:

4.4.5 *Deciding Between a Pop-Up Menu and Push Buttons.* Pop-up menus provide users with quick access to application functions. So do control panels containing push buttons. Generally, pop-up menus are preferable when users are focused on their work areas. In these situations, moving the mouse between a control panel and the work area would be distracting.

Push buttons and a control panel are preferable when users make frequent selections, need to make several selections at the same time, or are already manipulating the mouse primarily in the control panel area. (OSF, 1990, p. 4-13)

While this appears to give rather useful guidance, closer inspection shows that it still needs much interpretation. For example, can a designer always know "when users are focused on their work areas"? Also, how long should they be focused there in order to use a pop-up menu rather than push buttons?

The foregoing guideline recommends providing interaction objects and feedback in the local area where a user currently is doing work. However, there seems to be no evidence that moving between a control panel and a work area is indeed distracting. Nonetheless, this movement could be distracting if the screen surface were large, the distance between the work area and the control panel were great, and/or the effort to make such a move required a user to transfer complete attention to performing the move.

This seemingly innocent situation illustrates a major issue with various types of user interaction design guidance: *A large number of factors can make one technique appropriate in one situation and inappropriate in a situation that appears, at least initially, to be similar.* Numerous other questions would surely arise, which are not answered by either of the passages from the style guide that has been shown so far.

Please note that the Motif™ style guide is not unique in terms of determining its applicability. In fact, all style guides—either commercial or customized—are fraught with these same kinds of problems. The foregoing example simply points out some of the reasons why styles guides are not, in and of themselves, the answer to all user interaction development problems. Producing a style guide that could answer every design question is, of course, impossible, and probably even undesirable—it would inhibit the creativity of designers.

In sum, commercial style guides, unlike standards or even guidelines, are very specific as to the look and feel of different interaction objects. If well-written, they will not require too much interpretation. Their main advantage is to improve consistency of the user interaction design.

> **Acquire at least one commercial style guide, particularly if you are developing your application on a hardware/software platform that supports a particular one. Use them to help produce a customized style guide (see below) for individual interface projects.**

2.2.4   Customized Style Guides

An important early activity for a user interface development team is to produce and internally document their own customized style guide. This can be done for a particular interface development project or for a set of projects. The team can draw on user interaction standards and guidelines, commercial style guides, and possibly even existing customized style guides from other projects. Customized style guides contain quite specifically worded recommendations for various aspects of the user interaction design. Management can mandate the use of a specific style guide for a particular project. A main difference between guidelines and commercial style guides, as compared with customized style guides, is that customized style guides are usually for a specific project, product, and/or organization, while guidelines and commercial guides are generally applicable across a broad range of user interfaces.

Developing an appropriate customized project- or organization-specific style guide is a critical part of user interaction design. It gets the team working together and focusing on human factors issues. Once a customized style guide has been approved by the development team(s), it can serve to mediate decision making throughout the design process. It serves as a record of decisions that have been made about a user interaction design, so that these decisions are not constantly revisited and remade.

The following examples of the kinds of information contained in a customized style guide illustrate how they can be used to help ensure consistency across a user interface:

- Display the time in hh:mm AM/PM (e.g., "10:13 PM") in the upper right corner of the screen.

- Center the name of the application in the middle of the title bar, at the top of the window.

- If a list does not fill the on-screen area allocated to it, do not display an elevator in the vertical scroll bar.

- If a list does fill the on-screen area allocated to it, display an elevator, such that its location in the scroll bar is relative to the portion of the list that is visible.

- Use a blue background color for all displays.

These kinds of very specifically worded rules serve as important components of a customized style guide. In particular, they fit very well into the section that describes the screen templates (see third item in the following list). They remove ambiguities that can leave designers wondering about specific placement, wording, content, and other aspects of interaction objects. Note also that, if accompanied by toolkits, much of this appearance and behavior can be encapsulated in customized precoded interaction objects (or widgets) and is not determined by either an interaction designer or a programmer.

Customized style guides, like commercial style guides, are also based on various interaction objects and interaction styles (see Chapter 3) that the design team considers appropriate for the user interface(s) being developed. A customized style guide should contain at least the following information:

- An *introduction* that explains the basic user interface paradigm used in the guide (e.g., direct manipulation, multiwindow interface), why this paradigm was chosen, and any other project- or organization-specific information that might have influenced this choice (e.g., corporate culture, usability goals, hardware and/or software limitations, constraints, philosophy, politics).

- A short section on *input and output devices* for which the guide is appropriate, and the intended use of these devices in an interface. Because the style guide is typically written very early in the development process, perhaps even before the final application platform has been decided, it may be necessary in the style guide to refer only to generic I/O devices, such as pointer, keyboard, button, or screen. Later, when a decision has been made about platform, specific I/O devices can be indicated as a revision or an addendum to the style guide.

- A section that shows a sketch of a *representative screen template* and describes a typical screen format and layout, such as the main window of the application, in as much detail as is known. It should also include sketches to cover as many situations as possible. These sample representative screen templates are very valuable in ensuring consistency of the screen appearance throughout an interface.

- A separate section for each *interaction object* and *interaction style* that is included in the guide, such as windows, menus, buttons, forms, boxes, command languages, direct manipulation objects, and so on. Each style should be described in terms of what it is (at least for the current user interface); what it looks like, in as much detail as possible, including a good sketch (even a screen dump, if available); how the user interacts with it; and—as much as possible—*when* it should be used in the interface. The guide should be as specific as possible here, in order to remove individual interpretation by designers using the guide, thus aiding consistency of the interface. Again, much of the look and feel will be determined by a toolkit if one is used.

- A section on *messages*, including error messages, informative messages, warning messages, and other feedback, with specific suggested wordings and/or graphics, as appropriate.

Obviously, developing a detailed customized style guide can require a great deal of effort and expertise. However, an initial basic customized style guide might contain no more than a few dozen specific rules and a few screen sketches. It can be expanded as development work progresses. To produce a really effective customized style guide, it may be necessary to enlist expertise from a professional human factors expert early in the development process. The effort and cost of producing a customized style guide should quickly be amortized as members of the development team refer to it for design decisions that do not have to be remade constantly.

A customized style guide document should be produced by one primary author (with outside expertise if necessary), acting as caretaker and documentation specialist for the team. This person should be an expert user interaction designer and should also know much about the applications that will be developed using the customized style guide. Unfortunately, in some current interface development cultures, accepting responsibility for a customized style guide is not a popular activity. It is even viewed as busywork, a superfluous part of the development effort. However, this document is a *critical component* of any interface development project, and it simply cannot be written effectively by someone with little or no user interaction design training and experience.

The author of a customized style guide should interact with and coordinate other appropriate people in the group who are designing the user interface(s) for which the customized style guide is intended. The author should draw on existing standards, guidelines, and commercial style guides, selecting appropriate subsets from each of these. The author should tailor the chosen subsets to the particular design(s) by converting them to rules that are as specific as possible.

Wherever possible, the customized style guide should include information that has been validated through user evaluation, preferably by the group that will be using the customized style guide. It is not feasible to evaluate every suggestion and style in a customized style guide, but those that are most critical and most pervasive throughout an interface should somehow be evaluated. Final approval of a customized style guide requires that members of the development team should accept at least the bulk of it, understand it, and consult it as needed—a process of "buying in."

In sum, producing a customized style guide is a key activity in developing user interaction. It is very specific to a particular application or set of applications within an organization or group. Its main advantage is providing consistent, explicit, unambiguous information for a design, but by its very nature, it lacks the general broad applicability that can be needed to deal with contingencies where specific design rules may cause conflicts. Some customized style guides are beginning to be primarily graphic design standards that provide a corporate look while maintaining a generic (e.g., Motif™ or OpenLook™) feel. This kind of style guide is likely to appear often in the future.

> **Develop at least a simple customized style guide as a record of decisions on specific rules to guide the user interaction design. A more fully developed guide can provide additional guidance for designing other parts of the user interaction.**

2.2.5   Some Cautions on Use of Human Factors Information

One of the biggest concerns about the various kinds of human factors information is the many ways in which they can be misused. In particular, by their very nature, they can be either *too vague* (standards and guidelines) or *too specific* (commercial and customized style guides). Style guides, for example, may very clearly describe *what* particular interaction styles or devices might be used but fail to say *when* that style or device is appropriate. Even when they make an attempt to give guidance on when to use, say, a specific interaction style, there can still be ambiguities. For example, the Apple Guidelines make a suggestion on when to use pop-up menus: "pop-up menus are used for setting values or choosing from lists of related items" (Apple Computer, Inc., 1988). Although this provides some guidance, there are also other ways to set values (e.g., dials), or to choose an item from a list (e.g., pull-down menus). So the interaction designer still must decide when to use which style, given a particular situation.

Perhaps the greatest pitfall in using these kinds of human factors information is the very real *danger* that developers will use them as an *excuse for no longer doing usability evaluation* with human users. One horror story involves a multiyear, multibillion-dollar military weapons system development effort. The development team consisted of more than 100 people. Of these, the person who was designing the user interaction component of the interface was a 26-year-old physicist, straight out of graduate school, who had never even used a graphics package, and who had been given the assignment of working on the user interaction design in his spare time! He waved the OSF Motif™ style guide, asking hopefully, "This will give me a good user interface, won't it?"

Developing and/or using a style guide, with specific design rules, is only a small portion of the effort involved in ensuring usability in an interface. Style guides may contain a lot of good human factors information, but that information alone is not enough. The *process* by which that information is used, and the way in which the resulting interfaces are evaluated, constitutes a major portion of the effort involved in producing a high-quality user interface. This process is discussed in detail in Part II of this book.

An analogy based on the popular toy Legos™ helps people understand why guidelines and rules alone are not enough. It is entirely feasible that someone can be given a box of very fancy Legos™, each of which is individually perfect, and then use those Legos™ to build a structure that will collapse. If the person does not know the process by which Legos™ can be properly put together to construct things, the resulting product will probably crumble. Similarly, following every known guideline and rule in a series of isolated design decisions does not ensure that users will like or be able to use the resulting interface. The only way to evaluate the usability of an interface is to test the whole interface with appropriate users.

2.3   GUIDELINES

As already discussed earlier in this chapter (Section 2.2.2), guidelines represent the common sense side of user interaction design. They typically are general in nature, but, by their very breadth, cover many different facets that must be taken into consideration when designing user interaction. Because of the importance of guidelines in interaction design, this chapter presents those guidelines we have found to be most relevant to designing a usable interface, with examples and anecdotes for each. Again, recall that *this is an overview* and in no way a complete set of guidelines. For much more detail, refer to any of the references cited in Section 2.1. Also recall that *guidelines are just that*: a set of strong, reasonable suggestions for interaction design, which—to be properly applied—must be evaluated in each individual design situation.

2.3.1   User-Centered Design

▶ Practice user-centered design.

User-centered design (Norman & Draper, 1986) has emerged as one of the most compelling mandates for developing user interaction. It is closely related to the notion of behavioral design (see Chapter 1), producing the interaction from the view of the user, rather than the view of the system. Unfortunately, what is best for the user may not be natural for the designer. What is easiest for the user to use is rarely easiest for the interaction designer to design or for the programmer to implement. In fact, exactly the opposite is often true. Having the role of interaction designer distinguished from that of software engineer helps to meet this guideline.

User-centered design takes time, effort, and expertise. Producing effective user interaction requires focusing on what is best for the user, rather than what is quickest and easiest to implement. Ted Nelson, creator of the Xanadu hypertext system of online publications, states it beautifully:

> Designing an object to be simple and clear takes at least twice as long as the usual way. It requires concentration at the outset on how a clear and simple system would work, followed by the steps required to make it come out that way—steps which are often much harder and more complex than the ordinary ones. It also requires relentless pursuit of that simplicity even when obstacles appear which would seem to stand in the way of that simplicity. (T.H. Nelson, *The Home Computer Revolution*, 1977, as quoted in Shneiderman, 1992)

▶ Know the user.

This maxim of user-centered design, originally from Hansen (1971), appears simple on the surface but is difficult to accomplish. To know the user means to understand human behavior. More particularly, it means to know the characteristics of the classes of users that will be using a particular interface. Designers should give early and continual attention to the user throughout the development process. They need to *understand*—not just identify, describe, or stereotype—users of the system. Designers can begin to understand users by interviewing them and observing them at work both before and during interaction design.

You don't, however, get to "know the user" by simple observation or arbitrary interviews. Such techniques as user analysis, task analysis, information flow analysis, and, when appropriate, time-and-motion studies can be used to obtain a better understanding of the characteristics of users of an application. These techniques require some skill and analysis to be effective and are often best used in combination with each other. Many questions have to be answered, for example: What are the expected users' cognitive, behavioral, anthropometric, ergonomic, and attitudinal characteristics? What education, training, skills, and experience will they have?

To know the user also means to know what tasks users need to perform, with or without a computer-based system. In fact, one of our colleagues talks about "*use*-centered design," as well as user-centered design (George Casaday, c. 1991). That is, the design should be tailored to facilitate the use that a user will make of the system—the tasks a user will perform in order to achieve some purpose. The important development activity of task analysis is discussed further in Chapter 5. Giving early and continual attention to the user's tasks will help designers understand the nature of the work that users want to do with the system. Study of how users currently are accomplishing their tasks—with or without an interactive system—will help designers to understand users and their work.

▶ Involve the user via participatory design.

Getting users involved in interaction development is now widely recognized as a key to improved usability of the interface. The payoffs are tremendous. Designers benefit from the problem domain knowledge that only users can have. This is, in fact, the role of the problem domain expert that was mentioned in Chapter 1. Users feel as if they have a stake in producing a good interface, rather than sitting around waiting for it to appear on the scene, with little or no warning.

For production workers in a factory, for example, who have never used a computer, finding out that their job is going to become dependent on their ability to use a computer can be frightening. Their very livelihood is threatened. Having some of the workers involved in interaction development increases their ownership of the product and decreases their fear of it. They can also serve as advocates of the system to their coworkers, thereby increasing psychological acceptance of and "buy in" to the system.

The precise role of users in participatory design is still somewhat an open issue. However, users can help designers understand what tasks the users need to perform, how often the tasks are performed, conditions under which those tasks currently are being performed, and so on. If the current system supporting those tasks is computer-based, users can tell a designer what they do and don't like about it. They can show what is easy and what is hard to accomplish. They can also tell a designer how they might like to do tasks differently or can suggest other tasks that they would like to perform. If the current system is manual, rather than computer-supported, users can convey much of the same information, as well as indicating ways in which their tasks can be made easier by automation.

We are not advocating involvement of large numbers of potential users of an interactive system in its development. A few carefully chosen representatives of each appropriate class of user, even a single representative, can provide designers with invaluable information. That person can also serve as a good-news messenger to others who might be threatened by the thought of a computer.

▶ Prevent user errors.

To "engineer for errors" or to "make things goof proof" for the user is an excellent way to practice user-centered design. This means to anticipate possible user errors and head them off. In a good interaction design, almost no action a user takes is unanticipated. Like many other aspects of user-centered design, this may be easier said than done; user error analysis is a major field of study in its own right.

There are, however, many ways an interaction designer can anticipate potential problem areas and help the user avoid mistakes. For example, in typed .command interaction, the system can adopt the approach of syntax-directed editing. When the user types a left parenthesis or left bracket, the system immediately displays the right parenthesis or bracket also. The user can then type the desired characters between the parentheses or brackets, not having to worry about remembering to close the parentheses or brackets.

Many graphical user interfaces help the user avoid errors by making erroneous choices unavailable. Graying out menu choices or buttons when they are not available is a good example. This is especially appropriate for direct manipulation, asynchronous interfaces, when many choices exist in the design, but only a subset of those choices might be enabled and available to the user at any given time. This is a good example of what is best for the user not being easiest for the designer and implementer. Graying out choices when they are not enabled requires the designer and implementer to determine extensive state information. At the same time, though, it prevents them from having to design and implement error messages that would be needed if the user could choose unavailable commands.

The graying-out approach can lead to frustration, however, for users who do not know why the desired choice is not available. This can be solved by displaying a help message if a user attempts to make a grayed-out choice anyway. For this approach to be successful, a designer needs to establish, as part of the user's system model, that this is the way in which grayed-out choices work throughout the interface.

Designing to prevent errors can go beyond the syntactic kinds of errors just described and can protect users at the semantic level, as well. One way to do this is to require user confirmation for potentially destructive actions. For example, the interaction should be designed so that if a user tries to delete an entire directory of files, that action must be confirmed by the user. That is, the interface should warn the user of the potential annihilation of a directory and should ask the user whether that is the intended task. In one popular operating system, a user can type

```
delete *.*.*
```

and the system—having deleted all files in the user's current directory—responds with nothing more than the operating-system-level prompt.

This guideline is best summed up by a paraphrasing of a well-known saying: "To err is human; forgive by design." Another philosophy (contributed by Jon Meads) espouses making the cost of an error and its correction so cheap that users can make all the errors they want without great adverse effects.

▶ Optimize user operations.

Designers should strive toward the most effect for the least user effort, offering the user—especially the frequent user—increased efficiency as much as possible. Good examples include use of accelerator keys (e.g., "Ctrl-s", which means to depress the "control" key together with the "s" key, for the "save" command) or function keys as alternative methods for selecting from a menu. If accelerator keys or function keys are available, then a frequent user, who knows the selections on a menu (or at least the selections the user most often makes), does not have to use the menu to make the desired choice.

More sophisticated users may want to use macros and abbreviations to optimize their actions. Macros, including user-defined ones, allow users to define a sequence of frequently used actions or tasks with a single name, so that they do not have to type each step of the complete sequence every time they wish to perform those tasks. Similarly, abbreviations increase user performance by reducing typing.

▶ Keep the locus of control with the user.

It is vitally important that the user feels in charge at all times, rather than feeling as if the computer is in charge. The user should have the impression that the computer is prepared to respond whenever the user is ready to issue a command. Subtle differences in wording of messages can convey this in a surprisingly forceful way. Think about the difference between "enter next command" and "ready for next command." "Enter next command" is a very demanding message from the computer, to which the user may feel pressure to take action. However, "ready for next command" is a message that implies to the user that the computer is prepared to respond on demand from the user.

Inappropriate time-outs, such as a screen display disappearing because the user didn't enter anything for a few seconds, can also make users feel as if they are not in control. Locus of control, and the user's perception of it, has great psychological impact and can strongly influence the user's impression of an interface.

▶ Help the user get started with the system.

In general, a user should need no more than one page (or screenful) of information before being able to begin useful work with a new (to the user) interactive system. Provide a simple overview (either a page or a screen) that explains such basic information as conventions for mouse buttons, where to look for messages, how to get more extensive help, what the basic core functions are and what they do, and how to select them. Such minimalist introduction to a system will help to make the user more comfortable more quickly with a new system. After all, if users find that they can indeed do useful work after reading only one page of information, how bad can the system be?

2.3.2 System Model

▶ Give the user a mental model of the system, based on user tasks.

Developing a good system model is very important during interaction design. Too many systems, lacking a good system model, incorporate features in an ad hoc fashion. Lack of a well-developed system model is one of the root causes for poor user interfaces.

A system model sets the architectural framework for a system. It typically is device-, data-, and operation-oriented and represents flow of data and operations performed on those data. This maps into a conceptual model, which is the view of typical sequencing and functionality being offered to a user by a developer (and therefore a system). This, in turn, translates into a user's mental model, which is how a user perceives a system (Mayhew, 1992). The mental model governs how a user understands a system and interacts with it. If the mental model does not correspond well to the system model—because a system model is poorly done or lacking altogether, or because the mapping was not done reasonably—the user will have a difficult time understanding and interacting with a system.

A consistent user mental model, based on the tasks a user performs, will guide a user in accomplishing tasks in a general way. For example, in a direct manipulation interface, a user typically accomplishes tasks by first selecting an object, such as an icon, and then performing an action on that object, such as opening it. A user will quickly learn this object–action paradigm and will apply it throughout the interface. In a typed-command-line interface, the user often performs tasks via the opposite paradigm. That is, the user first types in the action, such as "show," followed by the object on which to perform the action, such as "dir" (for directory).

Visual cues can be especially effective in helping a user understand the system model and thereby formulate a mental model. A vertically (top to bottom) scrollable window, for example, has a scroll bar, usually on the window's right side, in which an iconic elevator is positioned, to indicate where in the file the current contents of the window are positioned. If the elevator is not at the top or the bottom of the scroll bar, the user can move forward and backward in the file, examining more of its contents. A window that is also horizontally (side to side) scrollable has a scroll bar, usually at the bottom of the window, that shows the user the left-to-right position of the current contents of the window. This kind of cue tells users where they are (position within the file) and what they can do from this point (move up or down or side to side).

2.3.3 Consistency and Simplicity

▶ Be consistent.

This has been called the "principle of least astonishment." On the surface, this guideline is easy to understand. If something is done a certain way in an interface (e.g., a task has a specific name, or an icon has a certain appearance [look] or behavior [feel]), users expect the same thing to be done the same way throughout the rest of the interface. Thus, similar things are expected to be done in similar ways.

Much has been written about the need for consistency in user interaction. On the other hand, much has also been written about the difficulty in understanding what consistency is and how to apply it effectively (e.g., Grudin, 1989). Consistency can have many different interpretations. It can be looked at with respect to many different attributes (e.g., size, location, color, wording, function, sequencing, and so on). Consistency by one criterion can conflict with consistency by another. This guideline of consistency can even conflict or trade off with other guidelines.

Nonetheless, consistency is one of the most significant factors affecting usability. Users expect certain aspects of an interface to behave in certain ways, and when that does not happen, it can be very confusing. For similar semantics in an interface, similar syntax should be used, and vice versa. This is true within a single interface and even across a product line or organization. For example, in a word processor, the command to replicate selected text should not be named "duplicate" in one menu and "copy" in another.

While the Macintosh™ desktop interface is one of the most consistent, there are a couple of glaring instances of inconsistency in its design. Our favorite is found in the commands for deleting a file and for ejecting a floppy disk. In order to delete (erase) a file or folder, as well as its contents (so that they can never be used again), the user uses the mouse to select and drag the file's icon to the trash icon. To eject a floppy disk, the user uses the mouse in the same way to select and drag the disk's icon to the trash icon. In this case, however, the contents of the floppy disk are preserved for future use: same syntax (user actions), very different semantics (final results).

First-time users sometimes refuse to use the action of dragging the disk icon to the trash to eject the disk, fearing—and rightfully so—that the contents of the floppy could be destroyed (at least prior to System 7.0) when they release it into the trash. Most users, however, adapt to this inconsistency, and a user is not required to use this action to eject a disk (there is also a menu command). The Macintosh™ interface designers contend that this is an example of an inconsistency that is practical and acceptable. Users certainly learn it, but many still don't care for it. In System 7.0, this inconsistency is fixed, to the extent that the user has control over when the trash is emptied (just as in real life), so that files and folders put in it by the user are not dumped at some seemingly random time.

▶ Keep it simple.

This certainly is not simple to do! Today's interactive systems are inherently complex, resulting in a user interface that is also complex. However, as Alan Kay (c. 1973) suggests, interaction designers can make an effort to keep simple tasks easy for the user, and to make complex tasks possible.

Simple tasks can be kept easy by using actions, icons, words, and other interaction objects that are natural to the user. For those aspects of the interaction that are difficult, designers should attempt to make them as straightforward and understandable as possible by breaking complex tasks into simpler subtasks, using objects that are natural to the user, and so on. Reducing complexity for users is still a very difficult aspect of interaction design.

2.3.4   Human Memory Issues

▶ Account for human memory limitations by giving the user frequent closure on tasks.

Someone once said that memory is what people forget with. Because of this, the capacity and duration of a human's short-term or working memory must be taken into account when designing user interaction. That capacity is normally measured as the famous "seven plus or minus two chunks" (Miller, 1956). A *chunk* is a basic unit of information, in this case, to be remembered. It could be a person's name; it could be a word, a phrase, or a larger concept. The main thing is that it is a single entity. Just as is the case with computers, humans can trade off processing time for memory. Humans can encode several chunks into one chunk for storage, and decode again at retrieval time. As a very simple example, a person can remember a string of 15 binary bits (ones and zeroes) more easily by encoding these into 5 octal digits. Recalling the original bits requires decoding back to the binary.

The next natural question is, How short is short-term memory? This is the *duration*, the length of time that information can be held in memory (and, as we are discovering, is inversely proportional to age). Actually, it is approximately 30 seconds to a maximum of about 2 minutes. How often have you—at least in the days before phones had a redial feature—looked up the number of a restaurant to make a dinner reservation, dialed the number, gotten a busy signal, and hung up. A moment later, you pick up the receiver to dial again and . . . you've forgotten the number—you have experienced short-term memory limitations in action!

How is this applied in user interaction design? These limitations of human memory indicate, for example, that an interaction design should limit the number of items a user has to deal with at any particular moment. A bad design might have the first few choices of a long menu scrolling off the top of the screen where a user can no longer see them and certainly won't remember them. Information on screens should be organized so that a user does not have to buffer information from one screen to the next by remembering it or writing it down.

For example, information must sometimes be brought from a list in one screen to a field of a form in another screen that is not visible at the same time as the first screen. The user must either carry this information in short-term memory or write it down on a piece of paper and then reenter it. One way to relieve the user's short-term memory burden in this case is to have the user select a value from the list, have the system fill the selected value into the next screen's form as a default, and then allow the user to modify it as necessary. In order to handle this situation correctly, a designer must thoroughly understand the user's task context, realizing that the form field is logically connected to the list choice.

Another way human memory plays a part in interaction design has to do with how humans handle interruptions while they are performing tasks. For example, you may be in the middle of replying to a somewhat urgent electronic mail message when someone knocks on the door. You answer the door and start a discussion with the visitor, only to have the phone ring. You answer it and start another conversation. Each of these interruptions has caused mental stacking, which requires considerable effort by the human. When you finish on the phone and come back to the visitor, you may try to remember what you were discussing. This requires unstacking and restoring your previous mental working environment.

Because the mental stack is implemented in a human's short-term, or working, memory, there is a loss of information over relatively short periods of time. It takes extra effort, too, to recall the discussion with the visitor. You pay in additional time and effort when you return to work on your electronic mail, and by this time, you're likely to get interrupted again. Thus, the overhead cost, due to interruption, of stacking and restoring task environments is high.

The solution to this problem of interruption as it relates to user interaction is to design for task closure. An interaction designer should think carefully about how large tasks are decomposed into smaller tasks for the user. For example, if the decomposition is done on a depth-first basis within a hierarchical task/subtask structure, the user must first begin the overall task and then set it aside to do the first subtask at the next level down, then set it aside, and so on, leaving a whole series of containing tasks and subtasks suspended until the lowest-level subtask is completed. Then the user can come back up a level at a time, finally getting closure at each level. This approach of opening a new subtask at each level of decomposition causes a great deal of stacking for the user.

As an alternative, starting at the bottom, subtasks can be completed first, allowing the user to get closure on each one in turn. Then results of the subtasks can be combined to perform the highest-level task. In this approach, interruptions will not have as great an impact on user performance. Users can complete a task and return to the point of zero working-memory load, clearing their mental stacks, and starting fresh with a new task.

In sum, short linear sequences of actions by the user—rather than deep, involved task and subtask hierarchies—will facilitate task closure. Using small sequences allows a user to chunk activity with closure after each. Short sequences should not require a user to mentally transfer much information from one sequence to the next. A good design can guide the user through tasks with mileposts (e.g., short messages) indicating closure while maintaining status and presenting what may be done next.

► Let the user recognize, rather than having to recall, whenever feasible.

Human memory limitations can also be overcome in interaction design by using recognition, rather than recall. That is, allow the user to make a selection from a displayed list (*recognition*), rather than having to remember (*recall*) a specific string of characters that must be typed in to accomplish a task. For example, recognizing a choice from a menu is much easier for the user than having to remember all possible choices and then type in one of them as a command. In addition to reducing memory load, recognition also reduces typing errors.

2.3.5   Cognitive Issues

▶ Use cognitive directness.

Cognitive directness involves minimizing mental transformations that a user must make. Even small cognitive transformations by a user take effort away from the intended task. Minimization of mental transformations by a user can be accomplished by the use of appropriate mnemonics, or memory aids. For example, in a pull-down menu, an accelerator-key sequence such as "Command-c" for the "cut" command is much easier for the user to learn and remember than some meaningless sequence such as "Esc-F7". (However, if the usability of the interface is really poor, at some point, "escape" may appeal to a user.)

As much as possible, use of a meaningful leading letter for a menu selection is desirable, but clashes will arise inevitably and quickly (e.g., "cut" and "copy" in a word processor). When this happens, there is no easy solution; the designer might decide which command is likely to be the one most often selected and use the obvious mnemonic for it. Instead, the designer could give a different name, and therefore mnemonic, to one of the commands. These must simply be dealt with on a case-by-case basis, using good judgment.

Appropriate visual cues, such as the layout of arrow keys and carefully designed graphical icons, also contribute to cognitive directness. For example, some keyboards have the arrow keys for cursor movement all in one row. Users must look at the arrow symbol on each key and make a mental connection between the cursor movement they want and the appropriate symbol. Many users never really learn the arrow-key layout, especially if they are infrequent users, so a mental transformation must be performed every time the arrow keys are used. In an alternative layout, the left- and right-arrow keys can be placed side by side, with the up-arrow key centered above them and the down-arrow key centered beneath. With this simple change in layout, users do not have to look at the symbols on the keys; they need only glance at the keys themselves or even use them by touch. The relative position of each key directly implies the direction in which that key will move the cursor.

► Draw on real-world analogies.

By using situations, words, pictures, and metaphors that are natural and known to most users, a user's expectations about an interface are supported, and cognitive directness is increased. An electronic spreadsheet uses the metaphor of the familiar rows and columns used by accountants; users more easily understand its use than if some unfamiliar layout were used. The Macintosh™ desktop metaphor is an excellent example, where folders look like the familiar real-world manila file folders and can be treated like real folders by putting documents and even other folders into them. They can be stacked, moved around on the desktop, and renamed, and they are even deleted by throwing them in the trash.

Be forewarned, however, that design based on analogy, to mimic a real-world counterpart, can sometimes be a tricky proposition. This is especially true for the appearance of an icon. An interface can quickly become too cluttered and busy by the use of too many icons; some interfaces have more than 1000 different icons. Sometimes, when a picture simply isn't enough, a label should be added to an icon; a user can hardly distinguish among this number of different pictures.

There are numerous limitations on icon design imposed by such constraints as screen real estate, screen resolution, and even cultural biases. Consider, for example, the design of an icon to represent a "help" command. We have used this many times as an exercise for interaction design students. Think about it for a minute, and decide what kind of sketch you might use to indicate the help command. A typical one is that of a swimmer, either grasping for a life preserver of some sort, or "going down," with a hand sticking out of the water. The meaning of these visual representations is always very clear, but think about what this inadvertently and very subtly conveys to a user about the interface. To users, this becomes a "horror-glyph" (George Casaday, c. 1991), implying that this interface is so hard to use that they are going to need a life preserver or else they'll sink!

Some commands (e.g., undo, redo, and even help) may simply be best represented as a short word, rather than trying to use an icon. Another option is the *picon* (for picture icon)—a term denoting a visual icon that is a photograph, rather than a line drawing or cartoonlike image, of some interaction object. It can sometimes denote more clearly the desired meaning of an object than can a drawing.

2.3.6   Feedback

► Use informative feedback.

Closed-loop communication is always better than is open loop. Effective feedback is a part of the interaction that has a significant psychological impact on the user. Via good feedback, users can gauge the effects of their actions. Unfortunately, computer feedback is often just "backtalk." When users perform actions, they want to know what happened. When the outline of a folder icon is shown as it is dragged across a desktop, it lets the user know that the folder is, in fact, moving. When the trash can icon expands as the user drops a folder into it (if there is not already an undisposed item in the trash), the user knows that the folder was indeed put in the trash. Conversely, when the user types "delete *somefilename*" and the response is the operating system prompt, the user may still wonder whether, in fact, the *somefilename* file was removed or if something else happened instead.

A user often needs both articulatory feedback and semantic feedback. *Articulatory feedback* tells users that their hands worked correctly, while *semantic feedback* tells them that their heads worked correctly. For example, when the user selects "open" from a pull-down menu, the choice may blink briefly just before the menu disappears. This is articulatory feedback indicating to users that they picked their intended choice. Then a dialogue box appears that lists the possible files that can be opened; this is semantic feedback, confirming that the intended choice was indeed right for the task the user wished to perform.

Visual cues—either textual or graphical—are most commonly used for feedback. They show users the effects of their actions and can show users what is available at a given time.

▶ Give the user appropriate status indicators.

Whenever the system is performing a potentially lengthy process (e.g., making a lengthy computation), a user should be given feedback, such as the display of an hourglass, a clock face with moving hands, or even a simple "working . . ." message. Otherwise, after only a few seconds, the user will begin to wonder whether the system is really doing something useful or has somehow gotten into a suspended state. In general, a system should have a response time appropriate for the task (Shneiderman, 1992). For example, for typing, cursor movement, and mouse clicking, a response time of 50 to 150 milliseconds is recommended. Response time should be less than 1 second for simple frequent tasks in order for the user not to become annoyed with delays. For common tasks, the recommendation is 2 to 4 seconds. Users will tolerate somewhat longer response times, up to about 12 seconds or so, for more complex tasks.

For response times greater than 2 to 4 seconds, the user should be given some sort of status indicator. This is particularly true if the user cannot interact with the system while a system process is in progress, which is usually the case. The status indicator should disappear automatically, on completion of the process; the system should not need any input (e.g., selecting an "ok" button) from the user to remove a status indicator from the screen. In any case, a status indicator should remain on the screen long enough for a user to read it—at least a couple of seconds.

Some other examples of situations in which a status indicator is appropriate are found when the system is performing a long search throughout a network, formatting a disk, or transferring several files. Here, it is most helpful to a user to display an indicator showing what portion of the task is completed (e.g., what percentage of the network has been searched or how many of the files have been transferred). For particularly lengthy computations (greater than a few seconds), this more detailed feedback is particularly important.

2.3.7   System Messages

▶ Use user-centered wording in messages.

Obviously, the reason for displaying a message to a user is to communicate information. Users should be thinking about their tasks and not about how things are implemented within the system. Use of user-centered and task-centered, rather than system-centered, wording will greatly contribute to this communication.

A few years ago, the secretaries in our Computer Science department were using a popular mainframe word processor. Occasionally they received a rather bizarre message on the screen: "505 hex 0001F9 doublewords of storage were not recovered." You can imagine the panic and fear this caused, especially when the secretaries discovered that none of the professors seemed to know for sure what this message meant. The secretaries thought some of their work was gone, and indeed, from this message, that was as good a guess as any as to what had happened. Eventually, they were told by some systems guru that the system apparently was doing some automatic internal storage reallocation that was of no interest whatsoever to any user except perhaps the system manager. Why on earth was a poor unsuspecting word-processing user ever given this strange message?

Even the most innocent and seemingly straightforward message can be misunderstood or misinterpreted. A caller to a user-support desk reported receiving a message from the system that said, "Hit any key to continue." However, the caller stated, "I can't find the 'any' key." The person at the support desk calmly and effectively replied, "It's the space bar; they just failed to label it."

Protect users from system-related jargon, especially information presented in a way that is confusing or threatening. Communicate with users in terms of their tasks, in words that are familiar to them.

▶ Use positive, nonthreatening wording in error messages.

Error messages may be the part of an interactive system that have the greatest psychological impact on a user. Users may already know they are in trouble, and the last thing they need is to feel chastised or punished by the system. People who have been using computers for years have seen many negative, threatening, even demeaning, error messages, including old favorites (many of these from B. Shneiderman): "fatal error, run aborted"; "disastrous string overflow, job abandoned"; "catastrophic error, logged with operator." As if it is not bad enough that these messages sound so sinister, some almost violent, they give the user absolutely no information about what error was made or how to go about correcting that error.

Designers should also avoid chastising the user with violent, negative, or demeaning terms in error messages. Instead, use positive wording; remember that the user, in this situation, needs help and encouragement, not punishment. In addition, interaction designers should avoid the temptation to use humor; if users are making a lot of errors, they may be in a bad mood and may respond poorly to attempted humor. What is humorous in one language or culture may be humorless or even insulting in another.

▶ Use specific, constructive terms in error messages.

Be specific in the wording of error messages. Wordings such as "syntax error" or "incorrect data" do little more than puzzle or frustrate a user. Clearly, in order to determine that a syntax error has occurred or that the input data were incorrect, the system had to analyze the situation. Error messages should be worded so that any information the system may have about errors is given to the user. This is a good example of what is best for the user being harder for the designer and implementer. It is obviously much easier for the designer to write one simple "syntax error" message to cover a multitude of user input errors, rather than worrying about all possible erroneous kinds of input the user might make and writing a separate, lucid, informative message for each.

When users make errors, they often also need constructive information about how to get out of the jam. A simple message such as "invalid entry" as a response to erroneous input to a field of a form is useless to the user. A more specific message may be needed, such as "Inventory part number is out of allowable range." An even more constructive and specific message would be "Inventory numbers range from 0000 to 9999."

It can be difficult to give the user constructive, helpful messages without getting verbose, but messages should be brief and concise. One approach to this is to give as concise a message as possible, but allow the user to select help (e.g., from a menu or a button) to get additional information.

▶ Make the system take the blame for errors.

One of the fastest ways to strip users of the feeling that they are in charge—shifting the locus of control from the user to the computer—is through error messages that make users feel blamed for a problem. Very subtle differences in wording can have a tremendous impact on a user's feeling of guilt. Think about the difference in the two messages: "illegal command" and "unrecognized command." In the first message, the users are immediately put on the defensive; they did something illegal; they broke the law. In the second message, the system is "admitting" to the users that it can't recognize what the users are trying to tell it; the system is taking the blame. One simple word change very effectively shifts the blame from the user to the system. The phone company rather nicely handles some dialing error situations with system-blaming words: "We are unable to complete your call as dialed. Please hang up and try again." Sometimes, even more constructive messages are given, such as "You must first dial a '1' in order to complete your call. Please hang up and try again."

Novice user interaction designers are often surprised at the amount of work required to write positive, specific, constructive, user-centered messages. Constructing concise, yet informative, messages requires careful thinking and wording. The importance of every single word that a user sees cannot be emphasized enough. Very subtle differences in wording, seemingly inconsequential at first blush, can have great impact on a user's overall impression of the system and in fact on a user's performance with the system.

2.3.8   Anthropomorphization

▶ Do not anthropomorphize.

Anthropomorphization means attributing human characteristics to nonhuman objects, such as cars or computers. Talking heads, sometimes called "agents," are a good example. These are the little faces that pop up, usually in their own small window in a corner of the screen, and proceed to talk to the user in a very friendly fashion. A more common example is use of wording so that it appears to the user as if the computer is talking to them: "Good morning, John. How are you today?" First of all, the computer doesn't know what morning means and certainly doesn't care how John is. Why be cute?

The point is that anthropomorphization is very easy to do badly. The results can be patronizing, irritating, deceitful, and even demeaning. Naïve users, especially, can get the wrong impression about the computer, and if they are turned off by personal words or talking heads, they may develop distrust for the system. Even the much-hackneyed term "user-friendly" is anthropomorphic. Users don't want computers to be their friends; what they really want is for computers to help them to perform desired tasks easily. While talking heads and other such clever things can indeed be effective in, for example, training systems, they must be used judiciously and designed carefully (Shneiderman, 1992).

2.3.9   Modality and Reversible Actions

► Use modes cautiously.

A *mode* is an interface state in which a user action has a different meaning (and result) than it has in some other state. Modality is virtually impossible to avoid in interaction designs. When it is used, the designer should be careful to distinguish different interaction modes for the user, so the user clearly knows at all times which mode is active. Visual cues are often a good approach to distinguishing such modes. For example, in a modal graphics editor, the shape of the cursor might change to indicate whether the editor is in the mode for creating circles or lines.

A *preemptive mode* is one in which a user must complete one task before going to another. There are modal (preemptive) and modeless dialogue boxes, for example. In a modal dialogue box, the user must complete some task shown in the box before the box will become inactive or disappear. While the box is displayed, no user action can be performed outside the box. Such preemption is effective at focusing user activity, but it eliminates the rest of the application (outside the box) from the user's current task domain. Most of the time, preemptive modes are to be avoided, except when a user must commit to a response (e.g., to save a file or not) before a task can proceed.

In a modeless dialogue box, on the other hand, the user can either choose a task from within the box or choose some other task (e.g., an icon or a choice from a menu) not in the box. This keeps virtually the whole application task domain available to the user at any time. The dialogue box may or may not disappear if the user chooses a task outside the box, depending on the design.

► Make user actions easily reversible.

Direct manipulation interfaces, especially for text editing and graphics, typically have an "undo" command. This allows users to reverse undesirable or accidental actions they may make. This is an obvious example of a design feature that is good for the users but rather difficult for the designer and implementer of an interface. Designing an "undo" is quite tricky, and there is still no consensus on how far back users should be able to go with a series of "undos" or on what an "undo" of an "undo" should do. Should it take users back to where they were before the first "undo," or should it "redo" what the users did previous to the second "undo?" Also, what is an "undo" of an "undo" of an "undo?"

Reversibility applies to actions for navigating through the system, as well. Allowing a user to return to previous levels or screens is a way to make this kind of action easily reversible. Users should be able to return to at least the previous screen they came from. Also, if there are appropriate points partway through a task, they should be able to cancel a task without having to complete it. In most systems, a user should be able to escape or exit or quit from the application from any point in the system, without having to back up through previous levels or screens to get to an exclusive exit point.

Such mechanisms for allowing users easily to reverse their actions will encourage exploration of a system. With a good interaction design, users can be confident that they will not, indeed cannot, paint themselves into a corner. Under these conditions, when they are not fearful of getting trapped or of taking potentially destructive actions by accident, users will explore many more features of a system.

2.3.10 Getting the User's Attention

▶ Get the user's attention judiciously.

With advances in technology, there are almost limitless ways to get the user's attention while working with an interface. The key is to use attention-getting techniques *judiciously*. Among the many kinds of interaction features, these techniques are among the easiest to overuse and misuse. Note that our discussion addresses this guideline mainly in terms of simple text and graphical interfaces. Although it is also applicable to the complex graphical, visualization interfaces that are emerging, it is not yet known how specifically to interpret the guideline for these complicated new kinds of interfaces.

For text, the general rule is to use only two levels of *intensity* on a single screen. Use *underlining, bold, inverse video*, and other forms of marking sparingly. They draw the user's eye to the marked object. For predominantly textual screens, generally use no more than three different *fonts* on a single screen, no more than four different font sizes on a single screen. Fonts with a serif are easier to read, because the serifs help a user's eye glide across the text. (The letters on this page have a serif, those little marks that hang off the edges of many of the letters. Helvetica type, a sans serif type, is plain and boxy, without the little serif decorations. Sans serif typically makes the reading a bit harder and slower, but this also can depend on display characteristics such as resolution and contrast. Some people prefer it, despite somewhat less readability.)

Use uppercase and lowercase letters, not all uppercase. An exception here might be the title of the screen, but in general, capitalize as you would in a normal sentence. For some reason, probably dating back to teletype terminals, some people believe that all uppercase is appropriate for computer input and output. However, all capital letters not only take up a good deal more space on the screen, where real estate is usually at a premium, but also they have been shown to slow down reading speed by more than 10%.

Blinking is a particularly intense attention grabber, so use it only for very important items. If these items are text messages, for example, they should be fairly short (a few words), or only some portion of the message should blink. A screen on which more than a few words are blinking will irritate a user very quickly and may also frighten a novice user.

Audio can be used as a cue for important events and is often effective as a redundant output channel. For example, the user may see words on the screen warning of an alarm situation, while simultaneously hearing an alarm bell. Audio is particularly effective when one channel might not be enough, as when the user might not see an important message that appears, for example, on a rather busy screen. Soft tones should be used for positive or nonemergency feedback, such as a quiet beep to confirm successful completion of a print request, or to warn the user that the printer is out of paper. Use harsher tones for emergencies or to get immediate attention. Beeps for systems that are going to be used in open, office-type environments, such as word processors or spreadsheets, should have minimal audio output. Obviously, a constant barrage of beeps and blips will irritate officemates and can even embarrass the user if those beeps might be construed by coworkers as errors.

One of the most obnoxious examples of computer-generated speech (if it can be called that) is in the Atlanta airport people-mover. It sounds somewhat like the dying HAL in the movie *2001* as it loudly admonishes the riders to "Please stand away from the door. The train is leaving the station." The first few times we heard this, we could not understand why such harsh, loud tones were necessary. Then it occurred to us that unless the sound was quite loud and different from the normal human voice, it would not be distinguished from all the talking and other ambient noise that is a part of a busy airport and subway system. It was necessary in order to get the user's attention in this context.

Color is perhaps the single most overused feature in user interaction designs. Only clowns and comic-strip characters can get away with using too much color! Interaction designers, especially novice ones, often think they should use lots of color just because it is available to them. Granted, it's nice to know that 16 million colors are available on today's fancy workstations, but developers rarely need to use more than a handful of them, especially on a single screen. In fact, it is often a good idea to design screens in black and white (monochrome) first. Color monitors are not always available for all installations of a system. Also, about 8%

of Caucasian men are color-deficient in their vision, and use of color is therefore lost on them. The point is that the layout and content of the user interaction should make sense independently of color.

Generally, use no more than four different colors on a single screen, especially if it is mostly text, and no more than seven different colors throughout a single application. While numerous studies give different results, a general rule is that blue or black is best as a background color, especially for text, with white or yellow characters, respectively. Blue should not be used for text; it is one of the hardest colors to read because the color receptors in the eye, the cones, are particularly insensitive to blue. Because of this, blue is a good color for background and for large areas, but not for details. These guidelines are, of course, variable, depending on the interaction style, and, indeed, on user preference. Designers often think that because people are mostly used to reading dark letters on light paper, that same combination can be the most effective for computer screens. However, staring at a constant bright background (e.g., white) for long periods of time can cause eye strain. Unfortunately, various studies have produced contradictory results as to guidelines for foreground and background color, so it is impossible to say what the best combination is. However, one important point is that a good combination of foreground and background colors is one with a good contrast between the two.

Color can, of course, be used effectively as a coding technique, but it should be used conservatively and redundantly. Use color coding, for example, to show relationships of objects on screens, such as related fields in a single screen form, or related fields across several forms. Windows generated, for example, from different tasks can be related by their color. Color will also effectively call attention to important or changing information. It can be used to make objects, especially icons, on the screen look more realistic. Redundancy is important because of the color-perception deficiencies of some users; for example, using both shape and color to distinguish classes of items is an effective approach.

Always consider familiar color conventions carefully. Green, yellow, and especially red have special connotations, at least to Americans, and their use in an interface should not violate user expectations. When users see a green object, they automatically think "Go" or "Everything is OK." Yellow raises a caution flag in their minds. Red causes them to immediately think "Stop" or "Something is wrong." Red should be reserved for emergency messages or critical icons, such as the "fire" button in a weapons launching system.

Especially because of the wide diversity of opinions about use of color and the relatively few concrete rules, designers often think that the best solution is to let users customize their displays to their own personal preferences. If color has not been used significantly in the design, then it is usually acceptable to give users control over their own color choices. However, such flexibility doesn't work, obviously, if color has special meaning in the design. In this case, you might give the user a set of preferences that will automatically maintain the appropriate color codings (e.g., choices among pastels, primary colors, or even monochrome with appropriate patterns rather than colors).

Graphics can effectively allow more use of color than just a simple alphanumeric interface, but graphical interface designs are likely to overuse color severely. For example, in a workstation-based military flight system, the main screen was a large map of Europe. The oceans were brilliant blue, each country was a different strong color, and aircraft and their tracks were all bright red. Instead, the use of more subtle, even pastel, colors, would be much easier on the user who has to sit in front of this screen for several hours at a time. In fact, the map had been originally designed and implemented using fewer and less intense colors, but when the Admiral who was funding the project came to inspect the system, he demanded that all the colors be changed because the map looked too feminine. Of course, he had to look at it for only a few minutes once, not hours and days on end. In another interface involving battlefield maps, some of the color adjacencies produced potentially lethal color misperceptions because of bleeding, jitter, and other hardware-specific technological deficiencies.

In sum, there are many situations in which an interaction designer needs to get a user's attention. The really big attention-getters should be saved for the most important situations. For example, some screen designs have a small area, usually a single line near the bottom of the screen, reserved for feedback messages. As the user performs tasks, various short messages appear in this little out-of-the-way space. Many of these messages are just status messages that the user doesn't really need, which is fortunate because most users don't even notice these messages flashing away down there. Surprisingly, many users will not even be aware of this message area on the screen, despite the fact that it is always there and is constantly changing. Sometimes, though, a message is important, and that can lead to trouble. Perhaps the user cannot proceed with a task and does not know why. For the important messages (only), the interaction designer could use a small audio beep or one of the other attention-getting techniques to shift the user's focus to the message area for a moment.

2.3.11 Display Issues

▶ Maintain display inertia.

A good interaction design changes as little as possible from one screen to the next. Obviously, static objects such as buttons, words, and icons that appear on many screens should always appear in exactly the same location on all screens, for consistency. However, if an icon or some text on one screen moves by even a pixel on the subsequent screen, users may be annoyed by the jerky, flashing objects on the display, and their eyes will have to adjust to the new screen. This also increases eye fatigue and therefore general fatigue for a user, which can reduce accuracy and productivity.

It is still possible to maintain screen inertia even when objects change their appearance a little bit. For example an "ok" button that appears to be depressed (selected) as the default is essentially the same as the "ok" button that does not appear to be depressed. Inertia is important primarily in location, shape, and size of objects, but not necessarily in the labels, default indicators, and so on.

For example, a pinball game, running on a PC, has a rather realistic screen image of an actual pinball game layout. However, as the user paddles the ball around the screen with mouse clicks, the area of the screen that is being displayed changes with almost every hit of the ball, moving up or down, left or right, depending on which way the ball is rolling. The screen is so jerky that it is almost impossible for users to have any sense of what portion of the layout they are in, and therefore they become easily disoriented and rarely make many points because they don't even know in which direction to go for the big points. The problem, of course, is that the screen real estate on a PC is simply too small to display the entire layout for the pinball game all at once. The designers' solution—constantly moving the view window around the layout, displaying only a small portion at a time—is very ineffective, and users rarely play with this game for any length of time.

▶ Organize the screen to manage complexity.

Elimination of unnecessary information can greatly simplify a screen design. Using concise wording of instructions, messages, and other text, or easy-to-recognize icons can help with this. Minimizing the overall density of the screen, especially for text, is important, as is minimizing the local density in subareas of the screen. Closely packed words, and even icons, are very hard for a user to read and recognize, and they can obscure important information that the user needs to perform tasks.

A balanced layout of the display should avoid having too much information at the top or bottom, left or right of the screen. Novice designers tend to put too much information at the top of the screen, even when they don't have enough to fill a screen, and they tend to left-justify the contents of the screen. This produces an unbalanced format that can be aesthetically unpleasing to the user. Imagine the screen drawn into quadrants, and generally put about the same amount of content into each quadrant. Use plenty of *white (empty) space*, especially around blocks of text. User performance suffers when less than 25% of the screen is white space (Tullis, 1988); 50% white space is recommended for primarily textual displays.

Related information should be grouped logically on the screen, using wording and icons that are familiar to the user. Use an imaginary grid layout, to give a reasonable alignment of columns and rows; this contributes to effective grouping and balancing of screen contents. Emphasis on information relevant to the tasks will help users perform those tasks more effectively and efficiently. Avoid clutter on the screen; don't overuse the "*" or ":" or other special characters, heavy lines, or graphics to set off titles or groups.

This guideline is not just for the sake of aesthetics. Organization and layout of a screen display can have a dramatic effect on user performance. An empirical study (Tullis, 1981) used two different formats for the same user task. The task was to perform some diagnostic tests on telephone circuits, based on information presented on the screen. Figure 2.1a shows the narrative format that was used, and Figure 2.1b shows the same information in a structured format. The narrative format had all the textual information densely grouped together, with no delineation of, or emphasis on, important information. The structured format made use of white space, grouping of related information, obvious titles for groups, and a columnar presentation. Results showed that users interpreted the information in the narrative format on average in 8.3 seconds, and the information in the structured format on average in 5.0 seconds. That is, users interpreted the structured format information about 40% more quickly than information in the narrative format. A time savings for users of nearly 80 person-years over the life of the

```
        TEST RESULTS    SUMMARY: GROUND

        GROUND, FAULT T-G
        3 TERMINAL DC RESISTANCE
        >   3500.00 K OHMS T-R
        =     14.21 K OHMS T-G
        >   3500.00 K OHMS R-G
        3 TERMINAL DC VOLTAGE
        =      0.00 VOLTS  T-G
        =      0.00 VOLTS  R-G
        VALID AC SIGNATURE
        3 TERMINAL AC RESISTANCE
        =      8.82 K OHMS T-R
        =     14.17 K OHMS T-G
        =    628.52 K OHMS R-G
        LONGITUDINAL BALANCE POOR
        =     39     DB
        COULD NOT COUNT RINGERS DUE TO
          LOW RESISTANCE
        VALID LINE CKT CONFIGURATION
        CAN DRAW AND BREAK DIAL TONE
```

Figure 2.1a. Narrative format—average 8.3 seconds to perform typical task. Reprinted with permission from *Human Factors*, Vol. 23, No. 5. 1981. Copyright 1981 by The Human Factors Society, Inc. All rights reserved.

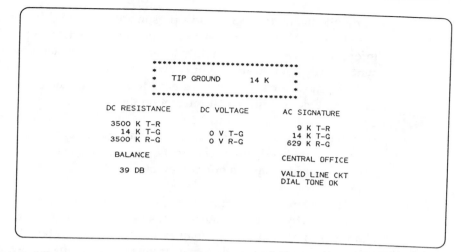

```
        *********************************
        *                               *
        *   TIP GROUND        14 K       *
        *                               *
        *********************************

    DC RESISTANCE        DC VOLTAGE          AC SIGNATURE

    3500 K  T-R                              9 K  T-R
      14 K  T-G          0 V  T-G           14 K  T-G
    3500 K  R-G          0 V  R-G          629 K  R-G

    BALANCE                                CENTRAL OFFICE

      39 DB                                VALID LINE CKT
                                           DIAL TONE OK
```

Figure 2.1b. Structured format—average 5.0 seconds to perform same task. Reprinted with permission from *Human Factors*, Vol. 23, No. 5. 1981. Copyright 1981 by The Human Factors Society, Inc. All rights reserved.

system was estimated from these results.

2.3.12 Individual User Differences

▶ Accommodate individual user experiences and differences.

Many systems, especially public-access systems, will have a broad variety of user types. Studies have shown that user differences account for much more variability in task performance than either system design or training procedures. Much of this variability comes from making and recovering from errors.

Everyone from toddlers learning to count with computer-aided instruction to grandmothers using online storage and retrieval systems in the library are using computers. No matter how computer-literate a user may be, that user is a novice during the first time for using a system the user has never used before. Even frequent users need good usability. In one study of a library system (Borgman, 1986), it was discovered that the most frequent users were nontechnical types, and had the most trouble learning to use the online catalogue system.

Factors that predict differences in computer-based skills include user experience, particular technical aptitudes, age, and domain- (problem area) specific skills and knowledge. Technical aptitudes that are good predictors of user performance include spatial visualization ability, vocabulary, and logical reasoning ability. Just being intelligent does not mean a person will have no difficulties with computer-based tasks. Also, age makes a substantial contribution to prediction of errors in information searching, the ability to learn complex systems, and the generation of syntactically complicated commands.

Thus, most computer systems have to accommodate broad and varied classes of users. One way in which interaction designers can accommodate user differences is to allow users to make decisions about the interface based on their own preferences, such as short or long versions of menu choices or no help messages. On the other hand, users should be able to request short menus with simple functions or long menus offering greater, and probably more complex, functionality.

User preferences are part of the larger concept of user customizability, which allows users to make even more extensive changes in the user interaction design—changing command or menu names, changing the locations of interaction objects, and so on. Users have to do less learning if they can make new interactive systems look like the interactive systems they already know. Also, of course, the interface changes made by users must persist across sessions of use. An application design should not discard all of the user's customization when the user shuts down that application.

▶ Accommodate user experience levels.

There are at least three levels of user experience (Shneiderman, 1992) that have to be addressed in many interaction designs. A *novice* user has no syntactic knowledge of the system and only a little semantic knowledge. Such users often approach a system with anxiety, possibly even fear. In the interface, they need clarity and simplicity, a small number of meaningful functions, lucid error messages, and informative feedback. They may also need comprehensible manuals and online tutorials and demonstrations. These needs, of course, are not unique just to novice users; they can be good guidelines to follow for all levels of users.

An *intermittent* user maintains semantic knowledge of the system over time but loses syntactic knowledge. In the interface, such users prefer simple consistent commands, meaningful sequencing of steps, easy-to-remember functions and tasks, perhaps some prompting as a reminder, online assistance and help, and concise manuals.

A *frequent* user has both semantic and syntactic knowledge about the system; this is the typical "power" user. These users want fast interaction, powerful commands and possibly even typed-command strings, reduced keystrokes, brief error messages with access to detail at their own request, concise feedback, and customization of their own interface.

An individual user often represents a mixture of experience levels—expert with some systems but novice with others. Even for a single interactive system, an individual can be an expert at some tasks but be a novice at other tasks. With practice, novices become experts. Without practice, experts can forget and may even fall back into the novice realm.

The challenge for the interaction designer, of course, is to meet all these different user needs in one design. Some suggestions to help meet this challenge include providing novice users with an easy core set of commands, then allowing them to progress, at their own pace, to more commands. This technique of progressive disclosure allows more complex interaction as user needs become more sophisticated and customized.

Another approach is, for example, to allow novice users to select commands from a menu and simultaneously echo, perhaps at the bottom of the window, the associated textual (typed) form of the command. This will help teach them the typed forms. Allow frequent users access to more functionality, and allow them to work faster, by providing them with typed commands, macros, accelerators, abbreviations, and function keys. Also allow all users to control the density of the feedback and messages they receive from the system.

2.3.13   Examples of Guideline Conflicts

As you are producing your interaction designs, you will constantly encounter guideline conflicts. One example of this is found in a rather old operating system that had a "daytime" command; users (back in those days, mostly programmers) could type in "daytime" and get the time of day. However, many users on this system also had access to an electronic-mail application. This system used *immediate commands*—that is, a single character without a "Return" or "Enter" keystroke following it. This supports the guideline to optimize user actions, but this also conflicted with the guideline to prevent user errors.

Sometimes the users forgot whether they were in the operating system or in the mail system. If they typed "daytime" while in the mail system, can you guess what happened? The "d" deleted mail messages, and the "a" made it all messages. Now a good interaction designer would never violate a guideline and allow the user to delete all of anything without confirming it, but the next immediate command the mail system got was a "y"—yes. The "t" meant type out the messages, "i" meant in inverted order, and so on—the rest hardly matters; there were no mail messages left to operate on. The final immediate command, "e," meant to exit the mail system, making certain that recovery would be impossible!

Another example of a conflict that could arise in a design situation is in the display and removal of messages from the screen. As mentioned previously, an important guideline is to ensure that the locus of control makes the user feel in charge. This implies that a user should take some explicit action to make a message disappear. However, you could encounter a design situation in which you want to give users a status-indicator message while they are blocked from interacting with the system, for example, during a potentially lengthy system process. Status-indicator messages typically stay on the screen only as long as the system process is in progress and then disappear automatically, upon completion of the process. This presents a conflict: Should the system remove control from the user and have the message automatically disappear or force the user to have to deal with removing a message that really should need no action by the user? The best solution is indeed to remove the message automatically when the process is complete, but make sure that it does not disappear too soon, so that the user is left wondering, "What just flashed across the screen?"

A third example of a guideline conflict is found in the use of default choices for buttons. Suppose that, in your design, you want to follow the guideline of consistency and always have three buttons, labeled "help," "cancel," and "ok," available in a message box. Further, you want the "help" button to be on the left, "cancel" in the middle, and "ok" on the right. Also in your consistent design, you want the rightmost button, in this case the "ok" button, to be the default choice because you think it is the one that users are most likely to choose. You design the default button to be indicated by some visual cue (e.g., highlighting or a bold outline for the button). Users can select this default button by simply pressing the "Enter" key rather than moving their hand away from the keyboard to the mouse. So far, this sounds very consistent and reasonable.

However, later in your design, you find that, in response to a potentially destructive situation, you prefer that the default button be the "cancel" button because it will do the least harm if a user chooses it by accident. To be consistent, you must put the default button on the right. Now you need to put the "ok" button in the middle. Remembering the guideline to make the system goof proof and protect the user, you now must decide between two design options. You must decide whether to reorder the buttons in all boxes, making the "cancel" button the consistent default, and thereby probably making users move their hand to the mouse more frequently to select the "ok" button. Alternatively, you can have your design be inconsistent for the few situations in which "cancel" is a more appropriate default. Most designers would probably opt in favor of the latter option, despite violating the consistency guideline. If users recognize a potentially destructive situation, they will usually look more carefully at their choices, rather than just automatically hitting some key to make the default choice. Also, if they do not recognize a potentially destructive situation, then you have protected them by making "cancel" the default. Instead, if you choose the first option, users are forced to do much more hand movement because the button choice they are most likely to want is not the default. The consistency guideline is undoubtedly one of the guidelines most frequently encountered in design conflict decisions.

As mentioned previously, design guidelines are not strict rules to be blindly followed to the letter. They are reasonable, common sense suggestions for user interaction design. Guidelines require interpretation and perhaps tailoring for specificity within a particular design situation. Inevitably, conflicts arise when you are applying guidelines in interaction design, and you must make trade-offs when deciding how to apply them.

REFERENCES

Apple Computer, Inc. (1988). *Inside Macintosh*. Reading, MA: Addison-Wesley.

Borgman, C. L. (1986). Why Are Online Catalogs Hard to Use? Lessons Learned from Information-Retrieval Studies. *Journal of the American Society for Information Science*, 37(6), 387–400.

Grudin, J. (1989). The Case Against User Interface Consistency. *Communications of the ACM*, 32, 1164–1173.

Hansen, W. J. (1971). User Engineering Principles for Interactive Systems. *Proceedings of Fall Joint Computer Conference*, Montvale, NJ: AFIPS Press, 523–532.

Marcus, A. (1992). *Graphic Design for Electronic Documents and User Interfaces*. New York: ACM Press/Addison-Wesley.

Mayhew, D. J. (1992). *Principles and Guidelines in Software User Interface Design*. Englewood Cliffs, NJ: Prentice-Hall.

Miller, G. A. (1956). The Magical Number Seven, Plus or Minus Two: Some Limits on Our Capability for Processing Information. *Psychological Science*, 63, 81–97.

Norman, D. A. & Draper, S. W. (1986). *User Centered System Design: New Perspectives on Human-Computer Interaction*. Hillsdale, NJ: Erlbaum.

Open Software Foundation. (1990). *OSF/Motif Style Guide*. Englewood Cliffs, NJ: Prentice-Hall.

Powell, J. E. (1990). *Designing User Interfaces* . San Marcos, CA: Microtrend Books.

Shneiderman, B. (1992). *Designing the User Interface: Strategies for Effective Human-Computer Interaction*. Reading, MA: Addison-Wesley.

Smith, S. L. & Mosier, J. N. (1986). *Guidelines for Designing User Interface Software* (ESD-TR-86-278/MTR 10090). Bedford, MA: MITRE Corporation.

Tullis, T. S. (1981). An Evaluation of Alphanumeric, Graphic, and Color Information Displays. *Human Factors*, 23, 541–550.

Tullis, T. S. (1988). A System for Evaluating Screen Formats: Research and Application. In H. R. Hartson & D. Hix (Ed.), *Advances in Human-Computer Interaction* (pp. 214–286). Norwood, NJ: Ablex Publishing.

☰ 3

Interaction Styles

3.1 WHAT ARE INTERACTION STYLES?

Mention the term interaction style to anyone who knows much about direct manipulation user interfaces, and you will conjure up visions of menus and mice, windows and widgets, icons and other images of objects that appear in a user interface. Interaction styles are a collection of interface objects and associated techniques from which an interaction designer can choose when designing the user interaction component of an interface. They provide a behavioral view of how the user communicates with the system.

However, interface objects and their behavior must eventually be programmed as interaction techniques in user interface software. In the constructional domain, interaction techniques can be instantiated as widgets (see Section 2.2.3 on Commercial Style Guides, and Section 11.4 on Toolkits). We use the term *interaction style* here to include the look (appearance) and feel (behavior) of interaction objects and associated interaction techniques, from a *behavioral) (*user's) *view.*

Before toolkits for user interface implementation existed, each interaction style (e.g., menu, form, and so on) was coded a line at a time. Now, however, toolkits facilitate implementation by encapsulating each interaction style as a widget that can be reused and often even modified as desired. In addition, toolkits offer support in consistently meeting many of the guidelines discussed here for each interaction style. Brad Myers, in conjunction with the Association for Computing Machinery, has produced a video entitled *All the Widgets,* which shows examples of many of these different interaction styles (Myers, 1990).

Many of the interaction styles presented here are used in direct manipulation interfaces. In a *direct manipulation interface,* the user performs the intended actions by immediately interacting with interaction objects, rather than by indirectly describing the actions to perform. Because direct manipulation interfaces visually present tasks to the user, the effect of user input is immediately and directly visible, without the need to run a program to produce the output. Examples include spreadsheets, full-page editors, and many graphics packages. They tend to be easy to learn and to retain. Users tend to make fewer errors and can become more readily engaged by such an interface. How often have you seen a kid (either a young or an old one) engrossed in a videogame world? Users generally have very high subjective satisfaction with this type of interface.

Such interfaces do, however, require more design and implementation effort; indeed, they are easy to do badly. There are even some times when a direct manipulation interface is not appropriate, when the system can automate a task better than the user can perform it directly. For example, the task of performing a database search via a direct manipulation interface could have the user checking every record in the database to see whether it matches the desired search conditions. The system can go through the database and find the appropriate records much more quickly and easily than can the user. On the other hand, a direct manipulation interface can be used for the task of building a query to do the search, such as seen in Query-By-Example and other graphical query languages.

Direct manipulation should not be forced on power users; they may want other interaction styles, even typed-command languages. Also, of course, visually impaired users may not be able to see the pretty pictures offered by graphical interfaces, and physically impaired users may not be able to manipulate a mouse or a trackball or other pointing devices that are typically used to interact with objects in direct manipulation interfaces.

This chapter presents several of the most popular interaction styles, each of which can be part of an interaction design with an overall direct manipulation flavor:

- Windows
- Menus
- Forms
- Boxes

- Typed-command languages
- Graphical interfaces
- Other interaction styles, including touchscreen and voice I/O

Each of these interaction styles is discussed, as follows: (1) *definition* of the generic form of the style; (2) some *advantages* and *disadvantages* of the style; (3) some of the *varieties* of each interaction style, with appropriate *examples;* and (4) some applicable *guidelines* about use of the style. Many of the general guidelines discussed in Chapter 2 reemerge here within the context of a particular interaction style. Some guidelines are repeated, as appropriate, with the hope that the repetition will serve as reinforcement of the importance of some of these general guidelines to many different interaction design situations. Although these styles are discussed individually, most user interfaces, of course, are made up of several of these interactions styles, not just one of them.

Each interaction style is presented independently of a particular implementation platform, such as CUA™ or OpenLook™ (see Chapter 2). However, a figure has been included as an example of each interaction style, and many of these figures are taken from the *OSF/Motif Style Guide* (1990). Motif™ was chosen rather than one of the other style guides because of its popularity and because it is representative of the more common styles across workstations, PCs, and Macintoshes™. A word of caution: Sometimes different style guides or toolkits will use different names for the same interaction style. Because the example figures included here are from Motif™, Motif™ names have generally been used in the discussion of interaction styles.

3.2   WINDOWS

A *window is* a screen object that provides an arena for presentation of, and interaction with, other interaction objects. All interaction between a user and the system occurs through a window. Via windows, a user can organize work by tasks and can work on several tasks at once. However, a user's interactive desktop can become as cluttered as a real desktop if there are too many windows open at once. Also, windows require management and manipulation; we have observed users loudly proclaiming, while struggling to manage a maze of overlapping windows, "I don't do windows!"

There are at least two kinds of windows, as shown in Figure 3.1:

- Primary windows
- Secondary windows

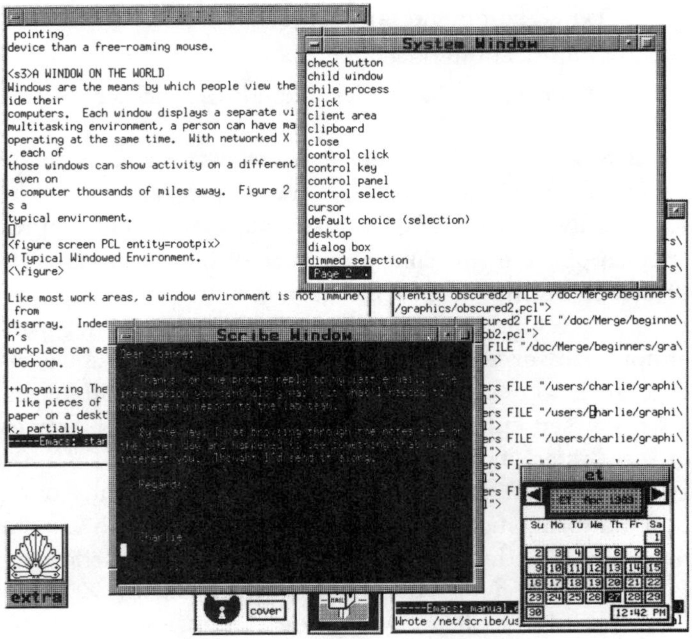

Figure 3.1. Primary and secondary windows.

3.2.1   Primary Windows

The primary window is the one through which all other windows in an application are generated. It is typically the only window through which an application can be closed.

3.2.2   Secondary Windows

A *secondary window* is generated through a primary window. For example, in a word processor, the first window that is opened in the application typically is the primary window, while other files may be opened for processing in secondary windows. A dialogue box or even a message box can also be considered a secondary window. When multiple windows are open on the screen at one time, generally only one is *active*—that is, it can accept user input. The user usually determines the active window by using a mouse to click anywhere in the window or by selecting from a menu of currently open windows that changes dynamically as the open windows change.

3.2.3   Windows Design Guidelines

▶ Don't overuse windows.

Minimize the amount of window manipulation that must be done by the user. Place a new window in a fixed position, then allow the user easily to reposition it. *Tiled windows* (i.e., nonoverlapping, as is characteristic of tiled floors or counters) generally seem to give better user performance, particularly for tasks that require little window manipulation. However, most users seem to prefer overlapping windows because they can control window placement more completely (Bly & Rosenberg, 1986). For most situations, users should also be able to resize windows.

▶ Appearance and behavior of the primary window should be consistent.

The primary window is an anchor for the user; especially as more windows are opened, the user can get lost in an ocean of windows and may want to return to the primary window as a sort of restarting point. Every time a user returns to the primary window, that window should appear exactly as the user left it. An exception to this would be when some user action taken in a secondary window is a deliberate modification of the content of the primary window, or if the primary window displays some dynamic state that is changing.

▶ Use different windows for different independent tasks.

Windows are an excellent way to allow users to work on more than one part of an application at once, or even to work within more than one application at a time. Electronic spreadsheets, for example, often allow users to display a "totals" line in one window, which is dynamically updated for users to see as they enter data in cells of the spreadsheet via another window. Users often have a word processor, a graphics editor, an electronic-mail application, and perhaps a clock, all running at once in different windows.

▶ Use different windows for different coordinated views of the same task.

Results of tasks can be made more understandable by presenting those results to the user in various forms. For example, numeric data being generated by a statistical package might be generated in one window while a graph of those data is being generated in an adjacent one.

3.3   MENUS

A *menu* is a list of items from which one or more selections are made by the user. It is one of the most popular interaction styles, partly because it reduces the need for memorization by the user (remember recognition over recall from Section 2.3.4). Because the user selects from a displayed list, typing is eliminated, which therefore reduces errors. Menus typically require little training over, for example, command line or even form-filling interaction styles. Users can become very proficient at menus, even using complicated cascading menus quite rapidly. Menus can, however, be overused; too many menus may slow down frequent users, especially if the hardware cannot support very rapid menu choices. Menus also require a lot of screen space when they are displayed.

Because the basic function of any menu is to offer choices to a user, this discussion includes sets of buttons as menus; several buttons on the screen at once do indeed act like a kind of menu. Of the numerous possible kinds of menus, this chapter discusses the following:

- Push-button menus
- Radio-button menus
- Check-button menus
- Pull-down menus
- Pop-up menus
- Option menus
- Toggle menus
- Cascading menus
- Pie menus
- Palette menus
- Embedded menus
- Dynamic menus

3.3.1   Push-Button Menus

In a *push-button menu*, choices are distributed over physically separate buttons, and the buttons are typically visible at all times. This type of button is very common in interfaces, and is often found in a *button bank* aligned across the bottom or down one side of a screen. Because buttons are usually permanent and therefore take up a lot of screen space, they should be used sparingly, only for the most frequent, basic commands. Some of the more common push buttons that appear throughout many interfaces include "cancel," "ok," "quit," "exit," and "help." Other very common application-specific commands might also be included on push buttons.

A word of caution about push buttons: Be sure that the label you put on a button makes sense for the situation in which that button is being used. The "cancel" and "ok" buttons are used at times when their meaning is unclear or even nonsensical as a response to the message currently displayed. For example, "cancel" as a choice for the warning message, "This action may cause loss of data" is ambiguous. Cancel what? The loss of data, or the action, or the window in which the message is shown? A designer who blindly follows a style guide, to maintain location and labeling consistency across button banks, can create this sort of nonsensical situation.

On a given bank of push buttons, one button is generally chosen as the default; its appearance is different from the rest of the buttons, to indicate this property. This different appearance is often a bold outline or an extra border surrounding the push button, to look as if it is already pressed in. The default button can usually by chosen by pressing the "Enter" or "Return" key, not requiring the hands to be removed from the keyboard to use the mouse.

Beyond this special default action, push buttons are usually chosen via a mouse click, but they can also be assigned to function keys or other accelerator-key combinations. Push buttons are often highlighted (e.g., reverse video, color change) in some way when chosen by the user. Some push buttons (e.g., those in Motif™) are shadowed to look three-dimensional, and the shadow appearance changes when they are selected, so that they look as if they have been pressed in. In Figure 3.2, the buttons across the bottom of the screen, labeled "OK," "Reset,"

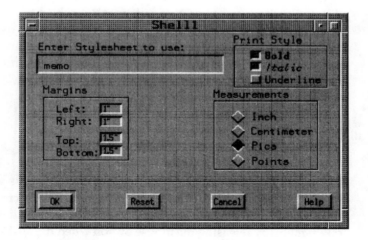

Figure 3.2. Push-button, radio-button, and check-button menus.

"Cancel," and "Help" are all push buttons. "OK" is the default button; note the extra border around it.

3.3.2   Radio-Button Menus

Radio-button menus offer choices that are exhaustive and mutually exclusive; just like the buttons on your car radio, on which exactly one station is chosen at any given time. The user makes exactly one choice from a set of two or more choices, usually by clicking with the mouse. The current choice is indicated by a visual cue (e.g., a small darkened circle or square beside the choice). An example is seen in Figure 3.2, in the group of diamond-shaped buttons from which a single unit of measure from the "Measurements" menu may be chosen. A good example of a radio-button menu is found in a word processor, from which a user can select the font (or size) for the text; text can be only one font and one size (e.g., Helvetica, 12 point) at a time. Radio-button menus are often found in dialogue or property boxes.

3.3.3   Check-Button Menus

Check-button menus offer choices that are not mutually exclusive. The user can make one or more choices from a set of two or more possibilities, again by clicking with the mouse. The current choices are indicated by a visual cue (e.g., a check (✓) or an "x" in a box beside the choice, or darkening of a small circle or box beside the choice). An example is seen in Figure 3.2, where the "Print Style" menu in the upper right shows a check-button menu. This might be used in a word processor, where a user can select properties for the text; text can have more than one display property (e.g., bold and italics) at a time. Like radio-button menus, check-button menus are often found in dialogue or property boxes.

3.3.4   Pull-Down Menus

Pull-down menus are a very popular interaction style. They are usually found across the top of a window or screen, and their title is always visible. Each pull-down menu appears—always in the same location on the screen—when the user depresses a mouse button over the menu title. The user makes a selection from a pull-down menu by releasing the mouse button when the desired choice is highlighted. Pull-down menus are used for access to major functionality of a system. Only the menu's title bar takes up permanent screen space. An example of a pull-down menu for a "File" option is shown in Figure 3.3.

3.3.5   Pop-Up Menus

Pop-up menus can appear in different places on the screen, determined by the current location of the cursor when the user depresses a specific mouse button; this is a pop-up menu as used in the Smalltalk environment. This interaction style is sometimes also called an "option menu," but most people use a different definition for an option menu (see next section). There is no visual cue to the availability of a pop-up menu.

Pop-up menus are often used to select functions and parameters. The contents of a pop-up menu can vary, too. The set of menu choices can be context dependent, based on the screen or window location of the cursor when the user requests the pop-up menu.

Because a pop-up menu appears wherever the cursor is located when the user requests the menu, it can save mouse movement, for example, over pull-down menus. In contrast, for a pull-down menu, the user must always move the mouse so that the cursor is over the permanently placed title. A pop-up menu uses no permanent screen space and is therefore useful when the screen's real estate is limited.

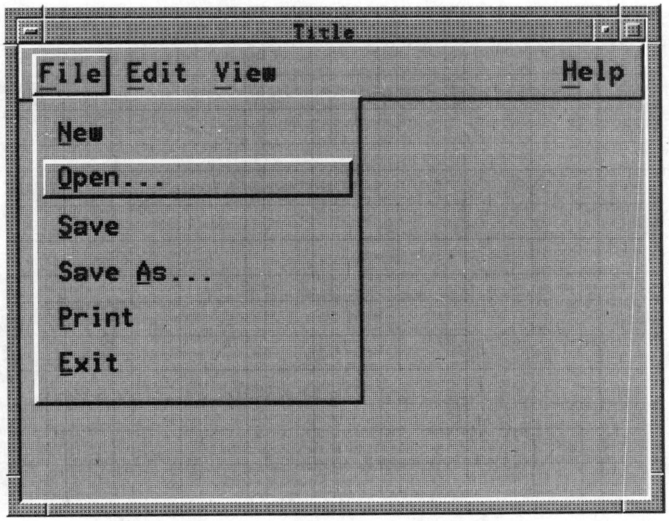

Figure 3.3. Pull-down menu.

3.3.6   Option Menus

An *option menu* looks much like a field (e.g., in a form), with its current value visible. Other values appear, in a list menu, when the user depresses the mouse button over the visible field. The user may then move the cursor up or down to select any one choice from the list menu by releasing the mouse button while that choice is highlighted. When the user releases the mouse button, the menu disappears, and the new choice appears as the value in the field. This interaction style is sometimes called a "pop-up menu," but we use a different definition for a pop-up menu (see previous section). Like pop-up menus, an option menu is most useful when screen space is limited. It also prevents a user from typing in an incorrect value to a field that has a known set of possible valid values. An example is shown in Figure 3.4 in the "Family" property of the "Font Attribute" selection box.

3.3.7   Toggle Menus

A to*ggle menu*, like an option menu, looks much like a field, with its current value visible, but a toggle menu rotates through all possible choices, one at a time, as the user clicks the mouse button over the field in which a selection of the menu appears. The user makes a selection simply by leaving the desired value visible in the field. This is useful for a small number of choices that can be put into some logical order (e.g., temporal, such as the days of the week). One of the most

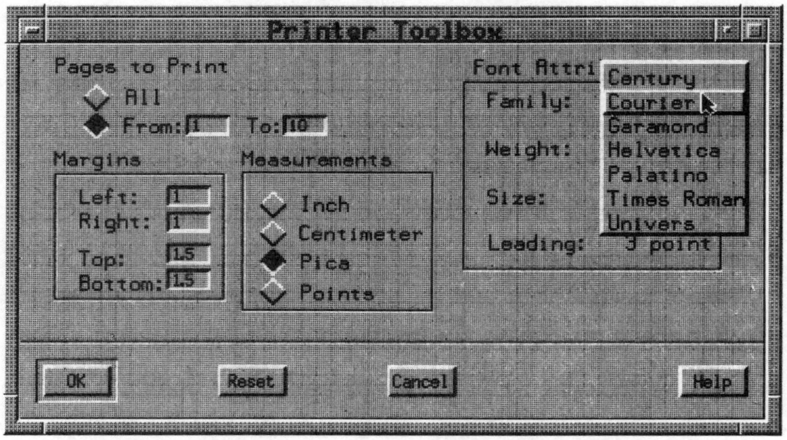

Figure 3.4. Option menu.

common uses of a toggle menu may be for offering binary choices (i.e., only two, probably opposite, possible selections) to a user. In contrast, if there are a large number of choices, a user will tire of having to toggle through them. Like the popup menu, a toggle menu is useful when screen space is limited. A disadvantage compared to the option menu is that the choices cannot all be made visible to the user simultaneously.

3.3.8   Cascading Menus

Cascading (hierarchical) *menus*, also called "walking menus," look and behave much like a sequence of pull-down menus. When a user depresses the mouse button over the title of the first menu in the sequence, that menu appears. The user may then move the cursor down to select a choice from that menu, leading to the appearance of another menu, usually to the right of the first one, from which the user may make another choice, and so on, while the mouse button is continually depressed. A final choice (of a whole path in the hierarchy) is made when the user releases the mouse button over a menu choice at the end of such a sequence.

Choices on the menus that lead to other menus should have a visual cue (e.g., an arrow pointing to the right) to indicate that another menu will appear. While such a series of menus is a good way to organize a hierarchical menu structure and to provide further selection detail, users sometimes have trouble with eye-hand coordination of cascading menus that go more than three levels deep. This difficulty may not be so much inherent in the basic concept of cascading menus as it is inherent in the design of a particular instance of a cascading menu (e.g., selection areas within each menu in the cascade are too small, or too close together, and so on). An example of a cascading menu is seen in Figure 3.5.

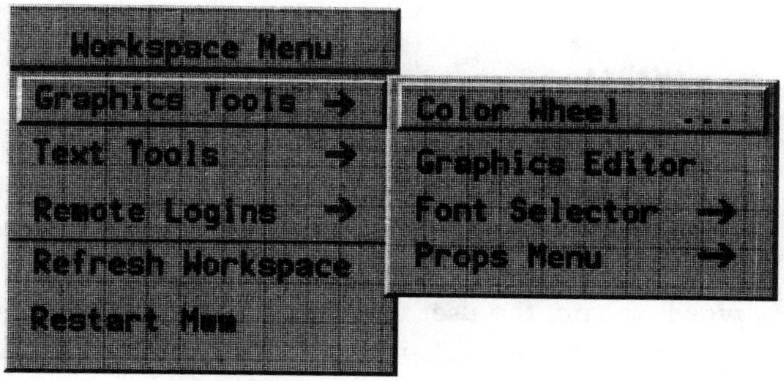

Figure 3.5. Cascading menu.

3.3.9   Pie Menus

Pie menus display choices in a circular or semicircular arrangement of labeled pie wedges. This is useful for a small to medium-sized number of selections. If there are several selections, and therefore several wedges, the wedges may be so small that there is not room to display the labels for the choices in the wedge. Pie menus minimize mouse movement; going from one wedge to the one directly across from it takes very little movement, unlike linear menus where the user must traverse from top to bottom. The user makes a selection by clicking in the desired wedge. When used for patterns or colors, for example, the pattern or color itself can serve as a label. The radius of a pie menu can also be meaningful, for example, to indicate that color intensity changes as the user moves the cursor along a radius from near the center of the circle toward the outside circumference. Relative sizes of wedges can be used to indicate proportionality—for example, of demographic data.

3.3.10   Palette Menus

Palette, or iconic, *menus* are menus in which the choices are represented as graphical icons, rather than as words, on what are essentially push buttons grouped together. The choices are usually mutually exclusive. They are often found in graphical editors and are used for selecting self-labeling visual choices, such as patterns, colors, shapes, and so on. The user makes a selection by clicking on or dragging the selection, such as clicking over the desired pattern in the menu, or by dragging an instance of a shape from the palette. Palette menus sometimes cause switches in the interaction mode, depending on what the user chooses from the palette. This mode switch (e.g., among text, graphic, or selection mode) is usually indicated by a change in the shape of the cursor. The icons along the left of the screen in Figure 3.6 make up a palette menu.

3.3.11   Embedded Menus

Embedded menus are found in what is more commonly called "hypertext" or "hypermedia." In a screen display of text and/or graphics, some of the objects are designated as selectable (e.g., by highlighting), usually with a mouse click or sometimes a touch on a touchscreen, by the user. Upon selection of a highlighted word or icon, the user can navigate to a different screen. Embedded menus, or hypertext "hot spots," are a good interaction style to use, for example, in an online information storage and retrieval system, where the user can click on a highlighted word in a screen full of information, to find more information about the

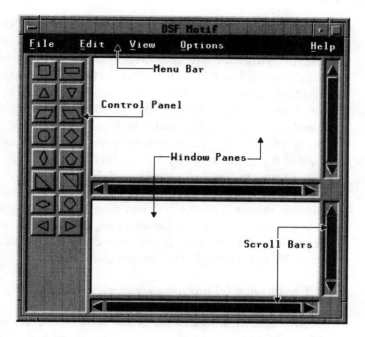

Figure 3.6. Palette menu.

chosen word. Sequences of these connections can be used to link related information together.

3.3.12 Dynamic Menus

Dynamic menus contain choices are that are runtime dependent. The choices vary, based on runtime conditions and/or values. A simple example of a dynamic menu is one in which currently unavailable choices are grayed out so that the user cannot select them. A more complicated example is a menu of possible flights between two cities, which can only be determined when the user requests specific cities at runtime. The content of the menu cannot be known until the request is processed.

3.3.13 Menu Design Guidelines

▶ Use the user tasks and system functions to organize hierarchical menus.

Menus are often organized into a hierarchical tree structure, with nodes of the tree representing various menu selections. A broad, shallow tree structure is preferred to a deep, narrow tree. Typically, there should be three to four levels in a menu tree structure, with four to eight items on each menu (Shneiderman, 1992). A structure much different than this may indicate that the interaction designer should look again at the tasks and functions represented by the items in the menus, to see whether they can be reorganized. However, there are also exceptions, depending on content. For example, it may be tolerable to have 12 choices for a listing of months. Applications with large sets of menus (e.g., CAD/CAM) may cause this suggested tree structure to be compromised.

A good way to decide on menus and their contents is to write down, on scraps of paper, the names of all choices (e.g., tasks and functions) the designer wants to include on menus. The designer can then move the pieces of paper around on a tabletop, easily arranging and rearranging the choices into menus until a desirable structure is found. Menus may also be organized into a network structure, but this is generally more complicated for the user to understand.

▶ Use meaningful groupings of menu choices.

Group together on one menu the items that are logically similar (e.g., font types and font sizes). Cover all choices in nonoverlapping groups, with each choice in one and only one menu.

▶ Use meaningful ordering of menu choices.

When deciding on the order of choices in a menu, use natural orderings, such as numeric, alphabetical, or temporal. Alphabetical orderings are good for longer menus but not as useful for short menus. In short menus, a different ordering, such as temporal (e.g., "open" before "close" because the user must open a file before closing it), may make more sense to the user. Other orderings to consider include listing the most frequently selected, the most recently selected, or the most important choice first. However, it is often difficult for the designer to know which choice will be most frequently made or which is more important.

▶ Use brief descriptions for menu choices.

Use single-word choices when the meaning of a choice is obvious. To make the words in a menu as clear as possible, consider the set of choices, the nature of each particular choice, and the likelihood that a user will recognize its meaning immediately or with a little investigation (e.g., calling up help, or trying out a choice to see what happens).

When it is not possible to use a single word, begin each choice with a key word, consistently choosing all nouns, all adjectives, or all verbs to begin every choice. Use descriptive, discriminating, nonoverlapping terms for choices. It is often difficult to decide on the best term for a function or task. For example, the task of removing text from a file could reasonably be called "delete" or "cut." Finishing work on a file could reasonably be called "exit" or "close." Some terminology, for example, for file handling, is now becoming more standardized, with conventional menu choice names (e.g., open, close, save, save as, delete, quit). Words used in menu choices must be chosen carefully and then be tested with users to make sure that the users understand their intended meanings.

▶ Use a consistent layout across all menus, and keep the screen uncluttered.

Menus are quite a prevalent interaction style, and, as such, should be clearly covered in a customized style guide. Defining and maintaining a consistent format among all menus will support users' expectations of the menu from which they are making a selection. Use white space or simple lines to separate small groups within a single menu, if needed, but don't overuse lines as separators on menus; they can be distracting. If instructions are needed for some menus, the wording of the instructions should be consistent and should appear in the same location for every menu. Error messages should also have a consistent wording and location for every menu, perhaps in a message box that pops up when needed. However, as we said in Section 2.3, an error message should rarely be needed for a menu choice.

▶ Allow shortcuts.

Accelerator keys should be provided for the user, when possible, to make choices—for example, from pull-down menus without having to pull down the menu or from pop-up menus without having to pop up the menu. Type-ahead, in which the system accepts typing of menu choices faster than it can display each successive menu, is also desirable for frequent users who will eventually memorize the menu hierarchy for their favorite commands and may not want to be forced to plod through the entire hierarchy one menu at a time.

Also desirable for frequent users might be one mnemonically meaningful key combination (e.g., a character string that they can define) that invokes a desired sequence of commands. This kind of macro helps translate a user's intent into a single muscle memory action, which is very desirable for frequently used commands.

3.4   FORMS

A *form* is a screen containing labeled fields that are to be filled in by a user, generally by typing or sometimes by making menu choices. On forms, the appropriate labels, blank fields, and buttons are visible to the user at any given time. Particularly on forms where the user can enter information into the fields in any order, the user feels in control. Forms are a simple means of data entry for the user and are similar to the very common real-world analogy of paper forms. However, it is easy to design forms that clutter the screen, and input to the forms is usually by typing, which may mean more errors.

There are several types of values for a field in a form, including

- User-typed strings
- User choices from a list
- Default values
- Required and optional values
- Dependent values

3.4.1   User-Typed Strings

There are two kinds of *user-typed strings:* unvalidated and validated. In an *unvalidated field*, the user can type any free-form character string, and it will be accepted by the system. In a *validated field*, the user must type in a string with a specific syntax (e.g., it might require that the first character be alphabetic, followed by six or fewer numeric characters). If the user does not follow this prescribed format, the string will not be accepted by the system, and the user will need to try again.

In a validated field, the designer should indicate the required syntax visually. For example, the maximum length of a string can be indicated by the length of the field. Alphabetic characters can be indicated by X's and numeric values by 9's (a la COBOL formatting). The preferred format for date fields can be indicated by an example, displayed as a sample default, or by displaying the familiar MM/DD/YY format in a field. Other examples of visually indicating a specified field format are given in Section 3.4.6.

3.4.2   User Choices from a List

In fields with *user choices from a list*, all allowable choices can be itemized. For example, a field for the value of "shirt color" might only accept one of six colors.

Use of an option or toggle menu to present the choices to the user will reduce errors due to typing and also remove the need for the user to remember all possible choices that could go into the field.

3.4.3   Default Values for Fields

Some fields have logical *default values,* such as current date. This value is easily obtained from the system and automatically filled in to the appropriate field on the form. The user may then change the value, if so desired. The user should never have to type in (or otherwise enter) values in a field for which a reasonable default value can be obtained from the system.

3.4.4   Required versus Optional Values

Required values in a form are just what the term implies; a valid value must be entered by the user before the form can be processed. *Optional values* are those that can remain empty; they do not require that a value be entered. On a form, required fields should be distinguished from optional fields, usually by different appearance. It is usually best to group these two kinds of fields separately on the screen, if possible.

3.4.5   Dependent Values

Fields for *dependent values* in a form need to be filled in only if another field has a particular value entered. For example, if the "marital status" field has a value of "m" (for married), then the "spouse's name" field must be completed. The spouse's name field, however, cannot be completed unless there is an "m" in the "marital status" field. The system can automate and enforce these interfield dependencies.

3.4.6   Forms Design Guidelines

▶ Use a consistent, visually appealing layout and content.

Each form should have a brief but meaningful title and should have concise, comprehensible instructions. Fields should be logically ordered and grouped, with groupings delineated by visual cues such as white space or limited use of simple lines around them. Resist the urge to separate parts of a form with an overabundance of lines or other characters such as "*" or ":" or "|." White space is preferred because the eye tends to group more effectively when presented with contrast clustering than with border tracing. Alignment within groups should be reasonable and attractive. Use consistent placement of the same fields across all forms.

▶ Do not assume that existing paper forms convert directly to screen designs and a good user interface.

A common but erroneous assumption is that existing paper forms will convert directly into a good computer-based interaction design. Almost invariably, if you closely scrutinize a set of paper forms, you will find redundancies among different forms. If you collect some of the completed forms from users who have been filling them out, perhaps for years, you will usually find extra information scribbled in the margins or on the back of the forms, and you will also find fields that are never filled in at all.

Converting an existing paper-based system to an interactive one provides an excellent opportunity to analyze the operations for which the paper forms have been used to capture data, as well as a chance to completely revise the needed data into a form that is consonant with what users actually are doing and with what actually is used in the system. The purview of this activity is task analysis, discussed in Chapter 5. Existing forms should be carefully studied for redundancies, omissions, and errors. Designers should query users of the paper forms to see what fields they have to fill out on more than one form, what information has to be captured somewhere other than a form, and what problems they have with the present forms.

Other problems also arise with attempting to do a translation from paper forms to computer screens. Paper forms may contain more on each line (especially if they are printed in landscape [horizontal] format) than a 13-inch monitor screen will accommodate. A user of the new automated system who was familiar with the paper forms probably will be surprised and confused to see that some information has moved for no apparent reason, while some of the familiar information is where it was expected. The best approach is simply to start over, revising the paper-based system so that the new interactive system will eliminate redundancies and omissions in the data, as well as unnecessary data. That is, design for the appropriate content and medium being used, not to suit the old forms.

▶ Use appropriate visual cues for fields on forms.

Visual cues should be used within fields to indicate the expected or maximum number of characters that can be filled in. Underscores in a field can show the number of characters, or a highlighted (e.g., reverse video or colored) box can indicate the length of the field. Dashes or slashes or other cues can be used to help the user know the format of a field and therefore its expected data values. For example, if a user must type in their social security number, the field should be formatted as three blanks, a dash, two blanks, a dash, and four blanks. The user should not have to type in the dash; the cursor should automatically skip from one part of the field across the dash to the next part of the field as the user types in the numbers. Nonetheless, if the user does type in the dash, the interface should accept it as a dash, essentially by ignoring it, and not give the user an error message.

Visual cues, such as different appearance, should also be used to distinguish optional from required fields. For example, a required field might be an empty outlined rectangle, while an optional field might be a subtly shaded outlined rectangle. Different locations on a form, with fields appropriately grouped and labeled as "required information" and "optional information" can also be used.

▶ Use familiar and consistent field labels and abbreviations.

Each field should always be labeled with a concise name indicating what the user should enter into that field. Unusual or unfamiliar labels (e.g., "domicile" rather than "address") will unnecessarily confuse a user (Shneiderman, 1992). These labels usually appear immediately to the left of the field to which they belong. There should be some sort of delimiter (e.g., a single blank space, or a colon and a space) between the label and the field. Each time the same field appears on a different form, it should have the same label and even be in the same location, as much as possible.

▶ Use logical navigation among fields.

Users should be able to move top-to-bottom, and vice versa, among all fields in a form. A form should also have a wraparound feature, so that when users reach the last field, they can get to the first field in only one move (and vice versa). The up- and down-arrow keys typically work best for sequential movement from field to field within a form, but the "Tab" and the "Return" keys are also frequently used. Best of all may be the order independent movement the user gets from using a mouse or a touchscreen to move directly from one field to another. Various standards committees (e.g., Institute for Electrical and Electronic Engineers [IEEE], International Standards Organization [ISO], and so on) are in the process of defining standard keys to use for navigation for fields in a form.

▶ Use logical navigation within fields.

The user should be able to move left-to-right, and vice versa, within a single field in a form. An individual field should also have wraparound for cursor movement, from last space to first space, and vice versa. The left- and right-arrow keys typically work best for movement within a single field, but the mouse again gives order independent movement.

▶ Support editing and error correction of fields.

A user obviously must be able to edit and correct an entire field. The user must also be able to correct individual erroneous characters within a field without having to retype the entire field, such as for one incorrect character. The use of insertion or overwriting is an acceptable way to accomplish this. It may be best to stop (and possibly beep) after a field is full. In today's interfaces, most text fields support full text-editing functions, including cut, copy, and paste among fields.

▶ Use consistent, informative error messages for unacceptable characters and values.

The same error message guidelines that were discussed at length in Section 2.3 apply to error messages for forms. Form-based systems often have a line either at the bottom or the top of the screen, where error (and perhaps other) messages always appear. A pop-up message box is perhaps even better for focusing user attention on important messages.

▶ Provide explanatory messages for expected field inputs.

If the label for a field is not understood, or if a user does not know what to enter into a field, that user should be able to request more information about the field. Such explanatory messages typically should be requestable by the user, but may also be displayed automatically in a consistent location on every screen (e.g., at the bottom or top), changing appropriately as the user moves from field to field. However, if messages are displayed automatically as the user moves through each field, they should be as short and unobtrusive as possible, to minimize the amount of the screen that is rewritten as the user moves around from field to field. A three-line message that is constantly changing can be very annoying for the user.

▶ Provide default values in fields whenever possible.

The user should not have to enter information that can be provided by the system or information that is not likely to vary much. If the value of the field is probably going to be the same almost every time a user must fill it in, provide the most likely default value, and allow the user to change it on those few occasions that it varies. This saves user effort, minimizes errors, and sometimes, as for a date, can indicate the correct format.

▶ Provide a completion indicator on each form-filling screen.

The screen should not flash away as soon as the user types in a value for the last required field on a form. The user should always have explicit control, via a button or a menu choice, for example, to indicate to the system that the form is completed. Just as with a paper form, a user should be able to correct it and make changes to it until the user is ready to submit the form. In most cases, the user should be able to exit a partially completed form, without having filled in all required fields, and the system should allow the user to return to that screen later for completion.

3.5   BOXES

A *box* is a rectangular, delineated screen area that is used for messages, text entry, commands, selection, and user control. Many kinds of boxes appear as a result of user actions (e.g., list boxes), while others (e.g., message boxes) are displayed by the system, to inform the user about a current situation. Boxes make temporary use of screen space and are a technique that supports the visual grouping of different kinds of functionally related objects, such as buttons, scrolling lists, and so on. Unless carefully designed, however, boxes (especially dialogue boxes) can get very cluttered in appearance. While visible, a box obscures the part of the screen on which it appears.

There are several kinds of boxes, including

- List boxes
- Entry boxes
- Message boxes
- Dialogue boxes

3.5.1   List Boxes

A *list box*, shown in Figure 3.7, is a scrollable sequence of user choices that appears in its own window. It can be used when the choice list is quite long and/or variable in length. The content of a list box is usually dynamic; the system can add choices to the list, based on runtime actions and results. A list box usually has a vertical and often a horizontal scroll bar, so the user can navigate in all directions within the box.

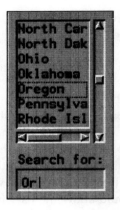

Figure 3.7. List box.

A user makes a selection from a list box by scrolling through the list until the desired selection is located, then clicking the mouse over the choice. Some list boxes allow a user to use the mouse to drag out a single selection over a range of adjacent choices. List boxes can also have a small text-entry field, usually at the bottom, into which a user can type a string, and the system will automatically scroll to the first selection or prefix that matches the string in the box.

3.5.2   Entry Boxes

An *entry box*, shown in Figure 3.8, allows a user to enter text; it usually has basic text-editing functions (such as wraparound, inserting, and deleting text) built in. It can be both vertically and horizontally scrollable. It can be a single line (even only a few characters), or a multiple-line area. A typical application of small, single-line entry boxes is for implementation of fields in forms. Preformatted entry boxes can be used to support automatic input validation, such as dates, numeric ranges, character strings, and so on.

3.5.3   Message Boxes

A *message box*, shown in Figure 3.9, is an interaction object that presents output to the user. It is usually displayed by the application, without the direct request of a user. It allows only limited user input, for example, for a user to respond to the message and have the message box then disappear. Message boxes are typically used for presenting information to the user, showing progress, asking the user a question, giving the user a warning, or requesting some action by the user. Mes-

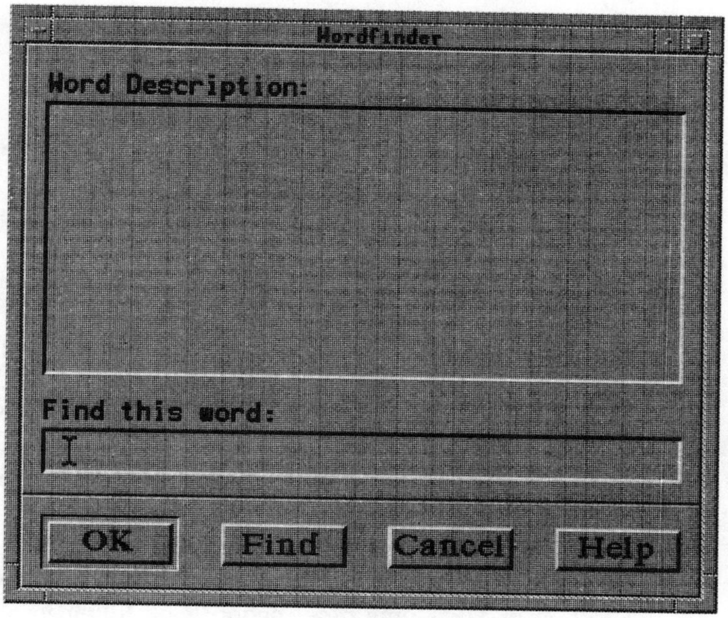

Figure 3.8. Entry box.

sage boxes are effective in focusing the user on a situation needing attention before a task can continue. Modal (preemptive) message boxes are often used to force this kind of user attention. Sometimes, the term *dialogue is* used to indicate what we call a "message box."

3.5.4   Dialogue Boxes

A *dialogue box is* a composite interaction object that can contain other interaction objects, such as lists, buttons, boxes, text-entry fields, valuators, and so on. It

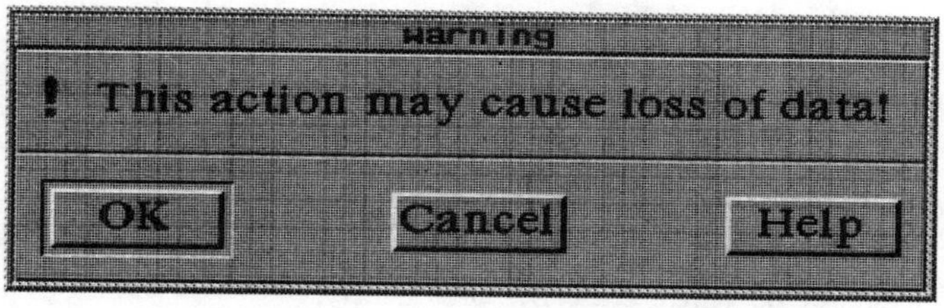

Figure 3.9. Message box.

allows a great deal of flexibility in the grouping of various related interaction objects. A dialogue box is typically displayed as part of a task sequence, often in response to a choice from a pull-down menu or an accelerator-key action. Dialogue boxes disappear as a result of a user action, usually within the box. Dialogue boxes are used to group functions for several related user tasks, as opposed to a menu, which allows a user to perform only one function at a time. Dialogue boxes are often (but not always) movable by a user but are rarely resizable.

Sometimes, dialogue boxes are a good approach for combining related user actions. For example, Microsoft Word™ requires a user to select text font and text size from the same pull-down menu; a user must first choose one and release the menu, then reopen the menu to make the second selection. It could have been more efficient for a user to have put both text-font selections and text-size selections (perhaps along with bold, italics, and so on) in a single dialogue box (such as with radio buttons), so a user could make both selections with fewer actions. There is rarely a visual cue to the availability of a dialogue box when it is not displayed, except for ellipsis (. . .) on a menu selection.

Dialogue boxes can be either modal (preemptive) or modeless (nonpreemptive). *Modal dialogue boxes* support sequential dialogue, in which a user must make some selection or take some other action (e.g., filling in a field) and dismiss the box before further actions can be made in the current (or any other) task. That is, when a modal dialogue box is being displayed, a user cannot simply click in another window and work on another task.

Modeless dialogue boxes, on the other hand, do not force the user to make a choice or take some other action from within the box before further work outside the box. A user can, for example, click on any other open window, and a modeless dialogue box will become inactive but will remain in the workspace, just as any secondary window would, even if the user has not interacted with the dialogue box. In Figure 3.2 the complete box, along with all the various kinds of buttons and the text field, is a dialogue box.

3.5.5 Box Design Guidelines

▶ Use brief but comprehensible instructions.

Because boxes often present multiple options, such as selecting from several menus, making a choice from a scrollable list, or typing a character string into a field, they can be confusing to the user. Simple, but clear, instructions may be needed, especially for modal dialogue boxes, in order for a user to know how to interact with the contents of the box.

▶ Use carefully worded messages.

Like any other message the user sees, messages that appear in boxes should be thoughtfully worded, from the user's—rather than the system's—view. The guidelines discussed previously for messages (see Section 2.3) all fully apply when writing messages to appear in boxes. This is, of course, especially true for alert or error messages that a user may see.

▶ Use logical groupings and orderings of objects in a box.

Because a box may contain several kinds of interaction objects, such as menus, scrollable lists, buttons, and text-entry fields all at once, the guidelines for each of those objects should apply. Different menus (e.g., two check-button banks) should be clearly separated in the box so that a user knows which choices belong to which button menu. Instructions for a text field should be close enough to that text field so that a user knows that the instructions apply to that field and not to a different object.

▶ Use visual cues to delineate groupings within boxes.

Just as with forms, white space and sometimes subtle lines should be used as visual cues for clearly indicating to a user the groups within boxes. Avoid overusing special characters—such as "*" or "/" or ":"—to delineate titles or groupings.

▶ Keep layout consistent and visually appealing.

If there are several message boxes in the interface, all of which offer the same three buttons for the user's response (e.g., "help," "ok," "cancel" are typical, although these are not necessarily good labels for many of their uses), generally use consistent placement and meaning of these buttons within all the boxes in which they appear. In dialogue boxes, do not overcrowd the format by trying to put too many different options into one box. Use reasonable alignment of objects within a box, left or right justifying the items, as appropriate.

▶ Make defaults, such as a button choice, visually distinctive.

If, in a message box, one of three buttons is the default choice (e.g., an "ok" button or a "cancel" button), show this to users via some visual cue such as highlighting, an extra border, or a deep shadow around the button. This will indicate to users that they can simply press the "Enter" key if they wish to select the default button, rather than having to move their hands from the keyboard to the mouse (or a bank of function keys) to make a selection. If they desire a selection other than the default, of course, they will have to use the mouse, the function keys, or whatever mechanism will allow traversal to the desired object.

▶ Menu selections that lead to dialogue boxes should contain a visual cue.

Dialogue boxes often appear after a user's menu selection (e.g., an "open" command in a graphics editor). Menu selections that will cause a dialogue box to be displayed to a user should somehow indicate that the user's choice will lead to the box, such as use of an ellipsis (. . .) following the choice. This may be the user's only visual cue that a dialogue box is available.

▶ Boxes should disappear under user control.

Boxes, especially those used to display messages to a user, sometimes appear momentarily on the screen, then magically disappear before a user can even read them. Any box displayed to the user should remain visible until the user performs some explicit action to deal with it, typically to make it go away or at least move it to the background. This can be accomplished by the use of one or more buttons in the box, to be chosen by the user to control the box. An example of an exception to user control of boxes is when they contain status indicators; these boxes generally should disappear automatically when the activity is completed for which the indicators are giving a status. However, these transient boxes should stay on the screen long enough for the user to read their content.

3.6   TYPED-COMMAND LANGUAGES

Typed-command languages, one of the earliest interaction styles found in user interfaces, are alphanumeric strings—representing commands, parameters, and/or options that are typed in by a user. They provide a powerful, brief, and rapid style of communication between user and system, and they often appeal to power (frequent) users who may not like the extra hand movements and desk scrubbing required by a mouse-driven direct manipulation interface. However, these commands often require extensive training, and a user must remember very precise and often arcane syntax (what does "grep" or "awk" mean, anyway?). Because they require typing, they lead to more user input errors, which necessitates the need for an interaction designer to produce more error messages.

The advent of direct manipulation interfaces has mercifully seen typed command languages become less prevalent, but they are still around in various forms in many user interfaces. An interesting recent application of command languages is typed commands in conjunction with speech input. Some interfaces (e.g., from NASA) have command languages that can be typed or unambiguously spoken by workers (e.g., astronauts) with otherwise-busy hands.

3.6.1   Typed-Command Languages Design Guidelines

▶ Use a consistent rule of formation for entering commands.

Because typed-command language interaction styles are more difficult for most users to learn than direct manipulation styles, the use of a consistent rule of formation is critical. That is, the format of each typed command should be the same throughout an interface. A common paradigm for typed commands has become the "action-modifier(s)-object(s)" convention of many of the UNIX functions (i.e., command, followed by options, followed by arguments). An example would be the command "ls -1 /usr," which displays a long (detailed) listing of a particular directory. This string indicates first the action the system is to perform ("ls," for "list"), next indicates the modifier ("-1," for long list, including date, size, and protection information), and then indicates the object on which to perform the action (the "usr" directory). Note that this recommended "action-object" model for typed command languages is just the opposite of the typical "object-action" paradigm (select an object, then indicate the action to be performed on it) found in most direct manipulation interfaces.

▶ Choose meaningful, specific, distinctive command names.

Determining names for typed commands is a very challenging task. The names should be meaningful yet should be nonoverlapping throughout an interface. Just as with menus and other interaction styles, it can be very difficult to decide, for example, whether the command to let a user leave the system should be "exit" or "quit," whether the command to remove selected objects should be "delete" or "cut," and so on. As mentioned earlier, conventions for many of these command names are now becoming standardized, at least for some platforms.

In an interface that allows abbreviations for typed commands, the inevitable collisions will occur; for example, it is desirable simply to be able to type "d," but does it stand for "down" or "delete"? Collisions can even occur with opposites, such as "k" for "kill" or "keep." The only way to resolve these kinds of design issues is to spend time working with possible command names, asking colleagues and potential users of an interface what words convey the most meaning to them for particular commands.

Use diametrical opposites (congruencies) for commands that are logically opposite (e.g., up and down, backward and forward, above and below). In one popular operating system, a user uses "connect" to attach to a system process, and "disconnect" to detach from a process. A user would logically assume that, when temporarily removed from a process by the system, the command to reestablish the process link would be "reconnect." For some inexplicable reason, however, designers of this interaction decided to use "resume."

▶ Apply consistent rules for abbreviating commands.

Users typically expect to use the first letter of a command as an abbreviation for that command. This is fine in a small command set where the designer may be able to come up with a set of good command names that have a unique first letter. In a larger command set, though, the designer will usually have to use more than the initial letter, often the first three, to achieve uniqueness. Another approach is to drop vowels, or to use only first and last letters of a command, but these are less obvious to a user.

In general, simple truncation is preferred by users to a single letter or to some other rule of abbreviation. Alternatively, a user can be allowed to type in characters while the system is doing character-at-a-time parsing, and as soon as the system recognizes a command unambiguously, it processes that command. The infamous "awk" command got its name from the first letter of the last names of its three creators. This command name is not user-centered, but it is perhaps more mnemonically meaningful than its creators expected.

▶ Allow easy correction of typing errors.

Some archaic typed-command language interfaces allowed a user to type in the full command line—perhaps 30 or 40 characters—and then, only after the user pressed the "Enter" key to end the command, informed the user that an error had occurred, usually about the second or third character. Good interfaces will provide an easy way for a user to correct the erroneous character or characters. Poor interfaces will require a user to retype the entire line, and the user will probably make a mistake in a different place on this attempt.

▶ Allow frequent users to develop macros.

Typed-command language interfaces are best suited for frequent, power users, because these users have the skills and the desire to work quickly with the system. Providing them with a mechanism through which they can develop their own macros, for example, for a sequence of commands that they may perform very often, can greatly accelerate their performance with the system. This capability reduces the amount of typing a user must do and therefore reduces errors. It can also help reduce the users' memory loads if they only have to remember a few macro names rather than the names of all the individual commands that make up those macros.

3.7   GRAPHICAL INTERFACES

Any user interaction that has windows, buttons, boxes, icons, and so on, is commonly called a graphical user interface, or GUI (pronounced "gooey"). They have also been fondly called "WIMP" (windows, icons, menus, and pointers) and "NERD" (navigation, evaluation, refinement, and demonstration) interfaces (Chignell & Waterworth, 1991). GUI appears to be the term that the industry is adopting. These graphical interfaces typically use direct manipulation, point-and-click interaction, following an object-action paradigm: Point to and click on an object to select it, then perform an action on it. Most graphical interfaces provide immediate visual feedback to a user. For example, as the user drags a folder across the screen, the folder (or its outline) follows the cursor movement, indicating to the user the exact current position of the folder on the screen.

All the interaction styles covered so far, with the exception of typed-command languages, could be classified as GUIs. This terminology seems unfortunate and inaccurate. There is a broader use of graphics in user interfaces that much more accurately deserves the appellation of graphical user interface, and that is the use of visual representations, rather than textual or numeric representations, to communicate with a user. We shall call these simply *graphical interfaces,* to at least somewhat distinguish them from the GUI realm. Graphics are important in user interfaces, to represent both input by a user to the application and output from the application to a user. Graphical objects can be, and often are, shared between the user and the system, and the actions of both can have an effect on those objects.

The main advantage of graphical interfaces is well-stated by Richard Hamming: "The purpose of computing is insight, not numbers" (1962). Even in days of inflation, a picture is still worth a thousand words. The graph of a function is much easier to understand than its formula or a table of values; graphics help to turn data into meaningful information. Graphics promote the exploration andmore importantlythe understanding of complex domains. However, graphical interfaces are easy to design badly and can quickly overload a user with information. They are typically more difficult to design and implement than more traditional interfaces, and the hardware for them can be more expensive. However, computing power has now improved to the point that graphical interfaces are available on desktop computers, and even on laptop and notebook computers.

Of the many kinds of graphical interfaces, this chapter briefly explores some of the most popular ones:

- Data and scientific visualization
- Visual databases
- Animation
- Video (and audio)
- Multimedia/hypermedia
- Virtual reality

3.7.1   Data and Scientific Visualization

Data and scientific visualization, one of the earliest uses of graphics in user inter-action, includes graphs, charts, histograms, and various kinds of elaborate screen images. Numerous application areas are making heavy use of visualization techniques. For example, computational chemists use three-dimensional rotating models of molecules and other kinds of visualization techniques to help predict the effects that will appear 10,000 years from now after toxic waste has been dumped on a particular area of land. Medical imaging of the interior of the human body is now extensively used by physicians to assist in diagnostic processes.

Space scientists discovered that data indicating the hole in the ozone layer had been available for more than a decade, in the form of numbers! Only the more recent advances in visualization techniques allowed scientists to see the hole. In fact, they discovered it in a visual display involving atmospheric data modeled around a spinning globe, which showed mysterious blobs being flung off into space as the earth rotated. Closer analysis showed that some of these blobs were, in fact, ozone. Had computer visualization techniques been utilized sooner, sci-entists might have known about the thinning ozone layer much earlier. Fluid flow (e.g., of air across an airplane wing, or of blood through the heart), weather patterns, heat transfer, and other such dynamic physical situations lend them-selves well to scientific visualization.

3.7.2   Visual Databases

Techniques for navigating and browsing through a *visual*, rather than the common textual, representation of a *database* are becoming popular. The Getty Museum has put digitized images of priceless Middle Ages illuminated manuscripts into a visual database, from which visitors to the museum can retrieve high-quality screen images of different pages and then can scan, pan, and zoom to examine the documents in detail. While no one except a few select museum curators are ever allowed to touch or see the actual manuscripts, an excellent reproduction of them is now available to the public, at least visually, if not tactilely.

Other kinds of visual representations are not digitized images, but rather computer-generated images. Imagine being able to drill a virtual oil well and to see the composition of the geology surrounding the drill hole (from a database of real geological data), represented by color coding at various depths of drilling. This can be much more effective for a petroleum engineer seeking to determine the likelihood of oil in a particular site than a table of values listing out the geological characteristics textually and/or numerically. The combination of these two techniques—the color representation and the table of values—can be extremely powerful as an analysis tool for a scientist.

3. 7.3 Animation

Animation, or simply cartoons, can represent the output of a simulation as it changes over time. It provides an excellent medium for producing training simulators and can include more than just visual images. Military tank drivers in the 1991 Desert Storm War in the Persian Gulf attributed much of their success to the use of extremely high-fidelity training simulators that exhibited not only realistic animated visual stimuli, but also other conditions, including sounds, vibrations, and the intense heat that can build up inside a tank. Animation simulators are very valuable for training in dangerous or inaccessible domains. Conditions that cannot feasibly be captured via real video footage, such as firefighting or deep underwater exploration, can be animated and used for training and other kinds of educational purposes.

3.7.4   Video

Full-motion *video,* and the audio that typically accompanies it, can be combined with other interaction styles in an interface—for example, in a window. Video gives the most realistic illustration of real-world activities and, like animation, can be used especially effectively for training. It is very easy to overuse full-motion video in a user interface, however; video in more than one place on the screen at a time can distract and indeed confuse a user. In addition, acquiring high-quality video footage is, in and of itself, a sizable task, as anyone who has ever shot serious amateur movies knows. Production of high-quality video involves numerous activities that require special skills and expensive equipment not usually available to user interaction designers.

3.7.5   Multimedia and Hypermedia

These are two of the most hyperused words in the area of user interfaces. Multimedia is itself a rather confused word because *media* is already plural, so why stick *multi-* in front of it? Simply put, multimedia and hypermedia involve the fusion of graphical, audio, and video media, often linked in an associative pattern. *Multimedia* user interfaces consist of more than one medium, typically video and/or animation and other interaction styles. *Hypermedia* interfaces provide links for a user to navigate among interaction objects, such as data, records, help information, documents, and even ideas and concepts, in a highly flexible fashion. This user navigation is a central concern in design of these kinds of interfaces; users can quickly get suspended in "hyperspace," completely losing track of where they are in the system, and indeed what task they might have been trying to accomplish.

3.7.6   Virtual Reality

Describing virtual reality by using words printed on a page is rather like trying verbally to describe falling in love to someone who never has. The term *virtual reality is* often used to refer to any interactive simulation. Virtual reality, or "artificial reality" as it is sometimes called, is perhaps the most interactive interaction style possible. Some of the most interesting applications involve a user's entire body. Rather than using a mouse, for example, to maneuver objects on a screen, people using virtual reality systems can project themselves into whatever three-dimensional environment the system is virtually creating. Through the use of special equipment with interesting names, such as data gloves, body gloves, and eye phones, users can enter the virtual world via these sensory-exchange devices and can manipulate objects in the virtual world by making motions with some parts of their bodies. For example, two people can play a game of virtual handball, using their real hands to volley a virtual ball that appears in their virtual shared handball court, and they can actually feel the pressure of the ball as it hits their hands, as simulated through the data glove. Users can walk through a virtual building, to see what their future offices, for example, might look like.

Virtual reality is not a new technology but is rather the amalgamation of existing complex technologies that have slowly evolved over the past few decades. A virtual reality system may be comprised of special high-performance interactive graphics computers, special displays, head-mounted displays that are essentially tiny TV sets mounted on a helmet, and electromagnetic trackers that sense and relay to the computer the position of the user's head, hand, and any other parts of the body to which the sensors are attached. Sophisticated robotics and artificial intelligence techniques are used in the tracking. As a user's head moves, the user's view of the virtual world changes correspondingly. Users can grasp an object in the virtual world by using their real hand to connect their virtual hand to the virtual object.

These systems can be extremely expensive, with even fairly simple ones costing hundreds of thousands of dollars. However, further technological advances promise to make them available to the masses. For several years, Nintendo, for example, marketed a Power Glove that cost well under $100. Pioneers in the field promise that virtual reality systems will change the way people use computers, the way people learn, and even the way people interact with each other. Imagine teleconferencing carried into a virtual world so that people in San Francisco, New York, Paris, and Osaka can see themselves assembled in a conference room in Atlanta. Imagine medical students being able to perform surgery—not on a cadaver, or even a live animal, which is how they currently learn many of their techniques—but on a virtual body using virtual tools that give the impression of actually performing the procedure. A goal of creating a virtual world is to design computer systems that communicate with human beings in human ways, rather than forcing the human to conform to the communication constraints of the computer. The sky is the limit.

3.7.7   Graphical Interface Design Guidelines

Guidelines for graphical interface design are very heuristic; there is very little firm evidence on this relatively new interaction style. It has taken well over a decade to assemble and organize the guidelines now available for fairly traditional user interfaces; now all bets are off as these exciting new interaction styles emerge in more and more systems. For example, the guideline that says a design should use no more than four different colors on a screen at one time is appropriate for textbased interfaces but may not apply to most graphical interfaces. Design of graphical, animated, potentially multidimensional interfaces is a huge design space that is still largely unexplored. The following guidelines are based heavily on common sense and experience.

▶ Use real-world analogies as much as possible.

Because these interaction styles are often used to convey real-world objects and real-world information to a user, designs that incorporate familiar analogs are most appropriate. Use graphical interaction styles for situations in which three-dimensional representation is appropriate. For example, using simulations or real video clips to show a process can be much more effective than screen after scrolling screen of text attempting to explain that process.

► Keep the visual representation as simple as possible.

Graphical interfaces offer a designer wonderful, innovative possibilities for interaction design, but there is such a thing as too much creativity. Making a visual representation more complex than it needs to be, just because it can be done, can actually hinder a user in accomplishing tasks. For example, imagine a system that displays all possible aircraft tracks on a single screen, just because the system is following all aircraft within a particular radius. If the user cannot filter the display to show only a few desired tracks at one time, the user may not be able to even find the aircraft to be tracked, with potentially disastrous results. Apply basic graphical design principles, including those for layout and typography. Use graphics meaningfully, rather than as useless, distracting decoration.

► Show different views of the same visual object.

This relates to keeping the visual representation simple, by allowing a user to see several different views of the same object. For example, an automotive engineer might like to work with a wire-frame representation of a new car design part of the time and a full realistic picture representation at other times.

► Use color sparingly and meaningfully.

Again, do not overuse color just because there are 16 million available choices. Even though more colors are allowable, and useful, in these graphical interfaces than in predominantly text-based interfaces, color is still very easy to overdo. Use color to highlight areas of interest, to monitor changes, to indicate targets, and so on.

► Use video sparingly.

As already discussed, production of high-quality video is itself a major undertaking. Nonetheless, only high-quality, well-produced video should be used in graphical interfaces, and then only for situations in which full-motion, realistic presentation is especially effective, such as training or other educational applications.

3.8   OTHER INTERACTION STYLES

While numerous other interaction styles could be discussed, we only briefly mention a few that are becoming more popular and feasible.

3.8.1   Touchscreens

Touchscreens are among the most durable of all input devices. They work beautifully in harsh, heavy-use environments, such as production floors and public access systems. Touchscreen-activated systems at Epcot Center work uninterrupted for weeks, with the only maintenance being a regular spritz of glass cleaner, despite having soft drinks spilled on them, high humidity, and literally millions of grimy fingers touching them.

Many improvements to touchscreens have appeared over the past few years. Early screens were notorious for causing arm fatigue, for having the hand moved far from the keyboard, and for imprecise reading of touches, among other drawbacks. More recent touchscreens now have much greater precision and a more comfortable tilted positioning. Touchscreens have no moving parts, resulting in high durability, and the price is reasonable. Touchscreens are desirable for novice users, especially for walk-up-and-use systems, because of their simplicity of use. They are also desirable for frequent users when space is very limited (e.g, with little room for a keyboard and/or mouse), when rugged design is important, or when users need to be guided through complex tasks (Shneiderman, 1992).

3.8.2   Speech Synthesis

Synthesis of speech—creating audible sounds and words with a computer—is a fairly well-developed technology. Computer-generated speech can range from very harsh, unrealistic sounds, to quite natural-sounding tones. Speech can be useful in a computer system as a redundant output channel, where users hear information from the computer as they read the same information on the screen. It is, of course, also desirable for visually and physically disabled users who may not be able to see the screen or to manipulate cursor-control devices effectively.

3.8.3   Speech Recognition: Natural Language

To date, computer recognition of speech is still fairly limited to discrete-word, domain-specific situations and vocabularies. Full speech recognition is, of course, the problem of natural language understanding, and a great deal of research is still needed before the development of a computer that can first recognize and then understand anything a user may speak to it. The difficulties with speech recognition are well-known and revolve around the lexical, syntactic, and semantic ambiguities inherent in all languages, especially English. A wonderful example of why it is so hard to develop a computer to recognize English is shown in the sequence of words "how view wonder stood mice peaches." Those words, individually, are each a real, meaningful English word. However, when assembled as shown here, they have no semantic meaning as a sentence. Now read the words, somewhat rapidly, out loud. What did you say? "Have you understood my speeches"! No wonder computers can't understand English—enough said.

REFERENCES

Bly, S. A. & Rosenberg, J. K. (1986). A Comparison of Tiled and Overlapping Windows. *Proceedings of CHI Conference on Human Factors in Computing Systems, New York: ACM, 101-106.*

Chignell, M. H. & Waterworth, J. A. (1991). WIMPS and NERDS: An Extended View of the User Interface. *SIGCHI Bulletin,* 23(2),15-21.

Hamming, R. W. (1962). *Numerical Methods for Scientists and Engineers.* New York: McGraw-Hill.

Myers, B. A. (1990). *All the Widgets* [two-hour video tape]: *SIGGRAPH Video Review* (Issue 57, Technical Video Program of CHI '90 Conference). New York: ACM.

Open Software Foundation. (1990). *OSF/Motif Style Guide.* Englewood Cliffs, NJ: Prentice-Hall.

Shneiderman, B. (1992). *Designing the User Interface: Strategies for Effective Human Computer Interaction.* Reading, MA: Addison-Wesley.

Part II

The Process

4

Iterative, Evaluation-Centered User Interaction Development

4.1 PRINCIPLES FOR THE PROCESS OF USER INTERACTION DEVELOPMENT AND ITS MANAGEMENT

Although it is always better to have a principled approach to development, the question is, What principles? We have adapted the following two principles from Gould, Boies, and Lewis's general principles for the process of user interaction development (Gould, Boies, & Lewis, 1991).

- Development should include early and continuous *empirical testing*, centered around appropriate users performing representative tasks.
- As development proceeds, it should incorporate subsequent *iterative refinement* procedures and *cost/benefit analyses* to determine the most cost-effective changes to make to the user interaction design.

To these, we add a third principle because management of the iterative refinement process is a critical aspect of user interaction development:

- The *management process should verify and control* the overall development life cycle and assign accountability for each step.

Perhaps these sound too obvious to be worth mentioning: "Of course we follow these principles," you're thinking. But do you really have detailed, structured procedures for interaction development, or are they fairly ad hoc? Gould and Lewis (1985)asked interaction developers to write down the major steps they used to develop and evaluate an interactive system. In a survey of 447 people, 26% of them did not mention use of any principles of user interaction development at all, and 35% mentioned only one. Only 2% mentioned four principles. Of the specific principles these developers mentioned, 62% mentioned early focus on users; 40% noted use of some sort of empirical, behavioral evaluation; and only 20% mentioned use of iterative design. Granted, this survey was performed in the early 1980s, and we would hope that results would be dramatically different today. Nonetheless, these results show that principles for user interaction development are *neither obvious nor intuitive*, and they are *not applied* nearly as often as they should be. This is hopefully due to a lack of knowledge about exactly how to apply the principles, not because of a lack of desire to develop a usable interface.

The life cycle concepts, methods, techniques, and tools discussed throughout the rest of this book are the mechanisms that support these development and management principles. Subsequent chapters present detailed approaches to the most critical activities in the user interaction development *process*, along with examples to illustrate these points and exercises for you to try yourself.

First, however, because user interaction development does not occur in a vacuum, it is important to talk a little bit about how the interaction development process fits together with the software (both interface software and noninterface software) development within the overall system development process. This discussion begins with what may be familiar to many readers, life cycle concepts for developing software, and then introduces life cycle concepts more appropriate for user interaction development.

4.2   LIFE CYCLE CONCEPTS FOR SOFTWARE DEVELOPMENT

If you are familiar with the software engineering world, you will know that a lot of software is developed using a top-down approach based on functional decomposition. The typical life cycle associated with this kind of methodology is one that begins with systems analysis and proceeds sequentially through phases of requirements specification, design, possibly prototyping, implementation, and testing.

Because the work flows from one phase to another, with management signing off on each phase, this kind of life cycle is sometimes termed the *waterfall method,* as shown in Figure 4.1 (adapted from Boehm, 1988).

Top-down development often begins with formal specifications. Formalizing specifications helps software engineers ensure completeness and understandability. In many software development environments, the process is *correctness-driven;* focusing on the fidelity with which implementation follows the specifications. The process is *essentially sequential,* as shown in the figure. There is, however, testing at various places in the sequence, and each of the activities has a feedback path to the previous activity.

Pragmatically, however, development of a complex system cannot go sequentially from beginning to end. Boehm (1988) recognized the need to iterate in software development when he introduced the *spiral methodology* for software development. The spiral approach involves a kind of large cycle moving several times through the whole top-down process, each time broadening the circle (thus, the name) to include more detail of the system. This kind of iteration is used in software engineering and user interaction development too, because of the inability to account for all the details at once.

However, iteration is used in user interaction development for an additional reason. Although some methods do exist for predicting software behavior, few or none exist for predicting human user behavior. As Gould and Lewis (1985, p. 305) say, an interactive system has a "coprocessor of largely unpredictable behavior"— the human user. The unpredictability stems in part from the limitations of psychological theory, but mostly from designers' lack of understanding of the specific context of use, an understanding that must be obtained, in large measure, from observing users.

As a result, user interface development, especially development of the interaction part (defined in Chapter 1), must be *essentially and inherently iterative.* That is, it must be a *self-correcting process.* This surely is not just a temporary situation, not just until developers learn how to do it right the first time. Carroll and Rosson (1985, p. 13) say that design is essentially empirical "not because we don't know enough yet, but because in a design domain we can never know enough." If this situation is not properly explained to others, however, it can lead to the comment, "These user interface people don't know what they are doing. They can't get it right the first time; they keep changing their minds."

4.3   OBSERVING HOW DEVELOPERS WORK: ALTERNATING WAVES OF ACTIVITY

The first section (4.1) of this chapter talked about some principles for interaction development. The preceding section (4.2) also began to note that for user interac-

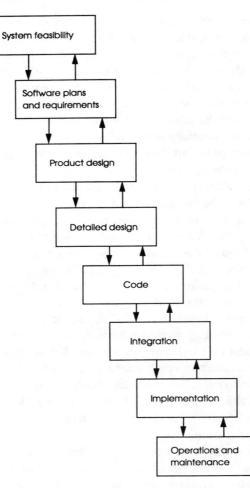

Figure 4.1. The waterfall method for software development. Adapted with permission from B. W. Boehm, A Spiral Model of Software Development, *IEEE Computer*, pp. 61–72. © 1988 IEEE.

tion development, developers need something different from the sequential and spiral life cycle concepts often used in software development. The next question is, What kinds of development activities (*methodology*) should be used to support these principles, and how can they be most effectively organized into a *life cycle*? The term methodology is often used in reference to how software is developed, and a similar development process is needed for the user interaction component. What development methodologies do you now use for developing software and for developing user interaction? Because software development methods are not necessarily suitable for developing the user interaction, it is important to find a life cycle that is more appropriate for user interaction development.

In order to understand the iterative development process better, we observed both interaction developers and software developers at work (Hartson & Hix, 1989). One thing we noticed is that a life cycle even for noninterface software would also benefit from a less rigid sequential process. There seems to be a natural need to alternate between top-down and bottom-up processes. Software engineers are familiar with this need and, when it becomes distracting, they call it "yo-yo-ing." Our observations were consistent with Piaget's idea that people learn better by starting with concrete examples (e.g., specific screen pictures for interaction design) and working toward the abstract. Iteration was the key, as also observed, for example, by Gould and Lewis (1985), and Carroll and Rosson (1985). This process involves even more iteration, and a different granularity of iteration, than is found in the spiral software methodology. For example, interaction designers may go through a dozen or more tight local cycles of iteration within an hour just to address one little point of interaction design, such as the labels on a set of buttons.

More generally, we observed developers, particularly interaction developers, operating in *alternating waves* of two complementary kinds of activities. Bottom-up, concrete, creative, and synthesizing activities tended to reflect the user's view, working toward the system. These were alternated with top-down, abstracting, structuring, and analyzing activities that tended to reflect a system view, working toward the user—a *synthesis* mode to create something and an *analysis* mode to evaluate it. This idea runs counter to traditional linear, sequential, top-down software engineering paradigms, but it more closely represents how people do most kinds of design, as most software developers would agree. It also fits well with the idea of rapid prototyping, which gives the interaction developer something to evaluate much sooner in the process (more about rapid prototyping later, in Chapter 9).

The early bottom-up activities we observed were based on partial trial designs of screen sketches, using scenarios and storyboarding techniques, often augmented with some kind of state diagram to represent sequencing. Subsequent activities often involved top-down task analysis, producing a hierarchical organization of user/system tasks. Often, evaluation is bottom-up because it deals with details, but top-down activities are needed to add structure. The wonderful power of abstraction (provided by a top-down approach), as applied by a good designer, relieves the need to worry about all the details at once.

The requirements process is strongly both top-down and bottom-up because both structure and details are important. Conventional life cycle concepts demand that requirements specification be essentially completed before beginning design activities. These two activities interact closely. Feedback from design played an important role in getting the requirements correct and complete, and many design issues surfaced during the requirements process. In some of our empirical observations of real-world developers at work, we noticed that iterative and alternating development activities occurred, but because corporate standards required it, they reported their work as having been done strictly top-down. Astonishingly, developers said that they performed the work basically using the alternating waves approach, then hid the results under their desk blotter and wrote up the final report based on the required corporate top-down approach.

Rosson, Maass, and Kellogg (1987) have shown how interaction developers might tend to emphasize either the top-down mode or the bottom-up mode, depending on their experience. The top-down, structuring mode tends to predominate when a developer has some experience and a priori knowledge of target system structure. Emphasis on the bottom-up, experimenting and synthesizing activity is more suitable in novel situations, where little about the target system structure is known in advance, and trial-and-error activity must augment experience and intuition to develop system structure.

In addition to top-down and bottom-up, software engineering activities often are performed from the inside out, with the major work being the development of a good impedance match between what is at hand at the bottom and what is expected at the top. Too much emphasis on top-down development can be detrimental to this impedance match.

One major reason for bottom-up work is to establish the low-level functions as building blocks for implementing the higher-level functions. Top-down work then deploys the resulting basic modules in developing an application solution. As toolkits, reusable objects, and standard library components become more prevalent, especially for user interface development, there may be a decline in the amount of bottom-up activity. It is not likely to disappear, though, because there will always be a need for a better, customized component to give the target product an edge over another that uses strictly standard components.

Exclusive use of a top-down approach in software engineering, or any development environment, can lead developers to defer some of the tough problems for too long, pushing them to the bottom. When they finally face these problems at the bottom, they may encounter the need for major changes that could affect the structure all the way back to the top.

To be effective, all developers must acquire a comprehensive and integrated understanding of the connections among development activities at all levels. Understanding and integrating the development process requires an understanding of how developers acquire this overview. This is true in user interface development and, to varying degrees, in the development of any large system (e.g., a new automobile, a large modern airplane, or a skyscraper). The section that follows describes a life cycle concept that helps an interaction developer acquire this comprehensive understanding because it accommodates the need to alternate between top-down and bottom-up development in an environment of constant evaluation and iteration. The design representation techniques discussed in Chapters 6 and 7 are also important in helping an interaction developer acquire a comprehensive overview of the interface.

4.4   A LIFE CYCLE FOR USER INTERACTION DEVELOPMENT

The following life cycle concept is based on extensive observations and is especially suited for the needs of user interaction development. It is intended to be equally supportive of both top-down and bottom-up development, plus inside-out and outside-in development, too. Also, of course, it was essential to support continual evaluation and iteration during interaction development, including much tighter, smaller loops of iteration than imagined in the spiral methodology. This life cycle minimizes the number of ordering constraints among the development activities. For example, you don't necessarily have to specify all requirements before working on design. In fact, you could start by playing with a design—such as by using a quick prototyping tool—and, in the process, learn a lot about what you want in the requirements.

All these considerations led to a different kind of development life cycle concept, shown here in Figure 4.2 (adapted from Hartson & Hix, 1989), termed the *star life cycle*, because of its shape. The points of the star are not ordered or connected in a sequence. This means that a user interaction developer can theoretically start with almost any development activity and move on to almost any other one. The various activities are highly interconnected, however, through the usability evaluation process in the center. Thus, this life cycle is evaluation-centered; results of each activity are evaluated before going on to the next activity. In general, a different kind of evaluation is required after each different activity in this life cycle. Conventional life cycles lean toward independent performance of each development activity, whereas the star life cycle supports interdependent, but still distinct, activities. The star life cycle described here is representative of the iterative process described throughout the book.

The user interaction development activities presented in subsequent chapters are shown in Figure 4.2, in the part labeled "Our area of interest," and include system (and other) analysis (in Chapter 5), usability specifications (in Chapter 8), design, design representation (in Chapters 6 and 7), rapid prototyping (in Chapter 9), and usability evaluation (in Chapter 10). These are shown here as representa-

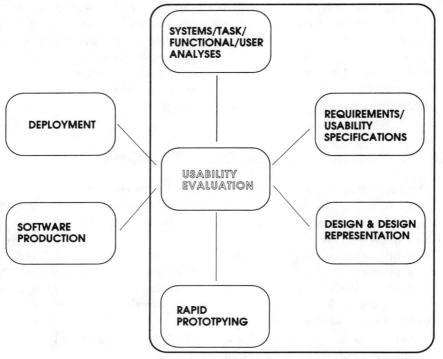

OUR AREA OF INTEREST

Figure 4.2. The star life cycle for user interaction development. Adapted with permission from Hartson and Hix, 1989.

tive development activities, ones that are common to almost any iterative approach, and you can probably add some of your own. Much of the rest of this book focuses on the development activities and not necessarily on this specific life cycle in which they can be set. The book also discusses how the activities fit together with each other and with the interface software life cycle to produce a user interface about which you can make and support specific, measurable usability claims.

The development activities of interest are predominantly in the behavioral domain (see Section 1.5). Although software production, final clean-up and optimization of code, and deployment are important parts of the overall process, they are largely in the constructional domain. Those activities are not discussed in this book. It is also important to remember that this representative user interaction development life cycle is set within the larger, and quite different, overall software and interactive system development life cycles.

4.5   USABILITY MANAGEMENT

The highly iterative process shown in Figure 4.2 is potentially one that never ends. Managers find this prospect scary and, besides, the process must end if a product is to get out the door. Managers would never permit the use of a development process that doesn't have a well-defined end point. So what's missing? A *control mechanism*. This book introduces you to a control mechanism that managers—and you—can use to decide when to stop iterating. It is based on establishing quantitative usability specifications (Chapter 8).

Formative evaluation, the kind of usability evaluation discussed in this book (Chapter 10), is used to compare actual usability of the interaction design with your usability specifications, as development progresses. You will learn methods for identifying problem areas and analysis techniques that you can use to determine which problems to address to get the most improvement in usability. Finally, you will learn to develop specific, measurable criteria for knowing when you should stop the iteration. These provide you with a control mechanism for managing the iterative process and help ensure usability in your interfaces. Before this chapter ends, however, the interaction development process is set into perspective within the broader area of software engineering.

4.6   CONNECTIONS TO SOFTWARE ENGINEERING

There are, as you might expect, both parallels and differences between user interaction development and software engineering. This section presents an overview of some of these differences and then discusses how user interaction development is connected to software engineering. There are many formal techniques in software engineering mentioned here, but detailed discussion of them is beyond our scope. To stay focused on user interaction, this overview offers a context for how user interaction development fits into the overall system development process.

4.6.1   A Comparison

The critical goals of software engineering as a technology are sometimes said to be software producibility and software quality. Software producibility addresses the difficulty and labor intensiveness of producing software. Weapons in the fight for producibility include high-level languages, abstraction, development environments, Computer-Aided Software Engineering (CASE) tools, and software reusability. Software quality usually means correctness, reliability, and maintainability. Techniques for formal specification and program proving have been developed to verify that implementation is faithful to design. Seldom, if ever, does software quality include quality of the user interface. So this book is about a new critical goal for user interface development as a technology: *software usability*.

User interaction development and software development have many similarities. They both produce parts of an interactive system. After all, user interfaces are built of software, so is there a difference? Because user interfaces are implemented with software, many software engineers believe that the well-established techniques for developing software in general will apply as well to user interface development. User interaction developers disagree. The real answer is yes and no. These techniques do apply to the user interface software, but not to designing what that software should implement—namely, the interaction with a user. Most significantly, the human element, brought into the equation by the user, is not a consideration of conventional software engineering as a discipline. To most software engineers, the system is the software, and possibly the hardware. To a user interaction developer, the system includes the human user, and the connection to the rest of the system is the user interface. Because of the "human factor," user interaction development represents a domain with its own special problems, requiring its own skills and its own special development techniques. In the sections that follow, these differences are formalized as a distinction of development processes and the new communication requirements that emerge as a result.

Can what is known about software engineering help with user interaction development? Well, it turns out that software engineering development techniques do not transfer well to engineering of user interaction. The same *kinds* of concepts apply—requirements, specifications, design, metrics, evaluation, maintenance, documentation, life cycle—but for user interaction, each has to be done in a different way, as shown in the chapters that follow.

4.6.2   User Interface Development as Part of Interactive System Development

User interface development is part of a larger set of development processes for an interactive system. Figure 4.3 shows how user interface development activities are related to other areas of interactive system development.

The *application software* referred to in the upper right box is the noninterface software, and established conventional software engineering techniques and methodologies apply to its development. The boundary between *interface software* development and application software development is not as sharp as this figure indicates. As most practitioners realize, there is unavoidable overlap between the two. The box on the upper left shows that the *user* is part of the system, and the user's knowledge must be developed, too. This usually means training. *Interactive*

User development (e.g. training)	Interactive medium, interaction device development	Interaction development	Interface software development	Application software development
		User interface development		
	Development of computer-based system			
Development of overall interactive system				

Figure 4.3. Areas of interactive system development. From Hartson, Brandenburg, & Hix, 1992, in *Languages for Developing User Interfaces.* © 1992. Boston: Jones and Bartlett Publishers. Reprinted by permission.

medium and device development has to do with the development of new hardware for user interfaces, which is outside the scope of this book. The hardware devices, of course, do have a strong influence on interaction styles used in development of the *interaction.* Interaction development is in the behavioral domain, while user interface software development is in the constructional domain.

4.6.3   Abstraction Buys Compartmentalization

A good way to see the relationship between user interaction development and software engineering is by looking at how development activities of each are modularized. In each case, the development process is broken into smaller subprocesses. By abstraction—elimination of all detail not germane to the domain of a given module—developers in either domain can control complexity by limiting the amount of detail they must handle at one time. The intention of this kind of compartmentalization is to try to separate issues by domain so that they can be considered independently of the other domains. Unfortunately, some issues tend to cross domains, preventing the creation of clean boundaries. That is why an integrated view is required of the development team. In any case, the boundaries introduce a new need—for *formal communication.* That, in turn, introduces new problems, such as how to handle incomplete or incorrect communication.

To illustrate these ideas, look at the distinction between *software design* and *software implementation,* a now-standard modularization within software engineering, as shown in Figure 4.4. Some software development teams treat the communication between these activities very formally. Others resolve problems between design and implementation in informal, face-to-face, fluid meetings. The style of interaction has a large influence on how development gets done and how *well* it gets done in practice. The following passages discuss some of the subprocesses of software development here, and then (in Section 4.6.6) develop the analogous case for user interface development.

Within the domain of software design, a software designer usually works at a reasonably high level of abstraction, considering algorithms, data structures, and the like, but not the details of coding. In contrast, the implementation domain requires concentration on coding. Here, a software implementer takes the design as a given and is not concerned about analyzing the design. The implementer avoids getting sidetracked with concerns over whether the software design should be improved, and so on.

In reality, however, the coupling between these modules is not always as low as would be desirable. For example, limitations of the programming language used for implementation may impose some very real constraints on what is practical in the design. Designers who take these limitations into account a priori will produce designs that are more likely to be implemented properly. It is because of the many ways the domains of these two modules of activity cannot be completely independent that Swartout and Balzer (1982) write about the "inevitable intertwining of specification and implementation."

So modularization solves some problems and introduces some new ones. With two modules instead of just one, a new communication need arises, as represented by the arrows between the modules in Figure 4.4. The vehicle for communicating the design to the implementer is often termed *specifications*, usually a formal set of statements about the design from which coding is to be done. The unfortunate thing about specifications is the difficulty in being sure they are complete and/or correct, but formal methods provide a way to increase the likelihood of correctness and completeness.

During the detailed coding process, a skilled implementer will often know

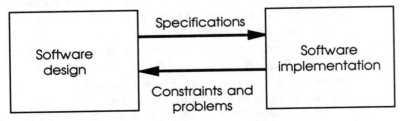

Figure 4.4. Distinction between software design and implementation.

when something is missing or something is wrong in the specifications. There are at least two possible courses of corrective action. The implementer can try to fill in or modify the specifications, or the implementer can communicate the shortcomings back to the designer. In the former case, the implementer is guilty of doing design, a violation of the distinction of design from implementation. The problem with this is that, although the implementer may also have good design skills, the implementer is not in the best position to do this design. The implementer will often not have easy access to the design rules agreed on by the designers, documentation of the design rationale that has guided design decisions, or methodology and structure used by the designers.

The result will be ad hoc design decisions with a very high probability of introducing inconsistencies, exceptions, and deviations from acceptable design style. The same missing or incorrect specifications will be corrected in different ways by different implementers at different times, resulting in nonuniformity and inconsistency. Errors and other new problems may be introduced when solutions to problems do not take into account the global view used by designers to fit all the pieces of the puzzle together.

As a result of these problems, most development projects have firm policies prohibiting implementers from doing on-the-fly design. As an alternative, it is important to establish an *effective communication channel*, indicated by the bottom arrow in Figure 4.4, feeding back from implementer to designer. In addition to this (possibly informal) feedback, formal program verification techniques are available to confirm that the implementation meets design specifications. Communication between these two parts of the development process has been the subject of much software engineering research, and is relatively well-understood.

4.6.4   Systems Analysis and Testing

In Figure 4.5, two more development activities have been added, for a more complete picture of the process. Chapter 5 gives an overview of some of the *systems analysis* activities having the most impact on the user interface, including needs analysis, task analysis, and user class analysis. In the present context, however, Figure 4.5 refers to development of only the noninterface part of the system and its software. The result of systems analysis is a set of design requirements for software designers. These requirements are high-level statements of system goals, needs, desired functionality, and features on which the software design is based.

While some of the feedback from *software testing* (for example, errors directly due to bugs in the code) are fed back to the implementation process, the main feedback path is to software design, where flaws and other problems are corrected, producing modifications to the specifications, which are then fed forward again to

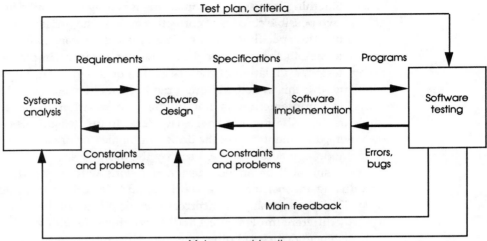

Figure 4.5. Adding systems analysis and testing.

implementation. Some problems discovered in testing may be fundamental enough to require more reconsideration in systems analysis. As a simple picture of the software development process, Figure 4.5 is nearly complete; there is just one more activity.

4.6.5   Design of the Problem Domain

That one more activity is important but is not obvious to everyone. In order to design the software in the software design box of Figure 4.5, a software designer must know what the software is supposed to do, and this is defined by the problem domain of the system. Problem domain design is added into the evolving diagram in Figure 4.6. Problem domain design is abstract design, in the sense that it is independent of software design and implementation.

The problem domain design is a formal model of the application, often made up of theory, engineering concepts, and equations. For example, if the problem domain of the interactive system is bridge building, it might contain a formal model for stress analysis that deals with information about stress, strength of materials, loading forces, and safety factors. The software design is then the design of data structures and algorithms to convert the problem domain design into a computer program.

Computers are used to help people solve problems in their own problem domain (e.g., bridge building, word processing, database storage and retrieval,

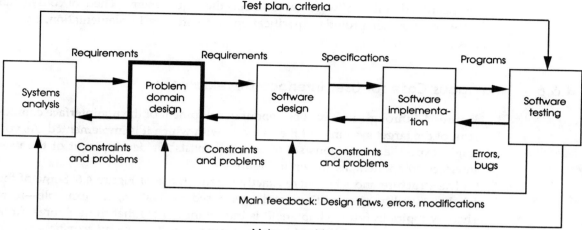

Test plan, criteria

Main feedback: Design flaws, errors, modifications

Major reconsiderations

Figure 4.6. Adding problem domain design.

analysis in physics or chemistry, numerical solutions to engineering applications). Inputs to the problem domain design box are from systems analysis, where it is decided what needs and features will be provided in the target system. This defines the underlying functionality of the developing system, the functionality that will also be supported in the user interaction design. Sometimes, development teams start thinking that software engineering is the whole process and, anxious to get on with development of the software, miss the opportunity to identify carefully what's really needed in the system. You know the story: "Hey, did you hear? We just got the contract! You start coding while I go find out what they want!" The result is often a poor match (even functionally) to the needs of the users.

Just as the software implementer in Figures 4.4 through 4.6 gives feedback to the software designer about incomplete and incorrect specifications, the problem domain designer gives feedback to the systems analyst regarding missing and inconsistent requirements for the formal model. The problem domain designer also produces requirements for the software design, which includes algorithms, data structures, definition of modules and the calling structure, data flow, and operations. The problem domain designer and the system analyst are two different roles. However, the activities are sometimes combined (e.g., as a systems engineering activity) because the problem domain designer is often viewed as a systems analysis resource rather than as a separate development role. The software designer provides feedback to the problem domain designer by reporting any inconsistencies, omissions, or ambiguities in the software requirements, and through verification that the software design meets the requirements. Then, of course, the software designer provides specifications for software implementation, as discussed earlier.

4.6.6   Analogous Case for User Interface Development

Figures 4.4 through 4.6 have been about development of the noninterface component of the target system, and the software with which it is implemented. As you might expect, an analogous set of activities exists for development of the user interface component, as shown in Figure 4.7.

The structure and labels here exactly parallel those of Figure 4.6. Some of the labels—usability specifications and user-based evaluation, for example—foreshadow topics in future chapters. It is important to note that these figures, from Figure 4.4 on, are depictions of *communication among development activities* and not depictions of relative timing or sequencing among them.

Figure 4.8 has extracted two important boxes from Figure 4.7, the two that deal with user interface design, for closer scrutiny. Figure 4.8 shows that interface design has both a part involving software and an interaction part independent of

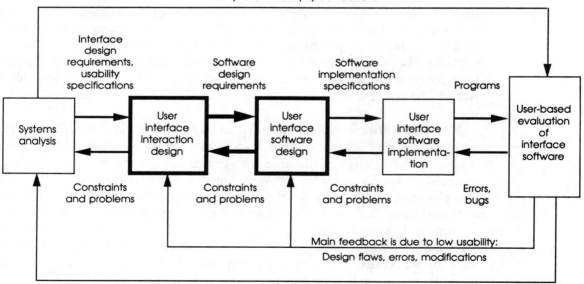

Figure 4.7. Analogous activities for user interface development.

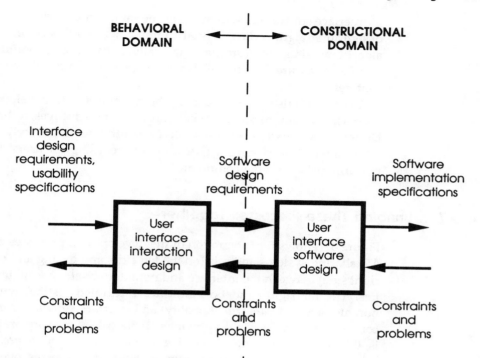

Figure 4.8. A closer look at the boxes for interface design.

software, just as was described earlier. Figure 4.7 showed these two related activities within the context of other interactive system development activities. Figure 4.8 illustrates the connection between the two different domains. In particular, the left box corresponds to the *behavioral domain* and the right box to the *constructional domain*. Communication between these boxes in Figure 4.8 is therefore the communication between the behavioral and the constructional domains. This communication is the subject of behavioral interaction design representation (e.g., the User Action Notation [UAN]), discussed in Chapters 6 and 7. Feedback—namely, constraints and problems—includes incomplete or incorrect requirements of specifications, infeasible design approaches, and limitations of development tools and environments.

The left box in Figure 4.8 is different from the right. As an activity, design of the interaction is very different from design of the interface software. As was discussed in Chapter 1, interaction design involves user actions, feedback, screen appearance, and user tasks, and it is also concerned with functionality, sequencing, content, and information access, as well as such details as designing interface objects, screen layout, and interaction styles.

Interface software design involves the same kinds of issues as for any software design. If straight coding is used to implement the interface, the issues include algorithms, data structures, and the calling structure of modules. Usually, user interface software design will also involve widgets and calls to toolkit and library routines.

The two kinds of design activity both contribute to development of the user interface but require different skills, attitudes, perspectives, techniques, and tools. Design of software, even user interface software, is properly system-centered, while interaction design is user-centered, focusing on users' behavior as they perform tasks with the computer.

4.6.7   Bringing These Processes Together

Figure 4.9 shows the integration of the development processes of Figures 4.6 and 4.7, sharing systems analysis (on the left side) and testing and evaluation (on the right side) between the interface and noninterface streams of development activities. The far right-hand box indicates integrated testing, with users, of both noninterface software (functionality) and interface software. Again, note that the connections here (and in the previous diagrams) are not temporal connections; that is, they are not showing sequencing in time. Rather, the *connections are communication paths (arcs) among the various activities (boxes)* in the overall development processes. Just as some development teams treat communication formally (see discussion of Figure 4.4) and some treat it informally, user interface developers can be formal in their communication, or they can discuss specifications and design in an informal, face-to-face manner.

This figure shows the parallelism between interface and noninterface development activities, in the lower and upper portions of the figure, respectively. It also shows the distinction between these parallel paths of development. In reality, of course, there is a need for many vertical communication channels connecting boxes of the two paths, communicating between developers of the interface and developers of the computational functionality connected to the interface. These interconnecting channels are essential to an integrated development team, but because these communication channels are not well understood, they are not included in this diagram. Also, this diagram is an idealized representation of communication paths but does not dictate anything about how that communication should occur. For example, Figure 4.9 shows the systems analysis group feeding requirements to both the problem domain design and the user interaction design groups. This could be accomplished within a single, informal, highly interactive team. Research is needed to better understand and support the real communication needs of this complex process.

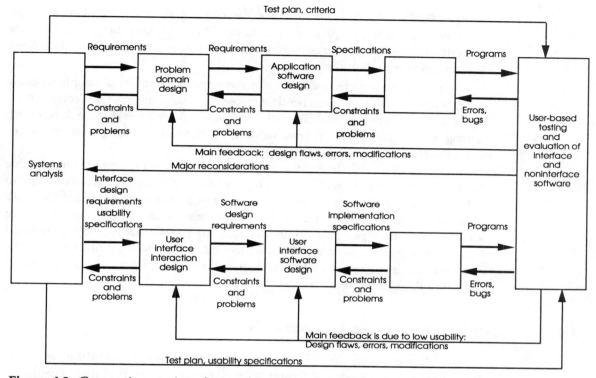

Figure 4.9. Connecting noninterface and interface development activities.

By the time you see Figure 4.9, you may say, "This sounds great for a large software house with large development teams, but what if there are only two or three of us; or what about the case where a single individual is responsible for developing a whole small system?" The answer is that these diagrams, starting with Figures 4.4, are not about individual versus team development; they are not about how many people are involved. They are about *structuring the process with clearly defined roles and clear-cut lines of communication,* having the right abstractions and activities in the appropriate domains. If you believe that, with a small group or a single individual, these activities would become so merged as to lose distinguishability, consider the analogous case in the early days of software engineering and structured programming. Regardless of the group size, it was shown that the discipline and structure in keeping the activities distinguished, right down to the resulting documentation, was the key to successful development.

Thus, these diagrams are about development *roles,* as well as *communication* among those roles, which were discussed in detail in Chapter 1. How people are mapped to the roles is a matter of the size of the project, the number of people involved, the management style, and so on. The important thing is to keep the roles distinct because that means keeping the activities, the communication lines, and the documentation distinct.

As the size of a system under development and the number of people working on it increase, communication needs increase. In reality, much of this communication occurs via very informal channels, and people sometimes drift back and forth among roles in the process. Yet maintaining the distinction among roles can reduce side effects and unwanted dependencies.

Applied to the entire interactive system development process, distinguishable roles filled with people working as a team of closely integrated peers can lead to better designs, better code, and ultimately ensure a more usable product. One way to achieve integration in practice is to have one person in the role of system architect, usually a person who understands the goals broadly and has invested heavily in achieving success. The system architect, who may not have all the needed expertise alone, will interact closely with all major contributors throughout the entire development process.

4.6.8   Rapid Prototyping and Formative Evaluation

Finally, the development picture is completed with the addition of rapid prototyping (discussed in Chapter 9) and formative, or usability, evaluation (discussed in Chapter 10) in Figure 4.10.

The loop in bold at the lower left corner of the diagram shows the short communication path for early evaluation of the interface prototype; design and prototyping are quickly followed by formative evaluation and then redesign, and so on. It is also interesting to note the very large communication distance—fully across the diagonal—shown in this diagram between the user interface prototype (at the lower left) and application (noninterface) software (in the upper right). This indicates the current gap in technology needed to test the functional software along with the interface prototype, as a whole-system prototype (see Chapter 9, on rapid prototyping).

As a final note, pertaining to all the diagrams in Figures 4.4 through 4.10, these diagrams depict a clean separation between user interface software and the rest of the system software. In reality, such separation is usually not easy (possible? desirable?) to achieve. These diagrams depict an idealized distinction, and communication paths, among development activities and corresponding roles. As mentioned previously, it is clear that many useful and even necessary paths of communication are not shown in these diagrams. The entire process of interactive system development would benefit from a model that recognizes these communi-

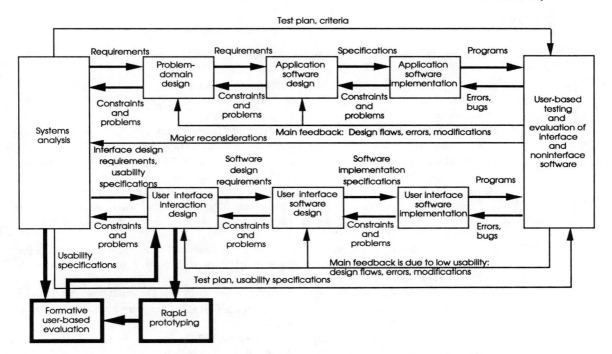

Figure 4.10. Completing the picture with rapid prototying and formative evaluation.

cation needs and provides the necessary channels and internal connections for them.

4.7   SUMMARY

This chapter introduced the focus of Part II, the *interaction development process*. The discussion of parallel paths for development of interface and noninterface components of an interactive system should reinforce both the similarities and the differences between development of interaction design and development of software. The comparison of development activities that occur in the behavioral domain with those in the constructional domain should reinforce the need for a user interaction development approach that is different from traditional software engineering approaches. The most important point as you continue through this book is the *distinction between interaction design and interface software design*. Again, the focus on development in the behavioral domain and detailed exploration of activities in this domain continues in subsequent chapters.

REFERENCES

Boehm, B. W. (1988). A Spiral Model of Software Development and Enhancement. *IEEE Computer*, *21*(5), 61–72.

Carroll, J. M. & Rosson, M. B. (1985). Usability Specifications as a Tool in Iterative Development. In H. R. Hartson (Ed.), *Advances in Human-Computer Interaction* (pp. 1–28). Norwood, NJ: Ablex.

Gould, J. D., Boies, S. J., & Lewis, C. (1991). Making Usable, Useful, Productivity-Enhancing Computer Applications. *Communications of the ACM*, *34*(1), 74–85.

Gould, J. D. & Lewis, C. (1985). Designing for Usability: Key Principles and What Designers Think. *Communications of the ACM*, *28*(3), 300–311.

Hartson, H. R., Brandenburg, J. L., & Hix, D. (1992). Different Languages for Different Development Activities: Behavioral Representation Techniques for User Interface Design. In B. A. Myers (Ed.), *Languages for Developing User Interfaces* (pp. 303–326). Boston: Jones and Bartlett.

Hartson, H. R. & Hix, D. (1989). Toward Empirically Derived Methodologies and Tools for Human-Computer Interface Development. *International Journal of Man-Machine Studies*, *31*, 477–494.

Rosson, M. B., Maass, S., & Kellogg, W. A. (1987). Designing for Designers: An Analysis of Design Practice in the Real World. *Proceedings of CHI+GI Conference on Human Factor in Computing Systems*, New York: ACM, 137–142.

Swartout, W. & Balzer, R. (1982). On the Inevitable Intertwining of Specification and Implementation. *Communications of the ACM*, *25*(7), 438–445.

≡ 5

An Overview of Systems Analysis and Design

Starting in this chapter and continuing through Chapter 10, we discuss each of the major user interaction development activities introduced in Chapter 4. Those major activities are the ones labeled as "our area of interest" in Figure 4.2. First is an introduction to systems analysis.

5.1   EARLY ANALYSIS ACTIVITIES

Many books have been written on the topic of systems analysis. Here you will be given only a flavor of the kinds of early analysis that lead to, among other things, interaction design for the user interface. A very informal capsule summary of some of these kinds of analyses, which can be considered as part of systems analysis, includes the following:

- *Needs analysis*—This establishes that a new system is in fact needed, based on goals of the organization and demands of the marketplace, and it determines the basic goals, purpose, and features desired for the application system. Features are characteristics and capabilities of the system as they appear to users. The result is an external view of what a user will be able to do with the application system.

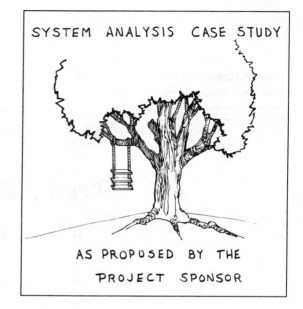

SYSTEM ANALYSIS CASE STUDY

AS PROPOSED BY THE PROJECT SPONSOR

- *User analysis*—This combines cognitive theory of human users, specific information about job functions and tasks of potential users, plus social and organizational work-flow considerations, to define representative classes of users in terms of the tasks to be performed and the skills and knowledge those users bring to the tasks. The result is a set of user class definitions, also called "user profiles."

AS SPECIFIED IN THE PROJECT REQUEST

- *Task analysis*—This provides a complete description of the tasks, subtasks, and methods involved in using the new system, identifying resources necessary for users and the system cooperatively to perform these tasks. Task analysis usually results in a top-down decomposition of detailed task descriptions. The purpose of task analysis is not to duplicate a procedure currently in place with the substitution of a computer as the medium. Task analysis involves understanding the required sequences, why they are required, what the information flow is, what the user contributes to the procedure, and what can be automated with the objective of designing a better (more productive, more efficient, higher quality, more capable) procedure. Task analysis is one of the more important up-front analysis activities but is one of the most frequently overlooked. Many user interaction developers claim that insufficient or inaccurate task analysis is responsible for many terrible designs.

- *Functional analysis*—Similar to task analysis, this results in an internal view of the technical functions to be designed into the computational (noninterface) component of the system. These functions, when combined with the user interface, will provide the features promised in needs analysis. At this point, a kind of duality is taking shape for the user's part and the system's part of each operation that they will perform together.

- *Task/function allocation*—This produces decisions about which parts of the tasks will be performed by the human user and which will be performed by the system. Some tasks may be manual (and will be performed by the user), while others are automated (and will be performed by the system).

- *Requirements analysis*—This is the formal process of specifying design requirements for the system. Requirements analysis draws on needs analysis, user analysis, task analysis, and functional analysis to set formal requirements for design.

Figure 5.1 shows how these early analysis activities might be related and how the information flow among them might look. Like many other user interaction development activities, these, too, are iterative and interwoven with later activities such as design. It is obvious that careful attention in these early stages of interaction development can have an enormous impact on quality in the final product, and on the ease and cost of reaching it. Nonetheless, most developers want to get past the early activities as fast as they can and get on to the parts of the process they understand better, such as design and evaluation. Yet, much of the bad design that must later be filtered out in the iterative process can be avoided, if the real goals of the design, the characteristics of the users, and the tasks to be performed are more thoroughly considered early in the process. Many of the early analysis activities shown in Figure 5.1 are discussed in this chapter.

There are two (at least) ways you can make your early analysis work more effective. One is to follow the methods of contextual inquiry (Whiteside, Bennett, & Holtzblatt, 1988; Wixon, Holtzblatt, & Knox, 1990). Talk with users about their work within their real work environment, such as in the real context of interruptions and ringing phones. Challenge assumptions, investigate surprises. Collaboratively build an understanding of the job requirements and the tasks to carry them out.

The second way to help ensure the effectiveness of your analysis is to have an problem domain expert *on your development team*. A problem domain expert can help you accurately direct your focus on the most important issues in your needs

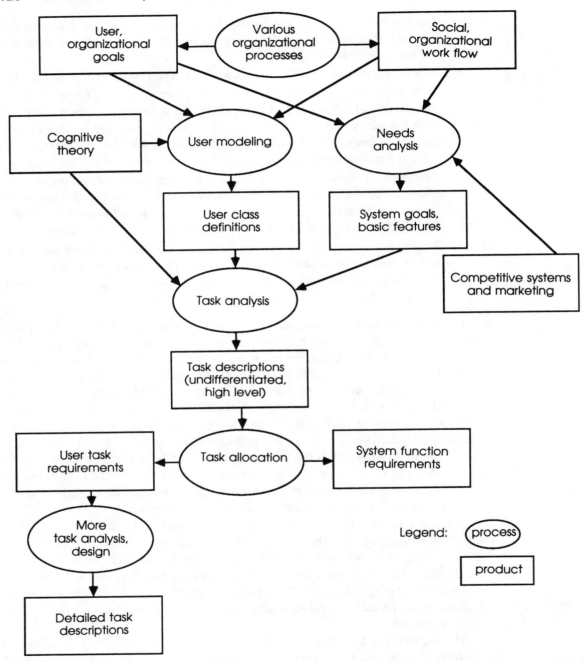

Figure 5.1. Early analysis activities.

analysis, user analysis, and task analysis, as well as design. A documentation specialist is also a valuable team member from the beginning.

5.1.1   Introducing the Exercises

Exercise—Introduction

When you see a header like the one above, it's time for an exercise for you to try, to help reinforce some of the concepts introduced in the preceding text.

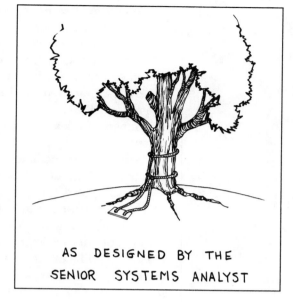

AS DESIGNED BY THE SENIOR SYSTEMS ANALYST

At this point, we introduce a simple application, a Calendar Management System, that will serve as an ongoing example to illustrate each major activity in the user interaction development process described in this book.

Following the presentation of each new topic, you will apply the material just covered to the Calendar Management System. Following each exercise is a possible solution—feedback about what might make a good answer. By the time you have completed the whole series of exercises, you will have created and analyzed your own design of a Calendar Management System.

Each exercise is presented in terms of its *goals*, a suggested minimum amount of *time* you should plan to spend on it, specific *activities* you are to perform during the exercise, and, where appropriate, *deliverables* you are to produce. Occasionally there are also some cautions, hints, and pointers to help you through an exercise.

An exercise and its possible solution are printed on separate pages. As you work through each exercise, please resist the urge to peek ahead to the example solution on the next page until you are satisfied you have gotten as much out of the exercise as you can, or until you decide that you just don't understand what to do and want to see an example.

Because the Calendar Management System is a running example for the rest of the book, most of the exercises build, at least to some extent, on results from previous exercises. Therefore, it is important that you have completed the material from one chapter and have performed the exercises before proceeding on to the next chapter.

A final word about the exercises: Clearly, the Calendar Management System is a simple application, far more so than any real-world development effort with which you are likely to be involved. However, our years of experience in using different applications and exercises indicate that the Calendar Management System and the exercises presented in this book work very well as pedagogical instruments for learning this material. The Calendar Management System represents a problem domain that is simple and familiar enough that everyone understands it immediately. Nonetheless, perhaps surprisingly, it is sufficiently rich to provide a nontrivial setting for the exercises.

The suggested solutions are not intended to serve as complete answers, as you would want for a real system and its user interface. The point of the exercises is, of course, to learn how each activity works. Later, you can give it the kind of time needed to put it to the test on a real development project, where the payoff will make it worth the investment. It is important to realize that there are no right or wrong answers. You just get better and better answers as you practice and gain experience.

Exercise—Team Work

These exercises are best done as a group effort. That is the best match to the way most of you will work as you develop interactive systems. Teams of three to five people work best for doing the exercises. You can, however, do most of these exercises on an individual basis, as many readers will find themselves without teammates to share in the experience. Nonetheless, the interaction among a few people working together provides a synergy one worker alone does not have. Also, one major exercise at the end of Chapter 10—the formative

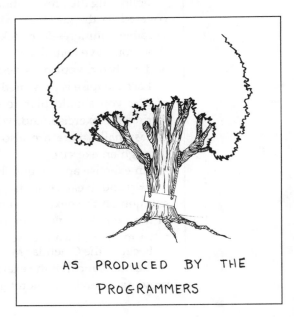

AS PRODUCED BY THE PROGRAMMERS

evaluation experiment—is necessarily a team effort and you will have to find some help (at the very least one other person, as a participant in usability evaluation) for that exercise.

Because the series of exercises is an ongoing team project, it is best to pick a team that can work together for several exercises. These are only suggestions, of course, for an approach to maximizing your benefits of the exercises; you can adapt them to your own situation in any way you desire.

5.1.2   Introducing the Calendar Management System

Let's assume that marketing and needs analysis has identified the need for a Calendar Management System. The goal is to serve as many of the functions of a paper pocket or desk calendar as reasonable. To give us a marketing edge, this product should have some advantage over these manual calendar systems, too.

So, to start with, this system is a simple, automated version of your pocket calendar. At a minimum, this means that you can put appointments and other events in it at certain times on specific dates, and you can look at the calendar and tell when you have appointments and what they are about. As you progress through your development efforts for the Calendar Management System, don't try to get fancy with lots of automated functions. Stick to the basics. Remember, the real goal from here on is to learn about user interaction development processes, not to produce a marketable automated calendar!

As mentioned previously, systems analysis for user interfaces is composed of several kinds of specific analyses, among which are needs analysis, user analysis, task analysis, functional analysis, task/function allocation, and requirements analysis. The overall goal of the following set of early analysis exercises is to make a fast tour through the

AS INSTALLED AT THE
USER'S SITE

systems analysis process, to determine the basic user and system requirements for the Calendar Management System. First is needs analysis.

5.1.3   Needs Analysis

Needs analysis is used to determine that a new system is, in fact, needed and what basic user and market needs it will be aimed at fulfilling. The preceding introduction of the Calendar Management System has already made a start on needs analysis, which can be expanded a little with an exercise.

Exercise—Needs Analysis

GOAL: To produce a single-sentence or single-phrase goal statement and some supporting descriptions of the terms used to state the goal(s).

MINIMUM TIME: About 20 minutes.

ACTIVITIES: Start by writing down a description of the overall goal of the whole system in a single phrase or sentence. *It is very important to be able to state the goal of a system in a single phrase or sentence.* If you can't do this, at least at a very high level, it is probably a sign that you don't understand what is needed. Include any assumptions that are needed, especially if they are important to achieving the goal of the system.

Next, expand on the goal statement by writing down a description of the basic features you expect in the Calendar Management System. Often, this can be just an elaboration and explanation of key terms used in the goal statement.

Possible Exercise Solution

Remember that solutions are not really right or wrong. Maybe it is better to say that there are many possible right solutions, some more right than others. The following solutions are not complete, although an attempt has been made to put enough in suggested solutions for you to get the idea about the process. The early analysis activities are especially sketchy because this is not a focus of the book. The analysis is conducted at a high level, though, in order to set a context for what follows. Needs analysis might be something like the following.

GOAL OF CALENDAR MANAGEMENT SYSTEM: Maintain appointments.

ASSUMPTION: Some boundaries (e.g., on hardware) will be set by management, marketing, the customers, and so on. Do not worry about those right now.

The goal statement is about the purpose of the system and the above example leads us directly to two concepts: one is *appointment*, an "object" concept, and the other is *maintain*, an "operation" concept. These require further description as features, or characteristics and capabilities of the system as they appear to a user.

FEATURES:

- An *appointment* is an object that has attributes such as date, time, place, and appointment description. These attributes take on specific values in instances of appointments.
- *Maintain* means to be able to add new appointments, modify existing appointments, and delete existing appointments. Additionally, an ability to view/display appointments is needed.

This obviously is only the beginning. For a real system, many more features will eventually be added to the list.

5.1.4   User Analysis

So far, analysis is based on best guesses about user characteristics. This is never enough. In every development project, and especially for a new or unfamiliar problem domain, it is necessary to *interview and survey potential users* to determine the information you will need. *Focus groups* and *search sessions*, in which users and developers interact to determine users needs and characteristics are a common approach.

For the Calendar Management System, there are many other characteristics of users that you could and should determine while doing user analysis and defining your user classes. These include characteristics such as

- Their general computer literacy
- Their expertise level (novice, intermittent, or frequent user)
- The hardware they are most familiar with (e.g., Mac, PC, workstation, mainframe)
- The software they are most familiar with (e.g., word processors, spreadsheets, databases)
- Job-related information access needs (e.g., summary versus detailed information)
- General experience with similar or related applications
- Skill base (e.g., typing)
- General education level
- Organization-specific knowledge and/or experience

A questionnaire can help to elicit this kind of information from users as you interview them during user analysis.

Exercise—User Analysis

GOAL: To make a characterization of various classes of potential users of the Calendar Management System.

MINIMUM TIME: About 15 minutes.

ACTIVITIES: Write down the defining characteristics—including required skills, knowledge, and limitations—of the users you expect to have for your Calendar Management System. Also note what you know about ways in which the system will be used by these users.

Possible Exercise Solution

Here are some things that could be said about expected users of the Calendar Management System.

USER CHARACTERISTICS:

- Professional, white collar (e.g., managers)
- Keeps schedule for self and/or others (e.g., clerical users)
- Sometimes just for personal use (e.g., anyone who owns a PC)
- Keeping a calendar is a very small part of the user's job
- Needs transparent tool (i.e., use without thinking much about the tool itself)

SKILLS:

- High general skill level
- Not necessarily computer skilled
- Some, but not necessarily all, will have some keyboard skills

CONCLUSIONS:

- Keep it simple
- Usability is as important as functionality (or more)
- Functionality must be greater than for paper calendar (or else why bother?)
- Usability must be no less than for paper calendar (hard to do!)
- Need to minimize typing
- Must be quick and easy to learn

WHAT THE USER NEEDED

The first conclusion, and maybe the second, can probably be derived from almost any user analysis. These apply to users of almost any interactive system but are especially important for users of the Calendar Management System. The other conclusions come from the more specific goals of the Calendar Management System.

To determine this kind of information, even interviews, surveys, and questionnaires are not enough; users can rarely articulate their real needs. Understanding users also means understanding how they will use the new system, and to do this, you must *observe users doing representative tasks* in their own work environment. This is often the only way to properly take into account elements of task context, such as interruptions, ringing telephones, and coffee breaks. Additionally, the problem domain expert can help significantly in ferreting out the real task-related needs.

Consulting with, and observing, users might, for example, lead someone to wonder whether an alarm feature should be provided in the Calendar Management System. Do you want to inform actively of appointments, with some kind of beeping, for example? To find the answer, study users. Observe how calendars are used. Calendars are used to remind people of appointments, and potential users say that an active reminder would be useful to a busy person who might not always look at the calendar in time for an appointment. The development team likes the idea, too, because an active reminder gives an advantage in functionality over a paper calendar. Thus, already, you need to iterate in the process and revise the needs statement to include an active reminder feature, and the goal is expanded slightly.

NEW GOAL: Maintain, and remind users of, appointments.

NEW FEATURE: An appointment can have an associated alarm.

The important concept to come out of this simple analysis is a recognition that what has been done so far *comes from the needs and user analyses*. Developers can sit around a table and brainstorm some parts of a system design, but there is no substitute for understanding system needs and users. This understanding is gained by observing and talking with users.

5.1.5 Task Analysis

Task analysis formalizes and extends some of what has already been done. The literature on task analysis in human–computer interaction is varied. Sometimes, task analysis is used to build an analytic model to predict user performance for existing interaction designs. Here, we use task analysis to help *drive design*. To do this, a hierarchical set of tasks must be identified that define how users will use the system. This hierarchical set of tasks evolves from a combination of top-down and bottom-up development. It is often useful to start with a single highest level task, the task of using the system itself, and decompose it into the next highest level—namely, those tasks through which a user manipulates main system functions to accomplish useful work. These tasks are each then decomposed into subtasks, perhaps the tasks through which users make use of each individual system function. Later, task analysis will also involve analysis of resources (e.g., information, feedback, visual cues) necessary for the user to perform the tasks.

Exercise—Task Analysis

GOAL: To identify the first two or three levels of tasks and subtasks in the task analysis hierarchy.

MINIMUM TIME: About 30 minutes.

ACTIVITIES: Write down a task name that describes use of the whole system. Then write down a list of task names that describe the highest level of subtasks in the Calendar Management System. Remember that these should be expressed as *tasks from the user's view*, not as functions from the system's view. Then pick a couple of these and try to describe how are they carried out by the user, still at a relatively high level.

HINT: Remember the goal of this system: Maintain, and remind users of, appointments.

Possible Exercise Solution

You can produce a task description of the Calendar Management System at its highest level of abstraction directly from the goal statement provided by needs analysis. This is "maintain, and remind users of, appointments." This sounds a little system-oriented. To make it a little more user-oriented, call the highest-level task, "manage appointments."

Now what about the major subtasks? Again, the needs analysis provides direct help. Drawing on the features that describe "manage appointments" yields a list of major subtasks something like this:

- Add (new) appointment
- View (existing) appointment
- Modify (existing) appointment
- Delete (existing) appointment
- Set alarm for (existing) appointment

Producing the top two levels in the task hierarchy for the Calendar Management System was easy, almost trivial. To develop the third level, descriptions of how users add new appointments and so on, you need some knowledge of the interaction design. This is because you are now at a level where interaction objects will be manipulated by a user, and you do not yet know much about what interaction objects and manipulations the system will have.

At this point, developers often make decisions (or assumptions) about the design for the first time. Here, task analysis becomes task synthesis and directly drives design. As interaction styles (e.g., use of pull-down menus and other design decisions) become established in the design, details about how styles are used will enter the growing task structure at lower levels. This interdependency between task analysis and design is just one of many reasons why an iterative development process is necessary. Chapter 7 shows a more complete task structure for the Calendar Management System.

5.1.6   Functional Analysis

Now that you have come this far, *functional analysis* is often pretty easy. It requires description of the internal system functions that must be designed and implemented into the noninterface software to support the tasks identified for the user. For the Calendar Management System, as is often the case, these functions just mirror the user tasks. For example, we have identified a user task for adding a new appointment. That means there must also be databaselike functionality, some program code to support adding appointments (e.g., accepting and storing new appointments). The databaselike subsystem must also support retrieval, updating, deletion, and so on.

5.1.7   Task/Function Allocation

Because use of an interactive system is a matter of cooperative task performance between user and system, there are times when decisions must be made about which/who does what. For many features, it will be easy; there will be both a user task and an associated system function. Some jobs will be allocated to the user only; these are the *manual tasks*. Some jobs will be allocated to the system only; these are the *automated functions*.

For example, the alarm feature added while iterating the needs analysis might introduce new tasks and/or functions, such as to set the alarm and its parameters. For one thing, given that some users would like the system to sound an alarm as the time for an appointment is near, how long before an appointment time should the alarm sound? The answer is, of course, determined from the users. Until user feedback is obtained, hard-wire the alarm lead time at, say, 10 minutes. (Future evaluation will probably show that this is not what the users need, but it serves the example here.) This means that the task of setting the lead time will be automatic; that is, the system determines the lead time. Thus, no new user tasks result for setting alarm parameters, but the user will still determine what appointments have alarms, and that will involve a user task to set an alarm for an appointment. In a more complicated design (but one that evaluation might show better meets user needs), the design could allow users to vary the lead time for each alarm, but it could leave 10 minutes as the default if a user does not wish to change it.

5.1.8   Iterating Task Analysis

As more users are observed performing tasks with calendars, their need for different levels of viewing the calendar—that is, by the month, by the week, by the day, or by the hour—becomes evident. The development group would like to provide this kind of flexibility, too. While the purchaser of a paper calendar must commit to just one of these view levels (week-at-a-glance, month-at-a-glance, and so on), the Calendar Management System will provide the advantage of having them all. Looking at how users use calendars, it is easy to see that the user must be in control of the view level. In terms of *task analysis*, this implies some kind of task(s) for controlling the view level, so "control view" is added to the task list.

As part of the iteration of task analysis, we go out and talk to potential users again. They suggest another possible advantage in functionality over a paper calendar: an ability to search the appointment database to find appointments by content—that is, by character strings found in values for appointment attributes. A simple example of this would be to find any appointment with Dr. Schulman. We add this new feature to our statements for needs, tasks, functions, and requirements.

5.2   DESIGN

Having completed the task analysis and determined the various features of the Calendar Management System, the next major activity in user interaction development is *design*. In human–computer interaction literature today, there is probably as much about user interaction *design* as any other single topic. Chapters 2 and 3 addressed this topic from a product view. Ironically, design as a *process* is one of the least understood development activities—for user interfaces or in any domain (Carroll & Rosson, 1985). Developers therefore must make up for the lack of knowledge through constant evaluation and midcourse corrections, and this situation is not likely to change. Design is a complex activity with infinite alternatives. To really understand user interaction design is to understand design in general, a topic that has been studied for many decades without yielding generally applicable formulas for success. It is certainly the most creative and individualized activity in the life cycle.

It is possible to carve design roughly into two (and probably many more) kinds: conceptual and detailed. *Conceptual design* is higher level and has to do with synthesizing objects and operations. *Detailed design* has to do with activities such as determining the wording of messages, labels, and menu choices, as well as the appearance of objects on the screen, navigation among screens, and much more. Although you will cycle among these kinds of design, too, you usually have to start with the more abstract conceptual design to establish the basic interaction/application objects, their properties, and relationships among them.

5.2.1   Conceptual Design

We will keep the Calendar Management System design simple here. In fact, we already have a good start on the design. You know that appointments are conceptual objects, and they have attributes such as date, time, place, and description. There are operations such as add, modify, delete, and view; these come directly from the user tasks. Next, you have to think about how these operations will be invoked and carried out. You often also have to think about how a user will gain access to the objects; this usually means enabling a user to get instances of them to be visible on the screen to operate on them.

Exercise—Conceptual Design

GOAL: To produce a conceptual (independent of appearance) user interaction design.

MINIMUM TIME: About 20 minutes.

ACTIVITIES: First, write down a list of some interaction objects for the Calendar Management System, their properties, and relationships among them. Decide how users will view those objects conceptually (not details of appearance) in the interface.

Next, decide how a user will gain access to those objects. Finally, determine operations to be performed on the objects as a result of user tasks. For example, how will appointments be represented, and what kind of containers will be used to hold appointments for editing by users?

Because conceptual design is one of the least understood activities in the development process, it is the most difficult to describe. So, if you get too frustrated with this exercise before giving it a reasonable amount of time and effort, proceed to the solution, and learn by example.

Possible Exercise Solution

It is clear that the Calendar Management System will have at least one kind of object: *appointments*. It is easy to identify the properties of appointment objects: date, time, description (what an appointment is for), and perhaps such things as person (whom an appointment is with), place, and length of time for which the appointment is scheduled. So far, there is only one object, so there are no relationships.

Next, ask how the objects will be represented conceptually. The concept of a calendar provides a set of hierarchically nested containers for appointments: years, months, weeks, days, and hours or other sizes of time slots. Of these, the one that really contains appointments is the *time slot*. A time slot can be empty or contain an appointment; that is, time slots exist whether or not appointments have been scheduled for them. In the user interaction design we are producing for the Calendar Management System, these containers will be treated as objects, too, because a user will view them, navigate among them, and manipulate them.

Next, consider the access methods, or ways in which a user will get to calendar objects. Again, the metaphor of the paper calendar offers some help. To navigate through a calendar, the user first finds the desired month (and year), then the desired week and/or day.

Next, think about the other operations needed. Task analysis directly states the need to view, add, delete, and modify appointments. How will users invoke and carry out these operations? To begin somewhat naïvely, suppose that you already know that people are using pull-down menus and buttons for a lot of interaction designs these days, so you decide to use these, too. Because you still have a small number of operations, you may decide to put the commands for them on buttons instead of, say, a pull-down menu. That will make them constantly visible and more directly accessible. Users also need something to select the view level (month, week, day) of the calendar, so add a pull-down menu for view-level control. Finally, the users need a text box of some kind in which to type and edit the appointment information.

5.2.2   Initial Scenario Design

As you may have noticed, in discussing a possible solution for the conceptual design exercise, buttons and menus and boxes popped up, which hints of doing some higher-level detailed design. You many even have a vision of some screens for the Calendar Management System beginning to form in your head. Perhaps, as you were working on the conceptual design, you started making some rough screen sketches. The next step is to formalize these ideas by producing an *initial scenario* of the Calendar Management System.

Exercise—Initial Scenario Design

GOAL: To develop an initial visual design/layout for a few screens of the Calendar Management System.

MINIMUM TIME: About one hour.

ACTIVITIES: Sketch some initial pictures of the screens, including the interaction/application objects, menus, buttons, and icons. Label the functions, and add notes about the behavior of objects, where appropriate. If you are working with a team, the process of arriving at your design should be very collaborative and cooperative.

DELIVERABLES: A few screen sketches on paper.

CAUTION: Don't get too involved in very low-level human factors issues (e.g., icon appearance or menu wording) yet. Keep things simple, and don't worry about too many different cases. At this point, it would be foolish to put too much time into the exact placement of an icon, when much of your design is likely to change anyway.

COMMENT: At this early stage of any interaction design, paper-and-pencil methods are often faster and easier than, say, a computer-based prototyping tool for exposing your very early designs to evaluation by users. On the other hand, some rapid prototyping tools allow you to make screen sketches about as fast (and possibly a lot more neatly) as you can manually. If you already are familiar with such a tool, feel free to use it for producing your screen sketches, if you wish.

Possible Exercise Solution

Almost everyone benefits from the concrete visual representations provided by early sketches of screens and objects. One possible initial screen layout is shown in Figure 5.2.

Although the way in which you write down, or represent, your design ideas to communicate them to others (and to yourself at a later time) is properly the subject of representation techniques (Chapters 6 and 7), it is difficult to separate this from design itself when you start doing it. Therefore, the present chapter uses scenarios—sequences of screen pictures—to get started now, and Chapters 6 and 7 present additional, more formal, techniques for design representation.

Scenarios are a good bottom-up way to get started; they are concrete representations of interaction objects that let you visualize the design, play with ideas, and try things out. Scenarios are a close fit to the idea of a prototype, which to some extent is just a more complete, executable set of scenarios.

The screen picture in Figure 5.2 is the beginning of a scenario, showing push buttons at the bottom of the screen, for invoking the functions to view, add, delete, and modify appointments. The box in the middle is the text box for editing the text describing an appointment. A user uses the pull-down menu in the upper right-hand corner to set (modally) the view level. The first design is rarely a very good design, but it is a start; it is sure to change a great deal during later iterations.

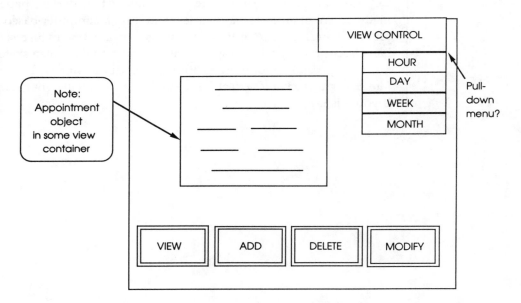

Figure 5.2. A possible first screen design for the Calendar Management System.

5.2.3   Early Usability Evaluation and Cognitive Analysis

At this point, it is opportune to demonstrate the importance of early design evaluation. It could not have been done much earlier in the development process, when there was no design to evaluate. On the other hand, it pays to stop now and do some evaluation, in order to move much more rapidly toward an optimal design.

What kind of early usability evaluation can you do when the design has just been born? Well, you can already show your initial screen pictures to users and explain how they would be used and ask how people like them. That is just what the following exercise asks you to do, because it is much more effective to experience this process than just to read about it.

Exercise—Early Usability Evaluation

GOAL: To get some early user feedback on your initial scenario design.

MINIMUM TIME: About 45 minutes.

ACTIVITIES: Show your initial screen sketches from the previous exercise to three people (one at a time). Explain the purpose of the new system, and ask each of them to visualize themselves using this design. Let them go through the motions of simulating the use of your system. Then ask them what they think about it, the good and bad points.

Possible Exercise Solution

To test the design of Figure 5.2 and other sample screen sketches, a few potential users played with the sketches and imagined themselves using the scenario design for some typical tasks (e.g., finding an existing appointment, adding a new appointment). It was immediately clear that these users didn't like the fact that the screen did not look very much like a calendar. They said they were used to the appearance of paper calendars; why should it be different in the Calendar Management System? They were also confused about what the view-control mechanism was used for and how to use it.

In addition to showing sketches to users, there are other ways you can evaluate an early design. For example, you can do some simple cognitive analysis. You can ask questions about what kind of working memory loads it imposes on a user. Does it require stacking (interrupting one task, doing another, and returning to the first, having to remember what you were doing there), or does it give closure at appropriate points? Does it match the skills brought to the task by the defined user classes?

It might be too early to get good answers for all these questions, but it is not too early to ask a question that bears on the design in a fundamental way, that gets to the root of the underlying metaphor in our design: Does the design reflect the way users think about calendars? This does not mean that developers always have to build automated systems to mimic the manual versions. It does mean, however, that the system has to offer a good match to the *users' concept* of a calendar in this design. Paper calendars have been around for so long and are used so frequently that some attention should be given to how they are used and how they look. When asking these questions about the initial scenario design, it shows a poor match to the concept of paper calendars. This analysis agrees with what the users said.

It is also important to determine whether the present design makes the most of cognitive directness. For example, does it use direct manipulation in a way that gives a direct cognitive mapping from the task to the interaction design? The answer, for the initial scenario design, is no. For example, the design in Figure 5.2 has a text box into which a user types and edits appointment information, but this text box has no visual relationship to the time slot on the calendar with which it is associated. This text editing box is *indirect*. How is this done on paper calendars? It is much more direct. A user writes the appointment information directly on the calendar, at the correct date and, often, into a specific time slot.

5.2.4   Iterating the Initial Design

From observations of users' comments and from some simple cognitive analysis, it is evident that the initial design must be changed in some fairly major ways.

Exercise—Improved Scenario Design

GOAL: To develop an improved, and more well-developed, visual design/layout for several screens of the Calendar Management System, based on results of early usability evaluation and cognitive analysis.

MINIMUM TIME: About one hour.

ACTIVITIES: Just as you did for design of the initial scenario in a previous exercise, draw pictures of the screens, including interaction/application objects, menus, buttons, and icons. Label the functions, and add notes about behavior of things where appropriate. If you are working in a team, put your design in the middle of a table, and let people walk around and attach buttons and other objects with sticky Post-It® notes or tape. Be democratic. Be collaborative and participatory. Be creative. Have fun!

DELIVERABLES: Start with few representative screen sketches, at first experimentally with paper and pencil. You may then wish to copy your design onto plastic transparencies to share with, and explain to, others, perhaps as a part of a design walk-through.

CAUTION: Again, don't get too involved in discussions over details (e.g., icon appearance or menu placement). Keep things simple, and don't worry about too many odd cases. At this point, it would be foolish to put too much time into the exact placement of an icon, when the next round of usability evaluation could tell you not to use the icon in the first place.

COMMENT: The value of paper and pencil (or even marking pens and transparent sheets of plastic) is not limited to this exercise. Paper and plastic are especially useful for getting feedback from a large group during early design walk-throughs. Other group techniques include drawing and tacking cutouts onto flip charts or bulletin boards. Use whatever medium works best for you (and your group, if applicable).

Possible Exercise Solution

Users indicated that it would be an improvement to replace the text box of the original design with a representation of a calendar itself. Next, we must decide which view of the calendar to show. Why not put them all on the screen (as in the desktop metaphor) and let the user select the one to work with at any given moment? This also solves the problem of the view control, eliminating the pull-down menu. This presentation empowers the user to bring the desired view directly to the top of the desktop by selecting a month view, a week view, a day view, or time slot view.

What about the operations on appointments? The directness of the calendar metaphor makes this easier, too. Now, the user can point to and click on a particular date and time slot on the calendar and can directly type in the appointment. The same approach works for modifying an existing appointment, too. The user can simply point to it and edit it right on the calendar, just as is done with paper calendars. This design has eliminated the view, add, and modify buttons from the design in Figure 5.2. For deletion, it might be best to leave the button, at least until the design has been tested more with users. It is pretty easy to delete even a large complicated appointment description by just selecting it and choosing the "Delete Appointment" button. The screen sketch of the revised scenario design is shown in Figure 5.3.

The early design has now been modified to eliminate the need for explicit view control commands, by adding tabs that let a user navigate to a month or a week. The user can gain access to appointment containers (years, months, weeks, days, hours, and time slots) by selecting and navigating among objects that look like a paper calendar on the desktop. Also, remember that when the task analysis was iterated in Section 5.1.8, users said that they wanted a direct search (by content) function. To facilitate this different way to access appointments, the design must add a search command, which leads to some kind of dialogue box with which to enter a search string to match against the text in existing appointments.

Tasks for adding new appointments and modifying or deleting existing appointments are piggybacked on the access methods. That is, the user first selects an appointment by directly navigating through the calendar, ending up at a particular time slot on a particular date. Once at the appropriate time slot, a user can then perform the operation directly on the calendar. For example, a user might type in a new appointment description or make changes in an existing appointment description.

The default calendar display will show the current month on top, with the next few months visible as the edge of pages underneath the current month. A user can bring any of these months to the top by selecting its edge, as it peeks out from the

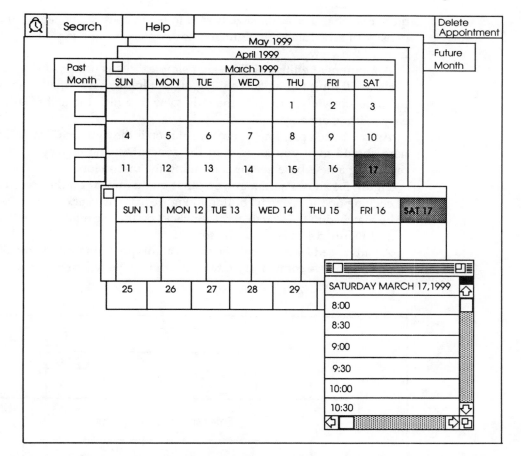

Figure 5.3. A sample screen picture for the revised design to the Calendar Management System. From Hartson & Gray, *Human-Computer Interaction*, pp. 1–45. © 1992. Reprinted by permission.

pile. To navigate to months beyond what are displayed (in either the past or future), the design can provide some tabs on the left and right sides of the calendar, labeled "Past Month" and "Future Month," respectively. These details are also shown in Figure 5.3.

Whenever possible, the design includes display of appointment information in every view. In the week and month views, resolution limitations of the display medium (not yet known for sure) may prevent the appointment descriptions from being very legible, but a scaled-down version of the text should still be displayed, anyway. This will be somewhat like the page preview feature of a word processor, which shows how text and graphics are arranged on a page, even if they are not quite readable. The advantage here is to retain context and show, at a glance, the density of scheduled appointments for any given time period, regardless of the level of the view.

Appointment editing will be kept simple. This is not a word processor, so the design will limit typing and editing of appointment information to occur only in the time slot view, probably the only view in which the text is large enough for easy editing, anyway.

As mentioned previously, no one solution is the right one. The solutions offered here should give you an idea of the concepts being conveyed in the exercise, providing a new baseline for continuing the discussion.

Figure 5.4 shows a dialogue box that might appear on the screen as the result of clicking on the "Search" button in Figure 5.3. The user enters a character string to be matched in the search and then clicks on the "Search" button in the dialogue box of Figure 5.4 to activate the search.

An advanced feature might be added at this point, to simplify making repetitive appointments. A command (button) much like the search command will be used

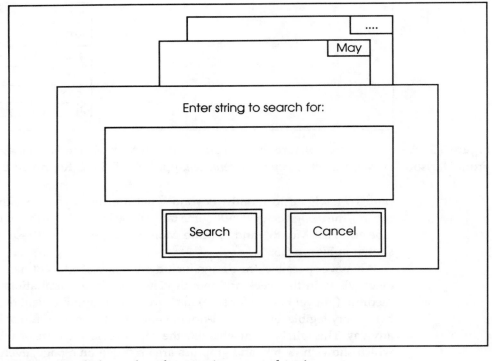

Figure 5.4. Search function dialogue box for entering a search string.

to bring up a dialogue box that facilitates the scheduling of appointments every week, every other week, or once a month so that, for example, it is possible to schedule, with one instance of this command, a meeting at 11:00 A.M. for the first Thursday of every month, for a specific range of months into the future.

Suppose that the week view, shown in Figure 5.5, was the cause of considerable group discussion in a subsequent design walk-through. Many users and developers were not content with this design. In response, the developers considered massive redesign and even considered not having a week view. They finally decided that these questions should be added to a list of issues to resolve by talking with marketing people and particularly to address in usability evaluation.

Next, the design team regarded the day view as very important and gave it lots of attention. The design for the day view is shown in Figure 5.6. Note its similarity to the appearance of a paper calendar. A user clicks the mouse with the cursor in a time slot and gets the "I"-shaped (I-beam) cursor for text editing, to enter and/ or modify appointment descriptions. The view for one day scrolls up and down over a 24-hour period. The "Delete Appointment" button is used to delete selected appointments from the calendar. It is grayed out (inactive) unless an appointment is selected.

As Figure 5.6 shows, the original design included a close box in the upper left-hand corner of each day, but—per the attached note—it was later removed, in

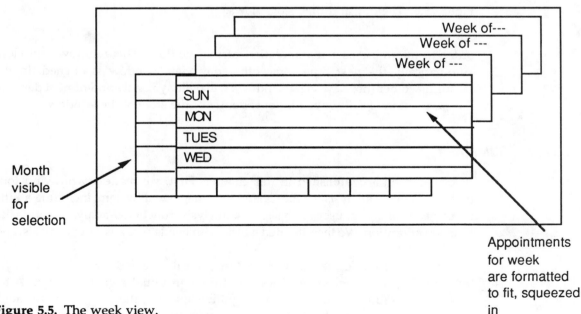

Month
visible
for
selection

Appointments
for week
are formatted
to fit, squeezed
in

Figure 5.5. The week view.

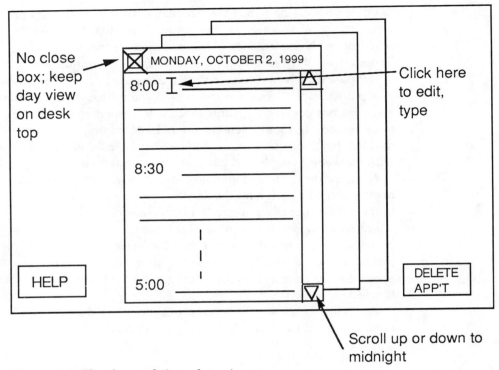

Figure 5.6. The day and time slots views.

order to minimize user manipulation of the window. This window will close automatically the next time some other day view window is opened. In the meantime, other (nonday) view windows will overlay it. All appointment descriptions are automatically saved independently of the state of the window.

5.3   SUMMARY

A lot has been accomplished in this chapter. First, we made a whirlwind tour through systems analysis for the Calendar Management System, including a little bit of needs analysis, user analysis, task analysis, functional analysis, and task/function allocation. We then iterated a little with needs analysis, user analysis, and task analysis.

Next was a sample user interaction design for the Calendar Management System, starting with conceptual design and then an initial scenario design. After some early usability evaluation and cognitive analysis, the design was iterated, too. The exercise begun here continues throughout most of the rest of the book.

REFERENCES

Carroll, J. M. & Rosson, M. B. (1985). Usability Specifications as a Tool in Iterative Development. In H. R. Hartson (Ed.), *Advances in Human-Computer Interaction*, Vol. 1, (pp. 1–28). Norwood, NJ: Ablex.

Whiteside, J., Bennett, J., & Holtzblatt, K. (1988). Usability Engineering: Our Experience and Evolution. In M. Helander (Ed.), *Handbook of Human-Computer Interaction* (pp. 791–817). Amsterdam: Elsevier North-Holland.

Wixon, D., Holtzblatt, K., & Knox, S. (1990). Contextual Design: An Emergent View of System Design. *Proceedings of CHI Conference on Human Factors in Computing Systems*, New York: ACM, 329–336.

≡ 6

Techniques for Representing User Interaction Designs

6.1   DESIGN REPRESENTATION AS A DEVELOPMENT ACTIVITY

Good user interaction designs invariably depend on an ability to understand and evaluate—and thereby improve—those designs during the development process. Understanding and evaluating designs depend, in part, on the techniques used to represent the designs. Design and representation are very closely related. *Design* is a creative, mental, problem-solving process; *representation* is the physical process of capturing or recording a design. *Design representations* are the means by which interaction designs are communicated and documented.

The need for effective design representation techniques is especially important with new interaction development methods that emphasize iterative refinement and involve *a multiplicity of separate but cooperating roles* for producing the interface. As already discussed (in Chapter 1), these roles include at least the following: designer, implementer, problem domain expert, evaluator, documentation specialist, marketer, customer, and user. There are also roles for developing the noninterface parts of an interactive system.

Each of these roles has its own, often different, *needs for communicating*—recording, conveying, reading, and understanding—an interaction design. This communication need translates into the need for a common set of *interaction design representation techniques*—the mechanism for completely and unambiguously capturing an interaction design as it evolves through all phases of the life cycle. Our main interest in design representation here is as a means for designers of the interaction component of a user interface to communicate their designs among all developers, and particularly to user interface software designers and implementers.

6.2   THE NEED FOR BEHAVIORAL REPRESENTATION

In software engineering, the distinction of design from implementation is an established principle. Chapter 1 established a similar distinction in user interface development, motivating the need for a behavioral domain in which to carry out and discuss the interaction development process, addressing user interaction distinctly from implementation (software) considerations. This chapter and the next introduce a design representation technique capable of specifying the *behavioral design* of an interactive system—the tasks and the actions a user performs to accomplish those tasks. Often, communication within a development group is informal, based mostly on implicit corporate culture. Typically, as Grudin (1991) claims, "for communicating a design, paper has been the preferred medium and brevity a preferred style." This book presents a more formal, tool-supportable design representation as a record of the design for all development roles.

Most representation techniques currently used for interface software development (e.g., state transition diagrams, event-based mechanisms, object orientation) are constructional—and properly so. Any technique that can be thought of as describing interaction from the system viewpoint is constructional. For example, a state transition diagram depicting interaction control flow represents the system view, looking out at the user and waiting for an input. State transition diagrams can also show the current system state and how each input takes the system to a new state. Constructional representation techniques support the designer and implementer of the interface software, but do not support design of the interaction part of the interface.

In the behavioral domain, an interaction developer gets away from software issues and (as discussed in Chapter 5) into the activities that precede software design, such as task analysis, functional analysis, task allocation, and user modeling. Consequently, behavioral representation techniques and supporting tools tend to be user centered and task oriented.

With the current emphasis on user-centered design, the interaction development process is driven heavily by user requirements and task analysis. Early evaluation of designs is based on user- and task-oriented models. In fact, the entire interaction development life cycle is becoming centered around the evaluation of users performing tasks. Thus, the *user task* has become a common element of interest among developer roles in the behavioral domain. The set of tasks that forms an interaction design becomes a set of requirements for the design and implementation of user interface software. A formal representation of interaction designs is, therefore, needed to convey these requirements.

Behavioral representation techniques are not replacements for constructional techniques; they just support a different domain. Each behavioral design must be translated into a constructional design that is the computer system's view of how the behavior is to be supported. *Behavioral design and representation* involve physical and cognitive user actions and interface feedback—that is, the behavior both of the user and of the interface as they interact with each other. This is the subject of this chapter and the next. Before describing this though, we briefly discuss some related existing representation techniques in the following section. If you are not interested in this related work, you can skip directly ahead to Section 6.4.

6.3   SOME EXISTING REPRESENTATION TECHNIQUES

This section first presents some representation techniques that are used in the constructional development domain and then discusses some that are used in the behavioral domain.

6.3.1   Constructional Representation Techniques for Sequential Interaction

In a *sequential interaction style,* control moves in a predictable way from one part of the dialogue to another. An example is navigation through a menu network. In sequential interaction, each user action leads to a predetermined successor menu, screen, window, or dialogue box.

State transition diagrams have long been used as a graphical representation of interaction control flow in sequential interaction (e.g., Wasserman & Shewmake, 1985; Jacob, 1986). *Nodes* represent interface states or screens; *arcs* represent state transitions based on inputs. Because the nodes of these diagrams usually do not represent interface feedback or screen appearance directly, the content of a node, a representation of what happens within that state, is often described in some other form, such as an *interface representation language.* These are high-level specialized programming languages with constructs especially for representing interaction design.

6.3.2   Constructional Representation Techniques for Asynchronous Interaction

Most interfaces today include both sequential and asynchronous styles. In an *asynchronous interaction style*, many tasks are available to a user at one time, and sequencing within each task is independent of sequencing within other tasks. Asynchronous interaction can be more difficult to represent than strict sequential interaction.

One kind of constructional representation technique especially for asynchronous interaction is event handlers (e.g., Green, 1985). With these, each user action or input is viewed by the system as an event and is sent to the appropriate *event handler*, a software routine associated with a class of events that can cause output, change the system state, and call computational routines.

Concurrent state diagrams (e.g., Jacob, 1986) are also used as constructional representations for control flow in asynchronous interaction. A mutually asynchronous set of state diagrams represents the interface, offering the graphical advantage of a diagrammatic approach but avoiding the complexity of a single large diagram. Multiple diagrams are active simultaneously, with control being transferred back and forth among the diagrams, in coroutine fashion.

Another popular method for constructional representation of asynchronous interaction is based on an *object-oriented approach* (e.g., Sibert, Hurley, & Bleser, 1988). This is a very good fit to today's interaction styles because the behavior of interaction objects is naturally event driven and asynchronous. In addition, high-level object classes contain default behavior, yet they can be specialized for specific behavior. However, a drawback is that the object-oriented approach distributes flow of control, and as a result, it is difficult to understand or trace the sequencing.

Other work has involved specifying *interaction by demonstration* (e.g., Peridot— Myers, 1988). This is a novel and creative approach and is very suitable for producing rapid prototypes. However, it produces only program code, with no behavioral representation of the interaction that can be analyzed.

Another approach, the User Interface Development Environment, or UIDE (Foley, Gibbs, Kim, & Kovacevic, 1988), involves building a *knowledge base* consisting of objects, attributes, actions, and pre- and post-conditions on actions that form a declarative description of an interface. From these descriptions, alternative interfaces are generated for the same underlying functionality.

6.3.3   Behavioral Representation Techniques for Asynchronous Interaction

The representation techniques discussed so far are all constructional, taking the system view of an interface—the view of the user interface software designer and implementer. Stop for a minute and think about how you write down your user interaction designs. You may describe the interaction objects and widgets and how they work, but how do you describe what the *user* does? Do you use just prose descriptions for this, perhaps with some state diagrams to keep track of major state changes? And, of course, you use screen pictures. What about behavioral ways of representing how it all works? This requires a task-oriented approach because tasks are how the user sees an interface.

The next section introduces a technique for representing user interaction designs from the behavioral view of the user: the *User Action Notation*, or *UAN*. Before describing this technique, however, we will briefly mention some other techniques used in the behavioral domain and the intended users of these techniques.

The existence of these other behavioral techniques might cause you to wonder why we are introducing yet another behavioral representation technique. Design of interactive systems, as with most kinds of design, involves an alternation of analysis and synthesis activities (Hartson & Hix, 1989). Most of these task-oriented models were originally oriented toward analysis; that is, they were not intended to capture a design as it is being created, but rather to build a detailed representation of an existing design with the purpose of predicting user performance for evaluating usability. In contrast, the UAN directly supports synthesis. That is, the UAN addresses the creative mental act of problem solving (i.e., creating new interaction designs) and the physical act of capturing (i.e., documenting) a representation of the design.

Some existing behavioral techniques that are user-task-oriented include the Goals, Operators, Methods, and Selection (GOMS) model (Card, Moran, & Newell, 1983), the Command Language Grammar (CLG) (Moran, 1981), the keystroke-level model (Card & Moran, 1980), the Task Action Grammar (TAG) (Payne & Green, 1986), and the work by Reisner (1981), and Kieras and Polson (1985).

In practice, most of these techniques can be used to support synthesis, as well as analysis, but typically, they cannot represent the direct association of feedback and state with user actions. Also, many of these models—the GOMS, CLG, and keystroke, in particular—are models of expert error-free task performance in contiguous time (without interruption, interleaving of tasks, and without considering interrelationships of concurrent tasks); these are not suitable assumptions for the synthesis-oriented aspects of interaction design.

On the other hand, the GOMS model is very important to task analysis for interaction design. However, although the amount of detail generated in a GOMS description of interaction allows for thorough analysis, it can be an enormous undertaking to produce. GOMS and the UAN have similarities, especially at higher levels of abstraction, where tasks are described in terms of subtasks. Given this brief description of several other behavioral representation techniques and their uses, the rest of this chapter and the next chapter discusses the UAN in detail.

6.4   INTRODUCING THE USER ACTION NOTATION (UAN)

The UAN was created within the Human–Computer Interaction Project at Virginia Tech (Hartson, Siochi, & Hix, 1990). Our friend and colleague, Antonio Siochi, is the originator of the UAN. Our project had a contract to develop a software tool, and Anton, the interaction designer for the tool, grew tired of struggling with the imprecision and verbosity of prose descriptions of how the interface should behave. In addition, our implementers grew tired of reading and trying to understand his prose descriptions. Out of this need arose the behavioral representation technique we called the User Action Notation, or UAN. Since its creation, many people, both at Virginia Tech and elsewhere, have contributed to extending and formalizing the UAN. So far, the UAN has been used by more than 50 interaction developers and researchers outside Virginia Tech.

6.4.1   Why Use UAN?

Before describing details of the UAN, it is important to explain why on earth such a level of detail is needed for an interaction design. Without such an explanation, it may not seem worth all the effort it will take to produce UAN descriptions. Much earlier, in Chapter 1 we espoused different roles for different activities in the user interface development process. We especially emphasized the different skills, attitudes, and perspectives needed to do design as compared to those needed to do implementation of a user interface. *The UAN is intended to be written primarily by someone designing the interaction component of an interface, and to be read by all developers, particularly those designing and implementing the user interface software.*

The UAN reader is, therefore, usually a software engineer or programmer. As discussed in Chapter 1, programmers probably should not be doing interaction design unless they are working closely with people who are trained specifically in interaction design; if so, then they can use the UAN to record their joint decisions. In most cases, however, by the time a programmer writes code, design decisions for the interaction component should already be made, in detail, and the programmer should simply implement that design. If details are omitted from a design, a programmer will have to make some guess about what the designer intended or will have to find the designer and ask, neither of which is a desirable situation. A technique such as the UAN is an appropriate mechanism for recording that design precisely, concisely, unambiguously, and in detail, so that decisions about interaction design are not left up to a programmer.

Another reason is sometimes given as to why the level of detail offered by the UAN isn't needed. In particular, people may say, "We've all worked together for so long, we don't need to record this kind of detail. We just know what every one else is thinking." Members of a user interface development team shouldn't believe in mind reading. Moreover, what happens when a new person joins the team? It normally takes someone from three months to a year to become acclimatized to a new environment, to pick up the vibes from everyone else, and to know what others are thinking. What happens to that new person (and other team members with whom the new person has to communicate) in the meantime? User interaction designers should not rely on corporate culture and philosophy as a communication technique for interaction designs. A structured approach such as the UAN can maximize the communication bandwidth among development team members as an interaction design evolves and can minimize misunderstandings and confusion about that design.

6.4.2   Overview of the UAN

The UAN is a user- and task-oriented notation that describes physical (and other) behavior of the user and interface as they perform a task together. The primary abstraction of the UAN is a *user task*. An interface is represented as a quasi-hierarchical structure of asynchronous tasks, the sequencing within each task being independent of that in the others. User actions, corresponding interface feedback, and state change information are represented at the lowest level. Levels of abstraction hide these details and are needed to build the task structure. At all levels, user actions and tasks are combined with temporal relations such as sequencing, interleaving, and concurrency, to describe allowable time-related user behavior.

The UAN is supplemented with scenarios, showing sequencing among screen pictures. The need for such detailed scenarios and task descriptions is articulated by Gould and Lewis (1985): "detailed scenarios [show] exactly how key tasks would be performed with the new system. It is extremely difficult for anybody, even its own designers, to understand an interface proposal, without this level of description." The UAN is also supplemented with state transition diagrams showing interface state changes resulting from user actions, and with discussion notes documenting the history and rationale of design decisions so that developers are not later doomed to repeat those decision processes. In sum, this whole set of representation techniques—the UAN task descriptions, scenarios, state transition diagrams, and discussion notes—is needed; a single one is not sufficient.

In teaching use of the UAN to interaction designers, we have found that teaching "by example" is an effective approach. Therefore, we begin presentation of the UAN with a simple example, at the lowest level of abstraction, the level of most detail in the UAN task descriptions. The discussion stays at this low level for the rest of Chapter 6, to establish notation for describing basic physical user actions. Then, Chapter 7 shows how you build up levels of abstraction to complete the whole task structure that comprises an interaction design.

6.5   INTRODUCING A SIMPLE EXAMPLE

Most of the following examples use a setting that is familiar to many of you: the desktop metaphor used in the Apple Macintosh™, Microsoft Windows™, and many workstations with a graphical direct manipulation interaction style. *The discussion and the notation are not limited to this interaction style*, but given its popularity and familiarity, it effectively illustrates the concepts herein.

Imagine a description in a user manual for the *task of selecting a file*, described in prose as

Step 1.   Move the cursor to the file icon.
Step 2.   Depress and immediately release the mouse button.

The UAN description corresponding to these two steps is as follows:

Step 1.   `~[file icon]`
Step 2.   `Mv^`

Note that a `typewriter-style` font is used to denote UAN expressions, including task names.

In step 1, the ~ denotes moving the cursor. The destination of the cursor movement is the context of some object represented in the `[]`. In this case, the object is a file icon. So we read step 1 of the UAN as "move the cursor to the context of the file icon." Step 2 represents depressing (v) and releasing (^) the mouse button (M). So we read step 2 of the UAN as "depress and release the mouse button," or simply "click the mouse button."

This task serves as an example for the next few sections, to explain, in detail, various aspects of the UAN. Our goal is to represent this, and other more complex user tasks, in a notation that is easy to read and write, but one that is more formal, clear, precise, and unambiguous than English prose.

6.5.1   Create Your Own Symbols

We tried to make the symbols in the UAN representation technique compact, to limit the amount of work designers have to do to record large amounts of notation.

Terse symbols are more difficult to remember, though, so the symbols must also be mnemonically suggestive of their function, a trait we call "visually onomatopoetic." For example, the tilde (~) represents "move the cursor to," because the curvy tilde gives the impression of motion. Similarly, v suggests a down arrow and ^ an up arrow.

If you don't like the symbols presented here for the UAN, you are welcome to create your own for any part of it. For example, you might prefer to use MOVE TO instead of the ~. However, anyone using the UAN for a serious design will write these expressions often and will probably be glad for the more terse symbols. The specific syntax of the UAN is not the most important concept here, but rather the expressive power, the levels of abstraction, and the design detail that can be obtained using the UAN. In fact, the UAN is an *open notation* in the sense that it can be adapted to the individual needs, standards, and styles of each development team. Symbols can be substituted, and as new devices requiring new kinds of user actions appear, appropriate new symbols should be added to the UAN by a development team using it.

6.5.2   Primitive User Actions

Because the task of selecting a file is directly made up of physical user actions on hardware devices (e.g., moving the cursor and clicking the mouse button), the UAN description of this task will reflect these low-level physical actions. Task descriptions can also include user actions other than physical ones—for example, memory, cognitive, perceptual, and decision-making actions (Sharratt, 1990). However, they are not discussed here because they are not (yet) formally included in the UAN.

The physical user actions are termed *primitive* because they are not decomposed into further details. We could go into detail about how cursor movement is accomplished, for example, by involving kinesthetics and eye–hand coordination. These pragmatic issues of devices involve important human factors issues. However, by being abstracted out of the notation, these issues can be settled independently and incorporated into the design. This means that, for the present purposes, these details can be ignored. Other task descriptions are built on top of these primitives, using levels of increasing abstraction that hide individual physical actions. In order to identify each of the primitives, the developer must first identify each device and the physical user actions that apply.

6.6   DEVICES AND PRIMITIVE USER ACTIONS

The UAN symbols discussed here are used to represent devices and user actions involving devices commonly found in many interaction designs.

6.6.1   Cursor Movement

In Step 1 of the example task of selecting a file, the first device mentioned is one for moving the cursor. Such a device is mentioned only indirectly, not indicating exactly how the cursor is to be moved. A cursor can be moved by a user in many different ways, such as by moving a mouse, a trackball, a joystick, the cross hairs on a digitizer, arrow keys, locations on a touch panel, or an eye tracker.

As in the preceding section, some levels of abstraction here may help to keep the concept of moving the cursor separate from the definition of how a user does it. This separation of definition from use is important because it allows a user interaction designer to change the definition of how a user is to move the cursor without having to find and change all the places in the design where the cursor can be moved. This is sometimes termed *locality of definition*, because the definition is in just one place. The notation for representing a user moving the cursor, then, must be independent of the way in which it is done.

6.6.2   Switchlike Devices

Step 2 in the prose task description of the example task involves another device— namely, the mouse button; the actions are depressing and releasing. This kind of pushing down and letting up action is used to operate many kinds of switchlike devices, such as a mouse button (there might be more than one on a mouse), a keyboard key, a special key (e.g., a "Ctrl", "Esc", or "Shift" key), a function key, a knee switch, a foot pedal, or a "puff-and-sip" tube. We usually use the letter M to represent the mouse button device, and you can use your imagination for others. Pushing down is mnemonically and visually represented with a small arrowhead pointing down (v), and letting up is represented with an upward arrowhead (^). Thus, depressing the mouse button is Mv, and releasing the mouse button is M^. Clicking the mouse button is Mv M^. Because clicking the mouse button is used quite often as a single action in itself, a click can be represented with this shorter idiomatic expression: Mv^.

6.6.3   Character String Generators

Another class of devices contains the ones from which user actions result in character strings. Examples are keyboards and voice-recognition devices. Although keyboards are comprised of keys, individual keys are abstracted out of the description because the significant feature is the character string that results from their use. For simplicity, K represents the keyboard as a device. In task descriptions, there are two kinds of strings, literal and variable.

When using a copy command, for example, it is possible that a user is required to type the *literal string* "copy." This is represented as

```
K"copy"
```

On the other hand, some strings typed by users are variable. For example, a user may be asked to enter his or her name, a string that varies with each user. This entry of a *variable string* is represented as

```
K(name)
```

If desired, a regular expression can be used additionally inside the parentheses to specify the lexical definition of the variable to be entered by a user, for example,

```
K(user id = [A-Z][A-Z 0-9]+)
```

The [A-Z] means the first character must be alphabetic, and the [A-Z 0-9]+ means there must be one or more alphanumeric characters to follow. Again, you may use your own favorite variation of regular expressions (including prose).

6.7   OBJECTS AND THEIR CONTEXTS

So far, the example of selecting a file has covered moving the cursor and depressing and releasing the mouse button. What about the part of the Step 1 prose description that says "to the file icon?" Well, when a user moves the cursor to an object, it is often for the purpose of manipulating that object in some way—for example, to click on it to select it, or it may be to grab it and move it or change its size or shape. The *context of an object* is that by which you manipulate the object. However, because a user can grab and manipulate an interaction object in different ways for different tasks, the meaning of the context of an object can be task dependent. In these cases, the difference must be made clear, often through use of a figure.

For example, to select a file on a desktop, a user uses the mouse to move the cursor to the file icon itself. The user of a graphical drawing application can use the mouse either to move a line segment or to change its length and/or orientation; the line serves as its own context for moving. However, for stretching or reorienting in some drawing applications, a user must move the cursor to one of the little square grab handles at an endpoint of the line. In this case, if the description of this task (either in prose or any other representation) simply says to move the cursor to the line, it would not be precise enough.

In the case of stretching or reorienting, the handles aid the user in discerning their function by being indicative of the task. However, this is a human factors issue, and it would be nice to abstract this issue out of the notation. To this end, the UAN includes the task-dependent notion of the *context of an object*, denoted by putting square brackets around the name of the object, like this:

```
[object]
```

visually indicating a kind of box, to represent context, around the object.
So,

```
[file icon]
```

denotes the context of `file icon`, which might be the icon itself. On the other hand,

```
[line]
```

represents the context of a line in a line drawing for the task of changing its length, and it might be a grab handle at one of the line endpoints. The distinction could be made more clear by using a subscript or some other explicit notation, to refer specifically to this kind of context:

$$[\texttt{line}]_{endpoint}$$

This little bit of abstraction, to keep the concept of grabbing an object separate from the definition of how a user does it, uses locality of definition, just as was done for moving the cursor at the beginning of Section 6.5. This allows a user interaction designer to change the definition of how a user grabs an object for a given task without having to find and change all the places in a design where that object can be grabbed.

This completes the detailed description of all the UAN needed to represent the user actions of the example file selection task, repeating as a summary:

Step 1. ~[file icon]
Step 2. Mv^

Even this simple example illustrates the brevity, readability, and precision of the UAN.

6.8   INTERFACE FEEDBACK

The preceding UAN captured the physical user actions in the example task, but what about feedback from the system in response to these user actions? Feedback is certainly part of interaction design; including it in these representations allows a more complete description of user and interface behavior as they interact. *Feedback* is displayed by the system, but *is included in our behavioral description* because it is so directly tied to the *user actions* and because it represents *perceptual actions* on the part of the user. Thus, it is an important factor in usability of the system and therefore is important in the behavioral design domain.

There are various kinds of feedback. In the example task of selecting a file, users generally expect (because this is the way it is done in most designs today) the icon of the selected file to be highlighted, indicating that the user has selected the file. Highlighting is the system's way of getting the user's attention, exclaiming a state change in response to the user's (or maybe the system's) action. It seemed natural to use an exclamation mark as a visual and mnemonic symbol for highlighting. Highlighting of a file icon is represented in UAN simply as

```
file icon!
```

Similarly, highlighting of any interaction object would be represented as

```
object name!
```

Notice that this does not say how highlighting is accomplished or how it looks or sounds (or feels?). Just as was done in representing both cursor movement and the context of an object, abstraction and locality of definition are used for separating the definition of the ! symbol from its use. In its definition, highlighting might be specified to mean reverse video (common for icons of selected objects), but it can also mean, for example, blinking, a change of color, putting a box around the object, and/or an audible beep.

Given the symbols to represent highlighting of the file icon in the file selection example, where should it be written? It would be nice to have each indication of feedback side-by-side with the user action that caused it, so the two can be associated. But what user action caused the file icon to highlight? Such details are not always apparent unless we especially look for them. You have surely seen the following kind of description in the manual for your computer, which is a variation on the previous description of selecting a file:

1. Move the cursor to the icon.
2. Click the mouse button, and the icon will be highlighted.

Technically, this seems to say that highlighting occurs after the button is clicked (i.e., depressed and released). That may be an accurate description for some computers, but on many computers, highlighting occurs when the mouse button is depressed. You can see how a small difference such as this can be the source of imprecision in documentation. When this documentation is used to tell an implementer, for the first time, how a particular interaction feature works, this imprecision can cause confusion and misinterpretation.

It is, of course, possible to be quite precise with prose descriptions, but people rarely take the time to write (or to read) lengthy, very precise descriptions. The UAN has the power to be both precise and concise. In order to associate highlighting feedback with depression of the mouse button, simply break up the Mv^ that represents a mouse click. The resulting task description, with feedback, looks like this:

TASK: **select file**	
USER ACTIONS	**INTERFACE FEEDBACK**
~[file icon'] Mv	file icon'!
M^	

Note that the UAN task descriptions have been made a bit more structured, by adding a *task name*, and headings for *User Actions* and *Interface Feedback* columns. Also, because the name file icon is like a general variable in mathematics and can therefore refer to any file icon, a prime has been added to the name, file icon', to indicate that *the name refers to some specific file icon*, thereby distinguishing this instance of the variable from other general references to the variable file icon.

As with most Western notations, the UAN is read top to bottom and left to right within a line. In the first line of this more structured format, highlighting of the file icon is associated (by being on the same line) with depressing of the mouse, Mv, with the cursor in the context of the file icon.

The way in which UAN represents that the file icon in the Interface Feedback column is the same one represented in the User Actions column is because exactly the same name is used. In mathematics, the name file icon is termed a *bound variable*, which means that all occurrences of that variable, within the scope of binding (here within the whole task description), refer to the same thing. The file icon to be highlighted is the same file icon over which the mouse button is clicked.

There is a little more to know about highlighting. First, the use of highlighting suggests the need for a way to represent unhighlighting. Removing something, such as highlighting, can be thought of as similar to subtracting, so the subtraction sign is the visually mnemonic UAN representation of unhighlighting:

```
file icon-!
```

Second, in a single interaction design there might be several different kinds of highlighting. There might even be more than one kind of highlighting within a single task description. Suppose a designer wants to design an interface so that file icons have a different kind of highlighting than, say, command icons. The designer can use

```
file icon!
```

for file icons and

```
cmd icon!!
```

for command icons. Then, ! and ! ! are defined elsewhere, again using the concept of locality of definition. Similarly, the meaning of ! can be specified as different for each kind of object.

The more experienced you are with interaction design, the more you become aware of all the details and hidden complexity. This awareness will lead you to more complete design descriptions. For example, feedback in the preceding task description is still not complete. In the desktop metaphor on some computers, ordinary selection of files (and, therefore, highlighting of file icons) is mutually exclusive. Unless a designer does something specifically to allow multiple selection (discussed in a later example), a user can select only one file at a time. Maybe this example task technically should be named, select one icon and deselect all others. To refer to "all others" in UAN, use the universal quantifier, ∀, from predicate calculus; literally it means "for all." For example, the expression

```
∀(file icon)
```

might be used to refer to all file icons. To refer to "all others," when "others" means all file icons other than the one that is being selected, is denoted by the UAN expression

```
∀file icon ≠ file icon':
```

which means "for all file icons except (not equal to) the specific one being selected."

Next, the designer has to say what should happen with all these other file icons when the specific one is selected by a user. In this case the designer wants them to unhighlight. This is represented in UAN as follows:

```
∀file icon ≠ file icon': file icon-!
```

Literally, this means "for all file icons except the selected one, unhighlight them."

When this is added into the task description, it yields a more precise representation of feedback behavior.

TASK: **select file**	
USER ACTIONS	**INTERFACE FEEDBACK**
~[file icon'] Mv	file icon'! ∀file icon ≠ file icon': file icon-!
M^	

This description of feedback in the UAN is more detailed, complete, and precise than the prose description, which said only, "click the mouse button, and the icon will be highlighted."

There is an alternative approach, however, to representing this mutually exclusive behavior—the unhighlighting of file icons other than the one selected—that you should consider for your interaction design representations. Some developers feel that this added detail (e.g., for unhighlighting all icons except the selected one) is not properly part of the mainline user task behavior. Thus, when it is included directly in a task description, it can detract from clarity and readability. The case could be made that this mutual exclusion under single icon selection is more properly expressed as a property of the whole set of file icons. In this case, it is better represented with a separate technique, perhaps as a declaration of an attribute of the set of objects that are file icons. It is possible to augment the UAN with declarative definitions of interaction objects and types, such as these:

```
file icon is an element of a set of type FI.

FI is mutually exclusive under single selection.
```

Another alternative, which works best with computer-based tool support, is to have two or more different views of task descriptions—one for mainline descriptions and one with all the ancillary details. Before pursuing this approach of including ancillary detail in task descriptions, you should realize that it is possible to get trapped into including details that really have little to do with the user task being described. For example, suppose that the containing window in which a file icon is being selected is not active. In some interaction designs, depressing the mouse button over the icon will activate the containing window, and a second mouse click is required to select the icon. In other designs, a single click will both activate the containing window *and* select the icon. In this situation, these extraneous concerns can be sorted out by, for example, requiring the containing window to be active as a condition of viability (discussed in Section 6.10) for the selection task. This has the effect of constraining a user to activate an inactive window before selecting a file icon in it. This constraint may or may not be appropriate for a particular design.

For the sake of clarity and simplicity, this discussion leaves out ancillary details from task descriptions in cases where they don't add any useful information concerning the design. When writing out a design (e.g., in UAN), you should use your own judgment to determine the appropriate level of detail, to give implementers sufficient unambiguous information without burying them with extraneous description.

That's enough for now about highlighting. There are other kinds of feedback, though. For example, how do you represent moving a box on the screen, as it is dragged by a user? For this, the UAN symbol is an arrow that is intended to show that the box follows the cursor as it moves:

```
box > ~
```

Don't mistake this > for the mathematical "greater than" symbol; when combined with the ~ symbol, it means "follows the cursor."

Also consider the case of "rubber-banding," where an object is stretched out by grabbing part of it and pulling it with the cursor. This might be used, for example, to change the size or shape of a box on the screen. After a user has moved to a corner of, say, a box and grabbed it with the cursor, the UAN represents the rubber-banding action with two arrowlike symbols written close together, as the box corner follows the cursor:

```
box corner >> ~
```

Even more detailed symbols can be used as an interaction design calls for them. For example, suppose that as feedback for the task of creating a new file icon, the system is to display that file icon at some specific location, (x',y'), on the screen. This could be represented in a UAN task description as

```
@(x',y') display(new file icon)
```

6.9   STATE INFORMATION

In addition to user actions and feedback, UAN task descriptions must somehow specify when information about interface state must be retained and/or changed. This must be specified because interface state can affect interaction within a task. A simple example is seen in the earlier example of the task of selecting a file icon. Being selected has to do with the state of the file represented by the icon. Modes are another kind of interface state. (Despite what you may hear to the contrary, not all modes are bad.) So how is state information represented in the UAN? A new column is simply added to the task description.

At this point, the abstraction used for locality of definition says that interface state information should be kept separate from the way it might be presented in a display. The simplest example of this is seen in the now-familiar selection task. You may have noticed that all along, this has been called the `select file` task and not the `select file icon` task. The difference is subtle but important and can be completely missed if design is carried out using constructional thinking, such as which widgets are needed, rather than focusing on the behavioral domain.

It might seem as though a user is selecting the file icon, but the purpose of this task is for a user to choose a specific *file*, possibly as the object of a subsequent file operation, such as opening or deleting. The physical file itself is stored somewhere on a disk and cannot be made visible or touchable by the user. So in a graphical direct manipulation interface, the *interaction object*, in this case the file *icon*, serves as a visual surrogate for the file. The extent to which a user can naturally operate within this illusion (Weller & Hartson, 1992) with a feeling of directly manipulating the file, while actually indirectly manipulating it through its iconic representation in the interface, is a measure of the cognitive directness and effectiveness of the desktop metaphor. Thus, this difference should not be visible to the user, but it is still very important for the designer.

How does this affect the task description for the selection task? It simply means that the file and the file icon referring to it are kept separate in that description, remembering that *it is the file that is selected but the associated file icon that is highlighted*. Thus, highlighting in the interface represents state information about selection in the file system. Here's what the task description becomes when a third column is added to hold Interface State information:

TASK: **select file**		
USER ACTIONS	INTERFACE FEEDBACK	INTERFACE STATE
~[file icon'] Mv	file icon'!	selected = file
M^		

Several parts of this task description must be defined further, probably in declarations. For example, `selected` is the name of a set that (in this case of single file selection) contains the name of the file that is currently selected. The user interaction designer must also explicitly declare the connection between the application entity (`file`) and the user interaction object (`file icon'`), in this general fashion:

```
file icon' ASSOCIATED WITH file
```

The final determination of how things such as selection are represented, though, should be based on what works best for the designer. The UAN is intended to be practical. Thus, the distinction between physical and logical selection should be maintained only as far as it is useful.

An example of a case where the distinction is, perhaps, not as useful to the designer is seen in the expression:

```
select (Open button)
```

Physical selection of the "Open" button causes logical selection (invocation) of the open command. In most direct manipulation interfaces, the task-oriented view does not include separate concepts for selecting a button and also for selecting the associated command. Even for the designer, the situation may be made simpler and/or clearer by referring only to the task or action of selecting the button. This same argument can, of course, be made for the case of the file icon and the file. If it suits the designer, the separate concept of a file icon can be omitted. Again, these fine distinctions are hidden from users but understood by designers.

6.10   CONDITIONS OF VIABILITY

A user interaction designer may not wish to deal with what it means to select something that is already selected. This difficulty can be avoided by allowing the `select file` task to apply only to files not already selected. This seems reasonable, but how can this be done in the UAN? We can qualify parts of the task description with a *condition of viability*. The `select file` task requires something that says,

```
for file icons not highlighted: ~[file icon] Mv^
```

The phrase before the colon is a condition of viability, and the expression after the colon is a conditional action. The general form for this kind of expression in the UAN is a condition, with a colon separating it from the action to which it applies:

```
condition: action
```

The scope of the condition is understood to include only the one action. Additionally, if the condition applies to a sequence of actions on the same line, it is written like this:

```
condition: action1 action2 action3
```

In such a statement, the scope is understood to include the actions in that one line. However, when the condition applies to actions on more than one line, parentheses are used to denote the scope in the following way:

```
condition:
  (action1
  action2
  action3)
```

A condition of viability acts as a precondition that must be satisfied—that is, have a true value—in order for user actions within its scope to be performed as part of the task being described. A condition of viability with a false value does not necessarily mean that a user cannot perform the corresponding actions; it just means that, even if they are performed, *the user is not performing this particular task.* The same actions, however, might be part of another task in the overall set of asynchronous tasks that comprise an interface.

When deciding how to use the UAN for a condition that requires the file icon to be unhighlighted, remember that for the file selection task, the following expression described the condition of being unhighlighted:

```
file icon-!
```

This is the same expression used for representing feedback earlier, where the expression served as an imperative; that is, it meant, "Make the file icon unhighlighted." Now we will use this expression as a condition of viability, where it says "file icon is unhighlighted," a logical proposition that can have a true or false value. The way you can tell the difference between the two cases is the context within a task description.

The first line of user actions of the select file task, with the new condition of viability, now becomes

```
file icon'-!: ~[file icon'] Mv
```

The colon indicates an if–then type of construct here, so you read this as follows:

"If the specific file icon of interest is not highlighted, then move the cursor to the context of that file icon and depress the mouse button."

As still more detail is added, the UAN task description now becomes

TASK: **select file**		
USER ACTIONS	**INTERFACE FEEDBACK**	**INTERFACE STATE**
file icon'-!: (~[file icon'] Mv	file icon'!	selected = file
M^)		

This example shows the use of parentheses in the User Action column to show that the whole task lies within the scope of the condition of viability. Just as before, the occurrence of file icon' in the condition of viability is bound to its other occurrences, meaning that they all refer to the same file icon. As a matter of practice, a shorter version of this expression may be easier to use. It amounts to a kind of built-in binding. Combining the conditional use of ! with the object of cursor movement, the following expression means, more directly, "move the cursor to a specific unhighlighted file icon and depress the mouse button":

~[file icon'-!] Mv

The task description, somewhat simpler than the previous one that describes exactly the same thing, becomes

TASK: **select file**		
USER ACTIONS	**INTERFACE FEEDBACK**	**INTERFACE STATE**
~[file icon'-!] Mv	file icon'!	selected = file
M^		

While this is a good way to represent the select file task, to be complete, the designer may also wish to specify what happens if the user does, in fact, try to select a file that is already selected. The most sensible result (and the one that happens on many computers) is that the file icon remains highlighted (and therefore the associated file remains selected) and nothing changes. How can this be included in the select file task description? The simplest way is to remove the condition of viability and define the meaning of ! as applied to file icons to be null (i.e., nothing changes in the icon appearance) if the file icon is already highlighted. The task description is correct in either case.

An alternative is to use a *condition of viability in the Interface Feedback column*, making the highlighting action dependent on the object's not being already highlighted. This covers both cases (i.e., selected icon already highlighted and not already highlighted). The line of feedback in the UAN description then becomes:

```
file icon'-!: file icon'!
```

This is read, "If a file icon is not highlighted, then highlight it" (in response to the Mv in the User Action column). Because it covers both cases, the following is probably a better task description than the previous ones:

TASK: **select file**		
USER ACTIONS	**INTERFACE FEEDBACK**	**INTERFACE STATE**
~[file icon'] Mv	file icon'-!: file icon'!	selected = file
M^		

6.11   EXTENSIBILITY OF THE UAN

To further extend your understanding of UAN, we will introduce a slightly different example: the task of moving a file icon on the desktop. Here is a prose description of that task:

1. Move the cursor to the file icon. Depress and hold down the mouse button. Depressing the mouse button selects the file, indicated by the highlighting of its icon.
2. With the button held down, move the cursor. An outline of the icon follows the cursor as you move it around.
3. Release the mouse button. The file icon is now moved to where you released the button, and the corresponding file remains selected.

Notice that, unlike the file selection task, this task changes the location of the file icon. Moving the file icon does not change the interface state relating to the file; it remains selected.

Exercise—UAN

GOAL: To produce a simple UAN task description.

MINIMUM TIME: About 10 minutes.

ACTIVITIES: Before looking at the development of the task description that follows, try to write a UAN task description for the `move file icon` task. You won't have all the notation you need, but this will give you a better appreciation for what is needed—and it won't take you much time. Start by drawing three columns—for the user actions, interface feedback, and interface state. Then go through the prose description line by line, trying to translate the prose words and phrases into UAN symbols. Also look back at the final UAN version of the `select file` task; you will find that much of it can be used in the UAN description of this new task.

For those parts of the prose you don't yet know how to represent in UAN, make up any symbols you might need to create a reasonably complete and precise description of this task. This will help you understand the power and the extensibility of the UAN.

DELIVERABLES: A UAN task description for the `move file icon` task.

Possible Exercise Solution

Here is the beginning of a task description for the move file icon task:

TASK: **move file icon**		
USER ACTIONS	**INTERFACE FEEDBACK**	**INTERFACE STATE**
~[file icon'] Mv	file icon'-!: file icon'!	selected = file
~[x,y]* ~[x',y']	file icon' > ~	
M^		

It was easy to get started on this task description because it begins the same way that the select file task did. The first line of user actions and its associated feedback and state are, in fact, identical. The second line of user actions contains something new. The notation

~[x,y]

means that a user moves the cursor to some arbitrary point on the screen, x, y. The star, or asterisk (*), is the Kleene iterative closure star from regular languages and refers to the *repetition* of user actions. Literally, it means to do the preceding action zero or more times. When you add the star to the cursor movement, you get

~[x,y]*

which means to move the cursor arbitrarily around the screen going to zero or more points.

If you have a mind for precision, you might think that because the name x, y is used for the point coordinates for every repetition, binding would require that to be the same point every time. To avoid this difficulty, because it is impossible to use different coordinate names for each instance of the repetition in

~[x,y]*

it is necessary to assume that instances of x, y are not bound to each other (i.e., are not the same point on the screen). This convention allows the reference to a point x, y in the expression

~[x,y]*

to be a reference to an arbitrary number of points on the screen.

The expression

```
~[x',y']
```

that follows is also a move of the cursor to some point, this time a single specific point x', y'. This point is special in the task description because it is the final point in the cursor movement. The primes in the point coordinates are used to indicate reference to that specific point. The feedback for this cursor movement

```
file icon > ~
```

is an example of an object following the cursor (specifically, dragging the file icon) that was introduced in Section 6.8.

A closer look at this UAN task description shows that it isn't precisely what the prose description of the task said. Namely, Step 2 said that just the outline of the file icon follows the cursor. However, the UAN so far has not given us any way to refer to the outline of an icon. This is where the extensibility of the notation comes in. Remember, that is the topic of this section. So make something up! How about a function such as

```
outline(file icon')
```

This function is used in the UAN task description to say that just an outline of the file icon follows the cursor when it moves, but what happens when the user releases the mouse button? Then the complete file icon, not just its outline, appears on the spot where the user releases the mouse button. This sounds like the display function introduced at the end of Section 6.8. Thus, the feedback associated with releasing the mouse button could be represented in UAN as

```
@x',y' display(file icon')
```

Note that a binding is being used with the coordinate name x', y' from the User Actions column, to specify that the file icon is displayed at the point where the cursor stops moving. Putting these changes into the task description gives

TASK: **move file icon**		
USER ACTIONS	**INTERFACE FEEDBACK**	**INTERFACE STATE**
~[file icon'] Mv	file icon'-!: file icon'!	selected = file
~[x,y]* ~[x',y']	outline(file icon') > ~	
M^	@x',y' display(file icon')	

There is still a small problem with precision here. While the file icon is displayed, in its final position ($@x'$, y'), technically, it is still displayed in its original position, too. To avoid this, we can precede the display function with another one:

```
erase(file icon)
```

This making up of new functions or other notation, as needed, is fully within the spirit of extensibility of the UAN and its *open* symbology and structure. As long as we are creating new functions, let's introduce a redisplay function to combine both the erase and the display functions:

```
@x',y' redisplay(file icon)
```

Notice also, in the Interface State column, that this task leaves the file icon selected. Putting these changes into the task description gives

TASK: **move file icon**		
USER ACTIONS	**INTERFACE FEEDBACK**	**INTERFACE STATE**
~[file icon'] Mv	file icon'-!: file icon'!	selected = file
~[x,y]* ~[x',y']	outline(file icon') > ~	
M^	@x',y' redisplay(file icon')	

Your possible solution may have been quite different from this one. However, if you captured this level of detail in your description, perhaps using different symbols or functions, your solution is probably a reasonable one. If you left out a lot of the detail, you might consider for a moment what would have happened in a real-world situation, where you, as the user interaction designer, handed your somewhat incomplete, imprecise UAN description to the user interface software designer and programmer. What would they have implemented? For how much of the design would they have had to guess what you meant? As stated earlier, when the interaction design is incomplete, the programmer sometimes ends up doing that design, often with unexpected or undesirable results. This is one of the situations that can be avoided by representing all details of the design using a technique such as the UAN.

6.12   TASK REPETITION

In the example of the move file icon task of the previous section, it was necessary to express arbitrary repetition of a user action or task. The UAN idiom

$$\sim[x,y]$$

denotes movement of the cursor to some (any) point on the screen. The expression

$$\sim[x,y]*$$

then refers to an arbitrary number (zero or more) of occurrences of this kind of cursor movement.

As a variation of this expression for task repetition, there is also the UAN expression

$$\sim[x,y]^+$$

which means that cursor movement will occur one or more times; that is, at least once. Here the + symbol, like the * symbol, is taken from the language of regular expressions.

Sometimes, an interaction designer will wish to require a user to perform an action or task some specific number of times. If, for example, you wished to represent exactly three cursor movements, then (per regular expression notation), you would use a 3 as a superscript for the expression, as follows:

$$\sim[x,y]^3$$

A special case of task repetition occurs when a task or action is *optional*—that is, a user may or may not perform it. As a regular expression, this might be written as

$$\sim[x,y]^{(0 \ or \ 1)}$$

literally meaning that the user performs the action either zero times or once. However, the UAN also distinguishes optionality as a special case and denotes it by enclosing the task or action in curly braces:

$$\{\sim[x,y]\}$$

6.13   MORE EXERCISES

To give you some more practice with UAN, let's try another task: Delete a file by dragging its icon on the desktop to the trash can icon. Details of this task vary, depending on your computer, so let's use the following prose description as the one for which you will write the UAN task description:

1. Move the cursor to the file icon representing the file to be deleted.
2. Depress the mouse button; the file icon highlights.
3. Keeping the mouse button depressed, move the cursor to drag an outline of the file icon over the trash icon. The trash icon highlights.
4. Release the mouse button; the file icon disappears, and the trash can does something else (e.g., bulges) to show that the file was removed.

Exercise—UAN

GOAL: To produce another UAN task description.

MINIMUM TIME: About 15 minutes.

ACTIVITIES: Now you have a little more experience with the UAN. Stretch your knowledge by trying to write a UAN task description for the task to delete a file, as described in the preceding prose. As with the previous exercise you tried, begin by drawing the three columns. Feel free to reuse any parts of the previous UAN descriptions as you write out this new task description.

DELIVERABLES: A UAN task description for the delete a file task.

Possible Exercise Solution

Because this starts out a lot like the move file icon task, use what you know from that task. That gets you this far into the task description:

TASK: **delete file**		
USER ACTIONS	INTERFACE FEEDBACK	INTERFACE STATE
~[file icon'] Mv	file icon'-!: file icon'!	selected = file
~[x,y]* ~[x',y']	outline(file icon') > ~	

This description still leaves the user stranded out in the middle of the screen at *x',y'*, holding down the mouse button. Instead of stopping at *x',y'*, the user needs to keep moving the file icon to the trash can icon, and then to release the mouse button there, deleting the file:

TASK: **delete file**		
USER ACTIONS	INTERFACE FEEDBACK	INTERFACE STATE
~[file icon'] Mv	file icon'-!: file icon'!	selected = file
~[x,y]*	outline(file icon') > ~	
~[trash icon]	outline(file icon') > ~ trash icon!	
M^	erase(file icon') erase(outline(file icon')) trash icon-! trash icon!!	selected = null

Note the second kind of highlighting for the trash icon, trash icon!!, which was used to indicate that the file was received in the trash can. Further note that in order to associate specific feedback—namely, highlighting of the trash icon when the cursor moves over it—the action

~[trash icon]

is written on a separate line from

~[x,y]*

This is in contrast to the move file icon task, which had no special feedback upon reaching x',y'. In that task, feedback occurred only upon release of the mouse button.

This leads to a realization about the expression

```
~[x,y]*
```

used to represent cursor movement. The ~ is used in the UAN to represent *path-independent cursor movement* of arbitrary distance. So the expression

```
~[object]
```

is a path-independent move to an object. Thus, the

```
~[x,y]*
```

is not really needed in front of a move to a specific location or object (icon), *unless* you want to use it as an action to associate with feedback for cursor movement, specifically to show the feedback for cursor movement at a given point within a task.

In the task descriptions for the move file icon task,

```
~[x,y]
```

and

```
~[x,y]*
```

were used as a user action to associate with the feedback

```
outline(file icon) > ~
```

to show feedback behavior during cursor movement. This separate user action is not needed for that purpose in the present task because it can be associated here with the path-independent movement to the trash icon. Here is the UAN description of the delete file task without that redundant step:

TASK: **delete file**		
USER ACTIONS	INTERFACE FEEDBACK	INTERFACE STATE
~[file icon'] Mv	file icon'-!: file icon'!	selected = file
~[trash icon]	outline(file icon') > ~ trash icon!	
M^	erase(file icon') erase(outline(file icon')) trash icon-! trash icon!!	selected = null

Up until this task, the UAN examples have been tasks that involve the interface only, without any connections to noninterface functionality. For these desktop examples, if there were some noninterface functionality, it would be in the computer's file system. The `select file` and `move file icon` tasks affected feedback and interface state but did not make any changes to the files themselves. (There is an assumption here that the system architecture is such that file selection state information resides in the interface, and the file system does not have *direct* access to such information.)

Although it is desirable, in reality this separation of user interface from noninterface functions often cannot be maintained and often simply cannot be done at all. In such cases, it is necessary to indicate connections that do exist. Thus, the present example, the task description for deleting a file, is the first one that has meaning (semantics) outside the user interface. Most user tasks do have semantic connections to noninterface functionality; after all, that's the real purpose of an interface—to give easy access to the functionality of the system. To serve this purpose, another column is needed—*Connection to Computation*—in the UAN task descriptions. This column is important to interaction designers because it is where they specify simple connections from the interface to the computational component. Software designers in the constructional domain might implement these connections, for example, as callbacks to functional routines from interface widgets.

TASK: **delete file**			
USER ACTIONS	**INTERFACE FEEDBACK**	**INTERFACE STATE**	**CONNECTION TO COMPUTATION**
~[file icon'] Mv	file icon'-!: file icon'!	selected = file	
~[trash icon]	outline(file icon') > ~ trash icon!		
M^	erase(file icon') erase(outline(file icon')) trash icon-! trash icon!!	selected = null	mark file for deletion

Notice that in the new column, the file is to be marked for deletion, rather than to be deleted immediately. This is what actually happens on many desktop interfaces. At some later time, by some mysterious algorithm, the system decides to do some garbage collection and actually deletes all files marked for deletion. In the meantime, the file continues to reside in the trash can, which acts pretty much like a regular file folder.

In the next example, you are to delete several files at once from the desktop. This task begins with selecting several files. Although there are many ways to do multiple file selection, each of which involves some complexity, only one way of performing this task is represented here. This method deletes files by using the *shift-select technique*, which involves holding the "Shift" key down while going around and clicking on file icons to be selected for deletion. When all the file icons the user wants to delete are selected, the user can then drag them as a group to the trash. Here is the prose description to be described in UAN:

1. Depress the "Shift" key, and hold it down.
2. Move the cursor to a file icon.
3. Click the mouse button; the file icon highlights.
4. Repeat the previous two steps as many times as desired.
5. Release the "Shift" key.
6. If desired, repeat the first five steps any number of times.
7. Move the cursor to any one of the selected file icons, depress the mouse button, and drag the selected group of file icons to the trash icon; the trash icon highlights.
8. Release the mouse button, dropping the file icons into the trash. The trash icon highlights (or bulges) again.

Exercise—UAN

GOAL: To produce a slightly more complicated UAN task description.

MINIMUM TIME: About 20 minutes.

ACTIVITIES: Even though this one is a bit more difficult, it still builds on what you have learned. Don't peek ahead to the possible solution! You need to be strengthening your UAN skills now. Make your best attempt at a UAN task description for the delete multiple files task just described in prose.

DELIVERABLES: A UAN task description for the delete multiple files task.

Possible Exercise Solution

This solution starts with just the part at the beginning, the first six steps in the prose description, which describe the multiple selection of files using the shift-select method:

TASK: **delete multiple files**			
USER ACTIONS	**INTERFACE FEEDBACK**	**INTERFACE STATE**	**CONNECTION TO COMPUTATION**

(Sv
 (~[file icon'-!]
  Mv
 	
  M^)$^+$
S^)$^+$
	file icon'!	selected =
		 selected ∪ file	

rest of "delete multiple files" task...			

Here, S denotes the "Shift" key, where one of the keyboard keys (the "Shift" key) is used as a switchlike device (see Section 6.6.2) rather than as a character-string generator. Note the use of the + symbol (introduced in Section 6.12) in two places, to specify that particular actions are performed one or more times. In the preceding task description, this repetition applies to moving to the file icons and clicking on them while the "Shift" is key depressed. It also applies to the whole set of actions between, and including, depressing and releasing the "Shift" key. This means that a user can release the "Shift" key and still continue selection by depressing it again and clicking on more file icons.

Also note the built-in condition of viability, denoted by the – ! in

```
[file icon'-!]
```

applied to the file icon in the user action on the second line. The icon cannot already be selected for a user to perform this action. If a user moves the cursor to a highlighted icon (in the second line) and depresses the mouse button, this task description simply does not indicate what would happen. Because the condition of viability is not met for this action, such a user action *does not apply to this task.* There may, however, be another task within the set of asynchronous tasks that comprise the interface (perhaps a deselect task), for which its conditions of viability are met and its description matches these user actions. That task description would say what results in this case.

As with many other formal specification techniques, the question of completeness is difficult. There is no way, in general, to determine whether all possible user behaviors are covered by the current set of task descriptions. This is an area of future work, drawing on software analysis techniques and tools that can process a set of task descriptions and identify problems with completeness, correctness, and consistency.

Returning to the present example, it is easy to make the case that a user might want to click on an already selected file icon during this task—perhaps due to a change of mind, deciding not to select it after all. As mentioned previously, the "Shift" key is used to allow multiple selection. The behavior of the "Shift" key when used for selection actually has slightly more meaning associated with it. In this case, holding down the "Shift" key puts the interface into a mode. (Remember, not all modes are bad; in fact, this one is pretty useful.) When the "Shift" key is depressed, a user can toggle between selection and deselection by successively clicking on the same file icon.

This provides an easy way to do multiple selection. Users can just hold down the "Shift" key and go around clicking on file icons. It also provides an easy way for users to change their minds about selecting some file; they can just click on its icon again, with the "Shift" key depressed, to deselect that file. This toggling behavior can easily be included in the task description. In the following UAN task description, note the interface feedback and interface state for the Mv action. Notice that the condition of functional viability on the file icon now moves from the User Actions column to the Interface Feedback column.

TASK: **delete multiple files**			
USER ACTIONS	**INTERFACE FEEDBACK**	**INTERFACE STATE**	**CONNECTION TO COMPUTATION**
`(Sv` `(~[file icon']` `Mv` `M^)` $^+$ `S^)` $^+$	`file icon'-!: file icon'!` `file icon'!: file icon'-!`	`selected = selected U file` `selected = selected - file`	
rest of "delete multiple files" task . . .			

To represent the rest of the delete multiple files task is just a matter of picking up any one of the selected file icons (denoted by file icon!!) and using it to drag the whole group of selected file icons to the trash, as shown in the following:

TASK: **delete multiple files**			
USER ACTIONS	INTERFACE FEEDBACK	INTERFACE STATE	CONNECTION TO COMPUTATION

(Sv
  (~[file icon']
    Mv
 	
    M^)$^+$
S^)$^+$
	file icon'-!: file icon'!
	
	file icon'!: file icon'-!
		selected =
		  selected ∪ file
		selected =
		  selected - file	

~[file icon''!] Mv			
~[trash icon]	outline(∀file icon'!) > ~ trash icon!		
M^	erase(∀file icon'!) erase(outline(∀file icon'!)) trash icon!!	selected = null	mark selected files for deletion

We will return to this example of deleting multiple files in Chapter 7.

6.14   CONCLUSIONS ABOUT USE OF THE UAN

Having reached the end of this chapter, you probably have come to think of the UAN as very complex—all the details discussed in this chapter about moving the cursor and pushing buttons, highlighting, and so on. The level of detail you see in UAN descriptions may have surprised you. The alternative, however, is not to include so much detail in your designs and to leave the decisions about them up to a programmer at implementation time. The reasons why this is not a good idea should be abundantly clear to you by now.

Beyond this, however, the truth is that only a very small portion of the representation of a user interaction design in the UAN contains this kind of complex detail. These primitive user actions make up the *articulatory level* of the UAN, referring to the movement of a user's fingers in performing the physical actions. This level contains the low-level details of physical user actions (e.g., moving the cursor and clicking the mouse button) as a user interacts with devices. A complete interaction description, however, is made up of many levels of abstraction built on top of the articulatory level, and these higher levels are made up of task names, not primitive user actions. These task macros and levels of abstraction are discussed in Chapter 7.

The complexity of the UAN as discussed in this present chapter is mostly hidden from readers and writers of the UAN, except when they are working at the articulatory level. Unless you are interested in exactly what physical actions are used to make selections, and so on, you need not see this level of complexity; instead you just see task names such as

```
select(object)
```

Above the articulatory level, interaction representations are in the form of a quasi-hierarchical task structure that looks very much like what you get from task analyses, except that the UAN also includes temporal relationships among tasks and subtasks, as discussed in Chapter 7. This next chapter also returns to the Calendar Management System and uses the UAN to represent its design.

REFERENCES

Card, S. K., & Moran, T. P. (1980). The Keystroke-Level Model for User Performance Time with Interactive Systems. *Communications of the ACM, 23,* 396–410.

Card, S. K., Moran, T. P., & Newell, A. (1983). *The Psychology of Human-Computer Interaction.* Hillsdale, NJ: Erlbaum.

Foley, J., Gibbs, C., Kim, W., & Kovacevic, S. (1988). A Knowledge-Based User Interface Management System. *Proceedings of CHI Conference on Human Factors in Computing Systems,* New York: ACM, 67–72.

Gould, J. D., & Lewis, C. (1985). Designing for Usability: Key Principles and What Designers Think. *Communications of the ACM, 28*(3), 300–311.

Green, M. (1985). The University of Alberta User Interface Management System. *Computer Graphics, 19*(3), 205–213.

Grudin, J. (1991). Systematic Sources of Suboptimal Interface Design in Large Product Development Organizations. *Human-Computer Interaction, 6*(2).

Hartson, H. R., & Hix, D. (1989). Toward Empirically Derived Methodologies and Tools for Human-Computer Interface Development. *International Journal of Man-Machine Studies, 31,* 477–494.

Hartson, H. R., Siochi, A. C., & Hix, D. (1990). The UAN: A User-Oriented Representation for Direct Manipulation Interface Designs. *ACM Transactions on Information Systems, 8*(3), 181–203.

Jacob, R. J. K. (1986). A Specification Language for Direct Manipulation User Interfaces. *ACM Transactions on Graphics, 5*(4), 283–317.

Kieras, D. & Polson, P. G. (1985). An Approach to the Formal Analysis of User Complexity. *International Journal of Man-Machine Studies, 22,* 365–394.

Moran, T. P. (1981). The Command Language Grammar: A Representation for the User Interface of Interactive Computer Systems. *International Journal of Man-Machine Studies, 15,* 3–51.

Myers, B. A. (1988). *Creating User Interfaces by Demonstration.* Boston: Academic Press.

Payne, S. J. & Green, T. R. G. (1986). Task-Action Grammars: A Model of the Mental Representation of Task Languages. *Human-Computer Interaction, 2,* 93–133.

Reisner, P. (1981). Formal Grammar and Human Factors Design of an Interactive Graphics System. *IEEE Transactions on Software Engineering, SE-7,* 229–240.

Sharratt, B. (1990). Memory-Cognition-Action Tables: A Pragmatic Approach to Analytical Modelling. *Proceedings of Interact '90,* Amsterdam: Elsevier Science Publishers, 271–275.

Sibert, J. L., Hurley, W. D., & Bleser, T. W. (1988). Design and Implementation of an Object-Oriented User Interface Management System. In H. R. Hartson & D. Hix (Eds.), *Advances in Human-Computer Interaction,* Vol. 2 (pp. 175–213). Norwood, NJ: Ablex.

Wasserman, A. I. & Shewmake, D. T. (1985). The Role of Prototypes in the User Software Engineering Methodology. In H. R. Hartson (Ed.), *Advances in Human-Computer Interaction* (pp. 191–210). Norwood, NJ: Ablex.

Weller, H. G., & Hartson, H. R. (1992). Metaphors for the Nature of Human-Computer Interaction in an Empowering Environment: Interaction Style Influences the Manner of Human Accomplishment. *Computers in Human Behavior, 8,* 313–333.

≡ 7

More on Using the User Action Notation

7.1   INTRODUCING TEMPORAL RELATIONS

The UAN was introduced in the previous chapter and now continues, with more examples and more about how to use the UAN to represent a user interaction design. In particular, this chapter discusses *temporal relations* that describe how user tasks and user actions are related over time. This chapter gives quite a different flavor to the UAN than was seen in Chapter 6. There, the UAN was used to describe low-level details of a design; in this chapter the UAN is used to present task descriptions at higher levels of abstraction, with emphasis on temporal relations. We will continue with use of the Calendar Management System example to illustrate application of the concepts.

Task descriptions cannot be represented in the UAN without the use of temporal relations. At a minimum, two simple user actions within a task are temporally related by being in a *sequence*—one occurs after the other in time. Chapter 6 included several examples of user actions in a sequence, as well as some examples of *iteration*, another kind of temporal relation. This chapter explores some additional temporal relations for use in UAN task descriptions. Formal definitions of the temporal relations are given in Hartson and Gray (1992). Table 7.1 shows a summary list of the temporal relations discussed in this chapter. Later we describe how each of these is used in interaction designs.

The question of temporal aspects enters into the user interaction design process when the relative timing of tasks is considered. The easiest case for an interaction designer is often the most constraining for a user. For example, a designer can easily specify a sequence, but in doing so, the designer is strictly requiring a user to complete one task before beginning another.

For example, in the Calendar Management System, to add a new appointment, a user must first access the proper day and time slot on the calendar, then type in the appointment. The two tasks of accessing and typing are related temporally by being in a *sequence*; they cannot both be active at the same time.

However, users often wish to interrupt a task and, while they are thinking of it, perform another task, later resuming the original one. For example, entering a new appointment may cause the user to remember a problem with an existing appointment; perhaps there is some missing information for an existing appointment that the user had intended to enter. In order not to forget it again, the user wishes immediately to interrupt the entry of the new appointment and go to the existing one to add the desired information. Then the user wishes to return to the new appointment without losing its context. This is a good example of a user need that might not be anticipated during task analysis unless it is supported by observation of users performing representative tasks.

A major purpose of asynchronous direct manipulation interaction styles is to support this kind of interleaved user task behavior. It follows that there is a need for a behavioral way to represent the designer's intention to allow interleaving of tasks by a user. This need is met by the *interleavability* temporal relation, which is used to connect these kinds of tasks in UAN task descriptions.

Most design representations and almost all task analysis techniques leave this

TABLE 7.1. TEMPORAL RELATIONS IN THE UAN

Sequence
Iteration
Optionality
Repeating choice
Order independence
Interruptibility
Interleavability
Concurrency
Waiting

question of intertask temporal relationships implicit, if not ambiguous or unde-fined. Such specifications often lead to arbitrary design on the part of the interface software designer or implementer. For example, in designing for the task of adding a new appointment to the calendar, a designer may look to an interface toolkit for an appropriate widget. It could be reasonable to the designer to use a preemptive style (modal) dialogue box, requiring the user to enter information for the current appointment before performing a different task. This, of course, does not support the needs of a user to go off and work on an existing appointment while in the midst of creating a new one, as was discussed earlier.

This illustrates the *danger of doing user interaction design in the constructional domain, letting the design be driven by available widgets rather than by users' task needs.* Unfortunately, much interaction design these days does, in fact, begin with, "What widget should we use?" A better question might be, "What widget do I need to use to support the behavioral design?" Unfortunately, the choice of available widgets is limited in many interface toolkits, and coding new ones can be very expensive in a commercial environment.

If developers do observe users during task analysis, though, they may also see a user who wishes to create two or more related appointments at once, or to set an alarm while still creating an appointment. If a user does somehow end up with a dialogue box, say, for typing in appointment information, good interaction design suggests that the user should be allowed to close the dialogue box without completing the associated data entry task for the current appointment, and any information entered so far should be retained. However, the user would still be left with the responsibility for temporarily ending (suspending) one task and starting the other, and would have to use human working memory to carry information from one task context to another. In such a case, it would be useful to provide copy and paste operations for the user to move information from one related ap-pointment to the other. From the user view, there is a task interruption, but the design still does not really support it well. Proper evaluation and design iteration can lead to an even better design, one that allows fully interleaved task perfor-mance.

These examples should motivate the usefulness of temporal relations in behav-ioral interaction design representations. First, temporal considerations might be in a design but cannot be explicit in its representation without temporal relations. The UAN temporal operators allow an interaction designer to represent explicit temporal relationships among and within tasks. Second, treatment of temporal aspects in the previous designs was informal, whereas temporal relations in the UAN help a designer to think a priori about temporally related issues as part of the design process.

7.2   SEQUENCE

Perhaps the simplest temporal relationship between two (or more) tasks is expressed by a *sequence*; one task is performed immediately and entirely after the other. This idea of sequence does not allow any intervening action between two actions in sequence, an observation that is important later in this chapter, when we examine the temporal relations of interleaving and interruption.

In the UAN, a temporal sequence is represented by writing the actions as a spatial sequence horizontally (left to right on the same line) or vertically (top to bottom, from line to line). Chapter 6 showed examples of both. For example, when writing

```
~[file icon] Mv
```

on a line, it is a sequence meaning first to move the cursor to the context of a file icon and then to depress the mouse button.

7.3   COMBINING SMALLER TASKS INTO LARGER ONES

A temporal relation combines pairs, and, more generally, groups of user actions or tasks into a larger single task. This means that whenever two user actions or tasks are connected with a temporal relation, a third task is created. For example,

```
~[file icon]
```

and

```
Mv
```

are each single user actions, but when combined in a sequence,

```
~[file icon] Mv
```

they form a third, new task—in this case, the sequence itself. Any task or grouping of tasks can be enclosed within parentheses. The result is a new task that is composed of the tasks and temporal relations contained within the parentheses. For example, if the preceding sequence

```
~[file icon] Mv
```

were enclosed in parentheses, it would create the new task:

```
(~[file icon] Mv)
```

This task, in turn, can be connected to another task via another temporal relation. The parentheses are generally used for clarity; they do not change the meaning of a task description.

The following definitions summarize the concept of *tasks and how tasks can be combined in the UAN*. Several of these terms and symbols are so far mentioned only in the list of temporal relations in Section 7.1. Each is explained later in this chapter.

- The primitive physical actions on devices described so far are tasks. Examples include all actions, such as ~[icon], Mv^, and so on.
- If A is a task, so are (A), A*, A⁺, <A>, and {A}.
- If A and B are tasks, so are A B, A (t > n) B, A|B, (A|B)*, A&B, A⟹B, A⟺B, and A||B.

By combining smaller tasks into larger ones, a designer can represent the complete task structure for an entire interaction design. The articulatory detail of the design appears only at the bottom-most levels.

7.4   TASK NAMES, MACROS, AND LEVELS OF ABSTRACTION

By the time you read through all the detail for describing simple tasks in Chapter 6, you may have been wondering, "If every task takes this much effort and detail, how will I ever get through a whole design?" The answer is that in Chapter 6, you were operating only at the level of abstraction with the most detail. This lowest level, where all the physical actions appear, is the *articulatory level*. The effort a designer puts into task descriptions at this level is an investment that can be reused. Most of a design represented in UAN is at higher levels of abstraction, where this detail is neither necessary nor visible.

A *task description* written in the UAN is a *set of actions, possibly grouped with parentheses and interspersed with temporal operators,* according to the rules for their use (defined later in this chapter). Each task thus formed can then be named and the name used as a reference to that task. A task name used as a reference to a task is termed a *macro task* because the name is used as a substitute for the whole task description. (Don't allow the analogy to programming macros cause you to forget that these procedures are *performed by the user* in the behavioral domain.) The effect is similar to combining tasks and grouping them with parentheses, as described in the previous section, except that now the resulting task is named. This *name ref-*

erence can be used as a user action in another higher level, or containing, task. The containing task is said to be at a higher level of abstraction because the macro task is only named there; the details of its description are hidden by abstraction at the higher level. A good example of macros, showing these levels of abstraction, is given in the next section, for the task of `delete multiple files`, which follows introduction of the concept of choice, or disjunction.

During a user's performance of a task, a task name in the User Actions column is an invocation of a user-performed procedure, serving two purposes (just as invocations do for procedures in programming). The first purpose is for *abstraction,* to hide details of the procedure; the second is for *instantiation,* to create a task instance. This abstraction operation can be applied repeatedly to build levels of abstraction, allowing the entire interaction design to be organized into a quasi-hierarchical user task structure. Just as in the case of program code, levels of abstraction are necessary in the UAN, for controlling complexity and to promote understanding by its readers and writers.

Because a physical user action is a (primitive) task, and a macro task name can be used as a user action, we use the terms *task* and *user action* interchangeably. They have essentially the same properties within a UAN task structure, except that primitives are not decomposed into more detailed user actions.

Getting back to macros, what else is involved in turning a task description into a macro? To gain the most benefit from packaging these task descriptions into macros, they must be general enough to be *reusable.* For example, the task description for the `select file` task from Chapter 6 can be generalized so that it can be used any time the design calls for a user to select a single object from a set of objects having the same mutually exclusive behavior for ordinary selection. That task description can also be extended to represent selection of lots of different interaction objects—any file icon, a specific file icon, a command icon, a button, and so on. This means that the object must be given parameters; that is, `file` can be made more general by making it a parameter of the task and calling it `object` (or `object'`, so that it is clear that it refers to a specific object, as explained in Chapter 6). Here is what the UAN description for a generalized selection task might look like:

TASK: select(object')	
USER ACTIONS	INTERFACE FEEDBACK
~[object'] Mv	object! ∀object !≠object': object −!
M^	

As an aside, the second line in the Feedback column describes the mutually exclusive property of objects that can be selected using this generic selection task. It says that when one object is highlighted (single selection) via this task, other selected objects (in this class of objects) become unhighlighted. By omitting this line, a different behavior can be specified—for example, one that just keeps adding to the set of highlighted objects as the user clicks on more icons.

When the designer needs to include in a task description the selection of something, such as an "open" command (using an "Open" button), the macro is invoked like this:

```
select(Open button)
```

This binds Open button as the object during instantiation of the select task.

Note that the Interface State column is not included here. In its more general form, the select task does not always cause a change in interface state. For example, selection of a button for a command (e.g., the "open" command) merely causes the command to be executed. There is no state change associated directly with this selection, as there is with the selection of a file.

This variability of the Interface State column information means that it must be factored out of the general form of the select task. Although the Interface State column was not needed for this task description, it would reappear, as needed, in association with an invocation of the select task as a step in another task, such as the following extract of an open file task:

TASK: **open file**		
USER ACTIONS	**INTERFACE FEEDBACK**	**INTERFACE STATE**
select (file icon')		selected = file
.		
.		
.		

One final issue arising in macro tasks is the treatment of feedback. There are no strict rules here; designers are advised to do what is most effective in communicating the design. If all else is equal, articulatory feedback is usually limited to the lowest level and is not included at the macro level. In the preceding example, the open file task is at a higher level of abstraction than that of the select task. It therefore does not show highlighting behavior of the file icon, which was already defined within the select task description. However, in general, it is acceptable to repeat the highlighting behavior in higher-level task descriptions if that will help to clarify the design.

Now that you know about macro task descriptions, you have a very important tool for building task structures. For example, you now can take advantage of a characteristic of top-down development, referring to something you want to have happen in your design before you have worked out the details of how it will happen. For example, you can define a high-level task for adding a new appointment to the Calendar Management System as a sequence of two other tasks, tasks that themselves have not yet been defined:

TASK: **add appointment**
access appointment
edit appointment

To add an appointment to the calendar, the user must first access the appointment (i.e., find day and time slot) and then edit (type, make corrections to) the appointment. Details of the `access appointment` and `edit appointment` tasks, developed later, will tell precisely how these tasks are performed by a user.

7.5   CHOICE

The *choice* relation is a disjunction, or logical "OR." It is used to describe a set of alternative ways to perform a task, or part of a task, from which a user chooses exactly one each time the task is performed. Because just one choice is made from the set of possibilities, the choice relation really corresponds to an exclusive "OR." The choice symbol | represents only the choices offered to the user, not anything about how the user might make the choice. Extensions to the UAN that include cognitive user actions, however, are being considered to describe, and help support in the design, how users make choices and other decisions.

Before introducing the choice symbol to the UAN, let's review the example task to `delete multiple files` from a desktop style interface, given at the end of Chapter 6. This example of choice also shows how task names as abstractions offer modularity, consistency, and reusability. To refresh your memory, here is the `delete multiple files` task description without use of abstraction:

TASK: **delete multiple files**			
USER ACTIONS	INTERFACE FEEDBACK	INTERFACE STATE	CONNECTION TO COMPUTATION
(Sv (~[file icon'] Mv M^)$^+$ S^)$^+$	file icon'-!: file icon'! file icon'!: file icon'-!	selected = selected ∪ file selected = selected - file	
~[file icon''!] Mv			
~[trash icon]	outline(∀file icon'!) > ~ trash icon!		
M^	erase(∀file icon'!) erase(outline(∀file icon'!)) trash icon!!	selected = null	mark selected files for deletion

The double line shows where this task of delete multiple files can be broken to decompose it into two tasks:

1. Select files (the top block in the preceding task description)
2. Delete selected files (the bottom three blocks in the task description)

Both these subtasks may be performed often and might appear as part of other tasks as well. Thus, they are good candidates for making into macros, called, respectively, select multiple files and delete multiple files.

Here is how the overall task description is stated in terms of names for these lower-level tasks, which are then defined, exactly as shown, elsewhere:

TASK: **delete multiple files**
select multiple files
delete selected files

As an aside, when the name of a task appears as a user action in the description of a given task definition, the named task is sometimes termed a *subtask* of the given task. A subtask is just a task; the term is used only when emphasizing the hierarchical relationship between two tasks, in cases where one task is defined in terms of the other. In the preceding example, `select multiple files` and `delete selected files` are subtasks of `delete multiple files`.

Chapter 6 described the task of selecting multiple files using the "Shift" key, as shown in the top block of the preceding detailed task description. That method could be called the `shift multiple select` task. Multiple file selection can also be accomplished in (at least) one other way. A user can drag out, on the desktop, a selection rectangle to enclose or intersect the desired file icons. This method could be called the `drag box multiple select` task. Now we can describe the task of multiple file selection as a choice between two alternative subtasks. This choice is represented in the UAN by the word OR or by a vertical bar (|):

TASK: **select multiple files**
shift multiple select
| drag box multiple select

This example is further expanded and completed in Section 7.14, when we discuss representation techniques to complement the UAN. By now, you can see the advantages of using task macros like this. They make higher-level task descriptions shorter and simpler, hiding details at the lower levels of abstraction. They also promote and support reuse of task descriptions and consistency across an interaction design.

7.6   REPEATING CHOICE

Combining the OR or choice, described in the previous section with the UAN iteration symbols * and + yields a combination used often enough to have its own name, the *repeating choice*. To start with,

(A|B|C)

denotes a single task that is a three-way choice among the user actions or tasks A, B, and C. To perform this choice task, a user chooses and performs one of the three tasks, and that is all that happens. Suppose, however, that the designer wants a user to be able to repeat this choice task—that is, to be able to choose a task from A, B, or C, perform it, choose one again, and so on. This could be the situation at a high level of design if, for example, A, B, and C are choices among major system functions. To represent this in UAN, the designer uses a repeating choice:

(A | B | C) *

The repeating choice is interpreted in the following way. First, the ordinary choice inside the parentheses means that tasks A, B, and C are simultaneously and equally available. The * means, as usual, that the whole phrase inside the parentheses (the choice itself) is performed zero or more times. Once a task from the choice is begun, it is performed to completion (a kind of modality), at which time the three tasks are equally available again. The cycle continues for as long as one of the three tasks is selected by a user and performed to completion.

To see how this notation can be used as a compact high-level description for a choice among major system functions, try it out on the Calendar Management System. Recalling, from Chapter 5, the five basic functions of the Calendar Management System, the highest-level task in this system can be defined as a repeating choice among tasks corresponding to these main user operations:

TASK: **manage calendar**
(access appointment
| add appointment
| update appointment
| delete appointment
| establish alarm) +

The use of + here, as opposed to *, illustrates a fine point—to rule out the case of a user performing the contents of the parentheses zero times, because that is the same as not performing the manage calendar task at all.

This kind of repeating choice can be implemented as a pull-down menu, for example. When the system in launched, the user is initially faced with a choice among these basic functions. When the user makes a choice, that function is carried to completion, and the user returns to the main menu, where the same choice for all functions is available again.

A repeating choice is also used in the access appointment task definition, as we begin to decompose this subtask for the manage calendar task:

TASK: **access appointment**	
USER ACTIONS	**INTERFACE STATE**
(search	
| access month	
| access week	
| access day) *	
access time slot	view level = time slot

This example shows how easy it is to use temporal relations to represent very specific combinations of tasks. The access appointment task is a sequence of two parts: the first part of the sequence is a repeating choice (in the parentheses), and the second-part is the access time slot task. If a system log were to record observable user behavior in performing the access appointment task it would record a series of zero or more instances from among its four subtasks of search, access month, access week, and access day, ending with a single instance of the access time slot subtask. This leaves the state of the view level at the time slot level.

Note that because these are higher-level tasks, interface feedback is not described here. Rather, it is detailed at lower levels, and so the Interface Feedback column has been omitted. You could have left that column in the task description and simply left it empty, if you wished.

7.7   ORDER INDEPENDENCE

In the use of interactive computer systems, as in the world in general, it is not uncommon to find situations where a number of tasks are to be performed, but the order of their performance is immaterial. Such tasks are represented in the UAN as an *order-independent* group. In this situation, a user must perform all the actions of the group, and each one must be completed before another is begun. There is no constraint on specific ordering among the actions. The UAN symbol to connect order-independent tasks or user actions is the & (ampersand). An example of order independence at the articulatory level is seen in the task of entering a command-X to delete some selected object(s) in many Macintosh™ applications. This is a combination of the ⌘ and X keys. because the ⌘ key must be depressed before the X key, but the order of their release does not matter, the task is defined in UAN as:

```
┌──────────────────────────────┐
│ TASK:  command-X             │
├──────────────────────────────┤
│   v Xv (  ^ & X^)            │
└──────────────────────────────┘
```

The `edit appointment` task provides an example of order independence in the Calendar Management System. Suppose that an appointment object has text fields for name of person, description of appointment, and location. The task of editing an appointment breaks down into the set of tasks for editing these smaller objects, but the order in which they are edited does not matter:

```
┌──────────────────────────────┐
│ TASK: edit appointment       │
├──────────────────────────────┤
│  view level = time slot:     │
├──────────────────────────────┤
│   (edit person               │
├──────────────────────────────┤
│   & edit description         │
├──────────────────────────────┤
│   & edit location)           │
└──────────────────────────────┘
```

7.8   INTERRUPTION

There are several ways in which tasks can be interrupted by other tasks, as the following subsections illustrate.

7.8.1   One Task Interrupting Another

Once a user begins a task, that task does not necessarily remain active until it is completed. One way that a task can become inactive is due to interruption by another task. An interruption occurs when the user and system activity of one task are suspended before that task is completed, and activity of another task is begun in its place. Task interruption often occurs due to actions initiated by the user, but it can also be the result of system-initiated actions (e.g., to update a clock or to announce the arrival of electronic mail).

7.8.2   Interruptibility

Because a design representation is intensional—that is, it describes what can happen rather that what does happen in any specific instance, there is no symbol in the UAN for *is interrupted by*. Rather, there is a temporal operator to denote cases of *interruptibility*, situations where interruption *can* occur. While order independence relaxes the sequentiality constraint, *interruptibility* goes even further by removing the constraint of one task having to be performed to completion before beginning another task. Interruptibility allows one task to be interrupted by another and then returned to later for completion.

In UAN, the symbol → denotes that one task can interrupt another. For example, the expression

```
help  →  edit document
```

represents the ability of the user to interrupt the document-editing task with a help task; literally read from the UAN, `help` can interrupt `edit   document`. In practical terms, this means that a user can invoke the help task at any time during editing, but closure of the help task is required before editing can continue. This ability to be interrupted naturally suggests the need to develop the notation used to express exceptions to interruptibility.

7.8.3   Uninterruptible Tasks

Sometimes a user interaction designer needs to define exceptions within some scope of interruptibility. That is, although a particular task is generally interruptible, there may be a couple of cases when it is important to prevent interruption. One kind of exception occurs when the user action in question is a primitive. For example, a designer should not have to think about another task interrupting the primitive user action of pushing down the mouse button; either the button was pushed or it was not. Thus, primitive user actions are generally defined as not interruptible.

A second situation where a task instance must be specified as uninterruptible occurs in preemptive (modal) interface features (Thimbleby, 1990). Certain kinds of dialogue boxes provide a good example. For example, while using a dialogue box in task A, a user cannot click in the window of task B to change tasks until the dialogue box is exited. While in the dialogue box, a user can still interleave tasks, but only among tasks available from within the dialogue box. In the UAN, angle brackets, < and >, are used to enclose those parts of a task description that are *uninterruptible* by other user actions at any level. For example, `<use dialogue box>` denotes that this task cannot be interrupted by any other user task.

7.9   INTERLEAVABILITY

Two tasks are *interleavable* if and only if they can interrupt each other. In practical terms, this means that a user can do part of one task, skip to another task and do part of it, then return to do more of the first task, and so on. Interleavability is represented in UAN with the ⟷ symbol, as in the following example from a desktop publishing application:

```
edit document text ⟷ create graphics
```

As an example from the Calendar Management System, consider the five main user operations discussed earlier as subtasks of the main task, manage calendar. As a reminder, those subtasks are access appointment, add appointment, update appointment, delete appointment, and establish alarm. In Section 7.6, these were represented as a repeating choice. A more asynchronous design would allow an instance of each subtask to be created in its own window. A user could go back and forth, interleaving the activity among instances of the subtasks by activating one window after another, say, by clicking in each window. The UAN task description for this interleaved design is:

TASK: **manage calendar**
(access appointment
⟷ add appointment
⟷ update appointment
⟷ delete appointment
⟷ establish alarm)⁺

Note once again use of the $^+$ to indicate that the entire construct can be repeated, allowing multiple instances of the same task and/or different tasks at once.

7.10   CONCURRENCY

With interleavability, user actions can be alternated among tasks; with *concurrency*, user actions for two or more tasks can occur simultaneously; that is, their physical actions overlap in time. Concurrency is a temporal relation that has not been greatly exploited in user interfaces. Nevertheless, there are cases in which it is possible and, indeed, preferable, for a user to carry out more than one task at the same time. For example, a user can be perceptually responsive to information on the display while typing or manipulating the mouse. Buxton has described input techniques that rely on concurrent use of both hands (Buxton, 1983). Such situations require the full representational power of the concurrency relation as just described.

Another kind of concurrency is seen in the actions of two or more users doing computer-supported cooperative work, or CSCW. These users, using different workstations, may be able to perform actions simultaneously on shared instances of application objects, possibly operating through different views.

The UAN symbol to represent a design that allows users to perform tasks concurrently is a symbol that implies parallelism—namely, ||. For a representation of the Calendar Management System in the case where periods of activity among tasks can overlap, the UAN task description becomes:

TASK: **manage calendar**
(access appointment
|| add appointment
|| update appointment
|| delete appointment
|| establish alarm)$^{+}$

7.11   INTERVALS AND WAITING

Time intervals are also important in task descriptions. For example, the prose description for a double click of a mouse button might tell a user to click the mouse button and immediately click it again. If the designer really wished to be precise, it requires the expression of a constraint on the time interval between clicks. In such cases where the time between user actions (e.g., clicks) is significant in a task description, the timing interval acts as a temporal relation between the actions, constraining the temporal distance between actions in a sequence. This task can be represented precisely in the UAN. The complete UAN task description for double clicking is

```
Mv^  (t<n)  Mv^
```

where t is the time between mouse clicks, and n is a numeric value in units of time (e.g., seconds). Often the value of n can be controlled by the user via a control panel setting, and an appropriate default setting can be empirically determined by developers.

Another way a time interval can be used in a UAN description as a temporal relation between two tasks is to indicate a minimum wait time to cause some kind of timeout by the system. A specific instance might be written as

```
Task1 (t > 5 seconds) Task2
```

7.12   SUMMARY OF UAN SYMBOLS

Tables 7.2 and 7.3 summarize the UAN symbols presented in Chapter 6 and this chapter. Table 7.2 summarizes all the temporal relations among user tasks discussed thus far, as well as all other UAN symbols currently in use in the UAN. The symbols in Table 7.2 are used in the User Actions column. The symbols for the basic physical user actions are at the lowest level of abstraction. Table 7.3 summarizes the symbols used in the Interface Feedback column. All symbols are suggested, in the sense that the UAN is, as discussed in Chapter 6, an open notation, often adapted and extended by interaction designers.

7.13   EXERCISES ON USING UAN

Now that you have been reading about the UAN, as well as seeing examples of it and doing small exercises for almost two chapters, it's time for you to try out the UAN yourself on your own Calendar Management System design. In the next several exercises, you will get practice in using the UAN for interaction representations in the design developed for the Calendar Management System in Chapter 5. At the end of this chapter, you will then write UAN descriptions for your own Calendar Management System design. Feel free to look back through this chapter and Chapter 6 to review the UAN, as needed, while doing the exercises. Most people learn the UAN pretty fast, with a little practice.

Much of the UAN representation of our Calendar Management System design has already appeared a bit at a time, as examples illustrating various aspects of the UAN. This set of exercises will pull it together into one place.

Exercise—High-Level Design Representation Using UAN

GOAL: To use the UAN to begin developing a behavioral representation of user tasks in the Calendar Management System's interaction design produced in Chapter 5, at the high levels of design.

MINIMUM TIME: About 10 minutes.

TABLE 7.2. UAN SYMBOLS FOR THE USER ACTIONS COLUMN.

What is Represented	UAN Symbols	Meaning
Cursor movement	~	move the cursor
Object context	[X]	the context of object X, the "handle" by which X is manipulated
Cursor movement	~[X]	move cursor into context of object X
Cursor movement	~[x,y]	move cursor to (arbitrary) point x,y
Cursor movement	~[x,y]*	move cursor to zero or more (arbitrary) points x,y
Cursor movement	~[x',y']	move cursor to specific point x',y'
Cursor movement	~[x,y in A]	move cursor to (arbitrary) point within object A
Cursor movement	~[X in Y]	move to object X within object Y
Cursor movement	[X]~	move cursor out of context of object X
Switch operation	v	depress
Switch operation	^	release
Switch operation	Xv	depress button, key, or switch X
Switch operation	X ^	release button, key, or switch X
Switch operation	Xv^	idiom for clicking button, key, or switch X
String value	K"abc"	enter literal string, abc, via device K
String value	K(xyz)	enter value for variable xyz via device K
Grouping	( )	grouping mechanism
Sequence	A B	tasks A and B are performed in order left to right, or top to bottom
Repetition	A*	task A is performed zero or more times
Repetition	A+	task A is performed one or more times
Repetition	A^n	task A is performed exactly n times
Optionality	{A}	enclosed task is optional (task A is performed zero or one time)
Choice	| , OR	choice of tasks (used to show alternative ways to perform a task)
Repeating choice	(A | B)*	choice of A or B is performed to completion, followed by another choice of A or B, etc.
Order independence	A & B	tasks A and B are order independent (order of their performance is immaterial)
Interruptibility	A → B	task A can interrupt task B
Uninterruptibility	<A>	task A cannot be interrupted
Interleavability	A ⇔ B	performance of tasks A and B can be interleaved in time
Concurrency	A || B	task A and task B can be performed simultaneously
Waiting	A (t > n) B	task B is performed after a delay of more than n units of time following task A

ACTIVITIES: Write a UAN task description for manage calendar, the task at the highest level of abstraction in the Calendar Management System. This task description should allow users to interleave major subtasks.

DELIVERABLES: One UAN task description for manage calendar, with appropriate temporal relations.

TABLE 7.3. UAN SYMBOLS FOR THE INTERFACE FEEDBACK COLUMN.

What is Represented	UAN Symbols	Meaning
Highlight	!	highlight object
Unhighlight	-!	unhighlight object
Highlight	!!	same as !, but use a different highlight
Location	@x',y'	at point x',y' (e.g., to display X)
Location	@X	at object X
Location	@x',y' in X	at point x',y' in object X
Display	display(X)	display object X
Erase	erase(X)	erase object X
Redisplay	redisplay(X)	erase X and display X again (in new location)
Outline	outline(X)	outline of object X
Dragging	X > ~	object X follows (is dragged by) cursor
Rubberbanding	X >> ~	object X is rubber-banded as its follows cursor
For all	∀	for all (e.g., ∀icons)

CAUTION: Many people, when beginning task descriptions, get involved in low-level details. The high-level descriptions are actually easier and are very important; they often form the bulk of your UAN design representation, and they bring task analysis and design together. Don't overdo on this exercise. This step takes lots of time for a real system, and it overlaps with task analysis and design, too.

Possible Exercise Solution

Because we wish, in our design, to let a user interleave tasks at the highest level, the UAN task description begins something like this, which is a group of previously shown interleaved tasks:

TASK: **manage calendar**
(access appointment
⟷ add appointment
⟷ update appointment
⟷ delete appointment
⟷ establish alarm)^t

Interleaving (⟷) and repetition (+) are the primary temporal relations in this task description. This means that the user can perform the set of tasks that appear within the parentheses one or more times. The expression within the parentheses is represented at runtime by a set of interleaved instances of the access appointment, add appointment, update appointment, delete appointment, and establish alarm tasks.

Exercise—Developing More Detail in Design Representations Using UAN

GOAL: To use the UAN to represent some middle-level user tasks.

MINIMUM TIME: About 10 minutes.

ACTIVITIES: Think about how you might successively decompose some of the subtasks from the previous exercise. Write a UAN task description for access appointment. As already shown, this involves tasks such as searching and accessing various view levels of the calendar. Because these subtasks really aren't interleavable, you will need a different temporal relation.

DELIVERABLES: One UAN task description for access appointment, with appropriate temporal relations.

Possible Exercise Solution

The subtask breakdown of the `access appointment` task might be described in the UAN as the group of disjoint subtasks shown here:

TASK: **access appointment**	
USER ACTIONS	**INTERFACE STATE**
(search	
| access month	
| access week	
| access day)*	
access time slot	view level = time slot

As stated previously, it doesn't make much sense to think of interleaving `access month`, `access week`, and `access day`. For example, if a user is in the month view level, any attempt at user actions involved in the `access week` task would change the current view level to the week level, and so the `access month` task would no longer be active. So the repeating choice is more realistic and accurate in describing the temporal relation among these `access appointment` subtasks. To access an appointment, then, this task description specifies that the user does any number of `search`, `access month`, `access week`, and `access day` tasks, followed sequentially by a single `access time slot` task (time slots can be considered as containers of appointments).

Exercise—Further Detail in Design Representations Using UAN

GOAL: To use the UAN to represent another middle-level user task.

MINIMUM TIME: About 15 minutes.

ACTIVITIES: Write a UAN task description for the `access month` task. This involves establishing the month level as the current view level and navigating back and forth among months. To establish the month view level, a user must select some (any) month from the screen. Use a parameterized invocation of a general `select` macro task to represent user selection of a month in the calendar.

DELIVERABLES: UAN task descriptions for `access month` and for `select(object)`, with appropriate temporal relations.

Possible Exercise Solution

The `access month` task description should look something like the following:

TASK: **access month**	
USER ACTIONS	**INTERFACE STATE**
(select(any month)	view level = month
| move forward by month	
| move backward by month)⁺	

The first subtask, `select(any month)`, allows a user to make the month view the current view level. By selecting a month on the screen, a user has instantiated the `select(object)` task, defined next. In this instantiation, the month object conceptually substituted for the `object` parameter, using the following task description for `select`:

TASK: **select(object)**		
USER ACTIONS	INTERFACE FEEDBACK	INTERFACE STATE
~[object icon'-!] Mv	object icon'!	selected = object
M^		

Exercise—More Practice with UAN

GOAL: To represent a couple more middle-level tasks.

MINIMUM TIME: About 10 minutes.

ACTIVITIES: Write a UAN task description for `access time slot`. This is similar to the `access month` task except that an initial condition of viability is added to ensure that the view is at the day level (you may remember this from Chapter 6). The user can then scroll up or down, finally selecting a time slot.

Next, write a task description for the `add appointment` task. This one is very brief.

HINT: Start by accessing an appointment, then editing it.

DELIVERABLES: UAN task descriptions for `access time slot` and `add appointment`.

Possible Exercise Solution

The `access time slot` task is a continuation of our decomposition of the `access appointment` task. It might look something like this:

TASK: **access time slot**	
USER ACTIONS	INTERFACE STATE
view level = day:	
((scroll up | scroll down)*	
select(any time slot))	view level = time slot

As you may recall from the discussion in Chapter 6, this task begins with a *condition of viability* requiring the view level for navigation to be at the day level. The current view level value is kept as interface state information. Each task that accesses a view level will reset the current value of the view level state, as shown in the preceding task description.

Next is the second task of the highest-level task, `manage calendar`—namely, the task for adding a new appointment. Its UAN description could be as simple as:

TASK: **add appointment**
access appointment
edit appointment

Notice how you can build on the `access appointment` task here, applying abstraction, as the details of task decomposition slowly unfold.

We will skip the two tasks of `update appointment` and `delete appointment`, since they are very similar to the ones we've just done. Now look at the last of the five tasks in the `manage calendar` task.

Exercise—Connecting to the Articulatory Level of the UAN

GOAL: To represent near-articulatory level tasks.

MINIMUM TIME: About 20 minutes.

ACTIVITIES: Write a UAN task description for the `establish alarm` task, to notify a user when an appointment is impending. A user must initially be at the time slot view level. The first part of establishing an alarm is to set the alarm, associating it with a specific time slot or appointment. This can be followed with a subtask for setting the alarm parameters (e.g., lead time for notification).

You are also to write a UAN description at the articulatory level for the set alarm task. A user accomplishes this association of an alarm with a time slot by dragging a copy of the alarm icon (from the top of the screen in Figure 5.3) to the desired time slot.

DELIVERABLES: UAN task descriptions for establish alarm and for set alarm.

Possible Exercise Solution

The establish alarm task description might look something like this:

TASK: **establish alarm**
view level = time slot:
(set alarm
set alarm parameters)

As pointed out in Chapter 6, the condition of viability in the first line ensures that there is a current appointment (or at least a specific time slot) with which to associate the alarm. The second line is a macro that establishes the association of an alarm with the appointment in that time slot. The third line is the macro for setting the alarm parameters, such as alarm lead time (how far in advance of an appointment to sound the alarm), perhaps by means of a dialogue box.

In the Calendar Management System design, the set alarm task is accomplished by dragging a copy of the alarm icon from the upper left-hand corner of the screen to the time slot of the appointment. You might want to look back at the screen design in Figure 5.3 and see the alarm clock icon. This task can be written in UAN as:

TASK: **set alarm**		
USER ACTIONS	**INTERFACE FEEDBACK**	**INTERFACE STATE**

view level = time slot:
  (~[alarm icon]
  Mv
	alarm icon-!: alarm icon!	set alarm mode = on

~[time slot']	outline(copy(alarm icon)) > ~ time slot'!	
M^)	@x',y' in time slot' display(copy(alarm icon))	set alarm mode = off

The first line here contains a condition of viability for the whole task. The feedback for the action of releasing the mouse button (M^) in the last block indicates that a copy of the alarm icon is affixed to the appointment display at a specific point x', y' (e.g., in the upper left corner) relative to the appointment itself.

This is the last task description we will develop for the Calendar Management System. The tasks already completed offer a start on the quasi-hierarchical task structure, as shown in Figure 7.1.

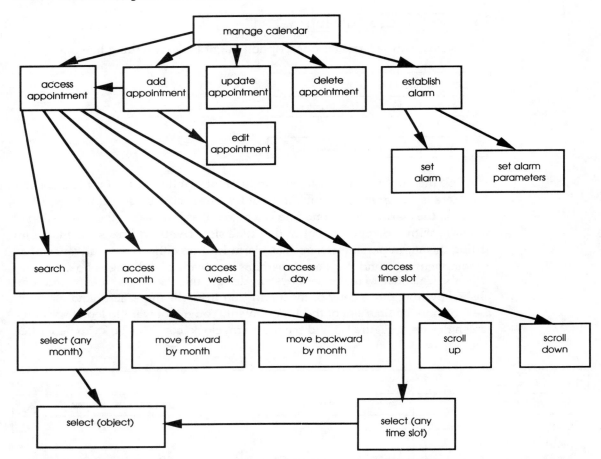

Figure 7.1. Beginnings of a quasi-hierarchical task structure for the Calendar Management System.

7.14   SUPPLEMENTARY REPRESENTATION TECHNIQUES

The UAN is effective in precisely and concisely describing user tasks. This is an important part of interaction design representation, but it is not complete. In addition, it is useful to complement UAN task descriptions with screen pictures and scenarios, interface state transition diagrams, and design rationale descriptions. Let's look at how we might use each of these other representation techniques in the Calendar Management System design.

7.14.1 Screen Pictures and Scenarios

The UAN is intended for describing user actions in the context of interaction objects, along with feedback and state information. Because the UAN does not show the appearance of screens and screen objects, it needs to be supplemented with pictures. For example, wherever the Interface Feedback column contains a description of something that is displayed, it usually should have a note that says, "See Figure XYZ," and Figure XYZ should accompany the design document. That is, UAN task descriptions should be supplemented with a set of screen pictures, such as the ones shown for the scenario designs in Chapter 5.

The following example, from the end of Section 7.5, continues the example of the task to `select multiple files`. One way this task allows a user to select is by dragging out a selection box to intersect or enclose the desired file icons. Section 7.5 didn't show visually how that would be done by a user. This could be difficult for an interface implementer to understand, even if it is completely and correctly written in UAN. Let's continue that example by using a screen sketch to accompany the UAN task description and clarify the design. Consider the following description of a task for selecting multiple files by dragging out a selection box:

TASK: **drag box multiple select**		
USER ACTIONS	INTERFACE FEEDBACK	INTERFACE STATE
~[x',y'] Mv		x',y' is fixed corner of rectangle
~[x',y']*	dotted rectangle >> ~ **See figure "selection rectangle"**	

~[x'',y''] M^	objects intersected and
	enclosed by rectangle are !
		selected = all
		  intersected and
		  enclosed objects

Notice the note in the Interface Feedback column referring to the figure called "selection rectangle." This figure would be part of the scenario design and would appear somewhat like Figure 7.2.

Note that the screen picture of Figure 7.2, showing an example layout of screen objects surrounded by the drag box (the dotted rectangle), is also annotated with

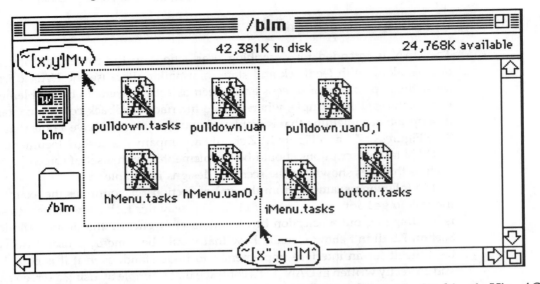

Figure 7.2. Scenario figure called "selection rectangle" From Hartson, Siochi, & Hix, *ACM Transactions on Information Systems*, p. 168. © 1990. Reprinted by permission.

UAN descriptions. Often UAN symbols can enhance the descriptive power of a screen picture by describing accompanying user actions.

7.14.2 Interface State Transition Diagrams

Many user interaction designs have lots of interface states. Often, the states are viewed by a user as modes. While the UAN has a column for Interface State, this often is not enough to represent a clear global picture of states and state transitions in an interaction design. Section 4.3 stated that early design activities can involve producing a state transition diagram to indicate sequencing and state or mode information. Indeed, it can be useful to supplement UAN task descriptions with *interface state transition diagrams*.

The different views within the Calendar Management System are modes. The way a user gets back and forth among them is by user actions that cause state transitions. The relationships among the views, and their corresponding modes, are not necessarily easy to see from individual task descriptions or scenario designs, so this provides an opportunity for us to improve the communication power of our design representations.

Exercise—Design Representation Using A State Transition Diagram

GOAL: To produce an interface state transition diagram to supplement the UAN task descriptions and scenario designs as a more complete set of design representations of the Calendar Management System.

MINIMUM TIME: About 30 minutes.

ACTIVITIES: Sketch a state transition diagram with the various views (which are states or modes of some kind in your design) as nodes, and with user actions that take a user to different modes or states as arcs.

DELIVERABLES: A state transition diagram drawn out on paper.

Possible Exercise Solution

Navigation among views within the Calendar Management System interaction design is shown in the diagram of Figure 7.3. There is clearly more than one possible correct solution, so your state transition diagram for the Calendar Management System design may differ from this one.

In this state transition diagram, the "START" arrow indicates that the month view is the default view; when the system is brought up, the month view is on top and therefore visible to a user. It is also easy to see in this diagram that, once in the month view, a user can go forward and backward among months. The same is true for the week and day views, going forward and backward among weeks and days, respectively. A user gets from either the month view or the day view to the week view by selecting any week. If some instance of a week is visible on the desktop, a user can click on it and bring it to the top, making the week view current. The month, week, and day views are identical with respect to all these navigational operations.

The day view has some additional features. This is the only view from which a user can move, by clicking on any time slot, to the time slot view, where appointments are kept. From here, a user can move to the type/edit state simply by typing on the keyboard. A user can return to the month, week, or day view from either the time slot view or the type/edit state by selecting (clicking on) any month, week, or day that is available from the desktop.

7.14.3 Design Rationale Descriptions

Because the design representation is a working document, as well as the means for communication among developer roles, designers would be wise to include, as part of the interaction design representation, their *design rationale*—comments about trade-offs they have faced and reasons behind their design decisions. These comments supplement UAN task descriptions, scenarios, and state diagrams, as a more complete representation of interaction designs. In an iterative development process involving several people in various roles, it is important to know *why* a certain design feature was used (and why others were rejected). If the feature itself fails in usability testing, the people in charge of redesign must understand the original goal of the feature. At a later time, the maintenance process also benefits from information on design decisions, often preventing repetition of an unsuccessful design previously tried and rejected by designers.

Implementers and evaluators also use design rationale descriptions to comment as early as possible on the design. Implementers are in the best position to estimate the cost of implementing certain features; evaluators must document their reasons

<u>VIEW LEVEL NAVIGATION</u>

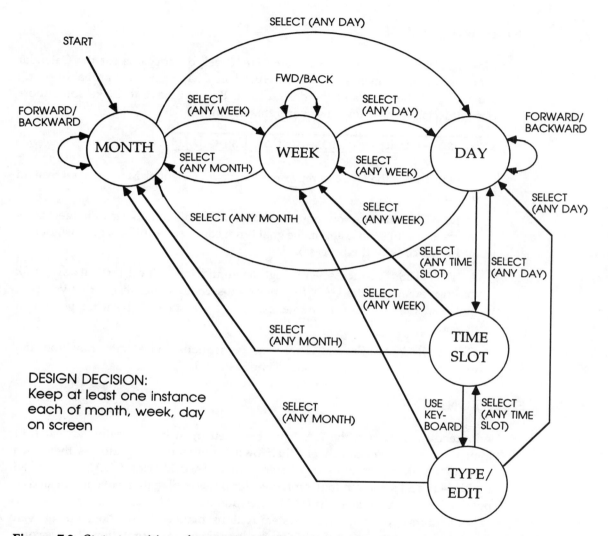

Figure 7.3. State transitions for navigating among views of the Calendar Management System. Adapted from Hartson & Gray, *Human-Computer Interaction*, pp. 1–45. © 1992. Reprinted by permission.

for suggested design changes. We do not offer any special notation for recording these decisions; use prose in whatever level of detail you deem necessary. Then, like screen sketches and figures, these descriptions can be referred to directly within any UAN task description to which they might be relevant.

7.15 FINAL UAN EXERCISE

Now it is time for you to write some UAN task descriptions for the Calendar Management System design you produced in Chapter 5. You probably didn't work out all the details of the design then. You will have to make some more design decisions now for those parts that are incomplete.

Exercise—Design Representation Using UAN

GOAL: To use the UAN to represent your own Calendar Management System design.

MINIMUM TIME: About one hour (obviously, this can take a lot longer; do as much as you like; once again, the goal is not complete solutions, but insight into and practice with the process).

ACTIVITIES: Produce several high-level and lower-level (articulatory) task descriptions using the UAN for your own scenarios and design that you produced in the exercise of Chapter 5. Also, try a state diagram for your own design.

DELIVERABLES: Several UAN task descriptions and a state transition diagram for your Calendar Management System design.

7.16 EXTENSIONS TO THE UAN

As already mentioned, the UAN has been left open intentionally, so that user interaction designers can invent their own UAN features to address their own particular task representation problems. In real-world use of UAN, almost all UAN users add a column for Comments, for prose explanations of complicated or potentially confusing steps in UAN descriptions.

Some users add a column for System Actions, making the relationship between system and user more symmetric in the interaction representation. This accommodates the need to represent actions that occur autonomously (not in response to a user action) within the system, but that have feedback in the interface to let a user know they have happened. For example, the system might need to announce the arrival of new mail or might simply need to update the display of a clock.

Some other extensions have also been tried. As the UAN has been presented here, user actions are limited to physical actions such as keystrokes and mouse movement. It could also be argued that the Interface Feedback column, which shows the system response to user actions, corresponds closely to desired perceptual actions of the user. To further support task analysis, columns sometimes have been added for user intentions and goals. Adding columns for cognitive actions, such as memory actions (e.g., recall, memory loading, closure) and decision making, have been done, to direct designs in supporting users' cognitive needs during task performance. This comes under the heading of ongoing research.

7.17   SOFTWARE TOOLS FOR UAN SUPPORT

It is obvious to most users of the UAN that its use could be greatly enhanced through software support tools. We (and others) are exploring a number of different tools to support the use of UAN in interaction design. The most fundamental UAN support tool is a UAN editor that developers can use to enter their interaction designs into the rows and columns of a UAN table. This aspect of the tool is similar to an engineering spreadsheet with simple text editing inside each cell and the ability to set the size of a row or column. Graphics editing facilitates development of screen pictures and scenarios. Finally, hypertext connections help a designer automate references from UAN descriptions to notes, figures, and state diagrams. The tool also supports some customization of UAN, such as the addition of new columns.

This UAN tool is part of a larger integrated set of tools to serve as a broad user interface development environment. This larger environment is called the Interface Development Environment and Analysis Lattice, or IDEAL; it will eventually have components to support much of the development work that occurs in the behavioral domain, including systems analysis, design and design representation, rapid prototyping, usability specifications, and formative evaluation. IDEAL is discussed in more detail in Chapter 10, on formative evaluation. Other tools presently being considered for UAN support include tools for analytic evaluation of interface usability, code generation and translation, and generation of end-user documentation from UAN task descriptions.

7.18   EXPERIENCE WITH THE UAN

As mentioned in Chapter 6, when we first began developing the UAN, we were doing it for our own internal need to communicate behavioral descriptions of interaction designs to implementers for construction and to evaluators for a preprototype view of the design. We used the UAN to conduct walk-throughs of the interaction design, and to check implementation against the design. We estimated that approximately 80% of the design of one system was implemented exactly as specified in UAN. Of the 20% that did not conform to the UAN design, 10% was due to misinterpretation of the UAN by the implementers, and 10% was due to their simply not wanting to implement it as represented. Other teams that have used the UAN report similar results.

To determine more about the usefulness of the UAN, we have promoted its use in commercial, government, and academic user interface development environments. The UAN has been used for the design of a telephone interface. A large government agency used the UAN to represent samples of a desired look and feel in a request for proposals (RFP) and to represent some prototype designs (Hix, Hartson, Siochi, & Ruppert, 1993). An interaction designer at a military installation, struggling through a several-inch-thick stack of human–computer interaction guidelines, used the UAN to document these guidelines precisely and to prevent repeated rereading of many lines of prose.

The UAN was also used to represent several multimedia interfaces involving full-motion video and audio for a digital video interactive (DVI) application being developed for a commercial company. Another multimedia system, called Project Envision, involves a database of computer science literature, including full text, audio and video clips, and animated algorithms. Interaction designs for a user interface management system and some interactive systems in Project DRUID at the University of Glasgow (Scotland) have been represented with the UAN. An interaction designer in Britain also used it to describe precisely what happens during a complex scrolling-in-a-window task for a new design. Designers at a commercial company used the UAN for the interface of a graphical editor. A data flow configuration system has been designed with the UAN at the Jet Propulsion Laboratory.

The UAN has been used by a producer of large-scale commercial security systems, such as might be used in airports and banks. The UAN was introduced into this project after a first design was complete (according to the designers). A number of significant design deficiencies were discovered while reverse engineering that design into UAN from the 400⁺-page prose-and-pictures design document. This caused the development team to rethink task analysis and to do substantial redesign. The UAN was also used as a review and presentation technique for walk-throughs during development. One of the development team members translated UAN task descriptions directly into user documentation. This diversity of uses of the UAN indicates the broad range of interaction styles it can represent.

The UAN has proven to be effective in conveying large and complex user interaction designs from designers to implementers and evaluators. The UAN has been found by many of its users to be expressive and highly readable because of its *simplicity*, natural enough so that it is *easily read and written with very little training*. In a typical training session, participants are reading UAN within half an hour and writing simple UAN task descriptions within one hour. In places where hands-on training for UAN has not been possible, developers have been provided with a tutorial containing much less detail than in Chapter 6 and this chapter, and they have picked up an adequate amount of UAN to get started.

User interaction developers find UAN symbols and idioms to be *mnemonic* and *intuitive*. Perhaps more important, they like the *thoroughness* of the descriptions and feel that it *facilitates communication* among interaction designers and implementers. They find it to be *precise, concise*, and easily *extensible*, as needed for their particular environment.

Among the negative comments are concerns that UAN descriptions may be too detailed to be used early in the design process, when too much specificity may limit a designer's creativity. One or two developers have commented that the symbols should be more expressive (e.g., they wanted to change the ~ to MOVE TO), or that the symbols or columns did not allow them to fully represent their design. For this reason, you should feel free to extend and customize UAN symbols, columns, or any other feature, so that the UAN technique will more completely support your own individual user interaction design needs during representation.

7.19   SUMMARY

Now that you have worked your way through two chapters on the UAN, you should have a much better appreciation for why such a behavioral design representation technique is needed in the user interaction development process. Now you can see how the precision of the UAN can help you alleviate many of the problems of ambiguity and incompleteness that are inherent in other design representation techniques, particularly prose. Regardless of the number of people on your interface development team (even if it's just you), you need some sort of technique for capturing designs as a record of decisions and for handing them over to a programmer. Even if you do the programming, too, you need a record of what you designed when it is time to implement the user interface.

If you feel you do not need the detail offered by the UAN for your entire interaction designs, perhaps you will find it useful for representing at least some portions of your designs. Some serious UAN users use mostly the levels above the articulation level, leaving the articulation level to widget definitions. We welcome feedback on your use of the UAN, and any suggestions you might have for its extension.

REFERENCES

Buxton, W. (1983). Lexical and Pragmatic Considerations of Input Structures. *Computer Graphics, 17*(1), 31–37.

Hartson, H. R., & Gray, P. (1992). Temporal Aspects of Tasks in the User Action Notation. *Human-Computer Interaction, 7,* 1–45.

Hix, D., Hartson, H. R., Siochi, A. C., & Ruppert, D. (1993). The Customer's Responsibility for Ensuring Usability: Requirements on the User Interface Development Process. To appear in *Journal of Systems and Software.*

Thimbleby, H. (1990). *User Interface Design.* New York: ACM Press/Addison-Wesley.

≡ 8

Usability Specification
Techniques

8.1   WHAT ARE USABILITY SPECIFICATIONS?

The activities described thus far pertain to the early phases of user interaction development—namely, systems (functional, task, and user) analysis, design (conceptual, scenario, and detailed), and design representation. Recall that each of these activities was part of the iterative refinement process represented in the star life cycle presented in Chapter 4. A pivotal activity in developing a user interface—and one that is often overlooked, either because of lack of knowledge or lack of time—is establishing *usability specifications*—quantitative usability goals, that are used as a guide for knowing when an interface is good enough.

This chapter presents techniques for specifying interface usability requirements. These usability specifications should be established as early as possible in the development process. Usability attributes, as target levels for usability, are operationally defined criteria for success of the user interface. They are key in determining usability of an interactive system, by providing a metric against which usability of the present version of a user interface can be measured.

Usability specifications also give an indication of whether the development process is converging toward a successful interface. The user-centered evaluation and iterative refinement approach, which is the theme of this book, guarantees that an interaction design will change from one iteration to the next, but without some sort of usability metric, it does not guarantee that the changes will result in an interface that is more usable than the interface of the previous iteration. In fact, without usability goals and metrics, it is impossible to assess the usability of any version of the interface. *By establishing usability specifications early in the development process, and monitoring them at each iteration, you can determine whether your interface is, indeed, converging toward an improved, more usable design.*

This chapter discusses how to establish usability specifications, and Chapter 10 details how to use those specifications during formative evaluation, to help ensure the usability of a user interface.

8.2   EXAMPLE OF A USABILITY SPECIFICATION TABLE

The concept of formal attribute specification in tabular form, with various metrics operationally defining success, was developed by Gilb (1981). The focus of Gilb's work was use of measurements in managing software development resources. Bennett (1984) adapted this approach to usability specifications as a technique for setting planned levels and managing development to meet those levels.

These ideas were refined and integrated into the usability engineering concept in Good, Spine, Whiteside, and George (1986) and in Whiteside, Bennett, and Holtzblatt (1988). *Usability engineering*, as defined in Good et al. (1986), is a process through which usability characteristics are specified, quantitatively and early in the development process, and measured throughout the process. Carroll and Rosson (1985) also stressed the need for quantifiable usability specifications, associated with appropriate benchmark tasks, in iterative development of user interfaces. Without measurable specifications, it is impossible to determine either the usability goals of a product or whether the final product meets those goals. The bottom line is that *if you can't measure it, you probably can't manage it.*

Through years of working with real-world developers and from our own usability evaluations, we have modified the format of a usability specification table to be as shown in Table 8.1 (adapted from Whiteside et al., 1988). We will set some usability specifications for the Calendar Management System, as an example to explain the various columns in this table.

8.2.1   Usability Attribute

The *usability attribute* is the *general usability characteristic to be measured* for an interface. Some common usability attributes include

TABLE 8.1. EXAMPLE OF A USABILITY SPECIFICATION TABLE FOR THE CALENDAR MANAGEMENT SYSTEM

Usability Attribute	Measuring Instrument	Value to be Measured	Current Level	Worst Acceptable Level	Planned Target Level	Best Possible Level	Observed Results
Initial performance	"Add appointment" task per Benchmark 1	Length of time to successfully add appointment on first trial	15 seconds (manually)	30 seconds	20 seconds	10 seconds	
Initial performance	"Delete appointment" task per Benchmark 2	Number of errors on first trial	0 errors	4 errors	3 errors	0 errors	
First impression	Questionnaire (adapted from QUIS)	Average score (range −2 to 2)	??	0	0.5	1.25	

From Whiteside, Bennett, & Holtzblatt, 1988. In *Handbook of Human-Computer Interaction*, Martin Helander, Ed., © 1988. Elsevier Science Publishing Company.

- Initial performance
- Long-term performance
- Learnability
- Retainability
- Advanced feature usage
- First impression
- Long-term user satisfaction

Initial performance refers to a user's performance during the very first use (somewhere between the first few minutes and first few hours, depending on the complexity of the system) of an interface by a user, while *long-term performance* typically refers to performance during more constant use over a lengthier period of time (fairly regular use over several weeks, perhaps). Initial performance is a key usability attribute because any user of a system must, at some point, use it for the first (initial) time. *Learnability* and *retainability* refer, respectively, to how quickly and easily users can learn to use a system, and how well they retain what they have learned over some period of time. *Advanced feature usage* is an attribute that helps determine usability of more complicated functions of an interface. The user's initial opinion of the system can be captured by a *first impression* attribute. *Long-term user satisfaction* refers to the user's opinion after using the system for some longer period of time.

For the Calendar Management System, let's start simply, with just two usability attributes: initial performance and first impression. The following sections discuss how specific values for each of the columns in Table 8.1 is decided. Section 8.5 provides some further general guidance on choosing values, as well.

In choosing usability attributes, you must think about *who the intended users of the system are*, and *what realistic, representative tasks are intended across all these users*. If there are several categories of users (e.g., intermittent and frequent), it can be useful to break down the usability attributes even further, with different tasks and/or levels for different user categories. For example, for complex tasks, you may also wish to establish an attribute for learnability and another for long-term performance after some measurable level of learning is reached.

The objective of this activity is to establish *what user performance will be acceptable*, based on user tasks and user classes, and then state that in terms of specific, quantifiable usability goals. It is also important to realize that it may not be possible to establish these goals for all possible classes of users or for all possible tasks. It is often stated that about 80% of users use only about 20% of the functionality of an interactive system; the remaining 80% of the functionality is accessed with any frequency by only about 20% of all users. While these figures obviously cannot be proven, they nonetheless can serve as a guide in targeting both classes of users and specific tasks in establishing usability specifications.

8.2.2   Measuring Instrument

The *measuring instrument* is a description of the *method for providing values for a particular usability attribute*. A measuring instrument for a usability specification is always quantitative (i.e., it can be numerically measured) and can be either objective or subjective. *Objective* measuring instruments are quantitative measures of observable user performance while performing tasks with the interface. *Subjective* measuring instruments are quantitative measures based on user opinion about the interface. The initial performance usability attribute in Table 8.1 is associated with two different objective measuring instruments (that are explained further subsequently), and the first impression usability attribute is associated with a subjective measuring instrument. Objective measures are commonly associated with a benchmark task, and subjective measures are commonly associated with a user questionnaire.

Because the setting of usability specification levels (described in Section 8.3) is indeed a subjective process, the usability specification technique is admittedly a subjective way of establishing objective metrics. It is therefore important to recognize that the terms subjective and objective refer here to the usability attribute, measuring instrument, and associated data. When the collected data are, for example, timed observations of user performance, those data are objective, and thus the associated usability attribute and measuring instrument are also objective. When the collected data are from a user preference questionnaire, those data are subjective, and the associated usability attribute and measuring instrument are also subjective. Both subjective and objective measures and data are equally important for establishing and evaluating usability of a design.

Most measuring instruments are associated with either benchmark tasks or user questionnaires, the most common measuring instruments for establishing and measuring appropriate usability specifications. A *benchmark task* (see further discussion of this in Chapter 10, on formative evaluation) is a typical, representative task a user will perform; measuring a user's performance on a benchmark task provides an *objective usability metric* for the related usability attribute.

For the Calendar Management System, a measuring instrument must be determined for each usability attribute. For the first usability attribute in Table 8.1, initial performance, an appropriate benchmark task would involve adding an appointment. This is a task that users will perform frequently and should therefore be very simple and quick for them to accomplish. The second row in the table is also the initial performance attribute, but this time, we use a different measuring instrument—namely, the task of deleting an appointment. This is also an important task that users will perform often, and its usability is therefore important to measure with a benchmark task.

Because a benchmark is a fixed point against which measurements can be made, a benchmark task must be very specifically worded in order to be the same for each participant (subject) who performs it during usability evaluation. So, for the first usability attribute for the Calendar Management System, initial performance, the "add appointment" benchmark task (referred to as Benchmark 1 in Table 8.1) might be, "Schedule a meeting with Dr. Ehrich for four weeks from today at 10 A.M. in 133 McBryde, concerning the HCI research project." This level of specificity is needed in order to make consistent measures across all participants, as each performs the task.

Benchmark tasks also must be specific, so that a participant doesn't get sidetracked on irrelevant details during testing. If, for example, the benchmark task had been simply stated as, "Add an appointment sometime next month," some participants might make it a long, elaborate task, while others would do the minimum. The length of time for each participant to perform the "add appointment" task would not be comparable in this situation. Benchmark 2, for the second row of Table 8.1, may be stated very precisely as follows: "Suppose you have decided that your dog is not worth spending money on. Delete your appointment with the vet for Mutt's annual checkup."

An important aspect of creating benchmark tasks is to state exactly *what* the user should do (e.g., "add a brown-bag lunch meeting with the HCI group every Tuesday at noon"), but *not how* the user should do it (e.g., "enter a brown bag lunch meeting with the HCI group at noon on the first Tuesday in the year, then select the 'repeat appointment' button, then select the 'weekly' button, to add the appointment at the same time every week for the whole year"). After all, the objective for the benchmark is to determine whether users can figure out how to perform various tasks, how long the tasks take, and how many errors they make. If users are told how to perform a task, then we have no indication of whether they can figure out how to do it for themselves, thus yielding little indication of the usability of the interface for that task.

In choosing benchmark tasks, it is best to use specific, single interface features or small groups of features so that problems discovered during evaluation can be more easily traced to specific parts of the design. Large, complicated tasks are not as suitable because they require more evaluation time and are less clear indicators of specific usability problems. Such large, complex tasks are usually covered by evaluating their constituent subtasks.

Although most tasks to be measured should be simple, there are situations in which it is desirable to measure user performance on small combinations of simple tasks, such as those that will frequently occur together. In these cases, you should set usability specifications for such combinations because difficulties related to usability that appear during performance of the combined tasks can be different than for the same tasks performed separately. For example, in the Calendar Management System, you may wish to measure user performance on the combined tasks of searching for and adding an appointment. A benchmark task requiring users to add a new appointment on the first available Monday morning at 9 A.M. could be used in conjunction with a calendar (probably a prototype) that has the next few Monday mornings already filled. This would force users to perform the task of searching through several Mondays, looking for the first free Monday morning before they could perform the task of adding a new appointment.

A *questionnaire* (see further discussion of this also in Chapter 10, on formative evaluation) related to various user interface features can be used to determine a user's subjective satisfaction with the interface; measuring a user's satisfaction provides a subjective (but still quantitative) usability metric for the related usability attribute. User opinion, measured subjectively, is a strong factor in user satisfaction, which may actually affect user performance over a long period of time. The better that users like the system, the more likely they are to have good performance with it over the long term. For the third row in Table 8.1, the first impression usability attribute, a questionnaire will allow us to determine each user's initial opinion of the system.

Although this kind of questionnaire or survey is inexpensive to administer, we strongly warn that there is a scientific method for producing and validating such scales; not just anyone can produce such a list of features and rankings and put them together in a questionnaire that will result in valid data. The Questionnaire for User Interface Satisfaction, or QUIS, developed at the University of Maryland (Chin, Diehl, & Norman, 1988) is the most extensive and most thoroughly validated questionnaire for determining subjective interface usability. It is organized around such general categories as *screen, terminology and system information, learning,* and *system capabilities.* Within each of these general categories are sets of detailed features, with scales from which a participant chooses a ranking. It also elicits some demographic information, as well as general user comments about the interface being evaluated. Many developers supplement the QUIS with some of their own questions, specific to the interface being evaluated. Although QUIS is quite thorough, it can be administered in a relatively short amount of time. QUIS is available for licensing in an online version from the University of Maryland.

Some examples of the general screen category, and its detailed features, from QUIS, are given in Figure 8.1. Also shown in Figure 8.1 is another category, overall

		1	2	3	4	5	6	7	8	9	NA
Characters on screen	hard to read									easy to read	
		1	2	3	4	5	6	7	8	9	NA
Image of characters	fuzzy									sharp	
		1	2	3	4	5	6	7	8	9	NA
Character shapes (fonts)	barely legible									very legible	
		1	2	3	4	5	6	7	8	9	NA
Was highlighting on the screen helpful?	not at all									very much	
		1	2	3	4	5	6	7	8	9	NA
Use of reverse video	unhelpful									helpful	
		1	2	3	4	5	6	7	8	9	NA
Use of blinking	unhelpful									helpful	
		1	2	3	4	5	6	7	8	9	NA
Were screen layouts helpful?	never									always	
		1	2	3	4	5	6	7	8	9	NA
Amount of information that can be displayed	inadequate									adequate	
		1	2	3	4	5	6	7	8	9	NA
Arrangement of information on screen	illogical									logical	
		1	2	3	4	5	6	7	8	9	NA
Sequence of screens	confusing									clear	
		1	2	3	4	5	6	7	8	9	NA
Next screen in sequence	unpredictable									predictable	
		1	2	3	4	5	6	7	8	9	NA
Going back to previous screen	impossible									easy	
		1	2	3	4	5	6	7	8	9	NA
Beginning, middle, and end of tasks	confusing									clearly marked	
		1	2	3	4	5	6	7	8	9	NA
Overall reactions to the system:	terrible									wonderful	
		1	2	3	4	5	6	7	8	9	NA
	frustrating									satisfying	
		1	2	3	4	5	6	7	8	9	NA
	dull									stimulating	
		1	2	3	4	5	6	7	8	9	NA
	difficult									easy	
		1	2	3	4	5	6	7	8	9	NA
	inadequate power									adequate power	
		1	2	3	4	5	6	7	8	9	NA
	rigid									flexible	
		1	2	3	4	5	6	7	8	9	NA

Figure 8.1. Some example questions adapted from QUIS (Chin, et al., 1988).

user reactions. We have found an adaptation of QUIS to work well. In this adaptation, we reduce the granularity of the scale from ten choices (1 through 9 and NA) to six (–2, –1, 0, 1, 2, and NA) for each question, centering the scale around zero. As a mid-scale reading, zero is an appropriately neutral value. Negative scale readings correspond to negative user opinions and positive readings to positive opinions. For the third usability attribute in Table 8.1, first impression, the user will complete a subset of QUIS, using our suggested adaptation of the scale.

8.2.3   Value to be Measured

The *value to be measured* is the *metric for which data values are collected*, the specific data to be collected during an evaluation session with a participant. Most commonly, this is what is measured using a benchmark task, or the kind of score to be computed from a questionnaire. For the initial performance attribute in the first row of Table 8.1, as already discussed in the previous section, the length of time to add a specific appointment is an appropriate value to measure.

A different measure would be the number of errors a user makes while deleting an appointment. This was chosen as the value to measure in the second row of Table 8.1. *Time to complete a task* and *number of errors during task performance* are, in fact, the most common objective values measured. In reality, you usually will want to measure both of these values, rather than choosing one or the other for a task, as was done here in the first two rows of Table 8.1.

An interesting issue that must be addressed when counting errors is determining exactly what constitutes an error. For example, an evaluator will certainly recognize when particular menu or button selections are not necessary to the task a user is attempting to perform, and those should count as errors. These are discussed further in Section 10.4.1, on quantitative data generation techniques.

For the third row of Table 8.1, the first impression attribute, the average score across all items in the questionnaire (e.g., QUIS or some other validated questionnaire) is a useful subjective metric. What to do with the data you collect from such a questionnaire is discussed in Chapter 10, on formative evaluation.

Interestingly, user perceptions of elapsed time can be an important attribute, such as for a usability test on a new software installation package. The old installation package required the user to perform repeated disk swaps during installation, while the new installation package required only one swap. Amazingly, users *thought* that using the new package took them longer to perform installation because they were not kept busy swapping disks. In reality, it took them one third less elapsed time to perform installation using the new package. User perception of task performance is testable in a postsession questionnaire or interview.

8.3   SETTING LEVELS IN THE USABILITY SPECIFICATION TABLE

So far so good: Coming up with attributes, instruments, and values to be measured doesn't appear to be too difficult. Now comes a bigger challenge. What values should be used to establish acceptable performance of the user, and therefore to reflect the level of usability of the interface? The answer to this requires determining what level of user behavior the system is to support. Columns four through seven in the usability specification table shown in Table 8.1 are key to *quantifying the usability* of an interface. These columns contain the values established to determine what user performance will be acceptable, both to the users and to the developers of the system. In Chapter 10, on formative evaluation we return to our usability specifications and compare them to our observed user performance, so choosing the values for the various levels in Table 8.1 is very important.

As mentioned, one of the measuring instruments most commonly used is length of time to perform a task. When first setting the levels, you may find that you have difficulty in establishing a value for timed tasks. Under different conditions, different lengths of time can be reasonable. For example, for a somewhat difficult task that will be done only once, such as configuring a database, a one-hour effort may not be unreasonable for user performance. However, if a task will be done frequently, a long performance time is rarely acceptable. If the database configuration task has to be performed by a database administrator on 500 different new PCs in the next two weeks, one hour is not an acceptable time for task performance. This kind of dilemma is solved by making the user class definition for a usability attribute and the task definition in the measuring instrument specific enough to narrow the cases so that only a small range of time values is reasonable for each case. In sum, different tasks and different users may indicate the need for different usability specifications, or at least for different tasks and different levels of task performance.

Although it is not explicitly indicated in Table 8.1, the *levels shown are the mean over all participants* who perform each task. That is, the levels shown do not have to be achieved by every participant in the formative evaluation sessions. So, for example, for Benchmark 2, the worst acceptable level of performance across all participants who perform the "delete appointment" task must be no more than *an average of* four errors. In these usability specification tables, we assume that each level is established as the mean over all participants.

8.3.1   Current Level

The *current level* is the *present level of the value to be measured* for the usability attribute in the present version of the system. A current level can be established whether the system is automated or is pencil and paper. For example, the Calendar Management System might be replacing a manual paper calendar. The difference between the current level and the planned target level (see Section 8.3.3) is a measure of the improvement that can be expected in the new interaction design for each of the usability attributes. Measuring a current level helps ensure that the other levels are, in fact, measurable. Measurements for the current level can come from an existing manual system, an existing automated system, or even from developer performance with a prototype of the new system. Sometimes, it is useful to know what the current level of performance is, relative to one or more competitive systems.

To determine the current level for the Calendar Management System, we can actually measure how long it takes someone to perform the benchmark tasks for adding an appointment and deleting an appointment, using a paper version of a calendar. Suppose that adding an appointment takes about 15 seconds. If so, this value, 15 seconds, becomes the current level for the first row in Table 8.1. Because most people are already experienced with paper calendars, this value, of course, is not really for initial performance, but it gives some idea of user performance with a paper calendar. This value probably won't change much, whether the user of a paper calendar is adding an appointment for the first time, or after the user has added 50 appointments.

To set a current value for the second row, for deleting an appointment, it can be assumed that almost no one should make any errors doing this on a paper calendar, so the current value for this attribute is 0 errors. To establish a current value for the first impression attribute in the third row, we could administer the questionnaire to some users of the paper calendar. However, because many of the items on the questionnaire relate specifically to an automated user interface, the results of a questionnaire based on a paper calendar would not be particularly useful, so a current level is not specified for the first impression attribute.

8.3.2   Worst Acceptable Level

The *worst acceptable level* is the *lowest acceptable level of user performance* for each usability attribute, *not the worst that can happen*. This border of failure for usability is the boundary between an acceptable and an unacceptable system for each specific attribute for the current version of the interface. As a usability specification table is defined, the worst levels for all attributes in the entire table must be simultaneously attained. If the observed value for even one attribute does not meet its worst level, then the whole system is formally unacceptable, at least in its present version. Therefore, mutually exclusive or contradictory levels guarantee failure, so be careful when setting your attributes and their levels.

It is important to note that developers sometimes mistakenly think that the various levels, especially worst acceptable level, are a prediction of how a user may perform. This is not the case. The levels indicate what developers agree on as the *acceptable* level of user performance to achieve the desired usability for an interface. For example, when developers are first learning to establish usability specifications, they may set a worst acceptable level of an average of 0 for a subjective user satisfaction questionnaire with rankings from 0 (worst) to 5 (best). Of course, the worst possible case is an average of 0, but this certainly would not be acceptable in terms of any reasonable measure of usability. Worst acceptable level is the minimum level of performance that users can attain and still consider the interface to have any credible usability.

How are the worst acceptable levels determined? There are no hard and fast rules for determining these values, but the following heuristics may help. The worst acceptable level should, when possible, be near the value for the current level of the present system and could be higher if the current level is not satisfactory. Ideally, a new automated system should not result in lower user performance than the current system, even for initial performance. In reality, however, user performance the very first time that users attempt a particular task with a new system is likely to be worse than their performance using the current system with which they are familiar, regardless of whether the current system is manual or automated. Obviously, a paper calendar is hard to beat for simple tasks such as adding an appointment.

For this reason, we set the worst acceptable level for the first initial performance attribute in Table 8.1 to be a value that is lower than the current level for the Calendar Management System. While this goes against the heuristic just stated, it makes sense here, because someone using the Calendar Management System simply would not be expected to perform the "add appointment" task for the very first time as quickly as that person could add an appointment to a paper calendar. When you feel that the current level is too stringent to be the worst acceptable level, then you have to make an educated estimate of a value for the worst acceptable level. Thus, if users can add an appointment in 30 seconds or less the very first time they try, then usability of that task is probably at least minimal. The second row in Table 8.1 also sets the worst acceptable level to be lower than the current level. Again, users could not be expected to make no errors the very first time they perform the "delete appointment" task. Assume, for this example, that four errors is a reasonable number of mistakes to allow a first-time user when deleting an appointment, and still have some minimal level of usability.

Finally, for the first impression attribute, we chose as the worst acceptable level a mean score of 0 on a rating scale of –2 to 2 on the questionnaire. Remember that in our adaptation of QUIS, the midrange of the rating scale is 0, and any negative rating indicates a negative user satisfaction. Thus, a system as simple as the Calendar Management System should rate no worse than a neutral (0) first impression from its users.

8.3.3   Planned Target Level

The planned *target level* is the target value indicating *attainment of unquestioned usability success* for the present version of the interface; it is the "what you would like" level. It is the nominal usability goal for each specific attribute. Attributes that have not yet achieved their planned levels serve as focal points for improvement by developers. Attributes for which planned levels have been attained no longer need attention.

Like the worst level, the planned levels for all attributes in the entire table must be simultaneously attainable. Also like the worst level, a value for the planned level is determined heuristically. It is usually set to be higher than the current level for the present system, if known, in order to give an improvement in user performance. Otherwise, why build a new system with which planned, desired user performance will be worse than the system presently being used? Of course, improved user performance is not the only motivation for building a new system; increased functionality over an old system is also a motivating factor in developing new systems. However, the focus here is on improving usability, which is most directly related to improved user performance. Another heuristic for setting a planned target level is to look at competitive systems; you want users to perform as well with your system as they would perform with a competitor's product.

For the first initial performance attribute in Table 8.1, let's set the target level to 20 seconds, a reasonable improvement over the worst acceptable level (which is 30 seconds). Similarly, for the second initial performance attribute, we set an improvement over the worst acceptable level, say three errors. For the first impression attribute, we set a level of a mean score of 0.5 on a scale of –2 to 2 as the desired planned level. An average questionnaire score of less than 70%, which 0.5 would be, seems a reasonable indication of failure in terms of usability for the first impression attribute. If these planned target levels are attained during formative evaluation with users, we can be confident of very good usability, at least for the attributes and tasks for which these levels were achieved.

You may be wondering why have planned target levels at all, if meeting all worst acceptable levels indicates the boundary between success and failure in terms of usability. Meeting a worst acceptable level is the absolute minimum performance that is acceptable for any usability attribute. Meeting all the worst acceptable levels formally meets the usability goals—but only barely. In reality, you hope to achieve better than the worst acceptable level on most usability attributes, hence, the planned target levels.

8.3.4   Best Possible Level

The *best possible level* is a *realistic state-of-the-art upper limit*, the inspiration level of a usability attribute. It should be an attainable level, not a total wild dream; all should agree that it is in fact achievable. The best possible level shows both management and developers the potential for an attribute and serves as a target for future versions of the interface. It also reinforces the idea of interaction development as a continual improvement cycle.

Like the other levels, the best possible level is the best level of performance you can hope for under ideal conditions and is heuristically set at what might be attainable for an expert user, the best design, and the best use of available technology. When you have a prototype of your design, you can have a developer who knows the design perform your benchmark tasks and take those measures indicated in the usability specification table (e.g., time, number of errors). It is unlikely that any user will do better than a developer who knows the design well, so this makes a realistic upper limit for an attribute. In fact, you may wish to measure a developer's performance to set best possible levels, and then double (e.g., allow twice as much time or twice as many errors) or triple those levels to set planned target levels and worst acceptable levels, respectively.

If the development team has members that are trained in use of analytic evaluation techniques (e.g., GOMS—Card, Moran, & Newell, 1983), these might be used to give theoretical estimates of expert error-free task performance. These estimates could be used to help set best possible levels. Such analytic evaluation techniques are beyond the scope of this discussion.

For now, set the best possible levels in Table 8.1 to be better than the planned levels for each of the three usability attributes, say, at 10 seconds for the first attribute, 0 errors for the second attribute, and a mean of 1.25 for the initial impression questionnaire score. If some of these best possible levels are attained during formative evaluation, it would indicate a high level of usability for the corresponding attributes and tasks.

8.3.5   Observed Results

Finally, the *observed results* are the *actual values obtained from observing users* performing the prescribed tasks during formative evaluation sessions. This column has been added to the usability specification table because it provides such a useful way to do quick comparisons between the specified levels and the actual results of user testing. Because you typically will have more than one user from which observed results are obtained, you can either record multiple values in a single Observed Results column or, if desired, add more than one column for observed results. You may also want to add another column to include the average of the observed values, if appropriate. The method for obtaining these observed results is detailed in Chapter 10, on formative evaluation.

8.4   ANOTHER EXAMPLE

The usability attributes described previously may not fully indicate the potential impact that usability specifications can have on interaction development. Simply adding an appointment is a pretty easy task, whether it is to a paper calendar or to an automated calendar. Realistically, automating that task is not going to give much in the way of improved user performance over a manual calendar. For example, consider a different task, one that potentially could, in fact, give quite an improvement in user performance and more functionality over a paper calendar—namely, the task of adding repeating appointments to a calendar. Suppose that you want to add an appointment for a particular meeting that is held every Wednesday at 9 A.M. for the next year. This might yield the usability specification table entry shown in Table 8.2.

Next, assume that you are designing this task for someone who is a frequent user of the Calendar Management System over a fairly lengthy period of time. The usability attribute is advanced feature usage, which indicates usability of more complex tasks, which frequent (as opposed to first-time) users are likely to perform. Because the Calendar Management System is quite a simple system, a user that has used it for, say, one hour or more should be reasonably expert with it and would be performing more complicated tasks, such as adding repeating appoint-

TABLE 8.2. ANOTHER USABILITY SPECIFICATION TABLE

Usability Attribute	Measuring Instrument	Value to be Measured	Current Level	Worst Acceptable Level	Planned Target Level	Best Possible Level	Observed Results
Advanced feature usage	"Add repeating appointment" task per Benchmark 3	Length of time to add a weekly appointment every week for one year after one hour of use	13 minutes (manually)	2 minutes	1 minute	30 seconds	

ments. Thus, the criterion for having users perform this more complicated task is that they must have used the Calendar Management System for one hour or more. When compiling a complete set of benchmark and other tasks in Section 10.2.2, on developing the tasks, we shall ensure that each user has, in fact, used the system for at least an hour.

The task used for determining the relevant measures is an "add repeating appointment" task, and the value measured is the length of time it takes users to add a weekly appointment, after they have used the system for at least an hour. Therefore, Benchmark 3 might be, "Enter a one hour weekly meeting with the HCI group every Wednesday at 9 A.M. for one year, beginning on the Wednesday of next week."

Although it is not explicitly shown in the partial design discussed in Chapter 5, assume that the Calendar Management System allows a user to add an appointment at the same time every week by entering one instance of the appointment (e.g., at 9 A.M. beginning with next Wednesday), and then indicating that the system should allocate that same time period for all Wednesdays for one year. Also assume that system performance is not an issue here; that is, the system can add the repeating appointments virtually instantly, so that system performance does not have to affect user performance. In this example, the current level for writing in an appointment by hand on a paper calendar is 52 Wednesdays multiplied by an estimate of 15 seconds per appointment (from measures taken earlier for the "add appointment" task), which equals 13 minutes. This can probably be reduced some, due to efficiency gained in repetition, but fatigue could cancel out some of the gains.

The Calendar Management System, if it is well-designed, should let a user perform this "add repeating appointment" task with only a little more effort than adding a single appointment. To be very conservative, because this is an advanced task, we set the worst acceptable level at 2 minutes, the planned target level at 1 minute (longer than the planned level for adding a single appointment discussed earlier), and the best possible case at 30 seconds (again, longer than adding a single appointment). These numbers show a much more dramatic improvement between the current level and the other levels than was demonstrated in the first usability specification table example.

8.5   HINTS TO HELP CREATE USABILITY SPECIFICATION TABLES

The first time you try to create some usability specification tables on your own, you are faced with a sheet of paper containing a blank table with lots of cells just waiting to be filled in. So how do you fill them in? In addition to using some of the aforementioned heuristics for choosing levels, some hints from Whiteside, Bennett, and Holtzblatt (1988) may serve as an aid to creativity for developing usability specifications, to help you know how to fill in the various columns. These suggestions are not intended to be requirements for items that must always be included, but rather to show the range of possibilities that can be incorporated into the tables. You should refer to these suggestions when you are choosing your own usability specifications, at least the first few times you try doing them for a design. Some of the previously mentioned possible ideas for *usability attributes* include initial performance, long-term performance, learnability, retainability, advanced feature usage, first impression, and long-term user satisfaction. Initial performance and first impression are appropriate usability attributes for virtually every interface.

The *measuring instrument* indicates the kind of user task that will be used to provide an observed measure. As already mentioned, this typically is done in one of two ways:

- User performance for specific benchmark tasks—Here, the user performs specific tasks that have been defined and pretested by the developers (see Chapter 10, on formative evaluation). Benchmark tasks provide quantitative, *objective* metrics that are the foundation of usability specifications. An explicit reference to a specific detailed benchmark task should be included as part of this kind of usability specification.

- Questionnaire scores—Here, the user completes a questionnaire assessing various aspects of the user interface. Questionnaires provide quantitative, but *subjective*, metrics that reflect user opinion.

The first example usability specification table (Table 8.1) had two usability specifications (the first two) associated with objective measures, and one usability specification (the third) associated with subjective measures.

The *value to be measured* relates either to the benchmark tasks or to the questionnaire chosen for the measuring instrument. When benchmark tasks are being used, a large number of measures can be taken from observations of users, including

- Time to complete task
- Number or percentage of errors
- Percentage of task completed in a given time
- Ratio of successes to failures
- Time spent in errors and recovery
- Number of commands/actions used to perform task(s)
- Frequency of help and documentation use

- Number of repetitions of failed commands
- Number of available commands not invoked
- Number of times user expresses frustration or satisfaction

As mentioned previously, values observed for any of these measures are typically averaged. Similarly for a questionnaire, an average of the measured ratings is typically computed. In both cases, the results are compared to the levels set in the usability specification.

Setting the various target *levels* is one of the hardest aspects of determining usability specifications. Obviously, they are often "best guesses," but it is far worse to attempt to develop a user interaction design without any usability specifications than to develop one while measuring against something, even "best guesses." With practice, developers become quite skilled at establishing credible usability specifications and setting reasonable levels. Sometimes, one of the results of early formative evaluation is realistic adjustments to usability specification levels—a reality check. As already indicated, the levels can be set in various ways, including with respect to

- An existing system or previous version of the new system under development
- Competitive systems, such as those with a large market share or with a widely acclaimed user interface
- Performing a task without use of a computer system (i.e., manually, using pencil and paper)
- Performance by developer(s) with your own prototype for some version of the interface
- Marketing input based on observations of desired user performance with existing similar systems
- Some absolute scale, when there is little else to compare against

8.6   CAUTIONS ON USE OF USABILITY SPECIFICATIONS

There are some cautions to be considered in developing and using usability specifications (Whiteside et al., 1988). In particular, you must consider the following kinds of issues.

▶ Is each usability attribute practically measurable?

It is possible to set usability attributes and measuring instruments that sound completely reasonable, but in actuality are unrealistic to observe, to collect data from, or to analyze. An extreme example of this might be setting a usability attribute of long-term performance and then attempting to record user keystrokes and count errors made in a two-week period of use.

▶ Are user classes specified clearly enough?

This is important when identifying representative users that will serve as participants in evaluation sessions (see Chapter 10, on formative evaluation). As already mentioned, the classes of users may also affect the setting of usability specifications, resulting in different measuring instruments and values to be measured for different user classes while performing the same task. If there are several user classes for which different usability specifications are appropriate, you may wish to have an additional User Class column in the table, which clearly specifies for which user class each usability attribute is intended. Probably a better approach is to use a completely separate table for each user class.

▶ Is the number of attributes to be measured reasonable?

The first time you develop a usability specification table, *start small*. Don't produce a table with even a dozen specifications. This will overwhelm you and discourage you for later use of the usability specification technique. In general, try to start with exactly what was given in the first example, Table 8.1: two specifications associated with objective measures and one associated with subjective measures. This is a manageable number but is also enough to let you get a feel for creating and measuring the usability specifications. Then gradually, as you become more skilled and confident at developing usability specifications, you can include more of them in the table.

▶ Do all project members agree on attributes and usability specification table values?

Creating usability specifications is not an activity that can be done by a dictator. They should be produced by at least a subset of the development team and must include an interaction designer and/or human factors engineer (and perhaps a marketing person, if appropriate). The entire team should review, negotiate, and eventually accept the usability specification table, so that the specifications are not perceived by the team as being externally imposed. Unless every member of the development team has committed to the usability specifications, different members will be striving for different goals—a guaranteed formula for frustration, if not failure.

► Are the values for the various levels reasonable?

This may be one of the hardest questions to answer. In fact, the first few times you develop usability specifications, you will probably be making a lot of guesses. What often happens is that when you observe users, you find that they perform dramatically differently than you had expected when you set the levels. Sometimes, the actual observed values, especially on the first cycle of evaluation, are a great deal better than the values for the levels in the table. When this occurs, it is generally the case that the levels have been set too leniently. This is a common mistake when setting usability specifications for the first time; members of the development team understandably want to protect themselves and not have users' actual performance be drastically worse than their specified acceptable levels of performance.

However, setting the levels too leniently does not serve their intended goal of achieving quantifiably good usability, if the lenient values do not, in fact, represent a level of acceptable usability for the interface. When observed values are much better than specified levels, particularly in the early cycles of evaluation, you may need to reassess the values of the specified levels to make sure they are reasonable. Modify them to be more stringent, if necessary.

The converse can also happen, especially in early cycles of iteration. When your observed results are much worse than specified levels, there typically are two possibilities. In the first (and preferable) case, the process of evaluation and refinement is working just as it should; the usability specifications are reasonable, and evaluation has shown that there are serious usability problems with the design. When these problems are solved, the design will meet the specified usability goals. In the second case, the usability specifications have been set unrealistically strictly, and no matter how much you improve the design and its usability, the usability goals might never be met. Sometimes, for example, a task simply takes longer than its designers first anticipated, even with a good design.

If you are not meeting your levels, especially after a few rounds of iteration, you will need to assess them to see whether they are unrealistically difficult to attain or whether the design simply needs a great deal of work. Determining which of these cases you have is, of course, not always easy. You will have to rely on your knowledge of interaction design, experience, intuition, and ultimately your best judgment to decide where the problem lies—with the specification levels or with the design. These issues are discussed in more detail in Chapter 10, on formative evaluation. Obviously, you should not change the usability levels once they are set, simply to claim that you have met them or to make them easier to meet. Sometimes, however, they may be too far to one extreme and will need modification in response to actual observations of user performance.

► How well do the attributes capture usability for the design?

Again, this is a very elusive situation to recognize. It is entirely possible to establish usability specifications that have little or nothing to do with assessing the real usability of a design. For example, a benchmark task might be very nonrepresentative, leading to design improvements in parts of the application that will rarely be used. It is equally easy to inadvertently omit usability specifications that are critical to assessing usability. Again, with experience, you will gain a better understanding of when you have established usability attributes and levels that capture the usability of the design.

8.7   SUMMARY

There are two important points to be made about usability specifications. The first is that developers of an interactive system wouldn't dream of developing it without first determining specifications for its functionality; similarly, they shouldn't dream of developing an interactive system without first *determining specifications for its usability*. We can hear it already: "Right! Usability specifications are just one more thing I have to do in an already too-tight schedule with too-limited resources. Not a chance!"

In reply to any potential protests, you can have your interface good, fast, or cheap, but not all of these all at once. Assuming you want it to be good, you therefore are interested in pursuing activities in the development process that will contribute to improved usability. Developing usability specifications, after a little practice, does not take much time. Also, if you believe in rapid prototyping (see Chapter 9) and formative evaluation (see Chapter 10), then you're going to be testing the interface with users anyway. Why not have specific quantified usability goals against which you are testing, rather than just waiting to see what happens when you put users in front of your interface? An ad hoc approach to interaction development, without measurable usability goals, can lead to the collection of large amounts of unusable and unneeded observational data from users. Usability specifications provide a feasible target for formative evaluation efforts, optimizing the results obtained from users.

The second point about usability specifications is that they are part of the *management and control mechanisms for the iterative refinement process*, as exemplified by the star life cycle described in Chapter 4. Usability specifications define a quantifiable end to the seemingly endless iterative refinement process. You can stop iterating for the present version of your interface when at least the worst level usability specifications are met for all attributes. When they are met, developers can be confident that the minimum usability for the interface has been achieved, at least for the present version of the interface. Without usability specifications, the key factors that generally determine an end to the iterative refinement process are when developers run out of time, patience, and/or money. Usability specifications provide a quantitative, not an arbitrary or political, basis for closure to the process, and as such are a significant technique in usability management and engineering.

8.8   EXERCISE ON USABILITY SPECIFICATIONS

Here is your exercise on establishing usability specifications for your Calendar Management System design, followed by a possible solution.

Exercise—Usability Specifications

GOAL: To gain experience in writing precise, measurable usability specifications and associated benchmark tasks.

MINIMUM TIME: About 30 minutes.

ACTIVITIES: Produce three usability specifications for your Calendar Management System design: two associated with objective measures and one associated with subjective measures. Obviously, they should be different than the ones used as examples in this chapter.

To accompany specifications with objective measures, write a very specific, brief benchmark task description for participants to perform. These two specifications should be testable in a later exercise on formative evaluation (at the end of Chapter 10). Expected average performance time for each task should be no more than three minutes (just to keep it short and simple for you).

The specification with subjective measures could be based on a few of the questions from the adapted QUIS questionnaire shown in Figure 8.1. Probably the best ones for evaluating your early prototype design are the questions about whether screen layouts are helpful, sequencing of screens, and the overall reaction.

DELIVERABLES: Your three usability specifications, filled into a blank usability specification table.

Possible Exercise Solution

The examples used for explaining usability specifications are one possible set of specifications that would satisfy this exercise. Because you were asked to produce different ones, here are a few others that may be similar to ones you produced. The first four are associated with objective measures; the fifth is associated with a subjective measure.

The usability attribute in the first row of the table is straightforward, and it uses the same benchmark task, Benchmark 1, that was created earlier for the "add appointment" task. This time, however, a different value—namely, errors, rather than time—is being measured. Levels here are a little more stringent than those for the "delete appointment" task in Table 8.1. The reason for this is that adding an appointment is a somewhat easier task than deleting an appointment, so the levels here should be a bit more stringent.

For any attribute with a benchmark task for which more than one measure (e.g., time and errors) is to be taken, you can, of course, measure both of these during a participant's performance of a single task. A participant does not, for example, need to perform one "add appointment" task while you time performance, and then do a different "add appointment" task while you count errors. Timing of tasks is usually fairly easy to do in real time, but counting errors can be trickier. Data collection is discussed in much more detail in Chapter 10, on formative evaluation.

The second row of Table 8.3 requires more explanation than the first row did. Suppose that Benchmark 4 for the "search for appointment" task of the second row is the following: "Find your next appointment with the dentist." The levels for the "search for appointment" task can vary quite considerably, depending on whether the user already knows the location/time slot of the task to be viewed, or at least its approximate time slot (e.g., sometime next Monday). However, if the user has no idea of the location of the appointment (other than, say, sometime in the next year), the user will probably want to do a search on a character string to help in locating the appointment.

Obviously, this is an example of greatly improved functionality of the automated calendar over the paper calendar. With a paper calendar, the user's only recourse is to manually turn through the pages of the calendar, looking for the dentist's appointment. The levels specified here are based on the premise that the user does not have much idea of when the next dental appointment is, and would have to search by hand for quite some time (approximately 2 minutes with the paper calendar) to find it. However, the string search capability of the Calendar Management System could be used to find it much more quickly. This suggests setting the worst acceptable level of performance at no more than 30 seconds, considerably better than the current level with a paper calendar.

TABLE 8.3. MORE USABILITY SPECIFICATIONS

Usability Attribute	Measuring Instrument	Value to be Measured	Current Level	Worst Acceptable Level	Planned Target Level	Best Possible Level	Observed Results
Initial performance	"Add appointment" task per Benchmark 1	Number of errors on first trial	0 errors (manually)	3 errors	2 errors	0 errors	
Initial performance	"Search for appointment" task per Benchmark 4	Length of time to successfully search for appointment	2 minutes (manually)	30 seconds	20 seconds	15 seconds	
Initial performance	"Delete appointment" task per Benchmark 2	Length of time to successfully delete appointment on first trial	12 seconds	20 seconds	12 seconds	8 seconds	
Learnability	"Add appointment" task per Benchmark 5	Length of time to successfully add appointment after one hour of use	15 seconds (manually)	15 seconds	12 seconds	8 seconds	
First impression	User reaction	Number of negative/positive remarks during session	??	10 negative/ 2 positive	5 negative/ 5 positive	2 negative/ 10 positive	

This example of finding the next dental appointment brings up another important consideration in setting levels for any usability attribute—namely, *establishing the task context*. In order for the measured data to be consistent and meaningful across all participants who perform the benchmark tasks, the location of that next dental appointment in the calendar must be controlled. All participants must start at approximately the same point in their search for the dental appointment. In fact, this same consideration of task context applies to the "delete appointment" task we established in Table 8.1, which is also shown in the third row of Table 8.3. The relationship between the starting point within the calendar for the task and the location of the appointment will give some indication of whether and how long a user must first search for an appointment before deleting it. If the established benchmark task is to delete the dentist's appointment immediately after the user just found that appointment (from the "search" task, for example), then obviously, it should only take a few seconds to delete the appointment.

If, however, users are given a different appointment to delete, one that they must first find, it may take much longer. When setting the usability levels and producing the associated benchmark tasks, you should decide whether you want the search included in the task and, if so, then uniformly include it as appropriate. This task context can be specified in rubrics (special instructions) for the benchmark task description, to be seen only by members of the development team (e.g., evaluator), but not by participants in evaluation sessions.

The third row of the table uses Benchmark 2, which was defined for the "delete appointment" task in Table 8.1, with the same usability attribute of initial performance. This example, however, measures a different value—specifically, length of time to successfully delete an appointment. Just as with Benchmark 1, two values are to be measured for this task: one for time to complete the task (in the third row of Table 8.3) and another for errors made (in Table 8.1). Suppose that we have decided not to include in the task a lengthy search for the appointment to be deleted, so we specify in the task context that the appointment to be deleted is not far from the task starting point and perhaps is even visible to participants when they begin the "delete appointment" task. In the table, we set the levels for the time values for the "delete appointment" task to be less than those for the "search for appointment" task. This is because the "delete appointment" task, as just described here, does not include time for searching.

If, instead, we had decided that the task context should be such that the user must first do some searching for an appointment before deleting it, the levels specified for deleting an appointment should be essentially the same as those specified for performing the "search for appointment" task plus a few seconds (say, 10 to 15 seconds) to delete the appointment once it is found.

For learnability, the usability attribute in the fourth row of Table 8.3, we measure participants' performance on an "add appointment" task after they have been using the Calendar Management System for an hour or so. We can then compare this performance to their performance the first time they added an appointment using Benchmark 1. To accomplish this, at least a couple more appointments must be added, interspersed with other tasks (e.g., deleting or modifying appointments) because the fourth row indicates that the time it takes the participant to successfully add an appointment will be measured after an hour of using the system. During this time, the participant presumably should have added a few more appointments; this permits assessment of learnability.

As Chapter 10, on formative evaluation, shows, a complete written description of all tasks is needed for the evaluator, and a different version of that list is needed to give to participants in the evaluation sessions. For example, the list must include the "add appointment" task, Benchmark 5, well into the session, as cited in Table 8.3. An appropriate set of tasks that specifically addresses this issue (that is, interspersing other tasks with the tasks of adding an appointment, and getting usage time to about an hour) is given in Chapter 10 (see Figure 10.1 and accompanying discussion). Task K in Figure 10.1 is Benchmark 5.

We still need to explain the levels set for the learnability attribute. The worst acceptable level was set to 15 seconds, half the worst acceptable level for the initial performance value (30 seconds, as shown in Table 8.1), because improvement would be expected between the very first try and the third or fourth try at adding an appointment after using the system for an hour or so. The planned target level was set to be 12 seconds, an improvement over the worst acceptable level; this improved the best possible level even more.

The attribute in the fifth row of the table shows a different instrument, other than a user questionnaire, to measure the user's first impression of the interface. For this, the number of negative and of positive remarks made by participants during their first session was used as an indicator of their first impression and satisfaction with the interface. This has been called the "cuss and aha count." Note that the worst level for negative remarks (10) was used as the best level for positive remarks, and vice versa. During a first session, the number of negative and positive remarks should be about the same (here, 5), for the planned level.

Of course, the number of remarks is directly related to the length of the session; this initial testing session for the simple Calendar Management System lasts a little over an hour, based on pilot test results. If it goes substantially longer (or shorter, for that matter), for whatever reason, you can handle this one of two ways. You can either measure the remarks made in just the first hour, or you can count the remarks throughout the entire session and indicate in your Observed Results column that the session took 75 minutes (or whatever). If the task time is variable, all values (both specified and observed) should be normalized to comments per minute. Admittedly, this measuring instrument is rather participant-dependent (whether a participant will talk much during a session, whether a participant is generally a complainer, and so on), but this instrument can produce some interesting results.

There are surely many other possibilities for usability attributes that you have chosen, which extend beyond the preceding samples of appropriate usability attributes for the Calendar Management System. We hope that these helped you to explore some of the interesting issues that must be resolved when determining usability attributes.

REFERENCES

Bennett, J. L. (1984). Managing to Meet Usability Requirements: Establishing and Meeting Software Development Goals. In J. Bennett, D. Case, J. Sandelin, & M. Smith (Ed.), *Visual Display Terminals* (pp. 161–184). Englewood Cliffs, NJ: Prentice-Hall.

Card, S. K., Moran, T. P., & Newell, A. (1983). *The Psychology of Human-Computer Interaction.* Hillsdale, NJ: Erlbaum.

Carroll, J. M. & Rosson, M. B. (1985). Usability Specifications as a Tool in Iterative Development. In H. R. Hartson (Ed.), *Advances in Human-Computer Interaction*, Vol. 1, (pp. 1–28). Norwood, NJ: Ablex.

Chin, J. P., Diehl, V. A., & Norman, K. L. (1988). Development of an Instrument Measuring User Satisfaction of the Human-Computer Interface. *Proceedings of CHI Conference on Human Factors in Computing Systems*, New York: ACM, 213–218.

Gilb, T. (1981). *Design by Objectives.* Unpublished manuscript.

Good, M., Spine, T., Whiteside, J., & George, P. (1986). User Derived Impact Analysis as a Tool for Usability Engineering. *Proceedings of CHI Conference on Human Factors in Computing Systems*, New York: ACM, 241–246.

Whiteside, J., Bennett, J., & Holtzblatt, K. (1988). Usability Engineering: Our Experience and Evolution. In M. Helander (Ed.), *Handbook of Human-Computer Interaction* (pp. 791–817). Amsterdam: Elsevier North-Holland.

≣9

Rapid Prototyping of Interaction Design

9.1   WHAT IS RAPID PROTOTYPING?

In a television interview, Anthony Perkins described a technique used by Alfred Hitchcock for developing and refining the plots of his movies. Hitchcock would tell the stories at cocktail parties and observe reactions of his listeners. He would experiment with various sequences and mechanisms for revealing the story line. Refinement of the story was based on listener reactions as an evaluation criterion. *Psycho* is one notable example of the results of this technique.

Automobile makers, architects, and sculptors make models; circuit designers use "bread-boards;" aircraft developers test "mockups;" artists experiment with working sketches. In each case, the goal is to provide an early ability to observe something about the nature of the final product, evaluating ideas and weighing alternatives before committing to one of them.

In contrast, conventional approaches to the development of large interactive software systems—a highly complex process that requires enormous quantities of time, money, and personnel—tend to force a commitment to large amounts of design detail without any means for visualizing and evaluating the product until it is too late to make significant changes. Construction and modification of software by ordinary programming techniques are notoriously expensive and time-consuming activities. It is little wonder that there is so much user dissatisfaction with many of the products developed this way.

The techniques of prototyping, especially *rapid prototyping*, and iterative design have emerged in the context of interactive software development, most importantly for the user interface. These techniques allow the software development process to share the essence of the Hitchcock story-development scheme: *refinement of the product based on feedback from users*.

People often voice concerns about testing with a prototype that might be quite different from the final product. If you are concerned, you should think about the Hitchcock case. In spite of the vast difference between prototype and finished product (i.e., verbal storytelling versus motion picture), no one can dispute that the prototyping technique was used to great effect by a master dialogue designer.

The prototyping approach to interactive system development involves production of at least one early version of the system that illustrates essential features of the later, operational system. With *rapid* prototyping, the process of constructing prototypes is accelerated, so that the time from beginning a prototype to evaluating user interaction with it is short enough to leave time for substantial changes, if needed, to the product. This, in turn, allows multiple iterations through the refinement process and a finer tuning to the needs of the user, helping ensure usability of the resulting system.

A rapid prototype lets potential users of an evolving interactive system "take it for a spin." Would you buy a car without taking it for a test drive, or buy a stereo system without first listening to it? Well, users should not be excluded from the development process, either; that is the whole premise behind the idea of participatory design. Used early in the development process, a prototype encourages user participation and involvement and allows developers to observe user behavior and reaction to the prototype. As such, it is the key to supporting the formative evaluation and iterative design process that is the heart of user interaction development.

This chapter motivates the need for rapid prototyping, and presents various types of prototypes. It discusses some advantages and pitfalls of prototyping and talks about what to put in prototypes at different stages of the development process. It briefly looks at interactive tools that support rapid prototyping and ends by presenting some details of experiences in prototyping a real-world development project.

9.1.1 The Need for Rapid Prototyping in Iterative Design

Using rapid prototyping to support iterative design does not mean that developers should be afforded a chance to be lazy or sloppy with the initial design. Rather, it is simply not possible, using design guidelines alone, to get it right the first time. Developers must thus adopt the "artillery" method, as shown in Figure 9.1: Ready, fire, aim. The first shot provides a reference point from which successive adjustments are made in order to hit the target.

The star life cycle introduced in Chapter 4 is evaluation-centered. The iterative development process exemplified by this life cycle is based on evaluating an interaction design with users. In doing so, however, developers face an inherent dilemma: *You can't evaluate an interaction design until it is built, but after building, changes to the design are difficult* (if not impossible). At the beginning of the development cycle there is nothing to test. Building something to test is expensive and time consuming and is a large investment in design concepts that have not been evaluated. These opposing realities can present an impasse in the development process, and a dilemma for the developer. The solution to this dilemma is the subject of this chapter: *rapid prototyping*. Through rapid prototyping, an interaction developer gets an opportunity to evaluate proposed designs very early in the life cycle and to ensure that usability gets built into the evolving interaction design.

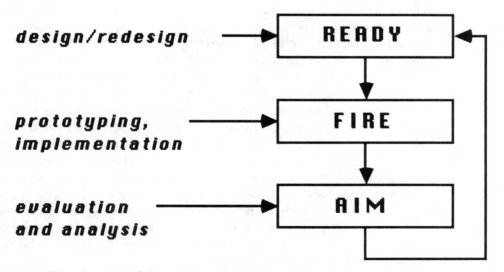

Figure 9.1. "Artillery" approach to rapid prototyping.

9.1.2   A Natural Technique

Although prototyping, especially rapid prototyping, has been closely associated in the literature with automated software tools, it is important to emphasize that *prototyping is a technique, not just a tool*. The technique can be effective even when used manually, especially in the early, conceptual stages of development. Creative use of paper-and-pencil prototypes, clear plastic overlays, flip charts, movable stick-on felt cutouts, and other props can sort out important aspects of an early design before any implementation effort is expended. One such prototype interaction design we saw included a borrowed telephone receiver for the user to seek help information. Another included a real keyboard and mouse that were used with screen sketches made on plastic transparencies.

In these creative prototypes, one member of the development team acts out the role of the computer, "executing" the prototype by moving paper and/or plastic (or whatever the prototype is built of) objects around within the prototype, in response to actions of another person acting as user. Users at this very early stage of rapid prototyping can be from the development team but should also include representative users. This method is surprisingly effective, especially very early in development, and is explained more fully in later sections. Typically, a great deal of discussion accompanies the interaction, and weaknesses in the design are highlighted by the amount of extra-system dialogue required to clarify the meaning of various features and how to use them. Such theatrical dialectics work best when oriented toward a specific task or situational context. Interaction between the user and the "computer" (the person manipulating the prototype), or an evaluator/observer, is typically concrete and fairly detailed. The results can often, however, be generalized to cover other parts of the interaction design as well.

There are, in fact, sound theoretical reasons for believing that rapid prototyping is a *natural technique*. Rapid prototyping is a technique that begins with rather specific details of an interaction design, then structures and refines them into a system. This approach is grounded in the precepts of developmental psychology (Piaget, 1950; Whiteside & Wixon, 1985). Working from concrete to abstract is the way humans naturally investigate, understand, and assimilate new concepts and solve problems. Teachers often begin with concrete, specific examples of the concept they are presenting, then move to a more abstract, theoretical presentation of that concept. To both users and developers, a prototype is concrete, while specifications are more abstract. The prototyping approach as a natural technique is supported by Ehn's (1990) assertion that design requirements are best conveyed by *showing* rather than by just *saying*.

Not only is rapid prototyping a natural technique, but it is also highly suitable for the special situation in which various members of the development team find themselves. As discussed in Chapter 1, in the cooperative development activity of behavioral scientists and computer scientists, a gap exists between the skills and goals brought to their tasks by each of these roles. Computer scientists often do not fully understand the need for user-centered design or the behavioral scientist's concern for human factors or for how human factors are incorporated into a design. Alternatively, behavioral scientists often do not appreciate the limitations and technical difficulties of building large interactive systems, and of integrating the user interface with the rest of the software. These two developer roles, along with a problem domain expert and other team members, must work together to achieve an artful—and *usable*—result. A prototype gives them a common communication technique for working toward this common goal.

9.2   TYPES OF PROTOTYPES

There are several ways to classify types of techniques for prototyping. The first classification presented here involves some dimensions of a prototype. This is followed by discussions of vertical versus horizontal prototyping, and global versus local prototyping.

9.2.1 Dimensions of Prototyping

From the perspective of the development process, four (more or less orthogonal) dimensions are useful for classifying approaches to prototyping (Hartson & Smith, 1991): representation, scope, executability, and maturation.

▶ *Representation*: How are interaction designs represented in the prototype?

Approaches to prototyping can be classified by the techniques used to represent interaction designs. Prototyping tools share this need for interaction design representation with other interface development tools. Interaction design representation techniques were discussed in Chapters 6 and 7. The more visual and user-task-oriented design representations are better for direct translation into a prototype—after all, this involves prototypes of the user interaction design, not of the interface program code.

For interaction developers who wish to concentrate on the interaction and not the problem of its representation, the less the representation technique is like a programming language, the better. This is especially true because interaction development is now falling more and more to behavioral specialists rather than to programmers (Richards, Boies, & Gould, 1986).

▶ *Scope*: Does the prototype include the whole system or just the interface?

When the scope of the prototype is limited to just the interface, this *interface-only prototype* is sometimes called a façade, interface simulation, or mockup (Gregory, 1984), and the drawbacks are obvious. Interface features dependent on computational actions can be difficult to anticipate. For example, the complicated dynamics of formatting displays for paging and scrolling of retrieved database records within a window are difficult to design and evaluate without some real output for testing. Also, the interaction developer cannot provide realistic messages in response to computational conditions that may not yet be fully known or understood. If the computational component cannot be tested with the prototype, it is more difficult to integrate the interaction component with the rest of the software. As computational functions come into existence, it is greatly beneficial to be able to see them in action in a *whole-system prototype*.

▶ *Executability*: Can the prototype be executed at any time?

One of the most common kinds of prototype is implementation as prototype. The idea is to code a mockup of the system to observe its behavior. Because the prototype is coded in a programming language, it is an effective way to construct a whole-system prototype. The disadvantage is that there are only *intermittent* times when the system is in a state that can be executed and evaluated. There are long intervals when, due to incomplete implementation of routines, syntax and semantic coding errors, data typing problems, unresolved symbolic references, and so on, it cannot run. Anything syntactically incomplete or erroneous in the partially developed code will prevent the prototype from executing. The result is slow prototyping, not a process that is useful for evaluating numerous different alternatives as an interaction design evolves. When each iteration is a lengthy process of programming and debugging, fewer iterations are possible, and users and evaluators have correspondingly less opportunity to participate in the design process. Also, of course, as the system grows, more and more delay is incurred from compiling, linking, and loading.

In contrast, prototypes that can be interpreted do not require compiling and linking, thereby allowing prototype modification and execution to be interleaved rapidly. Interpretable prototypes are *continuously* executable. Further, one of the most important features that a prototyping environment can provide is the ability for the developer to alter the design during running of the prototype and then restart testing from that same point in its execution. This is very rapid turnaround, indeed, and is perhaps the ultimate in continuous executability.

▶ *Maturation*: How does the prototype grow into a product?

During its maturation from prototype to product, it is not unusual for an interactive system to pass through several incarnations. Often, the following progression of deliverables comes from a development team:

1. One or more prototypes
2. A development implementation
3. The final product

Field, or beta, testing occurs between Steps 2 and 3. Step 3 is a software manufacturing step, in which the implementation code is streamlined and optimized by "code-smiths," often into assembly language. Step 3 is not considered to be part of the prototyping process. Thus, most of what is described in this book as development occurs in Steps 1 and 2.

The prototype-based development process is re*volutionary* in its maturation if the prototypes of Step 1 are discarded in the process of going to Step 2. That is, little or nothing from the prototype implementation is used in the development implementation; the prototype is eventually thrown away (or at least retired).

In *evolutionary* maturation, the Step 1 prototype eventually becomes complete enough to be a Step 2 implementation. That is, some or all of the prototype implementation can be used in the development implementation, and the prototype is not completely discarded. An automated tool can provide a support environment for executing partially specified and incompletely developed designs. As the design matures and becomes complete, the prototype evolves into a real, compilable implementation of the entire target system. The nature of the evolution to Step 2 depends on how the design is represented and captured in the prototype. If the prototype is coded, it may just be a matter of cleaning up the code and adding connections to the routines for computational functionality. If the interaction design is represented in other ways (e.g., state diagrams representing dialogue control), implementation can be achieved by manually coding the state diagrams or, if suitable tools are available, through compilation of the representation that previously was interpreted in the prototype.

Revolutionary prototyping is most useful when the prototype is built as early in the development process as possible and as rapidly as possible, without a large commitment of resources. Otherwise, deadline pressures make it difficult for managers and developers to work on a large prototype they know will be discarded. An early switch from a revolutionary prototype to a development implementation, however, means that development at the end, when changes can be surprisingly large and frequent, is done without benefit of a prototype. Revolutionary prototyping is the usual approach when the prototyping platform is different from the intended delivery platform of the final product.

For most applications, an evolutionary, whole-system, continuous prototype is a desirable choice for the user interaction developer. However, revolutionary, interface-only, intermittent prototypes are easier to produce, given the state of today's technology—the interactive support tools for rapid prototyping—mainly because most programming environments require programs to be correct and relatively complete before they can be executed.

9.2.2   Horizontal versus Vertical Prototypes

Nielsen (1987) describes types of prototypes based on how a target system is scaled down in the prototype. A *horizontal prototype* offers less depth in its coverage of functionality, but it is very broad in the features it incorporates. This results in a shallow, less detailed version of a prototype with more features. Usability evaluation with this kind of prototype is generally less realistic but covers more of the functionality of the final system.

In a *vertical prototype*, on the other hand, the number of features is reduced, yielding a prototype that covers a narrow range of possible functions. Those functions that are included are developed in detail. The advantage, of course, is that usability evaluation can be quite realistic, but only for a few functions.

Horizontal prototyping is generally best for very early prototypes because it is useful for more general concept proving and to help assess proposed functionality. Vertical prototyping serves well in later prototypes, when some selected functions can be developed in more detail for usability evaluation.

Either of these kinds of prototypes could also be classified along the dimensions presented in the previous section. Namely, either could be interface-only or whole-system (scope), intermittently or continuously executable (executability), and revolutionary or evolutionary (maturation).

9.2.3   Global versus Local Prototypes

Another way to classify prototypes, somewhat similar to Nielsen's, is based on content of the prototype. A *global prototype* is a prototype of much of the entire system, and a user can, from playing with it, get a good feel for the final product, both at a high, paradigmatic level and at a low, detailed level. It constitutes a rather complete instantiation of the current version of an interaction design. This is similar to the horizontal classification just presented, but a global prototype could, in addition to breadth, also have a good deal of depth (i.e., similar to the vertical prototype).

A *local prototype* is a prototype of a single specific detail, one that is important enough to potentially affect usability of the overall system. A local prototype is used to evaluate design alternatives for particular isolated interaction details (e.g., appearance of an icon, wording of a message, and behavior of an individual function). If developed in some detail, a local prototype can be similar to a vertical prototype. It is not, however, a horizontal prototype because it does not represent breadth in any way, but rather captures specific details.

A local prototype is typically stand-alone, not connected to the rest of the prototype, and has a very short life span. It is most effective when developers get into heated conversations about which design alternative is best, and all conversing parties are sure they are right! It is often useful to apply a *"five minute rule"* for such conversations. If one of these heated discussions goes on past five minutes, with essentially a stalemate occurring, we suggest allocating the point of discussion to be decided by use of a local prototype. It then becomes a candidate for appropriate testing with users at some later time.

Global prototypes are useful throughout the entire prototyping cycle, from beginning to end. Local prototypes tend to be more useful only for a brief time, when specific details of one or two particular design issues are being worked out. Both global and local prototypes can be classified along the scope, executability, and maturation dimensions. In reality, however, a local prototype would rarely be other than an interface-only, intermittently executable, revolutionary prototype. Global and local prototyping are discussed further, with examples of how each was used in an actual development situation, in Section 9.6, on examples from a development project.

9.3   WEIGHING RAPID PROTOTYPING

While rapid prototyping does address many needs in the iterative design process, there are trade-offs between its advantages and its pitfalls. There are only a few experimental studies on the subject of prototyping versus classical system development methods in which benefits to both developers and users are weighed.

9.3.1 Advantages

In an experiment conducted at the University of California, Los Angeles (UCLA) (Boehm, Gray, & Seewaldt, 1984), some development teams used conventional development methodologies while others employed prototypes in the software development process (with no particular emphasis on the user interface). Systems produced by the groups using prototypes were judged to be *easier to learn and use* than those produced by standard methods. Groups using the prototyping approach also appeared to be *less affected by deadline pressures*. The code of the final systems produced by prototyping groups was only about 40% as large as that of their counterparts. Finally, the prototyping groups accomplished their task with 45% *less effort* than the other groups.

In a similar study (Alavi, 1984), users of systems developed using the prototyping approach had a *higher level of satisfaction* than did users of nonprototyped systems. Developers felt that prototyping *enhanced communication* about the proposed system. The prototype created a *common baseline* or *reference point* from which potential problems and opportunities could be identified. Discussions could take place between developers and users about good and bad features in the evolving design. The prototype allowed these discussions to be conducted in concrete terms. Users also tended to be *more enthusiastic* about a project in which they were involved through the use and evaluation of prototypes. According to the developers, this enthusiasm, together with the *enhanced communication of requirements,* led to increased user acceptance of the systems.

A developer in Alavi (1984) commented that users were very good at criticizing an existing system (i.e., the prototype) but were not too good at anticipating or articulating needs. The first version that users can experiment with, whether prototype or real product, can cause them to change their view about what they want the system to do (Wasserman & Shewmake, 1985). Use of prototypes in design evaluation can *facilitate earlier developer response* to these changes and can increase the likelihood that the end product will be what users really want and need.

The advantage that rapid prototyping has to offer in addition to the prototyping concepts in the preceding studies is that of *iterative design.* In each of these studies, prototypes were manually coded by the developers. Due to time constraints, there was little opportunity for multiple passes through the prototype phase of development. In contrast, a rapid prototyping technique can be enhanced by automated support tools using noncoding techniques such as direct manipulation for construction of interface displays and state diagram representations of logical sequencing. This representation of the design can then be executed and used as a prototype. A prototype, however embryonic, can be available for experimentation and evaluation very early in the development cycle. Changes in the prototype can be made rapidly, using the same tools. Because the tools allow rapid representation of design ideas, users can be presented with many options instead of a single design, increasing their ability to move toward a design that meets their needs.

Another advantage of prototypes is their use in *effecting a paradigm shift for users* of an existing system (either manual or interactive) that are about to begin using a new interactive version of that system. Users of interactive systems, just like everyone else, get set in their ways, and don't always welcome change. Use of a prototype can be very effective in introducing a group of users to their new system. In one particular instance, we saw a development group present a simple version of an office automation prototype to users of an archaic existing interactive system. Even though the prototype was very early and of limited functionality, users got quite excited about it as they saw (admittedly carefully planned) demonstrations of how it would help them perform their jobs more effectively.

So prototypes are used primarily for communication and for evaluation with users but can also be used to encourage a shift from one system to another. Because of the many advantages of rapid prototyping—both empirically and anecdotally documented—it is difficult to avoid the conclusion that no interactive system ought to be produced without at least a simple paper-and-pencil prototype, evaluated with user feedback.

9.3.2   Pitfalls

Prototyping, however, is not without potential drawbacks as an approach to interactive system development. These are pitfalls, rather than real disadvantages, because with some caution, they can be avoided.

One of the biggest dangers is found in *attempts to use prototyping as a development technique without first securing cooperation from all parties* involved, and without establishing a thorough understanding of the process. Iterative design depends on the willingness and ability of customers and users to provide useful feedback. Also, established management procedures can make it difficult to deal with *planning and scheduling* of a development life cycle quite different from the traditional one. Managers may view allocation of resources to building a prototype, especially a throw-away one, as wasteful.

Developers also must have the proper attitude. For example, Alavi (1984) noticed a *reduction in programmer discipline*, possibly because the process of developing the prototype was viewed as an exercise rather than as the real thing. On the other hand, user and developer enthusiasm for continued development may diminish after some version of a working prototype is provided (Alavi, 1984). In addition, the prototypes of large systems can themselves be large and complex. For example, a Federal Aviation Administration (FAA) project to develop a new air traffic control system involved building a full-function prototype that took nearly two years and cost millions of dollars. The misconception that a prototype is just a toy can lead to its development without a methodology to aid in its management, resulting in a failed, unmanageable, useless prototype. These problems can be addressed by methodologies and tools built around a prototyping-based approach such as the star life cycle.

Some of the most serious problems occur if various parties—managers and/or customers and/or marketing—begin to *view the early prototypes they see as the final product*. There are horror stories of managers who, upon seeing a prototype that they like, profusely congratulated the development team on doing such a great job and being so far ahead of the delivery schedule. The manager then attempted to rush the prototype prematurely to market—to the astonishment and frustration of the developers! Marketing people who do not understand the purpose of prototyping have been known to have a similar reaction; upon seeing a good prototype, they may rush off and tell their potential customers that the product is going to be available far ahead of its original promised delivery date. These cases are abuses of the prototyping technique and represent problems that can be avoided by having an early agreement and understanding about the role of prototyping in the overall development process.

A prototype is a sort of scale-model of a real system and is therefore *limited regarding the accuracy with which it can represent the real system*. Prototypes usually focus on one aspect of a target system—the user interface, system functionality, or system performance. If a prototype is accurate in one of these areas, it usually must trade off accuracy in the other two. Scaling back up to the real system will require attention to where these inaccuracies occur.

Thus, an important aspect of prototyping is the *fidelity of the prototype* to the intended final product. Particularly if the prototype developer is using a prototyping tool, there will be some deviations between the prototype and the final delivered system. However, the prototype should be as true as possible to the final design. If it is not, there is the very real possibility of *overpromising with the prototype*, or of *misleading with the prototype*. For example, if the final delivery platform does not support use of a mouse, then the prototype should not use a mouse. Otherwise, users will expect a mouse in their final product and will be disappointed when they don't get it. In addition, users' evaluation of the prototype will not be as valuable, because of the potentially major difference that use of a mouse makes in an interface. Similarly, if there is to be a mouse in the final product, then the prototyping tool and platform should make it possible to include a mouse in the prototype. Otherwise, if the prototype is evaluated without a mouse, developers will have no way of knowing what to expect of users' performance with one.

Another aspect of promoting fidelity is the *choice of a prototyping tool and platform*, which can influence—sometimes quite dramatically—the user interaction design. If developers are using a prototyping tool to produce a prototype on a development platform that is different from the delivery platform for the final product, then that tool should be one that will support prototyping of as much of the final product design as possible. Developers should not have to compromise very much of the design because of the prototyping tool. The tool must allow developers to prototype most of what is desired in the final system, including interface appearance and behavior, and even as much of the delivery platform hardware as possible.

A throw-away, revolutionary prototype can seduce developers into the *trap of overdesign* (Mantei, 1986). Developers can fall in love with their prototype, becoming too attached to it and investing too much in its development, only to have it scrapped. The engineering maxim to "make it good enough" applies particularly to throw-away prototypes. The best way to avoid most of these problems is to adopt the evolutionary approach and not have to face the question of when to discard the prototype. Unfortunately, the industry still lacks good prototyping tools to support evolutionary development. Rapid prototyping tools are discussed more in Section 9.5.

Prototypes with emphasis on the user interaction design usually have a bottom-up flavor to their development because details of the interaction design tend to surface early in the development process. It can be difficult for a software engineer trained in the ways of top-down, stepwise decomposition to accept such a *different approach* to the interface component of the system. Also, emphasis on the interaction in the prototype almost always leads to stubbing of computational functionality. The temptation is to stub the difficult parts of the computational design without first understanding their design requirements. Later, development of the stubbed functions can reveal basic problems that affect the system at many levels above the stub in question. The result is upheaval rather than a smooth progression toward an implementation.

9.4   WHAT TO PUT IN A PROTOTYPE

So now you're convinced that you should be using rapid prototyping in your user interface development environment. Probably, indeed, you already have been involved in the development of a prototype. What should go into your prototypes? The answer depends on whether you're developing an early prototype, or whether you've progressed to working on a later, more mature one.

9.4.1   Early Prototypes

One purpose of the earliest user interface prototypes is *to test the overall interaction metaphor* you are designing. These early prototypes are a direct result of conceptual design (discussed in Chapter 5). To this end, the prototype should start with a few representative sample screens that include basic format and content, but will not have every detail of that format and content worked out. The representative screens should be ones that users of the final system are likely to see and use most often. What you are trying to find out with these early prototypes is, for example, whether users can understand and use the basic paradigm you are incorporating into the design, such as the desktop paradigm.

In early prototypes, you are looking at the big picture, not at tiny specific details. Thus, the *fidelity of early prototypes to the final design can be somewhat low*. If formative evaluation with early prototypes shows that users don't get along well with the basic metaphor, then the developers won't have wasted all the time it takes to work out design details of interaction objects such as screen icons, messages, and so on. Instead, they can try a different metaphor in a different prototype, and retest to see whether users like it better. Clearly, interaction details in these early prototypes cannot be too sloppy, or else they can influence the users' performance with and impression of the interaction metaphor you are trying to evaluate. Nonetheless, you can make good best guesses at iconic images, button and menu labels, and other specifics that are needed to evaluate early prototypes.

As you decide on which screens to include in your early prototype, you should develop a few representative functions that you expect the user to perform frequently. You should already have a good idea about this kind of information from your task analysis (discussed in Chapter 5). Choose a few functions that are the most important, and prototype them fairly completely; you will have less functionality but more usability. In order to mock up a representative function so that a user can be effective in evaluating the prototype, a user performing that function should be able to follow a representative functional thread—again, a series or group of commands or actions that a user will perform frequently. In a word processor, for example, this might be a cut/paste sequence, or setting up margins and tabs. In a spreadsheet, a representative function might be changing a formula in one cell and propagating that change to all logically related cells.

In order for developers to get maximum information from a user about the prototype, the prototype must support at least a few functional threads of the most common tasks. As Chapter 10, on formative evaluation, shows, a great deal can be learned from an incomplete design in a prototype, with every brand new user of it.

9.4.2 Later Prototypes

Eventually, the design of the interaction metaphor will settle down over a few iterations of formative evaluation, and you will move on to later versions of the prototype. The purpose of these later prototypes is *to test the details* of the design. After you are sure, from the early prototypes, that users are comfortable with the overall paradigmatic approach to the interface, then you can begin to focus on producing more detailed, refined screens for the interface. You can include more complete commands and more complete tasks and functional threads in the prototype. You can include well-designed icons, and carefully worded messages. These later, more detailed prototypes should have a higher fidelity to the final design.

In user testing with the early prototypes, you will certainly have collected lots of information about detailed changes that should be considered for the interaction design; later prototypes offer the chance to iron out all the details before actual implementation.

9.5   RAPID PROTOTYPING TOOLS

Prototyping can be accomplished without the aid of automated tool support, as the exercise on prototyping at the end of this chapter shows. However, without automated prototyping tools, management of the evolving design can quickly become intractable. Use of interactive tools in constructing and documenting designs and prototypes can be of great benefit. Because prototyping involves construction and modification of a software model of an interface or a system, it should not be surprising that much work to date has been devoted to the construction of special prototype definition and execution tools. These tools attempt to allow developers to construct useful prototypes while reducing the amount of conventional programming required.

These tools also can be used to maintain information about configurations, various versions, data and observations from evaluation, and reasons for design changes. This information, gathered as the tools are used, enables developers to track the fast pace of change during the design and prototyping phases of development. Automated tools can also provide instrumentation necessary to obtain objective measures for user performance with the prototype.

From the interaction developer's viewpoint, the important role of automated tools in rapid prototyping is to support the highly iterative cycles of design and evaluation. Any tool that is used for rapid prototyping should allow many alternative designs to be tried in a short period of time (hours as opposed to days or weeks). Although many tools concentrate on particular interaction styles or are limited to certain classes of application systems, they are still useful for trying out initial design ideas with users early in the development process.

Because of the ease with which many of them permit user interaction designs to be defined and modified, rapid prototyping tools may be the single most important class of tools in decreasing the time required for design and subsequent iteration based on evaluation with users. In addition to tools that are strictly for rapid prototyping, most User Interface Management Systems, or UIMSs, support rapid prototyping as well. At present, many tools for rapid prototyping run on microcomputers, while UIMSs often run on workstations. UIMSs typically support other activities in the interface development process, as well. UIMS are discussed in more detail in Chapter 11.

Many of the first tools for prototyping of interactive systems required a great deal of programming. Because of the amount of coding involved, these prototypes tended to be only intermittently executable. Because they were largely façades (interface-only), the prototypes tended to be revolutionary (throw-away), or a mixture of interface and some minimal functionality. Many of these early prototypes, however, were very realistic and could exhibit complex graphical behavior.

Other early tools produced interpreted interface definitions and offered the flexibility of an evolutionary approach, but they almost always caused the prototype to suffer slow performance. This trade-off still prevails in many of today's tools. As the ability to produce façades advanced in the tools, provision was made to program or at least stub noninterface functionality, moving the technology slowly toward whole-system prototypes. However, this technology still has not come nearly as far in this direction as is needed by real-world user interface development environments to truly make prototyping and iteration of a wide variety of interaction designs fast and easy.

9.5.1 Some Rapid Prototyping Tools

New user interface development tools appear at a prodigious rate, and almost all such tools now have some kind of prototyping capability. It is neither possible nor feasible to mention them all here. Because of their rapid proliferation, we do not attempt to give a survey or a consumer's guide to prototyping tools. Any details about specific tools would quickly be out of date. Therefore, what follows is a brief list of a few of the tools that have been most frequently used for rapid prototyping. Additional information about other classes of user interface development tools is given in Chapter 11.

Many people have speculated that the tool most frequently used for rapid prototyping is *HyperCard* ™, which runs on Macintosh™ computers. It was originally billed as "programming for the rest of us" and was not necessarily intended for prototyping. However, its ease of learning, ease of use, and built-in library of interaction objects (e.g., buttons, selectable hot spots, menus, and so on) give developers a running start on a rapid prototype. In addition, its HyperTalk™ scripting language allows extensions to the built-in objects to be done in a fairly easy manner. This greatly increases the functionality of the tool beyond just its built-in features. Some experiences with using *HyperCard* ™ as a prototyping tool are discussed in the next section.

Another similar product that runs on the Macintosh™ family of computers is *SuperCard*™, and also SmethersBarnes *Prototyper*™. MacroMind *Director*™ is another Mac-based product that was originally intended for instructional development and computer-aided learning programs, but because of its animation capabilities, it has been used quite a bit for prototyping.

There are also many non-Macintosh™ PC-based prototyping tools. One that is much like *HyperCard*™ and *SuperCard*™ is Asymetrix's *ToolBook*™, which runs under *Windows* 3.0™. *VisualBasic*™ and *ObjectScript*™ also run under *Windows* 3.0™. One of the earliest commercially available prototypers for personal computers was Bricklin's *Demo*™, now released as *Demo II*™.

9.5.2 Features to Look For in a Rapid Prototyping Tool

There are several important characteristics to look for as you choose a rapid prototyping tool for use in your user interface development environment. Choice of an inappropriate tool can lead to many of the pitfalls we discussed previously, such as overpromising (or underpromising) with the prototype, or having the prototyping tool affect the final design. On the other hand, choice of an appropriate tool can greatly facilitate your rapid prototyping effort and thereby expedite (and in many cases even make feasible) many cycles of formative evaluation and iterative design.

Some features that are most important when selecting a tool include the following (you will see many of these same characteristics mentioned in Chapter 11, in regard to choosing a user interface development tool):

▶ Easy to develop and modify screens

If a prototyping tool makes it difficult to create and difficult to change screen format and content, it's not the tool for you. In particular, a tool should allow you easily to create both graphics and text on a single screen, without having to go back and forth between a graphics editor and a text editor. Some tools make it quite easy to create interaction objects initially, but then make it difficult (or in a few cases, even impossible) to modify those objects. This is not acceptable; the whole concept of formative evaluation and iterative design is based on making changes to the user interaction design, quickly and easily. A tool must, at a minimum, give you fast and easy capability for modifying the design.

▶ Supports the type of interface you are developing

It is also important that the kinds of text and graphics, interaction styles, and other media a rapid prototyping tool supports are those that you intend to have in your final system. If there are particular interaction objects that you expect to have in your final interface, but that a particular tool makes very difficult to create and modify, then you should probably not consider using that tool. A tool should support interaction styles that are central to your project and environment. For example, a tool may support rather primitive text handling but has a wide variety of interaction styles that it produces. Perhaps you don't need much text handling in your design but do need several different interaction styles. Then if this tool provides those styles, it may be just the tool for you.

▶ Supports a variety of I/O devices

In addition to supporting the kinds of media and interaction styles you expect to have in your final interface, a tool should support use of the hardware devices you expect to have in the delivered system, as well. Some early prototypers supported only typed keyboard input in the interfaces they were used to prototype. This would obviously be a serious limitation today, and most current tools support keyboard and mouse input; a few support touchscreen input as well. The main output device supported in interfaces produced by tools is the cathode ray tube (CRT) terminal; more esoteric output devices are rarely supported by prototyping tools.

▶ Easy to link screens and to modify links

Some tools will allow you to create and modify individual screens but will not let you link them together in any fashion that will even vaguely resemble the final product. If this is the case, you might as well use a plain graphics editor and text editor and not waste your money on that tool. Be sure that you can create links among screens so that your prototypes can simulate real runtime navigational behavior for a user, and, again, that you can quickly and easily modify those links as necessary.

▶ Allows calling external procedures and programs

Many rapid prototyping tools provide a built-in library of user interaction objects and styles, which greatly expedites the prototype building process. However, if the tool provides only this built-in library, what happens if you want to include in your prototype something that isn't in that library? You're stuck—an example of where the tool can seriously (and probably negatively) influence the interaction design. Be sure the tool you choose either provides its own programming language and/or allows calls to external (outside the tool) program code. This will greatly extend the types of interaction features and interaction styles that can be produced by a tool.

▶ Allows importing of text, graphics, and other media

Although graphics capabilities are provided in most rapid prototyping tools, the graphics editors are sometimes fairly clumsy and may not allow you easily to produce more complex graphics. In this situation, you might wish to use a more powerful graphics package to create, say, some icons, and then import those icons into your prototype. You won't, of course, be able to modify whatever you import from within the prototyping tool. If you wish to make changes, you will have to use the graphics package that you used originally to create the imported graphics. Many prototyping tools allow you to import graphics, and, of course, text from other applications. In fact, some of them will even allow you to import video and/ or audio clips.

▶ Easy to learn and to use

The only way you can determine this for yourself is to try out a tool. As Chapter 11 stresses (in a discussion of selecting general user interface development tools), you must at least get evaluation copies of any tools you are considering. To try to make a decision after only watching a sales or marketing person give a snazzy demo, or after reading marketing glossies or even seeing a videotape, will not give you the information you need about either a tool's usability or its functionality. You must get hands-on experience with any tool that you are considering, in order to make a sensible choice.

▶ Good support from the vendor

Because so many new prototyping tools are constantly appearing, you should be sure that the company from which you are considering purchasing such a tool is a viable organization. Many of these tools are produced from brand new start-ups, with slim odds on their longevity. In all fairness, some of the best tools come from some of the newest companies, with the freshest ideas, but do be cautious about this. A phone and/or e-mail hotline, or some other sort of personal support, is highly desirable, especially when you are learning a tool and its basic capabilities. As with any software product, check the documentation as you are using the tool, and see whether it makes sense to you— or whether it is unclear, incomplete, or downright incorrect.

Increasingly, powerful automated tools to support rapid prototyping are becoming available. These tools allow more rapid production of executable designs or specifications. Improved development environments and other tool packages will allow better coordination of multiple designers. Development, management, and communication tools will become better integrated. The overall result will be faster iteration through the design/prototype loop, leading to systems that can be produced faster and less expensively and that are more satisfactory to users.

In sum, rapid prototyping tools can greatly facilitate the formative evaluation and iterative design process that is the very heart of the iterative refinement process. However, because of limitations in today's technology, choosing a tool for your development environment can be a difficult decision. We have offered these few basic features to look for when considering rapid prototyping tools. In Chapter 11, we offer a more structured, quantitative approach to evaluating and comparing general user interface development tools, and most of that approach is totally applicable to prototyping tools, as well.

9.6   EXAMPLES FROM A DEVELOPMENT PROJECT

The techniques described in this book have been used in numerous prototyping efforts with all sorts of organizations, in industrial, governmental, military, and academic environments. Rather than giving you hypothetical experiences with the rather simplistic design of the Calendar Management System, this chapter digresses from it to talk about some of our real-world experiences. You can gain some realistic ideas about prototyping based on a discussion of some experiences in a rather large development effort under a commercial contract. Prototyping of the user interaction design played an important role in development of a user interface management system called the Dialogue Management System (DMS). This development project was an 18-month effort of just under half a million dollars.

9.6.1   HyperCard as a Prototyping Tool

Our prototyping of DMS was done with *HyperCard*™ 1.0 on a Macintosh II™. Of several alternative tools considered, *HyperCard*™ offered advantages: It provided (through its built-in libraries, without the need for programming) many of the objects—namely, simple icons and some kinds of menus—anticipated in the final design. Developers learned it very quickly and were able to use it to produce screen mockups rapidly. Customized icons were simple to construct. The screen "hot spots" or "buttons" (selected screen areas) were easily definable to invoke arbitrary functions in response to selection by users.

Because *HyperCard*™ is interpreted, programs, written in a special *HyperCard*-ese called HyperTalk™, can be run immediately after changes are made to them. The cost for this feature is slow performance and some difficulty in tracing errors. *HyperCard*'s functionality is extensible, in the sense that any feature not already available in the built-in library (e.g., pop-up and pull-down menus) can be programmed in a compatible procedural language (e.g., in C or Pascal) and installed as an external function.

Because *HyperCard*™ was also used to document the user interaction designs, prototyping and design tools could be integrated in an interesting way. *Hyper-Card*™ buttons were associated with objects in screen pictures and other illustrations in the design documentation. If the reader of the online design documentation wished to explore the use of a feature, a mouse selection of the corresponding button took the reader to the *HyperCard*™ prototype for that feature. Ultimately, greater benefit can be gained from an even closer merging of the design documentation and prototype. Such connections to a prototype can offer interactive documentation and training for the user of an application.

The following two sections discuss some of our experiences on the DMS project, first with global prototyping, and then with local prototyping. These discussions illustrate some of the kinds of issues that can be addressed in various versions of your prototypes. *HyperCard*™ was used for both global and local prototypes.

DMS, as a user interface management system, contains several different interactive tools. The one used in this discussion and examples is the Graphical Programming Language, or GPL, tool, a graphical editor for constructing and maintaining a diagram of data and control flow, based on the concept of state transition diagrams. In particular, these diagrams are used to represent control and data flow in an interactive system design. The diagrams employ several different symbols for various kinds of nodes (e.g., entrances, exits, dialogue states, control states, computational states, and decision points), connected with arcs labeled with state transition conditions. The GPL tool is, in essence, a smart editor for a specific kind of state transition diagrams.

9.6.2 Global Prototyping

The DMS development team had distinct roles, including interaction developers, implementers, evaluators, and problem domain experts. In very early design stages, the primary user of the prototype was the interaction developer, who used the prototype almost daily to formatively evaluate and iterate designs. He also tested the prototype extensively to make sure that the programmers were implementing according to design (which, incidentally, was represented using UAN—see Chapters 6 and 7). During the first month of design, the prototype underwent fairly major redesign about twice a week. The goal was to iteratively refine the design via the prototype, which would later be discarded in favor of a Smalltalk implementation.

The GPL prototype was implemented by a newly hired programmer, who was unfamiliar with the project, *HyperCard*™, and Smalltalk. After he viewed a videotape of an earlier version of DMS that included a GPL tool, he was given the user interaction designs, written in UAN, for the new version of GPL. In two and a half weeks, he had the basic features of the GPL user interaction design incorporated into a *HyperCard*™ prototype, and required an additional week to polish it. During the ensuing iterations, most of the modifications were made by this programmer, although the interaction designer also had some experience with *HyperCard*™ and made occasional small changes.

During an 18-month development process, the global GPL prototype had a useful life of about 4 months, during which 3 cycles of formative evaluation were performed with users (see Chapter 10). At the 2-month point, a major design review was held, followed soon by delivery of a design document to the sponsor. Beyond this point, the GPL prototype continued to serve the development process, but more as a local prototyping tool for evaluating isolated design decisions. Having the prototype used by real users tremendously helped the designers of the GPL interface see the interaction from the user's viewpoint, exposing how users thought about the objects of the interface and their manipulation, relating them to task-performance issues in the design.

The main GPL screen, shown in Figure 9.2, was prototyped as a single card in *HyperCard*™ with buttons for each GPL icon and each GPL flow diagram object instance that a user can create. Mouse clicks within this screen are used to invoke the appropriate *HyperCard*™ scripts for the user's requested tasks (e.g., drawing lines, moving symbols). Each GPL flow diagram developed by a user is kept on a separate *HyperCard*™ card.

As a global prototype, the GPL prototype served to test many features, a couple of which are described here. For example, the GPL prototype helped provide insight into some questions about interface *modality*. This was a high-level issue, potentially affecting users virtually all the time they are using the GPL tool. As such, the global prototype incorporated our ideas about modality, in order to test them with users. Specifically, the prototype tested

- Whether modes were necessary in the design
- How often modes would be used by the user
- Whether modes would cause confusion for the user

The GPL tool is used to create GPL flow diagrams by creating various kinds of

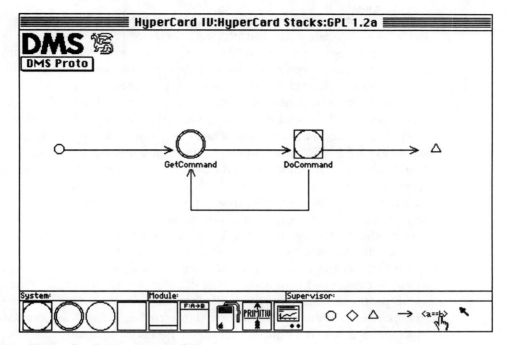

Figure 9.2. HyperCard™ prototype GPL screen.

node symbols on the screen and then connecting them with control flow arcs. A user must then do considerable detailed development in establishing attributes of both nodes and arcs in each GPL flow diagram. For these details, two modalities were incorporated into the prototype, so that the user must explicitly choose to be either in the mode for developing arcs or in the mode for developing nodes. A user selects the desired mode by clicking on the appropriate icon from the bottom of the screen (namely, the right-pointing arrow symbol for developing arcs, and one of the circular or square icons on the bottom left for developing nodes). The evaluation of the prototype with users showed that there is enough cognitive difference between developing nodes and developing arcs to justify separate modes in the design for these two kinds of objects.

Use of the prototype by potential DMS/GPL users showed that both modal and nonmodal usage was desirable, but the decision between them must be under user control. Observing users showed that some modes were acceptable and useful, as long as the appropriate visual cues were given as interface feedback—even something as simple as highlighting the selected icon representing a mode—to clearly indicate to users when a particular mode is active.

A specific question of modality arose when we considered whether the user should be able to select, say, the icon (e.g., circle or square) for a specific node type once and create several instances of it on the screen, or whether the user must select the icon for a node type each time a node type instance is added to the screen. Usability testing showed that users generally preferred to create several successive instances of the same node type without having to reselect the node icon each time.

Another specific modality question was related to the requirement that further design information about attributes must be given for each symbol: Should users be able to give that information successively for a number of existing symbols, or should they give the information for each symbol as the symbol is created? The answer was to give a user control of this situation by allowing the ability to enter all, some, or none of the information, upon creation of a new symbol instance. If the user does not enter all required information about some symbols before going on to another GPL diagram, the GPL tool informs the user of the missing information but still allows the user to work on another diagram if desired.

The GPL tool is fairly large and complex, and only a small portion of the prototype design is shown here. Figure 9.2, discussed earlier, shows the GPL tool prototype after construction of a GPL flow diagram consisting of a start symbol (small circle), a dialogue transaction (large circle) called "GetCommand," (for "getcommand"); a dialogue-computation function (box with inscribed circle) called DoCommand, and a triangular return symbol. A user creates the various symbols in this diagram by using the mouse to click on the corresponding node icon at the bottom of the screen, and positioning a new instance of that symbol on the screen with the mouse. When the user selects a node symbol (one of the nine leftmost icons across the bottom of the screen), the prototype is in node development mode. A user draws arcs by clicking the arc icon (the horizontal arrow just to the right of the triangle in the lower right part of the screen). This places the prototype in a different mode—namely, arc development mode—and then the user can click on the desired beginning and ending nodes for each arc, which the GPL tool automatically connects with an arc.

A user of the prototype can select one of the flow diagram symbols, for example GetCommand, to develop further (e.g., to define its attributes). This is possible when the prototype is in node development mode, as opposed to arc development mode. Because each symbol on the screen is defined as a *HyperCard*™ button, mouse selection capability is automatically provided in the prototype. The user can further develop a symbol by using a pop-up menu that appears when the user clicks on that symbol with the righthand mouse button. This pop-up menu allows the user to assign names, as well as documentation and other important information, to symbols. Although screens for them are not shown here, most of the commands on the pop-up menu and all the iconic commands along the bottom of the screen were incorporated into the prototype. Having such a complete proto-type as a guide proved invaluable during construction of the final product.

In addition to investigating modality questions, the GPL prototype was also used to experiment with screen layout for the tool, including

- Location of the command icon bar
- Visual design of each icon
- Relative location of textual labels for user-created GPL objects
- Location of information, such as names of user interaction objects

It is interesting to compare the final GPL prototype screen (shown in Figure 9.2) with the same screen, implemented later in Smalltalk (shown in Figure 9.3). This comparison reveals a side benefit of our prototyping: We were able to import the icons and other graphics from the prototype, via *MacPaint*™ files on the clipboard, directly into the Smalltalk application. This gave us a great appreciation for the

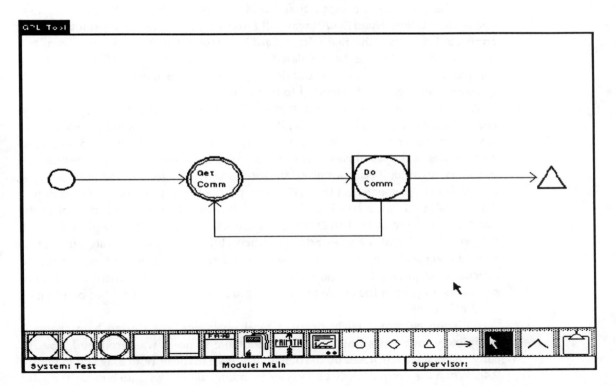

Figure 9.3. GPL tool screen as implemented in Smalltalk (compare with *Hypercard*™ prototype screen, Figure 9.2).

advantage of evolutionary prototyping: The icons that had come from detailed icon design work during prototyping could be reused.

9.6.3 Local Prototyping

During the design process, it can often be easier and faster for user interaction developers and evaluators to use a quick-and-dirty mock-up of a small excerpt of a design to answer isolated interaction design questions than to involve the full prototype. At some point, about 4 months into the 18-month project, the Smalltalk implementation version caught up with the *HyperCard*™ prototype version. Because Smalltalk is interpreted, that version was used as both prototype and implementation after that point. The *HyperCard*™ prototype was not kept up to date with all the user interaction design changes made after that point.

Nonetheless, isolated design questions still arose, especially during user interaction design walk-throughs, that could not be resolved without some user evaluation. Often, *HyperCard*™ was still faster for producing local prototypes (not connected to either the main *HyperCard*™ prototype or the evolving Smalltalk application) and testing these isolated detailed design features. While global prototypes are rather complete, our local prototypes focused on a few specific questions and were not intended to be extensible.

An example of a task-oriented issue studied with a local prototype involved the control flow arcs, which had several interdependent user-related problems. We wanted arcs to be responsive to direct manipulation by the user. Initial designs had ambiguities and special cases and did not address some important questions. A particularly difficult issue involved the mechanism for selecting and manipulating an arc. Must the user select the visible line precisely with the mouse (as in Figure 9.4a), or should "grab handles" be added? If a handle were needed, should the handle be in the middle of an arc (as in Figure 9.4b), or should one be placed at each endpoint? Will grab handles add too much clutter in crowded diagrams? How should a vertex be represented in a segmented arc? How can vertices be made to articulate as joints? Does movement of a vertex imply movement of adjacent segments only, or of the entire arc (as in Figure 9.4c)? How can rubber-banding be used effectively?

With the help of a fairly detailed local prototype, the design here changed completely four times until a design acceptable to users was produced. Specifically, users were surprised by the behavior shown in the bottom diagram in Figure 9.4c. When they moved only one vertex by manipulating its grab handle, they did not expect other vertices to move also. There was a strong user preference for the behavior shown in the middle diagram of Figure 9.4c, which gives users control of movement over each individual vertex.

Other kinds of issues that are appropriate for local prototyping would include

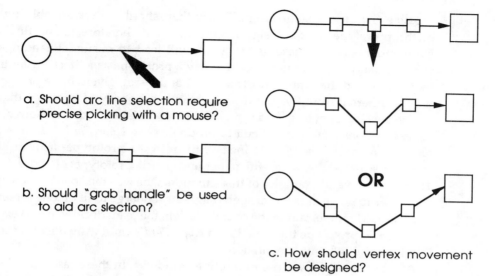

a. Should arc line selection require precise picking with a mouse?

b. Should "grab handle" be used to aid arc slection?

c. How should vertex movement be designed?

Figure 9.4. Local prototype used for answering design questions about manipulation of control flow arcs in the GPL tool.

wording of messages, icon design, use of color (or lack thereof), labels for buttons, and names for menu choices. A local prototype can be built quickly for each of these kinds of situations, giving two or more alternatives to the user. Then, a quick cycle of formative evaluation with a few users will help developers decide which of the alternatives will give the highest usability.

9.6.4   Lessons Learned

Two significant questions are repeatedly asked about using prototyping as a part of the development process:

1.   How much of the design should be included in the prototype?
2.   How far should development of the prototype be carried into the life cycle?

In response to the first question, developers often think that the prototype, being just a first draft, needs to bear only a loose resemblance to the real design. However, in order to have an effective global prototype, one that can be used by evaluators and users to get a reasonable feel for the evolving interface, it is useful to include as much functionality as possible, given constraints and resources (e.g., personnel, schedule). In addition, as the design becomes more complete and the prototype becomes more functional, it should be as similar in appearance as possible to the real system design. That is, there should be a reasonably high *fidelity* of the prototype to the design documents, and therefore to the final system. Differences between these, if too great, will lead to misunderstandings by the evaluator and potential users. Users view a prototype as a literal instantiation of the design, and they can only evaluate what they are given in the prototype. If it is very different from the real design, they have no way of knowing that.

The development team had to make difficult decisions at times, though, because some functions were too difficult to produce using *HyperCard™*. In this case, we *chose not to expend the effort* to include them in the prototype. Instead, the team sometimes opted for a careful paper-and-pencil prototype of those functions. There were several examples of this situation. One was the "pan" function, allowing a user to move around through diagrams too large to fit on one screen. While this was fairly important in the overall design, the team decided not to expend the resources to prototype this function in *HyperCard™*, and waited instead until well into the Smalltalk implementation.

Another example was use of multiple windows. In these cases, the limitations of *HyperCard™* prevented the fidelity of the prototype to the design from being as high as desired. Another option was to omit pop-up menus, which were tricky to implement in *HyperCard™*, and to use some other interaction style in the prototype. However, because pop-up menus were central to the design, the extra effort was expended to include them. The *HyperCard™* code was not aesthetic, but the pop-up menus worked well enough for the prototype.

It was relatively easy to answer the second question, how long to keep working on the prototype. Some of the Smalltalk implementation was developed more or less in parallel with the evolving *HyperCard™* prototype. The prototyping effort was stopped based on a simple criterion: *Cease development of the prototype when the effort of prototyping exceeds that for implementing the real system* (in this case, the Smalltalk version). Early in the development process, the prototype was invaluable in helping us make design decisions, but as the design progressed, conditions shifted so that using Smalltalk became faster and easier.

This shift in conditions was due to the trade-off between learnability and expressive power of the two languages. Developers were very proficient with *HyperCard™* in about two weeks, but Smalltalk has a much steeper learning curve: It generally takes a good programmer used to the procedural approach about three months to become proficient in Smalltalk. After the Smalltalk learning curve is climbed, however, the greater expressive power and flexibility of Smalltalk make it easier and, in many cases faster, to make changes directly to the Smalltalk implementation, rather than to the prototype. This same cross-over effect does not always hold for procedural implementation languages because they generally require more lines of code to be written, and they are typically compiled rather than interpreted.

The *learnability factor of a language* is always important; implementers learned both *HyperCard*™ and Smalltalk as the project proceeded. If implementers had been equally skilled in both at the outset, the cross-over just described would have occurred earlier. Nonetheless, our earliest global prototypes still would have been done in *HyperCard*™, because it is almost always easier and faster to do most screen mock-ups with *HyperCard*™. Additionally, using *HyperCard*™ for local prototyping of isolated specific design details generally continues to be useful beyond the cross-over point.

In this project, the choice of languages aided the transition from prototype to implementation. *HyperCard*™ has a strong object-oriented flavor; an input event, such as a mouse selection of an object, activates a programmed action. We deliberately exploited this in trying to make the prototype code as object-oriented as possible in order to match the object orientation of Smalltalk. For example, each card button corresponds to an object that contains the knowledge of how to display its own instances.

In conclusion, global prototyping, on the GPL tool and numerous other projects, serves a planned role in the development process very well. It indeed allows observation of early behavior and subsequent adjustment of the design. The prototypes allow interaction developers to be innovative, to dream a little, and to encourage them to play with design alternatives. Numerous instances of design incompleteness, ambiguity, and inconsistency are revealed through use of prototypes, allowing developers to resolve them while there is still enough flexibility in the design and its implementation to make changes.

Local prototyping, both for the GPL tool and in general, also offers benefits. Most local prototypes can be built in one to two hours, and give some very good information for decision making. It helps to adhere to the predefined purpose of these small prototypes, resisting the urge to make them more complete; it would be wasteful to develop the local prototypes beyond what is needed to answer specific design questions.

In sum, prototyping experiences strongly support the user interface development process. Nonetheless, numerous prototyping efforts report being affected by the limitations of *HyperCard*™ and other prototyping tools. More powerful prototyping tools, more integrated into the development environment, would make the transition from prototype to implementation more evolutionary.

9.7   SUMMARY AND FUTURE

Throughout this book we stress the importance of iterative design as an effective approach, possibly the only known effective approach for ensuring usability in user interfaces. Chapter 4 showed the special need in interaction development for a process that allows numerous cycles of redesign and evaluation for everything from a fairly detailed design to just a single interaction feature. Rapid prototyping provides the means by which such iteration can be accomplished.

The next chapter discusses the kind of empirical testing that is best suited for the user interaction development process—namely, formative evaluation. Rapid prototyping is an excellent technique to support this kind of formative testing. In fact, it is essentially the only way to achieve testing of designs early in the development process. Because prototypes are often produced from the bottom up, the technique is very compatible with the concrete, details-first approach often used with scenario designs. Formative evaluation approaches described in Chapter 10 are applicable to very early paper-and-pencil or plastic prototypes, as well as computer-based prototypes used throughout much of the development cycle.

Improved tools, set in better software development environments, coupled with rapid prototyping methodologies and a body of practical experience, are combining to revolutionize interactive system development, and especially development of the user interface. The future of rapid prototyping depends heavily on solutions to technical problems that presently limit effectiveness of the technique in the context of present software development environments.

9.8   EXERCISE ON RAPID PROTOTYPING

You are now ready to create a prototype for your Calendar Management System. This should be one of your most fun exercises.

Exercise—Building a Rapid Prototype

GOAL: To obtain some experience with rapid construction of a prototype.

MINIMUM TIME: About 1-$\frac{1}{2}$ hours, if you do the version using plastic transparencies who knows, if you use an interactive prototyping tool!

NOTE: You may have to do a bit more design work at some points during this exercise, to complete details that were not fully designed in previous exercises.

ACTIVITIES:

Build the prototype
Produce some pictures of screens in more detail than in your scenarios. There are two possible approaches here; either you can use plastic transparencies, or you can use an interactive tool.

If you decide to use the first approach, you should draw your screen pictures on plastic transparencies, using (washable!) colored marking pens. Draw various objects on different layers of transparencies so that they can be overlaid. Be as creative as you wish here. Make cutouts from the plastic, use paper to mask out various parts of the screen as appropriate (e.g., underneath a dialogue box).

Your plastic prototype should break down your design into a set of moving parts. You need separate pieces of plastic, sometimes just small pieces with handles, or strips for moving around (e.g., a cursor), or for picking pieces up and putting them down (e.g., pull-down menus), or for scrolling (e.g., a list). These separate pieces are needed for anything that can change dynamically during task performance—pull-down menus; highlighting of buttons, icons, and menu choices; text within appointments; scrolling lists; and so on. Do something clever for a mouse if you need one (we once saw one made from half a styrofoam cup and a string, complete with beady little eyes and a shredded plastic straw for whiskers).

In the exercise in Chapter 10, on formative evaluation, someone from your development team will "execute" your prototype by moving these different layers and pieces around, as appropriate, to demonstrate motion, dynamics, feedback, and so on as a user interacts with your prototype, based on the benchmark tasks you produced in the earlier exercise from Chapter 8. Thus, your prototype should support all benchmark tasks in your usability specifications (from Chapter 8).

If you have access to and/or wish to learn more about using interactive tools for rapid prototyping, you certainly can use one of them, instead of plastic transparencies, to produce your prototype for this exercise.

Pilot test the prototype

When you think that your prototype—either plastic or computer-based—is complete, be sure to pilot test it to make sure it can be used to perform your benchmark tasks, produced in the usability specification exercise at the end of Chapter 8. Also, make sure that your prototype won't blow up on you during "execution." In particular, don't assume error-free performance by your users; make sure that you have appropriate error messages where user errors might occur. Make sure that some sort of message can be presented to your users if they try to perform a task or command that isn't yet implemented in your prototype. In general, just make sure that your prototype is ready for evaluation.

If you developed a plastic prototype, have one member of your team play computer and "run" the prototype while another member plays user and tries to perform all the benchmark tasks. If you used an interactive prototyping tool, make sure that it can be used to perform all the benchmark tasks. In either case, whoever is trying out your prototype should deliberately make some mistakes and do goofy things, because—you can bet—your users will.

DELIVERABLES: An "executable" version of your prototype, either drawn on plastic transparencies or developed using an interactive tool, and pilot tested for readiness for formative evaluation.

Possible Exercise Solution

For this exercise, we obviously cannot give you a possible solution. This exercise has been used in classes with dozens of teams over the years, and some really innovative ideas have been incorporated into the plastic prototype. Use your and your team's imagination to produce a feasible prototype—either plastic or computer-based—that you can use in Chapter 10 for formative evaluation of your Calendar Management System interaction design.

REFERENCES

Alavi, M. (1984). An Assessment of the Prototyping Approach to Information Systems Development. *Communications of the ACM, 27*(6), 556–563.

Boehm, B. W., Gray, T. E., & Seewaldt, T. (1984). Prototyping vs. Specification: A Multi-Project Experiment. *Proceedings of Seventh International Conference on Software Engineering,* New York: ACM and IEEE, 473–484.

Ehn, P. (1990). *Work Oriented Design of Computer Artifacts.* Hillsdale, NJ: Erlbaum.

Gregory, S. T. (1984). On Prototype vs. Mockups. *SIGSOFT Software Engineering Notes, 9*(5), 13.

Hartson, H. R. & Smith, E. C. (1991). Rapid Prototyping in Human-Computer Interface Development. *Interacting with Computers, 3*(1), 51–91.

Mantei, M. (1986). Techniques for Incorporating Human Factors in the Software Lifecycle. *Proceedings of Structured Techniques Association Third Annual Conference,* 177–203.

Nielsen, J. (1987). Using Scenarios to Develop User Friendly Videotex Systems. *Proceedings of NordData87, Joint Scandanavian Computer Conference.*

Piaget, J. (1950). *The Psychology of Intelligence.* Orlando, FL: Harcourt Brace Jovanovich.

Richards, J. T., Boies, S. J., & Gould, J. D. (1986). Rapid Prototyping and System Development: Examination of an Interface Toolkit for Voice and Telephony Applications. *Proceedings of CHI Conference on Human Factors in Computing Systems,* New York: ACM, 216–220.

Wasserman, A. I. & Shewmake, D. T. (1985). The Role of Prototypes in the User Software Engineering Methodology. In H. R. Hartson (Ed.), *Advances in Human-Computer Interaction* (pp. 191–210). Norwood, NJ: Ablex.

Whiteside, J. & Wixon, D. (1985). Developmental Theory as a Framework for Studying Human-Computer Interaction. In H. R. Hartson (Ed.), *Advances in Human-Computer Interaction,* Vol. 1 (pp. 29–48). Norwood, NJ: Ablex.

☰ 10

Formative Evaluation

10.1 WHAT IS FORMATIVE EVALUATION?

To put formative evaluation into context, let's review the iterative refinement process represented in the star life cycle one more time. So far, we have designed the user interaction for the Calendar Management System, via some simple needs, user, functional, and task analysis; represented the user interaction design using the User Action Notation (UAN) as the representation technique; established some usability specifications; and prototyped the interface, either with plastic transparencies or with a computer-based tool. Now it is finally time for the user interaction design to undergo some usability evaluation, the central hub of the star life cycle. You already know that you are going to iteratively refine the user interaction design for the Calendar Management System based on the results of this evaluation. This approach has been called "Waffle Wisdom" or "Pancake Philosophy" (by our friend and colleague, George Casaday); like the first waffle or pancake, the first design (and maybe the next few, also) is made to be thrown away!

There are many stories about how *not* to evaluate an interaction design. A favorite came from an undergraduate student telling about her summer job. She was hired by a major government contractor to do some implementation on a portion of a huge federally-funded project. She had never worked for this company before, and the first day she went in, the module of the project she was to work on was not quite ready for her to begin. In an attempt to find something for her to do for the week or so until the module was ready, her supervisor decided, on the spur of the moment, that the student could evaluate the user interaction design. The student's instructions were to "go play around with this thing and tell us what to fix."

This company had planned no evaluation of the user interaction design for a multimillion-dollar project. In fact, the only evaluation the first version got—and this only by accident—was from a rising junior computer science major who knew absolutely nothing about human–computer interaction design and evaluation. She knew little about what the system was supposed to do and even less about evaluating an interaction design. By the way, the first release was such a disaster in terms of its usability that the contractor did formally include usability evaluation in its development plan for subsequent versions.

The kind of evaluation of the interaction design discussed here is *formative evaluation* (Carroll, Singley, & Rosson, 1992; Dick & Carey, 1978; Scriven, 1967; Williges, 1984). This is evaluation of the interaction design *as it is being developed*, early and continually throughout the interface development process. This is in comparison to *summative evaluation*, which is evaluation of the interaction design *after it is complete*, or nearly so. Summative evaluation is often used during field or beta testing, or to compare one product to another. For example, a summative evaluation of two systems, A and B, could show which one is better, where "better" is defined as "the user makes fewer errors with this one" or "the user subjectively prefers this one." In practice, summative evaluation is rarely used for usability testing.

On the other hand, formative evaluation, the mainstay of usability evaluation, is not to be confused with what is often thought of as typical human factors testing—for example, controlled hypothesis testing of an m by n factorial design with y independent variables, complete with quantitative data, statistical analyses, and numeric results. Controlled experimentation is valuable in contributing to the science and principles of human factors but does not produce results in a time frame that meets the needs of the fast, cyclical iterative development process.

In contrast, formative evaluation, performed in every cycle of iteration, produces quantitative data against which developers can compare the established usability specifications, and also produces qualitative data that can be used to help determine what changes to make to the interaction design to improve its usability. This *formative evaluation is begun as early in the development cycle as possible*, in order to discover usability problems while there is still plenty of time for modifications to be made to the design. By waiting until late in the development process, much of the interface will already be implemented, and it will be far more difficult to make changes indicated by usability evaluation.

Summative evaluation is usually performed only once, near the end of the user interface development process. Formative evaluation is performed several times throughout the process; the rule of thumb is that an average of *three major cycles of formative evaluation, each followed by iterative redesign,* will be completed for each significant version of an interaction design. There may be additional very short cycles, to check out quickly a few small changes made to the interaction design, while the major cycles will be longer, to evaluate more extensive issues. You will typically get the most data from the first major cycle of evaluation. If the process is working properly and the user interaction design is indeed improving, later cycles will generate fewer new discoveries and will generally necessitate fewer changes in the design. The first cycle can generate an enormous amount of data, enough to be overwhelming. This chapter tells you how to collect and analyze these data in order to optimize the usability of the interface.

Formative evaluation primarily addresses the path in the star life cycle between prototyping and design/redesign. People sometimes mistakenly think that formative evaluation is not as rigorous or as formal as summative evaluation. Actually, however, the distinction between formative and summative evaluation is not in its formality, but rather in the goal of each approach. Summative evaluation does not support the iterative refinement process represented in the star life cycle; waiting to evaluate an interface until it is almost complete will not allow much, if any, iterative refinement. Formative evaluation, because it is early and continual throughout the process, is most responsive to the iterative approach shown in the star life cycle.

It is important that members of the development team, and especially managers, understand this difference between formative and summative evaluation. Otherwise, because formative evaluation is not controlled testing and usually does not require many participants, your results may be discounted as being, for example, too informal, not scientifically rigorous, or not statistically significant. Formative evaluation is, indeed, rigorous and formal, in the sense of having an explicit and well-defined procedure, and it does result in quantitative data but is not intended to address statistical significance. It does address the needs of users, and therefore of developers, to ensure high usability in an interface.

Many people espouse a *"10% rule"* concerning evaluation: An interface development effort should have something that can be evaluated by the time the first 10% of the project resources (time and/or dollars) are expended. The previous chapter, on rapid prototyping, discussed how to quickly produce something testable; this chapter discusses in depth how to perform formative evaluation of early versions of the interaction design using prototypes.

The bottom line is this: *Users will evaluate your interface sooner or later*—either correctly, in-house, using the proper techniques and under the appropriate conditions, or after it's in the field, when it is too late. Why not do it *right*, and evaluate it *sooner*?

10.1.1 Types of Formative Evaluation Data

Several types of data are generated during formative evaluation, each of which can be used in making decisions about iterative redesign of the user interface. The following types of formative evaluation data are discussed throughout the rest of this chapter:

- *Objective*–These are directly observed measures, typically of user performance while using the interface to perform benchmark tasks.
- *Subjective*—These represent opinions, usually of the user, concerning usability of the interface.
- *Quantitative*—These are numeric data and results, such as user performance metrics or opinion ratings. This kind of data is key in helping to monitor convergence toward usability specifications during all cycles of iterative development.
- *Qualitative*—These are nonnumeric data and results, such as lists of problems users had while using the interface, and they result in suggestions for modifications to improve the interaction design. This kind of data is useful in identifying which design features are associated with measured usability problems during all cycles of iterative development.

Even though people often associate objective evaluation only with quantitative data and subjective evaluation with qualitative data, subjective evaluation (e.g., using user preference scales or questionnaires) can also produce quantitative data. Also, objective evaluation activities (e.g., benchmark task performance measurements) can produce qualitative data (e.g., critical incidents and verbal protocol, discussed later in Section 10.4, on generating and collecting the data).

10.1.2 Steps in Formative Evaluation

The remainder of this chapter elaborates on details of the major steps in formative evaluation. These include the following:

- Developing the experiment
- Directing the evaluation sessions

- Collecting the data
- Analyzing the data
- Drawing conclusions to form a resolution for each design problem
- Redesigning and implementing the revised interface

While many members of the interface development team may be involved in performing these steps at various times, we refer to the person who is primarily responsible as the *user interaction design evaluator*, or just *evaluator*, for short.

10.2   DEVELOPING THE EXPERIMENT

Developing an experiment to be used for formative evaluation involves four main activities, not necessarily in the order given:

- Selecting participants to perform tasks
- Developing tasks for participants to perform
- Determining protocol and procedures for the evaluation sessions
- Pilot testing to shake down the experiment

10.2.1   Selecting Participants

One of your first activities related to formative evaluation is *evaluation participant selection*—determining appropriate users for the experimental sessions. *Participant* is the term that most recent human factors literature now uses to indicate a human taking part in an experiment. There are good reasons for this change in terminology; people, on hearing themselves referred to as "subjects," will sometimes nervously joke about being attached to electrodes or ask to see the maze. It is better to *view the interface as the subject,* and the evaluation participant as helping you to evaluate the design.

The evaluator must determine the classes of representative users that will be used as participants to try out the interface. These participants should represent the typical kind of expected user of the interface being evaluated, including the users' general background, skill level, computer knowledge, application knowledge, and so on. Often, these attributes for expected user classes are explicitly stated in the usability specifications, and the participants should be chosen to match.

Appropriate users should be at least a little knowledgeable of the problem domain (e.g., word processing, accounting, graphical drawing, process control, airline reservations, or whatever the problem domain may be), but not necessarily knowledgeable of a specific interactive system within that domain. If an adequate user analysis was done up front (see Chapter 5), the evaluator will already have a good idea of the kinds of people who will fit the user profile to represent the various classes of users of the system being evaluated. If the user analysis was not sufficient, the evaluator can work with marketing people and other members of the development team to help define more clearly the user profile and appropriate population. For evaluating your Calendar Management System, appropriate participants should be rather easy to find; the most important criterion is that they need to know something about calendars.

The question arises, of course, as to where to find participants. Participants should not have to be coerced into taking part in an experiment, or they may come into it with a poor attitude and thereby color the results. Volunteers typically provide much better data. Often, people (coworkers, colleagues elsewhere in your organization, spouses, children, and so on) will volunteer their time to act as participants. Many organizations post notices in grocery stores or in other public places (e.g., libraries). Students at universities, community colleges, or even K–12, if appropriate, also work well. These people probably won't work for free; you will usually have to pay a modest hourly fee (for example, about a dollar above minimum wage is typical these days) in order to get the participants you need. In fact, it is always nice, and sometimes necessary, to offer bribes to get participants. Various kinds of inexpensive bribes include mugs with your company logo, T-shirts of some sort, or even chocolate chip cookies! Use any and all of these strategies, as needed, to assemble the participant pool for evaluating your user interaction design. While it is often necessary to offer compensation in order to recruit participants, some practitioners believe that monetary rewards may bias results. For example, paid participants with greater financial need could be more motivated than participants without financial need.

Another source you can use for finding participants is temporary employment agencies. A possible pitfall here: These agencies know nothing about usability evaluation, nor do they understand why it is so important to choose appropriate people as participants. These agencies' goal, after all, is to keep their pool of temporary workers employed. Particularly for potential participants sent from such an agency, as well as for those who respond to notices posted in public places, it is important to screen each person thoroughly to make sure each is appropriate for your current evaluation. You should have developed a good user profile for anticipated users of your system by now; use this as the basis for screening potential participants.

A common problem, particularly in a contractual development situation, is one in which an organization (e.g., a private company) is developing an interactive system under contract for a customer (e.g., some government agency). Sometimes, the customer—for whatever reasons—simply will not let the developer organization have access to representative users. The Navy, for example, can be rightfully hesitant about calling in its ships and shipboard personnel from the high seas to evaluate a system being developed to go on board.

We do not have a magic solution to this problem but we can offer encouragement: If the organization producing the interface informs the customer, at the beginning of the interface development process, about how the process will proceed, it will then have the highest likelihood of getting representative users from the customer involved at appropriate times. In fact, rather in-depth discussions of the user interface development process are sometimes included in proposals in response to RFPs (requests for proposal) during the bidding process to award a contract. Customers are now beginning to look closely in the response to an RFP for an explanation of the process by which a potential bidder expects to develop a user interface. If these customers do not see terms such as *user analysis, formative evaluation, rapid prototyping,* and *iterative refinement* in the bid description, then the likelihood of that bidder getting the contract falls drastically. In fact, more and more customers are starting to demand a user interface development process of their contractors, as this process becomes more widely known and understood.

When a customer knows up front exactly what to expect and approximately when to expect it, the customer is much more likely to cooperate and help provide appropriate participants for formative evaluation. However, it may still be difficult, in the beginning, to convince some customers that usability is crucial. Until the customer has personally observed a few evaluation sessions or read the results of a formative evaluation cycle and seen changes made that improved usability, the customer may be unwilling to help much with providing participants.

However, once the customer understands that the *success of the whole system revolves heavily around usability of the interface,* and that *usability of the interface revolves heavily around a development process involving usability testing,* the customer almost always will gladly supply the developer with appropriate participants. Once the customer sees the benefits of formative evaluation, the customer generally is very anxious to participate in any way possible to maximize its benefits. In addition, sometimes, when the customer has chosen a few representative users to be participants, these people have become so excited about the new system that lots of other people wanted to be participants, too—more people, in fact, than the formative evaluation schedule and resources could handle. The whole development process can, indeed, have a very positive effect on acceptance of a new interactive system by its customer.

In addition to representative users, the *human–computer interaction expert* plays an important part in formative evaluation. Evaluators sometimes overlook the need for critical review of the interface by a human–computer interaction expert when developing a formative evaluation plan. An expert will be broadly knowledgeable in the area of interaction development and will have extensive experience in evaluating a wide variety of interfaces. In particular, this person should know a great deal about interaction design and critiquing, as well as all activities of the user interaction development process. This expert particularly needs to be familiar with interaction design guidelines.

An expert does not necessarily have to know a great deal about the specific interactive system domain, but rather is interested in a more generic review of the interaction design. An expert will find subtle problems that a non–interface expert would be less likely to find (e.g., small inconsistencies, poor use of color, and confusing navigation). More importantly, a human–computer interaction expert will offer alternative suggestions for fixing problems, unlike the representative user, who typically tends to find a problem but cannot offer suggestions for resolving it. An expert can draw on knowledge of guidelines, design and critiquing experience, and familiarity with a broad spectrum of interfaces, to offer one or more feasible, guideline-based suggestions for modifications to improve usability.

What you do with a human–computer interaction expert during formative evaluation is somewhat different than what you do with participants representing typical users. Having the expert perform representative tasks, possibly your benchmark tasks, is a good place to start, but you probably do not want to time the expert or count the expert's errors. The expert is doing a critical review of the whole interaction design, so you typically will collect far more qualitative data than quantitative data during a review by an expert. If you give experts the benchmark tasks as a starting point, they may work through them all, or they may take their own path in exploring the rest of the interface. Either way will generally give you a great deal of valuable data to be used for design modifications—both problems in the design and guideline-based suggestions for improving the design. A word of caution: Do not think that a human–computer interaction expert can serve as a substitute for evaluation with representative users. You will get quite different data from the two different sources.

Nielsen (1992; Nielsen & Molich, 1990), in fact, espouses what he calls *heuristic evaluation* or *discount usability engineering*, which is related to the approach being described here. Heuristic evaluation is a technique for uncovering usability problems in a design by having a small set of participants (three to five) judge the compliance of the interaction design to a set of recognized usability guidelines (the heuristics). He has found, through empirical studies, that human–computer interaction experts make the best participants, in terms of discovering usability problems, and such experts with knowledge of the problem domain of the interface being evaluated are even better than those who do not have this specific knowledge. Nielsen states that heuristic evaluation has the advantages of being cheap, intuitive, and easy to motivate developers to do, and it is effective for use early in the development process.

You may be sitting there, saying to yourself, "Right! These people are still crazy. There's just not time to do all this evaluation with bunches of participants." Well, take heart. You don't need bunches of participants. You do need a few carefully chosen, really good representative users, and one or maybe two interaction experts. In fact, the purpose of formative evaluation is not to focus on a large number of experiments with a large number of participants for each one. Rather, it is to *focus on extracting as much information as possible from every participant who uses any part of the interface* (Carroll & Rosson, 1985; Whiteside, Bennett, & Holtzblatt, 1988).

As mentioned, some empirical work (Nielsen & Molich, 1990) has shown that the optimum number of participants for a cycle of formative evaluation is *three to five per user class*. Only one participant per class is typically not enough, but more than ten participants per class is not worth the diminishing returns obtained. After about five or six participants, they tend to cease finding new problems and mostly reiterate the ones already uncovered by prior participants. Often, three participants per well-defined user class is the most cost-effective number. The advice for getting started with usability specifications applies here again: *Start small*. Do a couple of cycles of testing with a couple of appropriate participants for your most representative user class. This is a perfectly manageable approach, and evaluators will become more skilled and more comfortable after going through the entire process a few times.

A question that commonly arises is whether you should use the same participants for more than one cycle of formative evaluation. Suppose that you use three participants per cycle. The best approach to participant selection for successive evaluation cycles is typically to use, for each cycle after the first, one participant from the previous cycle and two new participants. This way, you will get some feedback from the repeat participant on the reaction to the user interaction design changes from the previous cycle. You will also get a new set of data on the modified design from the two new participants.

10.2.2 Developing Tasks

By now, the evaluator should have participated with other members of the development team in *identifying usability specification attributes and levels*, as already discussed in Chapter 8. Because these specifications are the key to quantifiably—measurably—determining usability of the interface, they must be ready and waiting as a comparison point with actual results observed during formative evaluation sessions with participants.

In addition to the *benchmark tasks* developed for the usability attributes, the evaluator may also identify other *representative tasks* for participants to perform. These tasks will not be tested quantitatively (that is, against usability specifications) but are deemed, for whatever reason, to be important in adding breadth to evaluation of the user interaction design. These additional tasks, especially in early cycles of evaluation, should be ones that users are expected to perform often, and therefore should be easy for a user to accomplish.

In the early cycles of evaluation, these representative tasks might, for example, constitute a core set of tasks for the system being evaluated, without which a user cannot perform useful work. For the Calendar Management System, the task of adding an appointment is one a user will perform very often. In fact, it was included as the measuring instrument for a couple of usability attributes produced in Chapter 8. Just as with the benchmark tasks developed for testing usability attributes, additional representative tasks should, in general, be rather specific and should state *what* the user should do, rather than *how* the user should do it. Thus, if there is information about the design that is not related directly to usability specifications, but that an evaluator wishes to investigate, the evaluator can define any other desired tasks. The results of users performing those tasks will simply provide additional qualitative data for later analysis as input to the iterative refinement process. Some examples of this are given in Section 10.5, on analyzing the data.

To prepare for an evaluation session, the evaluator should write down all tasks (both the benchmark and representative tasks) in the order in which a participant will be asked to perform them. However, the evaluator can administer the tasks to a participant in several different ways. The evaluator can either hand the participant the written list and ask the participant to work through each task before going on to the next one, or the evaluator can read each task out loud to the participant, one task at a time, waiting until the participant completes a task before going on to the next one. The evaluator can, of course, also use a combination of these two approaches; for example, giving the participant some tasks in writing, and others orally. The nature of the tasks will help determine which approach is best, and pilot testing (see Section 10.2.4) will help verify the choice. For example, if a task (such as those given later, in Figure 10.1) is fairly specific and contains detailed information (e.g., particular time, place, and person for an appointment), it is best to write out the tasks and hand them to the participant. If a task can be stated in only a few words that are easy to remember (e.g., "Draw a rectangle;" "Go to the glossary;" "View Figure 3"), then it may be appropriate to simply read each one aloud to the participant. In general, it is preferable let the participant read written

Benchmark 1 (measure task performance time, count number of errors):

A. Schedule a meeting with Dr. Ehrich for four weeks from today at 10 A.M. in 133 McBryde, concerning the HCI research project.

Intervening nonbenchmark tasks:

B. Schedule an appointment for a physical exam with the vet for Pumpkin the cat on October 31.

C. Change the phone appointment with your book editor on Monday, December 1 at 1 P.M., to a meeting with Sam Smith about the usability lab.

D. To keep you from forgetting it, put an alarm on the meeting with Dr. Ehrich.

Benchmark 4 (measure task performance time):

E. Find your next appointment with the dentist.

Intervening nonbenchmark tasks:

F. Change the dentist's appointment you just found to the first available Tuesday morning (allow two hours) in May.

G. Schedule one week of vacation for the whole week during which the Fourth of July falls next year.

Benchmark 2 (measure task performance time, count number of errors):

H. Suppose that you have decided not to spend money on your dog. Delete your appointment with the vet for Mutt's annual checkup.

Intervening nonbenchmark task:

I. Look to see how many appointments you will have to cancel if you extend your vacation by another week.

Free use (to build up total usage time to at least one hour):

J. Play around with the system, exploring anything you would like to in the Calendar Management System, for as long as you would like to.

Benchmark 5 (measure task performance time):

K. Schedule an appointment for car maintenance on January 3 next year.

Benchmark 3 (measure task performance time):

L. Enter a one hour weekly meeting with the HCI group every Wednesday at 9 A.M. for one year, beginning on the Wednesday of next week.

Final task:

M. Add in the schedule for your HCI class, which meets every Tuesday during spring semester (January through May) from 2:00 to 3:30 P.M.

Figure 10.1. Some sample tasks for the Calendar Management System—the evaluator's version.

tasks, ensuring that each participant is given exactly the same instructions. Asking a participant to read each task description aloud before beginning it helps the evaluator know when to start timing the task performance (i.e., when the participant has finished reading the task aloud).

A sample set of tasks for the Calendar Management System is given in Figure 10.1, shown in the precise order in which a participant will perform them during a formative evaluation session. The benchmark numbers in this list are the same as those established in Chapter 8. Note that the benchmark numbers have nothing to do with the order in which a participant will perform the tasks (e.g., Benchmark 4 will be performed before Benchmark 2). These numbers are just identifiers that were assigned in the order in which a new benchmark number was needed while creating usability specifications in Chapter 8.

Benchmarks 1, 4, and 2 are indicated in Tasks A, E, and H, respectively. Of particular interest in Figure 10.1 is Benchmark 5 and the way in which this set of tasks addresses the usability attribute of learnability, from the table in the possible exercise solution at the end of Chapter 8. As was noted in discussing that attribute, an easy way to measure it for a system as simple as the Calendar Management System is to measure the participant's performance of the task of adding an appointment after an hour of using the system, and then to compare that to performance the first time the participant added an appointment.

To measure adequately the usability specification on learnability from Chapter 8, several other tasks must be included, to ensure that the participant will get an hour of system usage. In the set of tasks in Figure 10.1, a participant will attempt to add three different appointments—two (Tasks A and B) successively, and then add a third one (Task K) after trying a few other tasks (e.g., deleting and modifying an appointment, and adding an alarm). Note that some free use also is included (discussed below) before the participant is asked to perform Benchmark 5, to increase the participant's total usage time of the system to an hour or more. Benchmark 5, referred to in Table 8.1, is indicated as Task K in Figure 10.1.

Benchmark 3, described in Task L, is the more complex task, which will allow measurement of the usability attribute for advanced feature usage, also from Chapter 8. The other intervening representative nonbenchmark tasks in Figure 10.1 are intended to discover any problems that participants might have in performing some of the additional functions provided by the Calendar Management System, but they are not directly related to any specific usability attribute metric.

The list, as written out in Figure 10.1, showing specific benchmark numbers, is *for use by the evaluator*, to help keep track of specific benchmark tasks and to make it easier to later relate them back to the usability specifications. *Rubrics*—special instructions and comments—to the evaluator are indicated in bold italics. This is *not* the format that should be used for the list of tasks that is given to a participant during an evaluation session. That list, shown in Figure 10.2 just so you can see what it would look like, contains just the tasks, without the benchmark numbers, rubrics, or any extraneous remarks.

Note that some of these tasks imply that the Calendar Management System prototype already must have some specific appointments and other information in it before the participant begins an evaluation session. For example, Task H, deleting an appointment, means that the appointment must be in the version of the prototype or system the participant is evaluating. To be interesting, Task I needs some appointments during the weeks before and after vacation. Also, the prototype must be resettable between participants or else you should easily be able to make a new copy of the prototype (complete with appropriate appointments already in) for each participant, so that each evaluation session begins with the same known calendar content.

In addition to strictly specified benchmark and representative tasks, the evaluator may also find it useful to observe the participant in informal *free use* of the interface, without the constraints of predefined tasks. In fact, this was included as

---

A. Schedule a meeting with Dr. Ehrich for four weeks from today at 10 A.M. in 133 McBryde, concerning the HCI research project.

B. Schedule an appointment for a physical exam with the vet for Pumpkin the cat on October 31.

C. Change the phone appointment with your book editor on Monday, December 1 at 1 P.M., to a meeting with Sam Smith about the usability lab.

D. To keep you from forgetting it, put an alarm on the meeting with Dr. Ehrich.

E. Find your next appointment with the dentist.

F. Change the dentist's appointment you just found to the first available Tuesday morning (allow two hours) in May.

G. Schedule one week of vacation for the whole week during which the Fourth of July falls next year.

H. Suppose that you have decided not to spend money on your dog. Delete your appointment with the vet for Mutt's annual checkup.

I. Look to see how many appointments you will have to cancel if you extend your vacation by another week.

J. Play around with the system, exploring anything you would like to in the Calendar Management System, for as long as you would like to.

K. Schedule an appointment for car maintenance on January 3 next year.

L. Enter a one hour weekly meeting with the HCI group every Wednesday at 9 A.M. for one year, beginning on the Wednesday of next week.

M. Add in the schedule for your HCI class, which meets every Tuesday during spring semester (January through May) from 2:00 to 3:30 P.M.

Figure 10.2. Some sample tasks for the Calendar Management System—the participant's version.

a specific activity (Task J). To engage a participant in free use, the evaluator might simply say, "Play around with the interface for awhile, doing anything you would like to, and talk aloud while you are working." Free use is valuable for revealing participant and system behavior in situations not anticipated by designers, often situations that can break a poor design. Ways in which to take verbal protocol, such as during free use, are discussed in Section 10.4, on generating and collecting the data.

Benchmark tasks, other representative tasks, and free use are all key sources of critical incidents (again, see Section 10.4, on generating and collecting the data), a major form of the qualitative data to be collected. Free use by a participant can be performed after either some or all of the predefined tasks have been completed. Obviously, it should be performed after those tasks that are related to the initial use attribute.

Training materials and documentation are other aspects of developing the tasks to be performed by participants during formative evaluation. If the evaluator anticipates that a user's manual or quick reference cards or any sort of training material will be available to users of the system, the use of these materials should be explicit in the task descriptions.

Participants might be given time to read any training material at the beginning of the testing session, or they might be given the material and told they can refer to it, reading as necessary to find the desired information. The number of times participants refer to the training material, and the amount of assistance they are able to obtain from the material, for example, can also be important data about overall usability of the system.

Documentation and training materials for a system should also be evaluated, of course. Realistically, however, most systems are complicated enough that it is too difficult to evaluate documentation and the interface in the same session. It is better to develop separate formative evaluation plans for the documentation, the training material, and the user interface; don't try to test more than one unknown at a time.

10.2.3 Determining Protocol and Procedures

Finally, the evaluator must determine protocol and procedures for administering the experiment—exactly what will happen during an evaluation session with a participant. The evaluator must decide on whether laboratory testing or field testing, or both, will be performed. *Laboratory testing* involves bringing the participant to the interface; that is, participants are brought into a usability lab setting where they perform the benchmark tasks, performance measures are taken as appropriate, free use is encouraged, and so on. *Field testing* involves bringing the interface to the participant; that is, the present version is set up in situ, in the normal working environment in which users are expected to use the interface, and more qualitative, longer-term data can be collected.

Obviously lab and field testing each have pros and cons. In a laboratory setting, an evaluator can have greater control over the experiment, but the conditions are mostly artificial. On the other hand, in a field test, an evaluator has less control, yet the situation is more realistic. In general, laboratory testing yields more useful information for the earlier cycles of formative evaluation, when major problems with the interaction design are typically discovered. Field testing works well for later cycles, when data on long-term performance with the interface may be desirable. A combination of the two is the ideal circumstance for formative evaluation, but in real life, true field testing may be limited or even impossible. In this case, laboratory testing may have to suffice.

In conjunction with developing experimental procedures, the evaluator should prepare *introductory instructional remarks* that will be given uniformly to each participant. These remarks can be either written, to be read by the participant at the beginning of the experiment; or oral, to be read by the evaluator to the participant at the beginning of the experiment; or both. These remarks should briefly explain the purpose of the experiment, tell a little bit about the interface the participant will be using, state what the participant will be expected to do, and the procedure to be followed by the participant. For example, the instructions might state that a participant will be asked to perform some benchmark tasks that will be given by the evaluator, will be allowed to use the system freely for awhile, then will be given some more benchmark tasks, and finally will be asked to complete an exit questionnaire.

It is also important to specifically make clear to all participants that *the purpose of the session is to evaluate the system, not to evaluate them*. Some participants may be fearful that participation in this kind of test session will reflect poorly on them or even be used in their employment performance evaluations (if, for example, they work for the same organization that is developing the interface they are helping to evaluate), and they should be reassured that this is not the case. In this regard, it is effective to guarantee the confidentiality of individual information and anonymity of the data.

The instructions may ask participants to talk aloud while working or may indicate that they can ask the evaluator questions at any time. The expected length of time for the evaluation session, if known (the evaluator should have some idea of how long a session will take after performing pilot testing), can also be included. The important point is that all participants be given uniform instructions at the beginning, and the easiest way to ensure uniformity is through written instructions. This way, all participants start with the same level of knowledge about the system and the tasks they are to perform. This uniform instruction for each participant will help ensure consistency and remove some of the potential variance from the test sessions. An example of instructions you might give to a participant who is evaluating a prototype of the Calendar Management System is given in Figure 10.3.

One final, but important, activity that should be emphasized here is the preparation of an *informed consent form* for each participant to sign. This form states that the participant is volunteering for the experiment, that the data may be used if the participant's name or identity is not associated with those data, that the participant understands that the experiment is in no way harmful, and that the participant may discontinue the experiment at any time. The consent form should also include any nondisclosure requirements. This is standard protocol for performing experiments using human participants, and protects both the evaluator and the participant. The informed consent form is legally and ethically required; it is not optional.

There are experiments, of course, in which harm could come to a human participant, but the kind of experiments performed during formative evaluation of an interaction design are virtually never of this kind. (In fact, harm is more likely to come to the computer terminal, the evaluator, and/or the designers, inflicted by the participant frustrated by an interface with poor usability—fallout from a user melt-down!) The informed consent form is an obligation to the participant and a further indicator of the seriousness of the experiment. It is also a legal document to protect the organization performing the evaluation.

An example of a simple informed consent form is shown in Figure 10.4. The wording of this example shows quite a bit of overlap with the experimental instructions given in Figure 10.3, and some overlap is acceptable. It is also possible either to reduce the amount of explanation of the experiment given in the informed consent form, or, in fact, to include the whole explanation, resulting in just one document to be given to a participant. It is generally best to have a separate informed consent form, but the important point is to have some signed document ensuring that participants have been told their rights and are voluntarily taking part in the experiment.

10.2.4 Pilot Testing

Finally, once the benchmark tasks have been developed, the setting and procedures have been determined, and the types of participants chosen, the evaluator must perform some *pilot testing* to ensure that all parts of the experiment are ready.

Instructions for
Calendar Management System Evaluation

Thank you for agreeing to participate in this experiment. We would like you to help us evaluate a new system for managing your personal calendar, particularly to assist you with scheduling of appointments.

As you can see, the Calendar Management System runs on a Macintosh™ computer, and uses a mouse for cursor movement and to initiate task actions. Because you have some experience with the Macintosh™, the basic task interactions—pointing, clicking, dragging, and so on—involved in using this Calendar Management System will be familiar to you.

Several elements of this system make it similar to using your paper calendar: you can flip through the screens similarly to the way you would flip though the pages of a paper calendar; and you can add, delete, or change appointments. This automated system has several features that a paper calendar does not have, such as the following: you have the choice of viewing appointments by day, by week, or by month, and you can change this view at any time; you can search for specific appointments based on words or phrases in the appointment text (rather than manually hunting through all appointments until the desired ones are found); you can schedule repeating appointments (e.g., a research meeting that takes place every Tuesday afternoon at 1:00).

During this session, you will be asked to perform several specific tasks using this system, and you will also be given some time just to play around with it, to try whatever you would like to do. While you are performing some of the specific tasks, we may be timing how well the system helps you with these tasks. Therefore we would like for you to work through each task without taking a break; you can take time to relax between tasks if you wish. We would also like you to read each task aloud and make sure you understand it before commencing to perform the task.

Because we are interested in why this system is easy or difficult to use, we would like you to "think aloud." That is, we would like you to talk about what you are doing and why you are doing it. You should talk about what you expected to happen that perhaps did not when you perform an action. You should indicate both the positive (good) and negative (bad) aspects of how you have to perform the tasks. Remember to keep talking throughout the whole session. The evaluator may remind you to talk aloud sometimes and may ask you questions about why you have done something or how you feel about some part of the system. This will help us understand more about the system.

Remember that you are helping us evaluate the Calendar Management System; we are not evaluating you. You should feel free to say whatever you think about any aspect of the system or the tasks you are asked to perform.

Finally, to get your opinion of the system, we will ask you to complete a short questionnaire to rate the system, after you have finished using it.

This session should last a little over one hour. You will be videotaped during the entire session.

Before we begin, do you have any questions?

Figure 10.3. Sample instructions for an evaluation session.

Informed Consent Form

You have been solicited as a research participant for our evaluation of the design for a new interactive computer system. This evaluation is being conducted by _____ (include organization name, address, phone number). Your evaluation session will be run by _____ (include evaluator's name, position, address, phone number), who will be glad to answer any questions you have about the evaluation. As a participant, you have certain rights, which are listed below.

    You will be asked to perform various tasks with this system, including _____. We are evaluating the system, to make it as effective and usable as possible. We are not in any way evaluating you. We expect the session to last about _____ (length of time), and you will be videotaped during the session. During this session, (the computer screen, keyboard, and mouse, or whatever) will be videotaped; (your hands will be visible on the tape but not your face or body, or whatever is appropriate to say here). This videotape will be used only for purposes of evaluating and improving the system and will not be distributed nor viewed by anyone not associated with this evaluation process. Your name will not be associated with any data that are collected during this evaluation session. You will be paid _____ (amount). There are no known risks associated with this evaluation. (Include any other information that will be useful, such as whether the participant will be asked questions at the beginning or end of the session or will be asked to complete a questionnaire.)

    Your rights as a participant are as follows:

1. You have the right to withdraw from the session at any time for any reason.

2. At the conclusion of your session, you may see your data, if you so desire. If you decide to withdraw your data, please inform the evaluator immediately. Otherwise, identification of your data might not be possible because of our efforts to ensure anonymity.

3. You are requested not to discuss this session with other people who might be in the group from which other participants could be drawn, including _____. (Also include here, or elsewhere in this document as appropriate, any restriction on discussing the system with anyone {any appropriate nondisclosure regulations, for example, until the product is released or until five years after the evaluation session}.)

    Finally, we greatly appreciate your time and effort for participating in this computer system evaluation. Remember, you cannot fail any part of this session, and there are no right or wrong answers. The session is to identify usability problems with the system. Your signature below indicates that you have read this consent form in its entirety and that you voluntarily agree to participate.

    Do you have any questions?

NAME _____

ADDRESS _____

SIGNATURE _____

PHONE _____ DATE _____

Figure 10.4. Sample informed consent form.

The evaluator must make sure that all necessary equipment is available, installed, and working properly, whether it be in the laboratory or in the field. Obviously, you do not want the hardware or software to crash during an experimental session. The experimental tasks should be completely run through at least once, using the intended hardware and software (i.e., the interface prototype) by someone other than the person(s) who developed the tasks, to make sure, for example, that the prototype supports all the necessary user actions and that the instructions are unambiguously worded.

Because good representative participants may be hard to find, the evaluator will want to minimize the possibilities for problems that might invalidate a test session. It is very easy for an evaluator to inadvertently write a benchmark task in which the wording is unclear, and which can be misinterpreted by a participant during the experiment. For example, there is a subtle difference in the wording of the following two tasks: "Schedule an HCI meeting every Wednesday for one year, beginning on the next Wednesday" and "Schedule an HCI meeting every Wednesday for one year, beginning on next Wednesday." In the first wording, it is unclear whether a participant should schedule the weekly appointment beginning with whatever the next Wednesday from the *current* position on the calendar happens to be, regardless of today's date, or whether this implies, as the second wording intends, to schedule beginning on the next Wednesday from today. These kinds of problems can invalidate all data from a participant. (By the way, if you're still having trouble understanding these task descriptions after reading them several times, well, that's the point. Imagine how confused a participant might feel.)

Similarly, even more extensive pilot testing is needed prior to critical reviews by human–computer interaction experts. These experts do not work for free, and the evaluator will not want things going amiss during a session in which a hefty hourly fee is being paid for expert advice.

Sometimes, you will be pilot testing and evaluating a prototype that has known bugs and/or weaknesses. If this is the case, the best you can do is to include benchmark and representative tasks that avoid those problems as much as possible. However, nothing will ensure that a participant won't encounter them anyway, especially during free use. If the system does, in fact, blow up during an evaluation session, apologize to the participant, restart the system, and have the participant pick up where the crash occurred.

Test sessions will run much more smoothly and predictably if even a minimal amount of effort is put into pilot testing of procedures, hardware, software, instructions, and so on, in advance. Pilot testing requires a very small amount of time compared to all the other effort you put in setting up the experiment, and collecting and analyzing the data.

10.3   DIRECTING THE EVALUATION SESSION

So far, you have all the details of your experiment worked out, including bench-mark tasks, procedures, consent forms, and participant selection. It is finally time to bring a participant into the usability lab and get an evaluation session under-way. The evaluator is responsible for making sure that the session runs smoothly and efficiently. Typically, the evaluator, during a formative evaluation session, will be in the same room as the participant. For quantitative measures of perfor-mance, the evaluator should remain in the background, not interacting with the participant unless there is a problem. Sometimes even this is obtrusive, and the evaluator can be next door in a control room, if this is available. A video monitor and/or one-way mirror is helpful in this case for observing the session.

For taking qualitative data, it is best to have the evaluator sitting beside the participant. This approach is sometimes termed *codiscovery*, in which an evaluator and a participant work together to uncover usability problems. In this situation, the evaluator must be cautious not to lead the participant so much that the evaluator interferes with the goals of the session or of collecting appropriate data.

Usually, there is only one participant for a session, but occasionally, interesting data can be obtained from having two participants interact together while using an interface. Although the present discussion concentrates on how to direct the evaluation session with one participant, the same general procedures would apply to a session with two (or more) participants.

First, the evaluator should briefly show the participant the usability lab and equipment, including the other side of a one-way mirror, if there is one. The eval-uator can also briefly explain the lab setup from the evaluator's viewpoint, if the participant is interested. The evaluator should next get the participant settled com-fortably in front of the prototype, and then give the participant the written instruc-tions related to the evaluation session. Once the participant has read and under-stood the instructions, the evaluator should get the participant's signature on the informed consent form. The evaluator should ask if the participant has any ques-tions. When the participant is comfortable with the instructions, the evaluator can then commence with the evaluation portion of the session, according to the proto-col and procedures worked out during experiment development and pilot testing.

During the session, as the evaluator is administering the tasks and whatever else the participant is to do during the session, it may be necessary to prompt the participant, primarily during qualitative data collection, to obtain the desired information. For example, if the participant struggles for awhile with a particular task (see Section 10.4.2, on qualitative data generation techniques) without talking much, the evaluator might ask, "What are you trying to do?" or "What did you expect to happen when you clicked on the such-and-such icon?" or "What made you think that approach would work?" The evaluator may also ask such questions as "How would you like to perform that task?" or "What would make that icon easier to recognize?"

If, however, one of the objectives for formative evaluation is task completion and/or failure, the evaluator must be especially careful about the protocol for questioning and giving help to participants. The evaluator should, in general, *not* give a participant specific instructions on *how* to complete a task with which the participant may be struggling. By telling a participant the actions to perform, the evaluator obviously loses the information that would be acquired as a participant continues to attempt to accomplish the task.

The first question an evaluator might ask could be something like, "Are you stuck?" or "Do you need a hint?" If the answer is "No," the evaluator might then ask, "Please tell me what you are thinking" or "Please tell me what you are trying to do." If the participant's answer is "Yes," then a failure data point can be recorded and the evaluator can give help progressively. If the participant does ask for a hint, the evaluator might proceed, for example, by suggesting "Do you remember what you did before for such-and-such a task?" or "Do you see an icon (or a menu item or a button or whatever) anywhere on the screen that might help you perform the task?" or "Try using the help facility"—if there is one. The evaluator, however, should refrain from blatantly coaching the participant on *how* to perform a task.

Even if a participant asks for specific help ("What should I do now?" or "I'm really lost; can you help me?"), the evaluator should, at most, give hints, such as those just suggested, as to how to proceed. Sometimes, a participant will give up on a task, flatly stating, "I *quit*." When this happens, unless the evaluator can gently prod the participant into continuing to attempt the task, it is probably best to explain to the participant how to accomplish the task, lead the participant through the steps (especially if it is important to subsequent tasks that will be performed), and then let the participant go on to the next task. If participants become so disgusted that they want to quit the entire session, there is little an evaluator can or should do but thank them, pay them, and let them go.

The evaluator should ask any question that is likely to extract a useful response from the participant, as long as the evaluator does not lead too much with the question. The evaluator, after all, will not have another chance to get information related to this session from this participant after the session is finished and therefore should maximize the qualitative data obtained by asking appropriate questions. With experience, evaluators become very creative at being appropriately evasive while still helping a participant out of a problem without adversely affecting the data collected. Evaluators also become more comfortable with phrasing and interjecting questions to the participant.

Finally, when the participant has performed the desired tasks, including completion of any questionnaire (e.g., QUIS) or survey, the evaluator should answer any questions the participant may have, give the participant whatever reward has been determined (e.g., money, mug, T-shirt), then thank and dismiss the participant, concluding the evaluation session.

10.4 GENERATING AND COLLECTING THE DATA

Once the evaluation session is underway, lots of interesting things quickly start happening between the participant and the interface being evaluated. The data you need to collect may start arriving in a flood. It can be overwhelming, but, by being prepared, you can make it easy and fun, especially if you know what kinds of data to collect. It is very easy for inexperienced evaluators to collect reams of data that are later virtually worthless as far as providing information about improving the design and usability of the interface. To avoid this problem, let's look at the kinds of data that are most useful in helping us measure and achieve our usability goals. There are methods for generating and collecting both qualitative and quantitative data, discussed in the following sections.

10.4.1 Quantitative Data Generation Techniques

Quantitative techniques are used to measure directly the observed usability levels, in order to compare them against the specified levels set in the usability specifications. There are two main kinds of quantitative data generation techniques most often used in formative evaluation:

- Benchmark tasks
- User preference questionnaires

The development of *benchmark tasks* (see Chapter 8) has already been discussed extensively. During the experiment, each participant performs the prescribed benchmark tasks, and if appropriate, the evaluator takes numeric data, depending on what is being measured. For example, the evaluator may measure the time it takes the participant to perform a task, or count the number of errors a participant makes while performing a task, or count the number of tasks a participant can perform within a given time period. Again, remember the need for pretesting the benchmark tasks, to make sure that they are clearly stated for the participants, and also to make sure that the metrics they are intended to produce are practically measurable. Counting the number of tasks in either five seconds or five hours, for example, is not reasonable.

Counting errors sounds, on the surface, as if it would be straightforward. However, it can be rather tricky. The main difficulties are in deciding what constitutes an error, and also in recognizing that an error is occurring in real time during an evaluation session. There are several effective approaches for recognizing errors. In general, an error is a special case of a critical incident (see Section 10.4.2, on qualitative data generation techniques). Any time a participant *cannot take a task to completion,* an error (at least one, probably more) has occurred.

Another kind of error can be identified when the participant does something wrong—namely, taking *any action that does not lead to progress in performing the desired task.* Note that this definition does *not* count accessing online help or other documentation as an error. Another way to think of this would be that a participant takes a *"wrong turn" along the expected path of task performance,* such as choosing the incorrect item from a menu or selecting the wrong button, and these choices do not lead to progress in performing the desired task.

Sometimes, a participant takes a wrong turn and then *later backs up;* sometimes successfully (i.e., still is able to take the intended task to completion) and other times not successfully. In either case, an error (or errors) has still occurred. However, it is important to note the circumstances under which the participant attempted to back up, and whether the participant was successful in figuring out what was wrong. There are also incidents when a participant does something you did not expect, something that might initially appear to be a wrong turn but ends up being a different way to accomplish a task than you had in mind. This does not generally constitute an error but still could be considered a critical incident.

Error making and error recovery during a session are also a chance for the evaluator to take data on how much time a user spends dealing with errors. These data are used later in impact analysis (in Section 10.5.3, on the effects on user performance). Often, however, it is difficult to know exactly when an error situation has begun. Some are quite obvious, while you may not recognize others as errors until the participant has progressed further along a fruitless path and is therefore well into an error situation. Thus, it can be difficult to capture, in real time, the time spent in making and dealing with errors. You may not recognize that an error is occurring in time to start a timer. A note of the current video-frame counter (if available to you) at this point will facilitate obtaining these data by selective review of the videotape after the session.

The second quantitative data generation technique is *user preference questionnaires,* or semantic differential scales. These fancy terms refer to something you are already familiar with—namely, categorical rankings (e.g., from 0 to 9, or –2 to 2, or never to always, or strongly agree to strongly disagree) for different features that, in this case, are relevant to the usability of the interface being evaluated. As already discussed in Chapter 8, this kind of questionnaire or survey is inexpensive to administer but not easy to produce so that the data are valid and reliable. Questionnaires are the most effective technique for producing quantitative data on subjective user opinion of an interface. The QUIS survey (see Chapter 8) is one of the most comprehensive and readily available of these validated questionnaires.

Even these simple measuring instruments are, however, not without problems. For example, the phenomenon termed the *halo effect* sometimes occurs with user preference questionnaires: Participants will give unreasonably good rankings to an interface. This happens for a variety of reasons: Some people want to be nice; others don't want to be negative; some are looking for jobs. However, there is also the *pitchfork effect*, in which participants give unrealistically low rankings. Perhaps they're having a bad day, or they had a fight with their spouse, or they don't feel appreciated in their job and want to cause trouble. There is really very little way to control for these two phenomena across your participants. You can discard data from any participant you think is not cooperating or otherwise properly participating in the evaluation. The most important suggestion is to be aware of the possibility and to be consistent in collecting and analyzing the data from user preference questionnaires.

10.4.2 Qualitative Data Generation Techniques

Qualitative data are sometimes more mysterious and elusive than quantitative data. However, qualitative data are extremely important in performing formative evaluation of a user interaction design for usability. The kinds of techniques that are most effective for generating qualitative data include the following:

- Concurrent verbal protocol taking
- Retrospective verbal protocol taking
- Critical incident taking
- Structured interviews

Perhaps the most common technique for qualitative data generation is verbal protocol taking, sometimes also called "thinking aloud." This approach is immensely effective in determining what problems participants are having and what might be done to fix those problems. In *concurrent verbal protocol taking*, the evaluator asks participants to talk out loud while working during an evaluation session, indicating what they are trying to do, or why they are having a problem, what they expected to happen that didn't, what they wished had happened, and so on.

This technique obviously is invasive to a participant, so unless the participant offers it naturally, the evaluator should not actively elicit it for benchmark tasks where timing data are being taken. However, there is evidence that, except for very low-level tasks that occur in a very short time (a few seconds), thinking aloud does not measurably affect task performance. This is especially true if the participant is just thinking aloud and not being interrupted much by questions from the evaluator. So the verbal protocol technique is frequently employed during free use of the system, but it can also be effective during performance of timed tasks.

The evaluator will find that some participants are not good at thinking aloud while they work; they will not talk much, and the evaluator will have to prod them constantly to find out what they are thinking or trying to do. For tasks that are not timed, it is perfectly acceptable for the evaluator to query such reticent talkers, in order to discover the desired information. The previous section (Section 10.3, on directing the evaluation session) discussed various ways to prompt a reticent talker. Remember, one of the goals in formative evaluation is not to have a large number of participants, but rather to extract as much data as possible from each and every participant. Evaluators become more skilled at this as they work with more participants.

For *retrospective*, or *post hoc, verbal protocol taking*, the evaluator lets participants work relatively uninterrupted during a taped session, rather than prodding them to think aloud very much. Then, immediately after the session, the evaluator and each participant review the videotape together, and the evaluator asks the participant to analyze what was occurring during the session. The assumption here is that a participant is at least as good as an evaluator in analyzing the data, especially if guided with appropriate questions by the evaluator during the videotape review. This postsession discussion and questioning does not interfere in any way with real-time task performance or collection of timing data. Analyzing verbal protocol data that are collected by an evaluator during an evaluation session can force the evaluator to make assumptions, guesses, and interpretations about what the participant was really thinking or trying to do. In retrospective verbal protocol taking, an evaluator can find out directly from participants what they were thinking, without having to guess or infer it.

Retrospective verbal protocol taking works well with participants who have trouble performing tasks while simultaneously verbalizing what they are trying to do and/or what they are thinking. However, its biggest drawback is time and procedural constraints. It generally takes a minimum of three hours with a participant to conduct an evaluation session and then to follow it with retrospective analysis of a videotape. Also, it can take much longer than this, depending on the length of the actual evaluation session and the level of analysis given by the participant.

You don't have to look at everything on the tape during the postsession review.

Nonetheless, there are usually a large enough number of interesting incidents that you need to analyze with the participant that it typically takes at least twice as long to perform the retrospective analysis as it took for the session itself. It is very important to hold the review immediately after the session because the insights and ideas of the participant about the interface are very ephemeral and will be forgotten quickly. Retrospective verbal protocol taking is a good example of the codiscovery approach mentioned in Section 10.3.

During verbal protocol taking, you will find that many participants are able to express clearly what they don't like about an interaction design, but they often do not know what suggestions to make for changes. Some participants will, however, come up with a suggestion as an alternative design to something they don't like that will make the development team wonder why they didn't think of it earlier. Don't count on this happening very often, but this phenomenon can occur with both concurrent and retrospective verbal protocol taking.

Despite its popularity and usefulness, verbal protocol is not without its controversies. In particular, it is an invasive data generation technique, and if not properly handled by an evaluator, it can affect the data collected. It is easy to get people to rationalize anything they experience, and they can be easily convinced, especially by an unskilled evaluator, that the problems they had with the design were not so bad, after all, or that they just misunderstood the design or the task description or whatever.

Verbal protocol helps uncover the working knowledge and assumptions of a typical user, which help not only to uncover a usability problem but also to provide reasons as to why a specific incident occurred. It helps determine what information or knowledge a user was missing that would have allowed the user to successfully complete a task.

Another kind of qualitative data generation that is important, often in conjunction with verbal protocol taking, is *critical incident taking* (del Galdo, Williges, Williges, & Wixon, 1986). A *critical incident* is something that happens while a participant is working that has a significant effect, either positive or negative, on task performance or user satisfaction, and thus on usability of the interface. Critical incident data help focus analysis of the qualitative data, especially the verbal protocol data.

A bad, or *negative*, critical incident is typically a problem a participant encounters—something that causes an error, something that blocks (even temporarily) progress in task performance, something that results in a pejorative remark by the participant, and so on. For example, an evaluator might observe a participant try unsuccessfully five times to enlarge a graphical image on the screen, using a graphics editor. If it is taking the participant so many tries to perform the task, it is probably an indication that this particular part of the design should be improved. Similarly, the participant may begin to show signs of frustration, either with remarks (e.g., "What is this thing doing?" "Why did it do that?" "Why won't it do what I tell it to?") or actions (e.g., shaking a fist at the screen, shrugging shoulders defeatedly, drumming fingers impatiently on the table, or uttering various four-letter words—remember the "cuss count" from Chapter 8).

An occurrence that causes a participant to express satisfaction or closure in some way (e.g., "That was neat!" "Oh, now I see." "Cool!") is a good, or *positive*, critical incident. When a first-time participant immediately understands, for example, the metaphor of how to manipulate a graphical object, that can also be a positive critical incident. While negative critical incidents indicate problems in the interaction design, positive critical incidents indicate metaphors and details that, because they work well or a participant likes them, should be considered for use in other appropriate places throughout an interface. Critical incidents can be observed during performance of benchmark tasks, other representative tasks, or when a participant is freely using the system.

Structured interviews provide another form of qualitative data. These are typically in the form of a postexperiment interview, a series of preplanned questions that the evaluator asks each participant. A typical postsession interview might include, for example, such general questions as "What did you like best about the interface?" "What did you like least?" and "How would you change so-and-so?". An interesting question to ask is "What are the three most important pieces of information that a user must know to begin using this interface?" For example, in one design, some of the results of a database query were presented to the user as small circles. Most users did not at first realize that they could get more information if they clicked on a circle. So one very important piece of information users needed to know about the design was that they should treat a circle as an icon, and that they could manipulate it accordingly.

The interview questions may be asked by the evaluator, who writes down (or otherwise records) a participant's answers, or a participant may fill out the interview questionnaire. There is a danger of constructing an interview that will not produce valid and reliable data; it is therefore necessary to produce such a set of interview questions with assistance from someone who is skilled in interview development.

10.4.3 Data Collection Techniques

So far, this chapter has described ways of generating various kinds of data to collect, but not *how* to collect them. There are several recommended techniques for capturing both qualitative and quantitative data from participants during a formative evaluation experiment, including

- Real-time note-taking
- Videotaping
- Audiotaping
- Internal instrumentation of the interface

Our own experience and numerous conversations with other evaluators indicate that *real-time note-taking* is still the most effective technique to use for data (especially qualitative) capture during a formative evaluation session. The evaluator should be prepared to take copious notes as activities proceed during a session. When an evaluator is directing a test session for the first few times, it is a good idea to have a second evaluator also observing the session in order to help take notes. The primary evaluator is responsible for giving instructions, prompting the participant, administering appropriate tasks, timing tasks when necessary, and taking notes on the entire procedure. Until an evaluator is comfortable with this multitude of simultaneous activities that can happen quickly during an evaluation session, another person with the specific responsibility of taking notes and perhaps timing task performance can be invaluable. Even after becoming experienced with all aspects of directing an experiment, an evaluator may still find it helpful to have another evaluator observing the session, especially if the session is expected to be rather lengthy, say an hour or more.

To capture observations and notes, an evaluator can use either *pencil and paper* or *computer tools* such as word processors and/or spreadsheets. Many evaluators find that they can type data into a computer much faster than they can write (legibly). Then, during data analysis, even using a word processor's search facilities for such time-consuming activities as locating and counting similar incidents can be a huge time-saver. Using the computer may be more awkward than paper-and-pencil note-taking when the evaluator is in the same room as the participant. However, if the evaluator is using a laptop, or notebook computer, it seems to be much less invasive to the participant than a full-sized personal computer or workstation. The evaluator can explain why the computer is being used as part of the lab tour at the beginning of the evaluation session. Additionally, a person in a control room next door with a video monitor or one-way mirror could use a computer to take notes unobtrusively.

To collect quantitative data, the required equipment is minimal. Each evaluator who will be timing task performance by the participants will need a stopwatch or a clock with a seconds hand, and some kind of tally sheet for noting and/or counting errors, timings, and other observations. The simplest approach to capturing these data is to use a form such as shown in Figure 10.5, which has a column specifically for noting errors associated with each task. These forms can be either reproduced on paper or set up in advance in a word processor or a spreadsheet.

PARTICIPANT ID:		Session Date: Session Start Time: Session End Time:			
Task Description	Tape Counter	No. of Errors	Elapsed Time	Participant's Actions and Comments	Evaluator's Observations
A Schedule appt....					
B					

Figure 10.5. Sample form for collecting both quantitative and qualitative data during an evaluation session.

To collect qualitative data, the evaluator (or evaluators) should note all observed critical incidents, as well as any other observations, as a participant performs each task or uses the interface freely. A simple form such as shown in Figure 10.5 is useful to help structure the data collection. The evaluator should fill in the predefined tasks in the Task Description column before an evaluation session begins, leaving quite a bit of space between each one. The evaluator can also fill in the participant ID and session date before a session begins. This form can be used to record errors in the No. of Errors column, and elapsed time for task performance in the Elapsed Time column (when these are relevant measures for the task being performed). These values can then be later related to usability specifications as appropriate.

If the videotaping setup (see Section 10.8, on setting up a usability lab) has a frame counter or timing device, the evaluator can use the Tape Counter column to note the frame number or time associated with a particular task, action, comment, or observation. The Participant's Actions and Comments column will contain many of the critical incidents for each task. Often, direct quotes from participants are effective and easy to capture. (These also make good video clips for selling these ideas outside the lab.) The Evaluator's Observations column can be used to record any other interesting information (e.g., an idea for a design fix for an observed problem). Comments and observations may be lengthy, especially for complicated tasks. They describe the critical incidents that will be used to detect both problems and good features during the data analysis step of formative evaluation (see Section 10.5, on analyzing the data). You can also use this same form during free use.

Videotaping is a well-known and frequently used data collection technique. Many usability labs have an elaborate multicamera videotaping setup, with split-screen monitor for recording/editing capability, frame-accurate time tracking, and so on (see Section 10.8, on setting up a usability lab). Videotaping has many advantages, including the capture of every detail that occurs during an evaluation session. If multiple cameras are used, one can be aimed, for example, at the participant's hands and the screen, another at the participant's face, and perhaps a third can be capturing a wide-angle view of evaluator, participant, and computer. Generally, one camera is adequate, and more than two cameras may be excessive. A camera aimed at the participant's hands and the screen is the most important, and a second, if available, should be aimed for a broader view, including the participant's face.

Some people often ask, "Well, why not capture as much on tape as possible; you don't have to analyze it all if you don't want to." This is true, but the problem with analysis of videotape is twofold. First, it can take as much as eight hours to analyze each one hour of videotape (Mackay & Davenport, 1989). The chances of someone laboriously going back through several hours of videotape from half a dozen evaluation sessions is therefore very slim. Second, with multiple views and/or tapes of the same test session, there is a problem of synchronization of the tapes (e.g., was the participant grimacing when she was trying to move the icon, or when it disappeared unexpectedly just after she tried to move it?).

There is really no point in using two (or more) cameras unless you have very sophisticated (read: expensive) equipment to merge two views onto one tape, alleviating the second problem. Even so, the first problem remains. The *main use of videotape should be as a backup* for what happened during an evaluation session, not as the main source of data to be captured and analyzed.

The Tape Counter column shown in Figure 10.5 is invaluable when the videotape is used as a backup. Sometimes, during an evaluation session, things happen so fast that, even with two evaluators taking notes, it simply isn't possible to write down everything of interest that is going on. When this happens, the Tape Counter column provides a pointer back into the videotape. The evaluators can, after the session, go back to each such place on the videotape and review it efficiently at their leisure, and without the real-time stress of continuing the session in an orderly fashion. For example, in case of confusion, uncertainty about a specific detail, or some missed part of a critical incident that occurred during an evaluation session, the evaluator can—if the tape counter value was noted—quickly go to a specific point on the videotape and review a very short sequence to collect the missing data. If the tape counter value was not noted, then the evaluator can, of course, search for the desired spot on the tape, but this can obviously take much more time. There are some tools to make reviewing videotapes more efficient, and, when used, the usefulness of the videotape goes way up, but so does the cost of the equipment.

A few *carefully selected video clips (say, of five minutes each or less) can be of great influence on a development team that is resistant to making changes* to what the team members believe to be their already perfect design. Sometimes, programmers who have the major responsibility for an interaction design watch video clips in awe while a bewildered participant struggles to perform a task with an awkward interface. Interestingly, their response is sometimes "What a stupid user!" rather than the appropriate "Wow, do we need to work on that interaction design!" Fortunately, as an awareness of the importance of usability increases, such inappropriate comments are heard less and less. These same video clips can also be useful in convincing management that there is a usability problem in the first place.

Audiotaping of test sessions should be done when videotaping is not available (e.g., in field testing). It, too, should be used only as a backup, and not as the main data capture technique with the expectation of later going back and analyzing the full audiotaped session. While it does not capture the visual aspects of the test session, the oral exchanges that take place between an evaluator and a participant can be very valuable for later data analysis.

You probably are wondering just how much may be missed by an evaluator trying to take all the notes for an evaluation session in real time, without going back to review the videotape. We wondered this, too, and performed some simple studies to try to determine how much could be captured by evaluators taking real-time notes versus a complete review of the videotape. In one study, for example, two experienced evaluators observed an evaluation session of about two hours, capturing comments and observations by writing them down. The entire session was also videotaped, and a third experienced evaluator reviewed the videotape to capture comments and observations. The third evaluator could go back and forth and review any portion of the videotape as many times as desired. It took the third evaluator more than 12 tedious hours, over a 2-week period, to analyze the videotape in detail. The results were then compared from the real-time data collection to the data collected in the videotape review. On average, the postsession detailed videotape analysis resulted in an increase of observed critical incidents of no more than 10% over the real-time critical incident capture. Also, almost without exception, these few incidents were minor ones that had no real impact on the usability of the interface. We concluded, therefore, that postsession detailed videotape review has drastically diminishing returns for the amount of increased, useful data it provides. Thus, it appears that *real-time note-taking (either with pencil and paper or computer) is the most efficient means* of data capture during usability evaluation sessions.

Finally, another useful way to capture the kinds of data discussed in this chapter is *internally instrumenting the interface* being evaluated to capture individual events, from user keystrokes and mouse clicks to start and stop times of routines associated with specific tasks. For example, data on user errors or frequency of command usage, or elapsed task times taken from start–stop times, can be automatically collected by a fairly simple program. There is, however, a potential problem with this technique: what to do with the collected data. Evaluators, especially novice ones, may think "the more data, the better," but then find themselves inundated with details of keystrokes and mouse clicks. A fairly short session, say half an hour, can produce a several-megabyte user session transcript file. Manual analysis of a file dump printed as a 10-inch high (or even 10-foot high) stack of paper is totally untenable.

The difficult question is, What analysis should be done once such data are extracted from a transcript file? How can, for example, any of these keystrokes or cursor movements be associated with anything significant, good or bad, happening to the participant, and therefore related to usability? What do they mean in terms of the usability of the interface? What do they imply for the next iteration of modifications?

The only feasible way in which such data might be useful is if their analysis can be automated, and there appear to be very few workable techniques for analyzing (either manually or automatedly) user session transcripts. One such technique is Maximal Repeating Patterns, or MRPs (Siochi & Ehrich, 1991), in which repeating user action patterns of maximum length are extracted from a user session transcript, based on the hypothesis that repeated patterns of usage (e.g., sequences of repeated commands) contain *interesting* information about an interface's usability. In fact, this technique was compared empirically to observational evaluation of an interface (Siochi & Hix, 1991). Most problems discovered by observing participants of an interface were found independently by MRP analysis of user session transcripts. However, the MRP technique, too, produces voluminous data, and only a prototype tool for automated evaluation exists. Also, while the MRP technique does help to pinpoint specific problems, it does not indicate how the interaction design should be modified to fix those problems.

There are a few advantages of collecting user action data via instrumenting an interface. It can be employed in situ, thereby collecting real user data in field evaluation, which typically better represents a user's actual work context than data collected during laboratory evaluation. Collection of data via instrumentation is noninvasive (assuming it does not perceptibly slow down the system). This kind of data collection is cheaper than observational data because data can be automatically collected at multiple field sites without the need for dispatching platoons of evaluators to each site. However, until the information relating to usability that such data provide is better understood, and until satisfactory tools for automating such analysis are developed, its use is far less effective than direct observation of representative users, both in lab and field sites, for collecting data that will most influence the usability of an interface. We do not believe that any kind of analysis of user session transcripts will ever completely replace the kind of formative evaluation, involving observations of representative users, as described here.

10.4.4 Computer-Based Tool Support for Formative Evaluation

Finally, a few tools are emerging that support the formative evaluation process, by assisting in collection and analysis of observed user data during evaluation sessions. Most of these, however, seem to be in-house products and are not generally available commercially. Over the next few years, more tools to support formative evaluation are likely to appear.

The Interface Design Environment and Analysis Lattice, or IDEAL (Ashlund & Hix, 1992), is an interactive tool that supports the process of interaction design and usability evaluation. Components of IDEAL are based on user task descriptions that comprise the design. In particular, IDEAL allows a user interaction developer to attach specific benchmark task instances to UAN task descriptions. The developer can also create usability specifications, which are then stored and displayed in conjunction with the appropriate benchmark and other tasks.

During a formative evaluation session, the developer/evaluator can associate observed quantitative and qualitative (e.g., critical incidents) data directly with the benchmark and other task descriptions. IDEAL allows direct comparison between observed data and usability specifications. It also allows comparisons of measured usability for the present interface with previously measured usability, aiding developers and managers in seeing and understanding trends, convergence, and so on, in the usability of a design. These various components are connected via hypermedia links, based on task names.

Other features that are being built into IDEAL include the following:

- On-screen stopwatches to time user task performance
- On-screen counters for errors and critical incidents
- Automatic capture of videotape frame number/time
- Real-time video display in a window, for use by observers in a control room
- Multimedia connections to audio and video clips, particularly quick extraction of key segments to show to developers
- Management support for assessing convergence of a design over successive iterations

Early evaluation of a prototype of IDEAL has shown that it is useful in assisting and managing the inherently complex process of formative evaluation. We hope to see other tools emerging to support this process, as well.

10.5 ANALYZING THE DATA

After all evaluation sessions for a particular cycle of formative evaluation are completed, the data collected during those sessions must then be analyzed. In general, evaluators do not perform inferential statistical analyses, such as analyses of variance (ANOVAs) or t-tests or F-tests. Rather, they use data analysis techniques that will help determine whether the interface has met the usability specification levels, and if it has not, analysis indicates how to modify the design to help in converging toward those goals in subsequent cycles of formative evaluation.

This section discusses analysis of some of the data from a hypothetical formative evaluation session for the Calendar Management System, to bring this cycle of its development process to closure. All of this discussion is based on the design of the system described in Chapter 5. You might want to look back at the sample screen picture produced in Figure 5.3. In addition, when appropriate, this chapter also presents some real data collected and analyzed during formative evaluation of a graphical drawing application that we evaluated for a client. The graphical drawing application evaluation is included simply to give you further examples of how to analyze these kinds of data.

10.5.1 Initial Analysis: The Big Decision

At this point in the iterative cycle comes a major decision: Accept the interaction design as it is, or consider a redesign. This decision must be made at a global—interface metaphor—level, as well as a detailed—individual problem—level. To help make this decision, we now analyze the data collected.

The first step in analyzing the data is to compute averages and any other values stated in the usability specifications for timing, error counts, questionnaire ratings, and so on. A word of caution: Computing only the mean to determine whether usability specifications have been met can be misleading, because the mean is not resistant to outliers. With a small number of participants such as are typical in formative evaluation, it is possible for a mean to meet a reasonable preestablished usability specification, while there are serious usability problems. In fact, outliers may indicate serious usability problems. To help compensate for this, you may want also to report the standard deviation, and maybe the median.

Next, enter a summary of your results into the Observed Results column of the usability specification table. Partial results from a hypothetical evaluation of the Calendar Management System are shown in Table 10.1. This table contains four of the nine usability specifications that were established in Chapter 8. Table 10.1 shows observed results from three participants, using, for example, P1 to indicate

TABLE 10.1. PARTIAL RESULTS FROM A HYPOTHETICAL FORMATIVE EVALUATION SESSION OF THE CALENDAR MANAGEMENT SYSTEM

Usability Attribute	Measuring Instrument	Value to be Measured	Current Level	Worst Acceptable Level	Planned Target Level	Best Possible Level	Observed Results
Initial performance	"Add appointment" task per Benchmark 1	Length of time to successfully add appointment on first trial	15 seconds (manually)	30 seconds	20 seconds	10 seconds	P1=33 secs P2=42 secs P3=29 secs Mean = 35 seconds
Initial performance	"Add appointment" task per Benchmark 1	Number of errors on first trial	0 errors (manually)	3 errors	2 errors	0 errors	P1=2 P2=4 P3=1 Mean= 2.3 errors
Initial performance	"Delete appointment" task per Benchmark 2	Length of time to successfully delete appointment on first trial	12 seconds	20 seconds	12 seconds	8 seconds	P1=71 secs P2=42 secs P3=50 secs Mean= 54 seconds
Initial performance	"Delete appointment" task per Benchmark 2	Number of errors on first trial	0 errors	4 errors	3 errors	0 errors	P1=5 P2=5 P3=3 Mean= 4.3 errors

the first participant, and so on. The mean has also been computed and recorded here.

Now, by directly comparing the observed results with the specified usability goals, you can tell immediately which usability specifications have been met and which have not been met during this cycle of formative evaluation. In looking at the observed results, users did not meet the worst acceptable level for the "add appointment" task when their performance was timed (mean = 35 seconds), but they just met it for number of errors (mean = 2.3 errors). They did not come close to meeting the worst acceptable level for either of the measures (means = 54 seconds and 4.3 errors) for the "delete appointment" task. Because the mean time was so much greater than the worst acceptable level, this observed result serves as an example to carry on the data analysis. This section later discusses in more detail why user performance was so far off the usability specifications and what to do to improve performance.

After observed results have been recorded and compared to the established level, you can decide your next step. If all worst acceptable levels have been met and enough planned target levels have been met to satisfy the development team that usability of the present version of the interaction design is acceptable, then the design is satisfactory, and you can stop iterating for this version.

The one exception to terminating iteration when the minimum levels have been met is if, for whatever reason, you suspect that your usability specifications may be too lenient and therefore not a good indicator of high usability. For example, in a situation where all planned target levels were met or exceeded, but observations during evaluation sessions showed that participants were frustrated and performed tasks poorly, your intuition will probably tell you that the interface is, in fact, not acceptable in terms of its usability, despite having met all the specified goals. Then, obviously, the development team should reassess the usability specifications to see whether they should be more (or less) stringent.

In most cases where all usability specifications are met, though, you can stop iterating; you have reached the desired level of usability for the present version of the system. If you have not met your usability specifications (the most likely situation after the first cycle of testing), then you should continue with more in-depth data analysis, as described later.

The goal in further data analysis—much of which is qualitative data analysis—is structured identification of the observed problems and potential solutions to them. The subsequent activities address solving those problems in order of their potential impact on usability of the interface. The *process of determining how to convert the collected data into scheduled design and implementation solutions is essentially one of negotiation* in which, at various times, all members of the development team are involved.

In order to make final decisions, developers must also know the total amount of time allocated to making design changes for the current cycle of iteration. For example, suppose that for the Calendar Management System we have only a fairly small amount of time available in the schedule, about 25 person hours. This number is used a bit later in making redesign decisions (see Sections 10.6 and 10.7).

Figure 10.6 shows a form that is useful in enumerating and organizing the multitude of problems that will inevitably be uncovered during a cycle of formative evaluation. The data here for the Calendar Management System are again hypothetical and are used for explaining each column in this table in subsequent sections.

As mentioned earlier, we also use some data from an actual formative evaluation of a graphical drawing application as an example to further explain analysis of these kinds of data. These data are shown in Figure 10.7. This project had allocated 60 hours in its schedule for making modifications after this cycle of evaluation.

10.5.2 Problem

In Figures 10.6 and 10.7, the *problem* is an *interaction design flaw* or a *user difficulty directly associated with an interaction design flaw*. Problems are identified from observation of critical incidents (negative ones) and verbal protocol taking during evaluation sessions. Figure 10.6 listed three possible problems that might have been encountered in a formative evaluation of the design of the Calendar Management System.

The first problem arose as participants performed Benchmark 2, the "delete appointment" task. They had a great deal of trouble realizing that after finding the desired appointment, they had to first select it by double-clicking on it before they could delete that appointment (single-clicking is used to place the text editing cursor in an appointment). They would find the appointment and then perhaps have trouble finding the "Delete Appointment" button in the upper right corner of the screen in Figure 5.3 because it is rather far away from the appointment window. Once they found the button, still not having selected the appointment to delete, they would try single-clicking on the button, double-clicking on the button, even dragging the button toward the appointment, none of which worked. All they would get was a beep when they tried clicking on the button. All three participants did figure out after a time that they had to select the appointment, but each one tried several wrong actions (and therefore accumulated several errors, as recorded in Table 10.1 for Benchmark 2) before realizing this. They were very puzzled and frustrated during this time.

The other two problems were observed while participants were performing

Problem	Effect on User Performance	Importance	Solution(s)	Cost	Resolution
User did not know to select appointment before it could be deleted	115 of 163 seconds	High	Move delete button, gray it out until user selects appoint-ment, and add message to user	5 hours	
User can get to future years only by moving successively through months	N/A	Medium	Add navigation tabs for "future year" and "past year"	2 hours	
User did not understand need to drag the alarm icon to the desired appointment	N/A	High	When user clicks on alarm icon, change cursor to look like alarm icon, then user moves cursor to desired ap-pointment and single-clicks to add an alarm	2 hours	

Figure 10.6. Form for organizing and analyzing observed problems, showing data from the Calendar Management System.

some of the nonbenchmark tasks (in particular, Tasks G and D). In Task G, when participants were looking for the month of July in the next year, the only way they could get there was by clicking through the months sequentially, using the "Future Month" tab on the upper right of the screen in Figure 5.3. There is no provision in the current design to move to future (or past) years more directly. They found this very inefficient and annoying.

In Task D, participants did not understand how to set the alarm on an appointment. In the current design, to set an alarm, users should first locate the appointment for which they wish to set an alarm. They must then move the cursor so that it is over the alarm icon in the upper left corner of the screen in Figure 5.3 and depress the mouse button. Keeping the mouse button depressed causes a copy of the icon to follow the cursor, and users must drag this copy to the appointment for which the alarm is desired. Participants figured out that they needed to locate the desired appointment, and then they tried clicking on the alarm icon. However, neither single- nor double-clicking on this icon does anything. None of the participants figured out that they had to drag a copy of the alarm icon while keeping the mouse button depressed.

In actual evaluation sessions performed on the graphical drawing application, users had to do too much window manipulation, as indicated in Figure 10.7. The designers of the graphical drawing application had come up with what they thought was a great idea for handling the multiple windows that appeared during use of the system. Whenever a new window appeared, it remained connected to the cursor until the user clicked a mouse button to purposefully place the window somewhere. The designers thought this was a neat idea because it gave the user full control over window placement (remember the "keep the locus of control with the user" guideline way back in Chapter 2).

Well, participants hated it. They did not like having to do so much window manipulation. They were irritated by a window that wandered around, stuck to the cursor. In almost all situations where a new window appeared, the task the participant was attempting to perform was seriously interrupted by the need to park the "wandering window" somewhere on the screen. After repeated occurrences of this phenomenon, participants were shaking their fists at the screen and literally screaming, "I don't do windows!" This is an example of a serious negative critical incident.

An example of another problem encountered during evaluation of the graphical drawing application was simply an oversight on the part of the interaction designer. The cursor icon was a black arrow in one particular mode of the application. However, when the black arrow was moved over a black background, it stayed black and therefore disappeared. The black arrow should, of course, have become white (or reverse video, or whatever).

Each such problem observed during evaluation should be listed in the Problem column of this form—and there are potentially hundreds of problems, especially

Problem	Effect on User Performance	Importance	Solution(s)	Cost	Resolution
Too much window manipulation	10 of 35 minutes	High	Fix window placement automatically, but allow user to reposition it	6 hours	
Black arrow on black background	N/A	Low	Reverse arrow to white on black	1 hour	

Figure 10.7. Data from formative evaluation of a graphical drawing application.

in early cycles of formative evaluation. Any persons who observed any of the evaluation sessions should contribute a list of the problems they observed, and one person then typically takes responsibility for merging all the problems into a single list. In the graphical drawing application interface, after about five hours of the first cycle of evaluation sessions, there was a list of 54 problems to tackle, ranging from serious to trivial. Later cycles generally produce fewer changes, especially if the process is leading to convergence toward a more usable design.

10.5.3 Effect on User Performance

The *effect on user performance* is *data about the amount of time a user spends dealing with a specific problem.* Thus, comparing usability specification levels, observed values, and values from the Effect on User Performance column directly indicate which problems are the largest contributors to not achieving the desired usability specifications. Because this effect on user performance time is deducted from user performance times when the associated problem is solved, this will have the most impact on meeting the specifications. Because of this direct effect, a high importance rating (see Section 10.5.4) is generally assigned to problems with a high impact on performance.

Impact analysis (e.g., Good, Spine, Whiteside, & George, 1986) can be used to help determine the importance of problems listed in the tables of Figures 10.6 and 10.7, by deciding what problems most affect achievement of the usability specifications. This analysis is based on the time a user spends in various problems, recorded in the Effect on User Performance column. This effect on user performance is not just limited to error handling, but also should count the time during which a participant is sitting puzzled, being lost, fretting, and so on.

Recall in an earlier discussion, if the evaluator observes a problem just as it is occurring, a stopwatch can be used to measure the time spent by the participant in dealing with that problem. In reality, though, an evaluator often cannot determine that a problem is occurring until well after it has begun. This is where the videotape backup and tape counter are very helpful for later reviewing of the session.

For example, suppose that a quick review of the videotaped sessions for the Calendar Management System showed that of a total of 163 seconds (71 + 42 + 50 from row 3 of Table 10.1) for the "delete appointment" task, participants spent 115 seconds having problems. This means that more than 70% of the task performance time is attributable to trying to figure out how to perform the task. This obviously has a significant effect on user performance and on usability of the interface.

Most important, this 115-second value is a number that, when the associated problems causing it are solved, can be subtracted straight off the top of user performance times, contributing most directly to meeting the usability specifications. Specifically, subtracting 115 from 163 leaves 48 seconds, which was the total time the three participants spent productively in accomplishing the "delete appointment" task. Their average performance time, after removing the time spent in errors, is thus 16 seconds (48 ÷ 3), which is slightly better than the worst acceptable level (20 seconds) in the usability specification table. Now, by solving this problem, rather than being completely off the usability goal for this task, it can be within the minimum level. This shows the effect on user performance of removing time spent in errors, and says that if the design is modified so that this error time is eliminated (or at least drastically reduced), the usability goals can be met. Thus, impact analysis indicates that fixing the problems that users had in trying to perform the "delete appointment" task is of high importance (again, see the following section).

A value was not determined for the effect on user performance for either of the other two problems reported in Figure 10.6 because neither of the tasks (setting an alarm and adding an appointment far in the future) was associated with a specific usability specification. In retrospect, given that users were essentially unable to perform the "set alarm" task, this task should probably have been included in the usability specification table. When this kind of situation arises, you may want to add new specifications, even after you have conducted evaluation sessions with some of your participants. It's better to collect needed data from some of them than from none of them. Just be sure to note in making your summaries that the number of participants on which some values were taken is different than the number for other values.

In the wandering windows example for the graphical drawing application, a quick scan of the videotaped sessions showed that one participant spent 35 minutes attempting to perform several benchmark tasks, of which about 10 of those 35 minutes were wasted fretting about and manipulating the windows. Again, this 10-minute value can be subtracted off user performance times when the associated problems are fixed. Although the second problem, the black arrow on a black background, was annoying, participants spent very little of their time fretting over this problem. Therefore the videotapes were not reviewed in order to come up with an amount of time participants actually encountered this problem.

10.5.4 Importance

The *importance* rating is the *subjective (based on opinions of the development team) effect of an observed problem on user performance, interface usability, and overall system integrity.* The importance of a problem can be based on several different characteristics, including frequency, persistence, and impact on system integrity and consistency. On the other hand, it can simply be a subjective opinion about importance to the overall integrity or consistency of the design. Often, simply categorizing importance as low, moderate, or high provides an adequate level of granularity for most situations. First candidates for high importance ratings are those that, as revealed by impact analysis, have the greatest effect on meeting the established usability specifications. Low importance problems might be those that cause a user to become mildly confused; moderate importance problems might reflect an error a user made; and high importance problems might be those that prevent a user from completing a task—for example, because it was too difficult or too frustrating.

For the Calendar Management System, the impact analysis in the previous section showed that the problem with deleting an appointment is of high importance. This matches our intuitive feelings of importance, too, because it is a task that users will need to perform often, and all participants were puzzled as to how to perform this task. Similarly, setting an alarm is a task that gives the automated calendar a great deal of functionality over a paper calendar, yet participants could not figure out how to do this task. It is therefore of high importance. The problem of not having a direct method for getting to future years is of medium importance. Although it does provide substantial functional improvement over a paper calendar, this is probably not a task that users will perform very often.

In the graphical drawing application, impact analysis showed that the problem of the wandering windows was definitely of high importance. This, too, matches intuitive feelings of importance because of the constantly mounting irritation it caused participants. Although the arrow problem was a factor in system integrity, it did not really interfere with participants' performance at all, and its importance was therefore low.

Typically, via a group meeting, all who have been involved in observing the evaluation sessions contribute to the determination of the importance ratings. This dialectic decision-making process among development team members (possibly including some users) can take into account many factors. Most of these ratings are immediately obvious; in general, the really serious problems get a high importance rating, the inconsequential problems get a low rating, and everything else gets a moderate rating.

10.5.5 Solution

The development team, including the evaluator, must also propose one or more possible *solutions—that is, changes to the design to solve each of the observed problems on the list*. Ideas for these proposed design solutions can come from a variety of places. For example, in situations where design principles and guidelines have obviously been violated, a solution can be proposed that is *guideline based*. Solutions that may have been *suggested by participants*, and especially any suggestions made by a human–computer interaction *expert*, should be seriously considered. *Known available technology* and studies of other *similar designs* can also spark ideas for solutions to interface usability problems.

The development team, *brainstorming* together, can often come up with creative solutions. Sometimes, more than one good solution will be proposed. In this case, go ahead and list all the possible solutions. Often, different solutions will have different costs associated with them (that is, implementing one solution to a problem may be estimated to take two hours, while a different solution to the same problem may be estimated to take two days of coding time). When, in a later step of data analysis, you make decisions about which problems are most critical to fix, it may be useful to have alternative solutions with different costs, so that at least some sort of solution can be offered for a problem that might otherwise have to be ignored because the cost of the first-choice solution is too high.

Solving the first problem for the Calendar Management System means helping users to realize that they must use the "Delete Appointment" button, and that they first need to select an appointment before deleting it. This could be solved by modifying the current design in Figure 5.3 in several ways. First, a user would see the "Delete Appointment" button more easily if it were in the window with the appointment, rather than in the upper right corner of the screen. Thus, in the design the button is moved into the window. Also, the button will be grayed out (and therefore be disabled) until the user does, in fact, select an appointment. Upon selection, the button will no longer be grayed out, and hopefully users will realize that they can now delete the selected appointment. If users click on the button while it is grayed out (i.e., without first selecting an appointment), they will see a help message that says, "To delete an appointment, you must first select it by double-clicking on it," and the button will still remain grayed out until the user selects an appointment. This solution is good (if the paradigm of clicking on grayed-out choices for getting help is consistent throughout the interface), in that it helps a novice user who is having trouble but will not interfere with users who know how to perform the task.

To provide a more direct-access method for future and past years, the second problem in Figure 10.6, requires only a fairly simple change: Add a "Future Years" tab in the upper right of the screen in Figure 5.3 (near the one labeled "Future Months") and another labeled "Past Years" (on the upper left, near the tab labeled "Past Months"). These tabs will allow a user either to click through successive months or to navigate by successive years. Once the user is in a new year, the user can then click on the "Future Months" and "Past Months" tabs to navigate through that year.

The third problem with the Calendar Management System involves helping the user to understand how to set an alarm. All participants expected something to happen when they clicked on the alarm icon. In response to this observation, the design is modified so that when users click on the alarm icon, the cursor takes on the appearance of the alarm icon. Then users can move the cursor to the appointment for which they wish to set an alarm and single-click over that appointment to set the alarm. If users wish to get rid of the alarm cursor without setting an alarm for any appointment, they can move the cursor back over the alarm icon in the upper left corner of the screen and single-click, causing the cursor to change back to its normal (nonalarm) appearance. Because we can't predict for sure that users will understand this approach, we note to test it specifically in the next iteration.

For the wandering windows problem in the graphical drawing application, the solution was to fix window placement automatically at the center of the screen when a window first appears, but to allow a user to move and reposition it anywhere on the screen at any time. When this was retested in later formative evaluation cycles, users liked it much better. The solution for the black arrow on a black background was, of course, simply to reverse the arrow to white when it was over a black background.

All too often, "increased user training" or "cover in documentation" is a proposed solution for design problems. A word of caution: *Do not user either education or manuals as a crutch to overcome poor usability.* These solutions are often cop-outs to make up for poor interaction designs. Both of these should be last resorts, when there is no other feasible redesign alternative. It may take only an hour or so to add a paragraph to the user documentation, or a short while to add a little more information to the user training materials, but you can only document and train yourself out of so many problems! Such solutions do not improve poor usability that may be inherent in the interaction design; they only provide ways to work around it. There is no reason to believe, in most cases, that these solutions will have any real effect on user performance. Further, if you consider the cost of administering additional training to all users, or the cost in productivity if large numbers of users have to read extra documentation, these costs will surely be overwhelmingly greater than the cost of doing a proper fix to a usability problem by some redesign of the interaction.

10.5.6 Cost

For each proposed solution, a *cost* of implementing it must be estimated. This cost is usually the *amount of resources, usually time (sometimes money) needed for making the change indicated for each proposed solution.* Typically, it is measured in terms of the number of person hours needed to modify a prototype, or to modify existing source code or to write new code. If you cannot get reliable person hour estimates for proposed solutions, you can at least give them a high–medium–low rating.

The solution to the deletion problem in the Calendar Management System in Figure 10.6 requires about five hours of recoding time. This is a somewhat costly problem because of the fairly small amount of time for changes (25 hours, as mentioned earlier). To change the future and past year navigation scheme as proposed will probably take about two hours, a much lower cost. Modifying the alarm function will also probably take about two hours.

In the graphical drawing application, to fix the placement of a window, the programmer on the development team estimated, as shown in Figure 10.7, that six hours of recoding would be necessary. This therefore seemed to be a fairly high-cost problem. Reversing the arrow to be white over a black background was a very low-cost solution. The programmer estimated this would take no more than one hour to change.

Lower costs here are typically obtained when changes are made to a prototype, rather than to a version of the interface that has been coded. This reinforces the need to select good prototyping tools and to get a prototype running and testable as early in the development process as possible (see Chapter 9, on rapid prototyping).

10.5.7   Cost/Importance Analysis

Before completing the last column of Figures 10.6 and 10.7, the Resolution column, it is necessary to discuss cost/importance analysis. This is the next step toward resolving the list of usability problems. Once all columns *except* the Resolution column have been completed for all observed problems, some cost/importance analysis can be performed to help determine a resolution for each problem.

In a *cost/importance analysis*, the development team considers the relative importance of the problems and cost of the solutions as listed in a table like the one in Figures 10.6 and 10.7. The first step is to determine the resources (in particular, time and people) available to allocate for making modifications. For the Calendar Management System, we have already assumed that 25 hours have been allocated for making modifications to the design based on this cycle of formative evaluation. Totaling the Cost column in Figure 10.6 shows that only 9 hours have been used for these three changes. However, this is not a complete table of all problems. Because these data on the Calendar Management System are hypothetical anyway, there surely are at least half a dozen other problems, with costs of their solutions plus the ones in Figure 10.6 totaling more than 40 hours.

In the evaluation of the graphical drawing application, 60 hours (across two programmers) was allocated for modifications in the first cycle of formative evaluation. A total of the Cost column revealed more than 140 hours of suggested changes, even after selecting the lowest-cost suggestions to change for those problems for which there were multiple suggestions. This left some difficult decisions to make about which problems were going to get addressed, and which were going to remain unchanged, at least for the next cycle of evaluation.

Use a spreadsheet, or some word processing package, can help manage the list of problems, so that the problems can be sorted by cost and/or importance. Your initial sort (either automated or manual) should be first on importance (high to moderate to low) and then within each of these categories, on cost (low to high). Changes to high-importance problems obviously are most likely to improve usability, so look for high-importance but low-cost problems as those to address (i.e., to give a resolution of "Do it") first.

The sort just suggested will cause these to bubble to the top of the list. You will, in fact, find some high-importance/low-cost problems, despite your possible skepticism about whether this ideal combination will ever occur. In fact, a very common example is a badly worded message that completely confuses users. This is an example of an important problem that is cheap to fix. It may, of course, take a while to come up with a better wording (and this time should actually be included in the cost of fixing the problem), but once that wording is determined, replacing the confusing message with the revised message should take almost no time to implement.

Next, look for high-importance/high-cost problems. Some of these may be so severe that they must be fixed almost regardless of their cost, such as bugs that are causing the interface to blow up. Some severe problems may not be fixed because they are simply too costly. Next, look at moderate-importance/low-cost problems; often, you may find that there is simply not enough time to change very many of them. Continuing to work down the sorted list, you will find that in reality, low-importance/high-cost problems are rarely addressed; there simply won't be time or other resources.

This approach, and in fact much of the formative evaluation process described in this chapter, has similarities with Harlan Mills's *cleanroom approach* to software development (Dyer, 1992). The cleanroom method provides a technique for managing software development, as well as for quantitatively assessing software reliability and correctness. This method makes improvement of software integral to the process by which it is developed, in order to achieve specific quality objectives. The specific quality objectives are the usability goals, and formative evaluation and structured analysis is the method by which you can determine whether you have met those goals.

The graph shown in Figure 10.8 shows a simple way to compare costs and

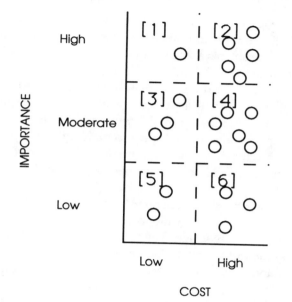

Figure 10.8. Graphical representation of problems for comparing cost and importance.

importances for all the problems in the list. By roughly graphing each problem within the appropriate cell along these axes, it is easy to see which problems should be addressed first. That is, the ones in the top left-hand cell are the high-importance/low-cost problems. Similarly, the low-importance/high-cost problems cluster in the bottom right-hand cell. The numbers in square brackets in the quadrants indicate the order in which to consider the various problems. Also, this kind of graph gives a quick view of where most of your problems cluster.

10.6   DRAWING CONCLUSIONS TO FORM A RESOLUTION FOR EACH PROBLEM

Finally, after impact analysis and/or cost/importance analysis of all problems in the list, developers must make a *resolution*—a final decision—about each problem. This is an indication of *how each problem will be addressed* (e.g., "do it;" "do it, time permitting;" "postpone it indefinitely") and which solutions will be implemented.

Having done both some impact and cost/importance analyses, at last, the Resolution column of Figures 10.6 and 10.7 can be completed. In fact, from the list ordered by importance (high to low) and, within that, cost (low to high), with high importance/low cost at the top of the list followed by high importance and moderate/high cost, you can determine the optimum choice of problems to address, given the time and other resources allotted for modifications.

Start with problems at the top of the list as candidates for priority. For example, look at some of the high-importance/high-cost problems perceived to be so critical that they must be fixed despite their high cost. Typically, it helps to prepare three separate lists: one for those problems that definitely are going to be addressed, one for those to be addressed if there is time, and one for those that are tabled for now (and perhaps for always). Also try to maintain some priority order within these lists, so that in the event that you run out of time before solving the problems you expected to fix, you have, at least, been attacking them in what you believe to be the best order.

After sorting the three Calendar Management System problems and associated solutions, there is one fairly low-cost (two hours) and high-importance problem— namely, the alarm redesign. The future and past navigation issue is also low cost but is only medium importance. The redesign for deleting an appointment is both high cost and high importance. As stated earlier, you would need to have a complete list of problems, with associated importance, solutions, and costs in order to make a final decision. However, we will assume that because the total cost for these three modifications is 9 hours, and 25 hours are available, all three of these suggested changes will, in fact, be made. Therefore, the resolution for each of these three is "Do it."

More realistically, for the graphical drawing application, some 24 different problems with high importance and low/moderate/high costs were consdered. Some of the high-importance/high-cost problems (e.g., the wandering windows) had to be included, to make parts of the interface robust or to modify a particularly troublesome aspect of the design. In addition, a few moderate-importance problems, and even a couple of low-importance ones (e.g., the black cursor on black background), were resolved. The basis for this decision was really more related to fixing a simple, but silly, oversight on the part of a designer, rather than modifying a problem that had a big impact on usability. In all, changes associated with 39 of the 54 problems listed were made, until the 60 hours of implementer time available for changes were allocated.

10.7   REDESIGNING AND IMPLEMENTING THE REVISED INTERFACE

Much of the work for this final phase of formative evaluation has already been done, when design solutions for each of the observed problems were proposed. At this point, developers need only to update the appropriate design documentation to reflect the decisions, and to resolve any conflicts or inconsistencies in the interaction design that might have resulted from the decisions. In addition, developers should make sure that the design is still a cohesive, comprehensive design that has not been affected, say, at a global level by any small detailed design decisions made to address specific low-level problems. It is then possible to proceed with confidence to implement the chosen design decisions. This is, of course, when developers realize the full benefits of formative evaluation, moving out of the current cycle of evaluation, and connecting back into the star life cycle, specifically into the subsequent cycle of (re)design, (re)implementation, and (re)evaluation.

10.8   SETTING UP A USABILITY LAB

This chapter has described in detail *why* and then *how* to evaluate an interaction design, but has not spent much time discussing *where* to evaluate it, other than alluding to the fact that you should consider both laboratory and field testing. We now describe the equipment and facilities layout of a *usability laboratory*.

In fact, you do not need a fancy usability laboratory with tens of thousands of dollars worth of equipment in order to perform a good usability study. A usability lab's fundamental requirement is that it be an enclosed space that is large enough to hold the participant, the evaluator(s), and the appropriate equipment. The room should have its own door, to shut out the rest of the world and to hold a sign announcing the room's purpose to the rest of the world. The most basic usability lab need be no more than, say, six feet by eight feet. Smaller than this and participants start to get claustrophobic. If you are really on a shoestring budget for setting up the lab, buy a stopwatch, a small portable tape recorder and some tapes, some pencils, and make your own copies of the various forms included throughout this and previous chapters (i.e., usability specifications table, problems table, and so on). This will be enough to get you started with some basic usability testing.

When the powers that be (i.e., the folks who hold the purse strings) become curious about what is going on behind that "Usability Laboratory" sign, and you have convinced them that the usability lab is indeed a useful facility, and it's time to buy some real equipment, add one simple video camera, a VCR and some tapes, and a small monitor. As the lab really starts to grow, you can upgrade to all sorts of fancy videotaping and playback equipment. This can have split-screen monitor and recording capability (e.g., you can use two cameras, with one aimed at a participant's face and hands, the other at the screen) so that you can capture and view more than one activity at a time. You can add microphones and headphones, too.

In fact, in a large enough space, you can put in a partition with a one-way mirror (although a wall will do just fine, too, if you can set up a viewing monitor in the part of the lab where the participant is not located). This divided space can house two rooms: an evaluation room and a control room, which are typically adjacent to each other. The *evaluation room* contains the participant and the primary evaluator, and therefore the equipment on which the interface runs. One or more cameras and microphones can be situated in this room to collect videotaped data during evaluation sessions.

The *control room* can contain one or more monitors and VCRs for the camera(s) in the evaluation room and may contain another evaluator, if there is someone else to help with, for example, critical incident taking and timing during sessions. Any others who would like to observe a test session, for whatever reason, can also sit in this room without disturbing the experimental sessions. Verbal data collected by the microphone in the evaluation room can be heard in this room, while simultaneously being recorded by the VCR(s). A second evaluator in this room can make suggestions to the primary evaluator, via a headphone intercom, in the evaluation room about, for example, refocusing or re-aiming a camera, or suggesting a question to ask the participant.

Recording equipment can get quite fancy, including a video/audio mixer; some equipment can generate, display, and time-stamp a numeric counter onto one or more of the videotapes as they are recorded. Lots of usability labs have literally hundreds of thousands of dollars worth of equipment. They may include such fancy gear as three or four ceiling-mounted, remotely pannable cameras with high-power zoom lenses; scan converters to convert the participant's screen to video; a mixer unit to convert up to four video streams into one, with numerous kinds of transitions such as fading, wiping, and screen splitting; recording capability from multiple cameras in which one image is the primary one and others appear as inset images from the other cameras; video special-effects generator to use in postproduction (e.g., to blur out the participant's face when you want to use a clip from the evaluation session to prove a point to unbelieving programmers); an eye-gaze system to track minute movements of participants' eyes; character generators for putting textual titles and comments on tapes; and lots of other equipment reminiscent of a full-blown video-production studio.

You don't need all this equipment to get started, and in fact, unless you are going into full-time usability evaluation, you will never need it. Instead, in addition to a stopwatch, pencil and paper, and audio recorder, first add a decent video camera, VCR, and color monitor; a setup that can given you a fairly accurate frame count also is very useful. This is all you need when you have only one room in which to work.

Later on, start thinking about things such as split-screen, multitape-synchronizing capability. If you get too much equipment in too fast, you will spend most of your time fiddling with it and not enough time concentrating on the participants. Get the basic procedures and protocol for conducting a usability evaluation session comfortably under your belt before you branch out into fancy electronics.

The layout for a usability lab can vary quite dramatically from site to site, but the fundamentals are usually the same. Figure 10.9 shows a typical layout for a small usability lab.

There is an interesting aside on setting up your own usability lab: When other teams hear about it and what goes on there, you may be able to rent it out to them for their own use. This can even eventually pay for your initial investment in the usability lab and its equipment.

Having said all this, it is possible, of course, to conduct usability evaluation sessions without a usability lab at all. You can always just put participants in a corner somewhere with the appropriate equipment and have at it. However, allocating some space—somewhere, anywhere—and putting a plaque on the door that says "Your Group's Name Usability Laboratory" has a tremendous psychological benefit. It makes the people serving as evaluators feel as if their work is important, when it has its own space. It means that management thinks usability evaluation is important enough to allocate a dedicated space to it. It impresses on the participants the importance of their contribution in the evaluation session. Also, *very* importantly—a company can say in its marketing materials that "This

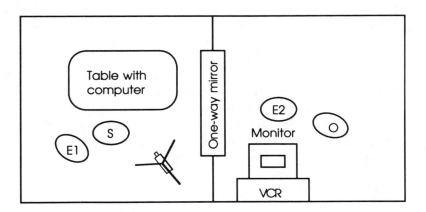

S: Subject
E1: Primary Evaluator
E2: Secondary Evaluator
O: Observer

Figure 10.9. Typical layout for a small usability lab.

product has been developed and evaluated in our usability lab." This simple statement will give more credence to a company's claims about the usability of a product than all the shallow, effusive hype typically seen about the "user-friend-liness" of a product. Impress your market and customers by stating proven facts, not untested fiction.

10.9   CONCLUSIONS

A summary of the main ways in which the various kinds of data—quantitative and qualitative data—are primarily used in formative evaluation is shown in Figure 10.10. Use quantitative data, such as data from benchmark tasks to compare to established usability specifications, and thereby determine that *something is wrong*—usability is not at an acceptable level. Specifically, this is true when any worst acceptable level usability specification is not met during evaluation with participants. Also, for each such occurrence, the reason for the poor performance must be pinpointed. For this, use qualitative data, such as data from observed critical incidents and/or verbal protocol of participants, to determine specifically *what is wrong*—what is causing the usability problems. Finally, use designers to determine *how to solve* the problems.

Clearly, there is considerable overlap among these categories. For example, participants themselves often suggest solutions for usability problems. Also, quantitative data from satisfaction questionnaires may reveal not only that something is wrong, but give an indication of what is wrong.

What this chapter has described, of course, is the very heart of the user interaction development process. This involves the management of very difficult decision-making as to which problems are most important in terms of interface usability. The point is that you are, in fact, *engineering* the interface, striving for the achievement of your usability specifications, rather than perfection. This approach recognizes diminishing economic returns in attempting to achieve perfection by trying to solve all known usability problems in a user interaction design. There-

USE THESE:	TO DECIDE THESE:
Quantitative data	Something is wrong
Qualitative data	What is wrong
Designers	How to fix what is wrong

Figure 10.10. Comparison of use of quantitative data and qualitative data.

fore, usability management includes quantitative techniques for making decisions about which changes to make to a design as a result of a cycle of formative evaluation.

A development process that does not have a well-defined ending point is unacceptable to most managers. A control mechanism is required, one that will help managers and developers alike know what design changes are most cost effective in meeting usability specifications—whether the iterative process is converging toward a usable interface, and when to stop iterating. Without such a control mechanism, interaction developers and evaluators can be caught in an infinite loop, thrashing about without any guidance and actually producing a *worse* interface (in terms of its usability) through this cyclic procedure.

We have now completed one full cycle through the star life cycle, showing all the major activities in the process of user interaction development—user, needs, functional, and task analyses; interaction design and representation; usability specification; rapid prototyping; and finally formative evaluation and the subsequent redesign. Development of an interactive system, of course, typically requires several iterations like this one. By this time, if you have followed the examples and done the exercises at the end of the appropriate chapters (including the one coming up), you should have a good grasp of how to perform these activities yourself. These are the most crucial activities in the process of developing a usable interface.

10.10 EXERCISE ON FORMATIVE EVALUATION

You are now ready to perform your very last exercise as a team. This is perhaps the most fun and most rewarding of all the exercises, when you finally get to see some users in action with your interaction design for the Calendar Management System. The following description of activities assumes that you have been working in a team of three. If you have more or fewer members in your team, it's easy to make adjustments. If there are only two of you, for example, one person can be the executor and the other person can record critical incidents and time the benchmark tasks. If there are four or five of you, just have the extra people help in recording critical incidents. If you have been working alone on all the previous exercises, you may want find at least one or two other people to help you run the experiment. In any case, you need to recruit two people to serve as participants, to evaluate your prototype.

The following description also assumes that you established a set of usability specifications in the exercise from Chapter 8 and created a plastic prototype in the exercise from Chapter 9; if you developed an interactive prototype, everything will be the same except that you won't need an interface executor. You will, instead, need someone to make sure the prototype hardware and software are set up, installed, and running properly for evaluation.

Exercise—Formative Evaluation

GOAL: To perform simple empirical evaluation of your user interaction design, along with data collection and analysis, as part of the user interaction development process.

MINIMUM TIME: Shown for each individual activity in the formative evaluation process.

NOTE: *Keep it simple* so that you can finish in a reasonable time!

ACTIVITIES:

Run the experiment (approximately 45 minutes)
Decide roles for your team members. You will need

- An evaluation *leader*, to keep the experiment moving and to record critical incidents
- A user performance *timer*, to time participants performing tasks
- A prototype *executor* (no pun intended!), to "play computer" and move transparencies, providing feedback to the participants

In addition to these roles for your three team members, you will also need (at least) two *participants*. These participants should not be anyone who knows much, if anything, about your Calendar Management System; if they've been involved with the design at all, they will already know at least something about how the interface is supposed to work, and you won't get much good information from them. Ask your coworkers, spouses, children, friends—anyone who ever uses a paper calendar would make a reasonable participant for evaluation.

Now, bring one of your participants into your usability lab. Give the participant brief, but uniform, written instructions, and then have them sign an informed consent form. This participant will use your prototype to perform the benchmark tasks for your objective usability specifications, the ones you produced in the exercise in Chapter 8.

For the plastic prototype, the person who is playing computer has to keep alert during this time, and make sure the prototype "executes" reasonably correctly and quickly in response to a participant's actions. This should not be a problem if you pilot tested your prototype, as was suggested in the previous exercise (Chapter 9) when you were building the prototype. As the executor moves transparencies in response to participant actions or as the interactive prototype executes, the performance timer should record times for the participant to perform each task and should count errors (assuming that these are metrics you included in your usability specifications). Use a copy of the form in Figure 10.6 to help with data collection. The evaluation leader should record critical incidents, using this same form.

Also have the participant perform one or more nontimed tasks and/or some free use of the system, being sure to have the participant talk aloud while working. When the participant has completed the tasks, have the participant answer the questionnaire.

Now have your second participant perform the tasks and complete the questionnaire. The first participant can stay and watch, if desired.

Important: The executor *must not* help the participants as they perform any of the tasks; the executor should just "do" (with the plastic prototype) what they say. Nor should the evaluator (or anyone else) coach the participants. If the participants cannot figure something out without help, you have probably found a usability problem—exactly what this process is intended to uncover! *Resist the urge to bail them out when they get stuck.* Just let them keep trying things, and don't tell them what to do. This is very difficult to do; you will be sitting there bursting to tell them how to get out of the jam they may have made their way into. Remember that there are appropriate questions that you can ask to give small hints to a participant, but don't just tell them how to do things.

Analyze data (approximately 30 minutes)
As a team, including your participants if they will stick around, compile your evaluation results to determine whether the participants met your usability specifications. Specifically, write a summary (e.g., average) of the observed results into the Observed Results column of your usability specification table. This will allow you easily to compare your observed values with your usability goals. At this point, your initial analysis will tell you whether you have met your usability goals and can therefore stop iterating.

Because this is your first cycle of evaluation, you probably have not met all of your usability specifications. If you did, it is almost certainly the case, as discussed earlier, that you did not set your usability specifications strictly enough to take best advantage of the iterative process. In any case, you should continue with this exercise so you will complete the entire development process.

Also compile your observed critical incidents to identify specific problems. Use a copy of the form in Figure 10.6 to help you organize the observed problems. Using this same form, assign an importance rating to some of the observed problems, based on an impact analysis, the severity of the problem, and the urgency to fix it. Use your intuition here.

Next, propose solutions for some of the problems on the problem list, without doing all the work of redesign. Write your solutions on the form. Assign cost values, again, intuitively, for each solution.

Resolution (approximately 30 minutes)
Using your cost/importance ratings, make some management decisions about which changes your development team will make in the next version of your Calendar Management System.

DELIVERABLES:
- A summary of quantitative results (task performance results), written into the Observed Results column of your usability specification table for comparison to the various levels
- A report of critical incidents, including both the main good and bad points
- A cost/importance table completed in a form like the one of Figure 10.6
- A brief management summary, including whether your usability specifications were met, and your decisions about redesign and what changes you will make to the user interaction design as a result of this evaluation cycle

Possible Exercise Solution

As in Chapter 9, it is not feasible to give you a possible solution here. Each evaluation session is unique, and yours will depend heavily on your Calendar Management System design and prototype, and on the benchmark tasks you establish for your participants. The point of this exercise is to increase your appreciation of both the intricacies and the fun of conducting formative evaluation sessions.

At the end of this exercise, you should treat yourself, and anyone else with whom you have worked through the other exercises, to a special lunch or dinner or happy hour, in celebration of successfully completing the series of exercises for the Calendar Management System. We hope you feel much better armed now to take on the development of your own user interface projects.

REFERENCES

Ashlund, S. & Hix, D. (1992). IDEAL: A Tool to Enable User-Centered Design. *Proceedings of CHI Conference on Human Factors in Computing Systems (Posters and Short Talk Supplement to Proceedings)*, New York: ACM, 119–120.

Carroll, J. M. & Rosson, M. B. (1985). Usability Specifications as a Tool in Iterative Development. In H. R. Hartson (Ed.), *Advances in Human–Computer Interaction,* Vol. 1 (pp. 1–28). Norwood, NJ: Ablex.

Carroll, J. M., Singley, M. K., & Rosson, M. B. (1992). Integrating Theory Development with Design Evaluation. *Journal of Behaviour and Information Technology.*

del Galdo, E. M., Williges, R. C., Williges, B. H., & Wixon, D. R. (1986). An Evaluation of Critical Incidents for Software Documentation Design. *Proceedings of Human Factors Society Conference*, Anaheim, CA: Human Factors Society, 19–23.

Dick, W. & Carey, L. (1978). *The Systematic Design of Instruction.* Glenview, IL: Scott, Foresman.

Dyer, M. (1992). *The Cleanroom Approach to Quality Software Development.* New York: Wiley.

Good, M., Spine, T., Whiteside, J., & George, P. (1986). User Derived Impact Analysis as a Tool for Usability Engineering. *Proceedings of CHI Conference on Human Factors in Computing Systems*, New York: ACM, 241–246.

Mackay, W. E. & Davenport, G. (1989). Virtual Video Editing in Interactive Multimedia Applications. *Communications of the ACM*, 32(7), 802–810.

Nielsen, J. (1992). Finding Usability Problems Through Heuristic Evaluation. *Proceedings of CHI Conference on Human Factors in Computing Systems*, New York: ACM, 373–380.

Nielsen, J. & Molich, R. (1990). Heuristic Evaluation of User Interfaces. *Proceedings of CHI Conference on Human Factors in Computing Systems*, New York: ACM, 249–256.

Scriven, M. (1967). The Methodology of Evaluation. In R. Tyler, R. Gagne, & M. Scriven (Ed.), *Perspectives of Curriculum Evaluation* (pp. 39–83). Chicago: Rand McNally.

Siochi, A. C. & Ehrich, R. W. (1991). Computer Analysis of User Interfaces Based on

Repetition in Transcripts of User Sessions. *Transactions on Information Systems*, 9(4), 309–335.

Siochi, A. C. & Hix, D. (1991). A Study of Computer-Supported User Interface Evaluation Using Maximal Repeating Pattern Analysis. *Proceedings of CHI Conference on Human Factors in Computing Systems*, New York: ACM, 301–305.

Whiteside, J., Bennett, J., & Holtzblatt, K. (1988). Usability Engineering: Our Experience and Evolution. In M. Helander (Ed.), *Handbook of Human–computer Interaction* (pp. 791–817). Amsterdam: Elsevier North-Holland.

Williges, R. C. (1984). Evaluating Human–Computer Software Interfaces. *Proceedings of International Conference on Occupational Ergonomics*.

≡ 11

User Interface Development Tools

11.1   CLASSES OF USER INTERFACE DEVELOPMENT TOOLS

Software tools for developing the user interface are among the most important aspects of the interface development process. Most tools currently available support implementation of the user interface—that is, they operate in the constructional domain. Tools are also among the most elusive and ephemeral aspects of the process; virtually weekly, some new software package claims that it will produce user friendly interfaces, or will produce the best user interface software—whatever that means. The spectrum of interface development tools ranges from libraries of device handling routines to toolkits to prototypers to user interface management systems.

Lest you be excitedly thinking, "Oh, boy; they're going to tell me all about all the different tools out there!"—this chapter does *not* present specific tools in detail. If it did, whatever details were included would probably be inaccurate, if not completely obsolete, by the time this book arrived in your hands. There are literally hundreds of tools available, both commercially and from research groups, and the number is ever-increasing. Therefore, this chapter describes only various *types of tools for developing the user interface* and discusses their characteristics in breadth rather than depth. In fact, this chapter actually mentions only a very few tools by name, and those are named only to illustrate a specific point and to help discuss the features and characteristics of the category to which that tool belongs. More complete discussion and surveys are available elsewhere (e.g., Myers, 1993).

There are numerous classifications of interface development tools; our presentation is simple and broad, again because of the volatile nature of this area. An overview of several classes of interface development tools includes the following:

- Interaction style support tools
- Toolkits
- User interface management systems

There is at least one other category of tool—interface design tools or IDTs—that you may hear mentioned. These tend basically to be graphics or drawing packages, and, as such, provide a developer with little more than the capability to produce static screen layouts. Because these are typically such simple tools, they have been omitted from this discussion. Finally, because choosing a particular tool for an interface development group is so important, but so confusing, the chapter concludes with an overview of an approach to evaluating and comparing user interface development tools.

11.2   ABOUT USER INTERFACE DEVELOPMENT TOOLS

User interface development tool is, not surprisingly, a much misunderstood and misused term. In this book, as in most current literature, *user interface development tool* is a very broad generic term to refer to *a software package that provides automated support for any part of the interface development process*, particularly the techniques discussed in this book. A tool can, therefore, be anything from a complete interface development environment to a single library routine. Most tools that are available today primarily support implementation activities in the constructional domain, but some are beginning to branch out and support more of the behavioral domain activities such as task analysis, detailed interaction design, and formative evaluation.

11.2.1   Advantages of Tools

Numerous advantages can come from using interface development tools (Myers, 1993), not the least of which is *improved interfaces*. Because many tools support rapid prototyping, *interfaces can be modified easily* in response to formative evaluation results. Tools support *reuse of interface components*, either interaction objects or code modules, allowing amortization of development efforts over numerous interfaces. That is, once a particular interaction style is developed using a particular tool, that style can be used again, either at other points in the same interface or in other interfaces. This reuse can promote *consistency* within a single interface as well as across multiple interfaces.

Slight *modifications to a particular style* are typically easy to make using a tool. Because user interface development tools represent a major move away from programming the user interaction component, it is now easier to involve interaction development specialists who are not themselves programmers, including graphic artists, human factors engineers, communication experts, and so on. As discussed at the beginning of the book, there are many nonprogrammer skills needed in producing interaction designs and we look forward to the day when tools fully support these skills, too.

From a constructional or implementation view, using specialized tools for interface development can result in interface *code that is more economical to create* (usually automatically generated by a tool) *and to maintain*. It can be more *structured* and *modular*, and therefore more *reusable*. If the tool has been well-tested, it should produce code that is highly *reliable*.

11.2.2 Shortcomings of Tools

Using interface development tools often implies that the interface and computational (application or noninterface) components of an application must be *logically and physically separated*, which obviously can be very difficult to do. Most tools that do more than allow a developer to display static screen pictures are often quite *difficult to learn and use*. It is ironic that the people building user interface development tools have, in many instances, completely overlooked the fact that their tool needs an interface with high usability, too! Further, the interaction *representation techniques that tools support are often difficult* to understand and use. This, in turn, can also contribute to making tools *difficult to use*.

Many tools have *limited functionality*; they may address only one part of the complete interface development process—for example, usually implementation. Tools are only now beginning to address, in any useful way, such difficult aspects of interface development as direct manipulation of application objects, application output, and semantic feedback. Interestingly, in these tools as in any interactive system, usability and functionality are often inversely related; the tool that is easiest to use may do very little, while the tool that has a great deal of functionality is often quite hard to use. *Portability*, also an important consideration in tools, is finally improving, thanks to common underlying software such as the *X Window System*™ (see Section 11.4) and *Windows*™ 3.0 (see Section 11.4).

There is also another danger with using interface development tools. People often say such things as, "If only I had the right tool, all my problems in developing the interface would be solved." This is, of course, dead wrong. *The problems with developing a usable interface are not necessarily solved by adding technology.* Also, there are definite limits to what these tools can do. In our classifications we discuss some of these limitations for each type of tool.

11.3 INTERACTION STYLE SUPPORT TOOLS

An *interaction style support tool* is an interactive system that enforces a particular, consistent interaction look and feel based on a specific style and standard. Two of the most popular commercial ones are OSF/Motif™ and OpenLook™. There are also several tools that support the Apple User Interface Guidelines in the interfaces they produce. Just as with commercial style guides (see Section 2.2), such tools generally help a developer know what an interaction object should look like, and perhaps even how it should behave, but not when to use it or how to use it most effectively for the user.

Interaction style support tools are based on specific interaction styles and can even enforce those interaction styles if the tool does not allow the interaction developer much flexibility in altering interaction components. However, as mentioned in the discussion about standards and style guides (see Chapter 2), having a style guide may be used as an excuse to avoid user testing of products. Even if every rule in a style guide is followed to the letter, the usability of an interface is still undetermined and must still be empirically evaluated and analyzed. Thus, *while tools that support and even enforce particular interaction styles provide a good mechanism for building consistency into an interaction design, they still do not guarantee a product with high usability.*

The goal, then, for using such tools often becomes interaction style *consistency*, at all levels, as much as possible. Nonetheless, the exceptions are inevitable and even acceptable, and they must be judiciously decided and carefully controlled. Bear in mind, of course, that styles can change, often and dramatically. Because of this, tools that support a specific interaction style—either an emerging commercial one or your own internal one—can be difficult to keep current.

A detailed comparison of most of these interaction styles and of the tools that support them shows that they are far more similar than they are different. Most of the tools are window-based, in fact X-based, and provide analogous components and controls. The tools provide a classic point-and-click, object–action paradigm for use by an interaction developer, and they support this in their products—the user interfaces they produce—as well. Most tools use pull-down and pop-up menus, cut/copy/paste with a clipboard, and bounding box selection of graphics. They run on either color or monochrome monitors and produce both two-dimensional and three-dimensional versions of the styles they support. They support production of numerous application components, including various kinds of buttons, boxes, valuators, menus, and usually multiple windows.

The *main difference among the style support tools* is generally in the *appearance* of the interaction components they produce. That is, the exact look of a pull-down menu or a push button may differ from one style support tool to the next. Generally to a lesser extent, the *behavior* of the supported components can also differ.

11.4   TOOLKITS

A user interface *toolkit* is a library of callable routines (code modules), used by programmers, for implementing low-level interface features. These routines are callable from within a UIMS (see Section 11.5) or from any other program. Global control for the application being developed using a toolkit is often in the computational (application or noninterface) component.

Toolkits provide code for various kinds of interaction techniques, which are ways of using different physical devices, typically for the user to enter a specific type of input. The ubiquitous *widget* has gained fame as the basic data type or object for encapsulating the look and feel of interaction techniques used in interactive applications. A widget holds information about graphical objects, and applications and their interfaces are built from instances of widget classes. Examples of widgets include text, graphics, boxes, buttons, menus, scroll bars, sliders, and so on (each interaction style in Chapter 3 could be instantiated as a widget).

Almost every toolkit also includes some kind of placement widget (e.g., bulletin board widgets, row–column widgets, canvases, frames) to control positioning of visual widgets on the screen. Users don't necessarily see these widgets, because they are the containers for the buttons, scroll bars, text entry boxes, and so on, and could actually be covered up by these visual widgets. However, users do see the effect of these widgets in moving, resizing, and redrawing.

Toolkits interact with computational code through *callbacks*, which are invocations of procedures defined by a programmer and executed by the application in response to some action taken by a user at runtime. That is, when a user interacts with a widget, the interface code calls back to the computational code in order to respond to the user's action. For example, the user might select an item from a pull-down menu, and the interface code (the widget instantiating that pull-down menu) would call back to the computational code in order to invoke the function selected from the menu by the user. Interfaces often consist of hundreds of widgets and callbacks, making the code harder to maintain (Myers, 1993).

The function of toolkits is very limited, when compared to other interface development tools, but they are very flexible in the programming sense. Still, they provide no support for any activity in the user interface development process except implementation.

Toolkits are often built on top of windowing systems, and several popular commercial windowing systems, including the *X Window System*™, provide an interface development toolkit. In fact, windowing systems have become such a fundamental part of user interface development tools that this discussion digresses a moment to talk about them.

Most windowing systems (the *X Window System*™ is an exception) include window managers. The early ideas on which *window managers* were based came largely from Xerox PARC (Palo Alto Research Center) and the Star interface (Smith, Irby, Kimball, Verplank, & Harslem, 1982). Later on, of course, they were popularized in the Lisa™ and subsequently in the Macintosh™. Through a windowing system, a user can interact with several tasks and/or applications, each in a different window. Typically, only one window is active—that is, attached to the keyboard and/or mouse (or other I/O devices)—at a time. Essentially, each window acts like a separate logical terminal with its own input and output. A user can manipulate windows in a variety of ways, including opening, closing, moving, and resizing them. Often, communication among different windows is via the clipboard concept. *Windows* 3.0™ is one of the most popular windowing systems, having revolutionized the PC/DOS world. There are a few toolkits for developing the user interface under *Windows* 3.0™.

One of the most popular windowing systems, this time in the UNIX world, is the *X Window System*™, which provides a toolkit, called *Xt*™, and a library, called *Xlib*™, for interface development. The Xlib™ functions are low-level callable procedures, similar to any graphics library. There are hundreds of these procedures that a programmer (yes, programmer, not interaction designer), coding an interactive system and its interface to run under X, must use to perform all windowing and drawing. Xt™ consists of routines built with Xlib™ functions. Xt™ defines only a very basic set of widgets (most of which are functional, not visual), providing a foundation on which to build the real widgets used to construct user interfaces. These claim to support rapid code development through a strong object orientation, and support quick prototyping by connecting readymade interface components. However, these routines must be called through *in-line code*, which means that the entire interface is produced by writing source code. There is, through X, no direct manipulation support for accessing and incorporating Xlib™ and Xt™ routines; all programming is done by writing code.

11.5   USER INTERFACE MANAGEMENT SYSTEMS

The term *user interface management system* or *UIMS* may be one of the most over-worked terms in the entire field of human–computer interaction. Software packages that even tangentially support some tiny aspect of user interface development (usually toolkits that support its construction) now often claim to be UIMSs, in hopes of cashing in on the current UIMS popularity. Many of these are simply too limited in their functionality to be called a UIMS; that is, they only support a few interaction styles such as menus or forms. They also lack good interaction design tools and are too "programmy."

Historically, the generally accepted use of the term UIMS referred primarily to runtime support for the user interface software. The term has now broadened to refer to an integrated set of interactive programs for the overall process of developing interfaces, including design, representation, prototyping, execution, evaluation, and maintenance of the interface. That is, they provide design-time support and a development environment for producing an interface, as well as runtime and/or prototyping support for executing an interface. A UIMS may contain or be built on a toolkit and may support a particular interaction style. A UIMS supports development and execution of user input, system output, and the linkage of these.

There are several basic elements needed in a UIMS to develop displays. A direct manipulation (nonprogramming) environment should support layout of displays, including the defining, positioning, resizing, moving, copying, and setting of display and object attributes and defaults. A UIMS should provide support for linking displays and their objects to the computational (application or noninterface) component of an interactive system via some mechanism other than programming (e.g., direct manipulation).

A UIMS also should provide runtime support mechanisms for sensing user actions on objects in a display and then provide feedback in the display. It needs runtime support mechanisms for communicating to the computational component when a user action causes changes in computational objects represented by interaction objects, as well as for communicating to the display when a computational component causes changes in interaction objects. It also needs a generator for producing interface code from interface definitions, as well as a database for storing those definitions and the generated code. There are many other characteristics that have been attributed to UIMSs, but these seem to be, from the literature and practical experience, the most important ones.

Many commercially available UIMSs (the real ones, not the pretenders) are based on the X Window System™ but protect an interface developer from the mysteries of X through a direct manipulation interface to the UIMS itself. They may be quite customizable, allowing an interface developer to create, modify, and/or add new widgets (or other toolkit library data structures).

11.6 STATUS OF USER INTERFACE DEVELOPMENT TOOLS

The state of the art in user interface development tools is not where interface developers would like it to be. Many tools are still hard to use, even for programmers. They may be limited in their functionality, which can force compromises in interaction designs when a tool does not support some neat new idea that a developer might have. Most tools are better at supporting the development of rather simple sequential dialogue than direct manipulation, asynchronous, graphical interfaces. Most tools do not easily support retrofitting interfaces to existing application code. Also, although user interface development tools may be a faster means to more consistent interfaces, there still is the very real risk that they are simply a faster means for producing poor, unevaluated interfaces.

Nonetheless, the available and emerging tools indicate progress. When work first began in the tool area, those in the field had to justify these tools' fundamental purpose: *to relieve as much of the programming burden as possible and to support all activities in the interface development life cycle.* People thought user interaction design by programming was just fine, and interfaces didn't need much evaluation, anyway—just let the user learn to live with it.

This has, gratifyingly, changed. The tools emerging now reflect more emphasis on the development of direct manipulation, multimedia, asynchronous, graphical interfaces. Incidentally, this applies both to the tools themselves and to the interactive systems they are being used to produce. Tools are now supporting extensions to direct manipulation interfaces, such as gestural interfaces and highly visual interfaces that emphasize a complex, dynamic, interactive output display. CSCW (computer-supported cooperative work) is another area that user interface development tools are beginning to address, and tools now support more reflection of semantics in the interface. Ideas such as these increase anticipation of still further advancements in user interface development tools.

11.7 EVALUATION OF USER INTERFACE DEVELOPMENT TOOLS

Imagine this scenario: You are a member of an interface development team for Project XYZ in your organization. Your boss comes to you and says, "I've decided we need to get some kind of user interface development tool to help us produce the interface for Project XYZ. Go out there and find out which one will be best for us to use." Gasp! There are literally hundreds of tools, and the number is growing constantly. Where do you begin?

Well, begin by telling the boss that to do a systematic, valid comparison of several interface tools is going to take some time. You won't be able to pull this off in a few days if you have little or no knowledge and hands-on use of them. You might also tell the boss that a structured, quantitative approach is very important in order to make the right choice. Warm fuzzy feelings and word-of-mouth won't get this job done well.

Selection of a tool for use in an interface development group can have a tremendous impact on the development team's productivity and morale, as well as the ultimate success of the product. The decision is important also because of the cost of these tools; it can range from free (usually from research groups in universities or research institutions; sometimes bundled with a commercial platform) to nominal (a few hundred dollars, which is the norm) to extremely expensive (tens of thousands of dollars for a site license). Interestingly, cost does not currently seem to be correlated with functionality or usability of available tools; that is, the more expensive tools are not necessarily the best ones. Tools for high-powered workstations and multiuser mainframes are usually much more expensive than those for personal computers.

Why is it so hard to evaluate and compare user interface development tools? There are several reasons. They are inherently complex software applications, and so their evaluation is bound to be complex. They are also relatively new, the earliest ones having been around for little more than a decade. Finally, many different kinds of software applications call themselves user interface development tools.

11.7.1 Discriminators for Tools

A number of high-level qualitative discriminators can be suggested as the minimal basis for selecting a tool for your interface development group. Following a description of these, we present a more detailed, quantitative approach to tool evaluation. Even if you do not have time for a thorough comparison of several tools, at least go through the basic discriminators. In fact, you can use these discriminators to make the first cut at a set of tools that might be appropriate for your group, to help you narrow down the dozens that are available to perhaps the half-dozen or fewer for which you want to make a detailed, quantitative comparison, perhaps using the approach presented in the next section.

One key to making a reasonable comparison is that *you must try out each tool that you are seriously considering*. Reading marketing glossies, watching a videotape, or even observing a salesperson (or anyone else, for that matter) put a tool through its paces will do little to give you a real feel for the capabilities and limitations, including usability, of a tool. No matter what it takes, you must get hands-on experience with these tools yourself. If you show some reasonably genuine interest in their products, most tool vendors will make a demo/evaluation copy available to you for 30 days or so. Get one for every tool you are seriously considering. If a vendor is hesitant or unwilling to let you have an evaluation copy, be very wary of the product. The vendor should also be willing to give you references to other organizations who are using the product. Again, if the vendor is not willing to do this, be wary.

There are a couple of ideas you might consider when you are ready to begin selecting a tool for your user interface development environment. You might try to arrange a *small in-house trade show* where vendors of the tools in which you are most interested can come and demonstrate their products, as well as give you some hands-on time with them. An even better idea is to set up a "petting zoo" of tools, purchasing full-version copies of those you can afford and acquiring evaluation versions of those you cannot afford or are less interested in. This way, people who will be using these tools can visit the "zoo" and try out the tools at their leisure, and you can solicit their opinions about the various tools. A word of caution: It's often difficult to get people to come in and just play around with tools; everyone already has more than enough to fill the hours in their day. Rather than asking them simply to play around with several tools, it will probably work better to take some specific representative portion of an interaction design that is currently being developed by the people looking for a tool, and encourage key people to try to produce that design using certain tools. A specific target, such as a portion of an actual design, will typically get better response than just asking for random efforts.

Once you have some tools in-house, there are myriad issues that must be addressed in order to select the tool that is right for your group. The following important characteristics must be considered when selecting a tool for an interface development group. They are very basic, and surely you will add your own discriminators to this list as you begin evaluating user interface tools yourself.

▶ Functionality of the tool

As we discuss in detail in the following section, the capabilities of a tool are one of its most important characteristics. You must make sure that the tool you acquire can produce the interaction styles you expect to have in the interfaces you will be developing. While this sounds painfully obvious, there have been many cases where an interface development group was swept off its feet by a flashy show-and-tell marketing presentation for a tool, purchased it, and then discovered that it would not produce all the various interaction styles the group needed the tool to produce. Think carefully about what you expect to be in your interaction designs—the kinds of menus, boxes, objects, icons, devices, and so on—and make sure the tool can produce these.

▶ Usability of the tool

As already mentioned, tool builders have been notoriously bad at practicing what they preach. That is, they have, in many cases, produced interface development tools that themselves had terrible user interfaces. This is much less an issue now than it used to be, but some user interface development tools still have poor usability. As with all interactive systems, functionality of a tool can be inversely proportional to usability, with the more functional systems being the hardest to use and the easier-to-use systems not having much functionality. However, many tools have found a successful compromise position and offer both reasonable functionality and ease of use. This is the sort of thing you should ask of the people who try out the various tools and of references given to you by the vendor of the tool.

▶ Easy-to-use graphical interface for the tool itself

This is closely related to usability. If it is important for the kinds of developers on your interface development team, the tool itself should have a graphical user interface. If people other than programmers will be constructing interfaces with this tool, this is particularly true. A graphical user interface to the tool needs to be weighed against the amount of programming that must be done in order to construct an interface. Most of today's better tools have the capability to produce a fairly broad variety of interaction styles without a programmer writing code.

▶ Ability to produce direct manipulation interfaces via direct manipulation

With the increase of direct manipulation in current interfaces, it is desirable that a tool be able to produce direct manipulation interface features via direct manipulation in its own interface. A tool that forces the interface implementer to resort to programming for difficult kinds of interfaces, such as direct manipulation, may not be the right tool for your development environment.

▶ Styles supported by the tool

This is closely related to functionality of the tool. Many tools come with a built-in set of widgets, often the Motif™ widget set or the MIT Athena widget set. If your organization is developing, for example, Motif™-compliant interfaces, then obviously the selected tool needs to support the Motif™ style. Otherwise, you will spend a great deal of time trying to customize (if possible) the tool product to match the Motif™ styles.

▶ Customization, including addition and modification, of widgets and widget sets

The built-in widgets that come with the tool you are considering will almost never provide all the kinds of interaction styles you expect to include in the interfaces to be developed with the tool. Thus, it is necessary that the widgets and the widget set be customizable. The ability to customize individual widgets is quite common in tools; the capability of adding completely new widgets to the widget set is more difficult and therefore more rare.

▶ Creation of dynamic interaction objects

Many user interface development tools do not support development of dynamic (runtime changeable, data dependent) interaction objects. Unless you are producing an extremely simplistic user interface, you will surely have some of these in your interface. The tool should be able to produce them, but here you may have to resort to programming in order to do so. Most tools still do not support creation of dynamic interaction objects via a graphical or direct manipulation interface.

▶ Support for formative evaluation and iterative refinement

Most tools do not provide direct support for formative evaluation and iterative refinement, other than claiming that modifications to an interface are easy to make using the tool. While this is, of course, very important, a tool that provides support for all user interface development activities, and particularly evaluation, is highly desirable. Some tools allow internal instrumentation of an interface being evaluated, and a few are beginning to support collection and analysis of both quantitative and qualitative data during formative evaluation sessions. This is a key area in which tools need to provide much more support.

▶ Type of control structure and callbacks

The type of control structure imposed by a tool on software may be important if you are trying to connect the output of the tool to existing software or to software being developed by other groups. There are at least three possible types of control structure that can affect the design and architecture of user interface software: *internal* (in the computational component), *external* (in the dialogue component), and *global*. The ability to define and manage callbacks is also important for coupling with other software. Some tools allow you to embed their output into existing software, and some tools allow you to embed existing software into the output of the tool. Few tools support both. Some tools maintain control of an event loop and decide how to respond to user actions. Depending on the overall architecture of your interactive system, these constructional domain issues can be important when choosing a tool.

▶ Portability of the interface produced by the tool

Often it is desirable that the interface produced by a tool be able to run on several different platforms. Some tools produce interfaces that will run on multiple platforms, but many do not yet do this. Some tools produce output that is portable across several platforms without delivering a different look and feel for each platform. Instead, they achieve portability by keeping the same look and feel on each platform. Being built on a standard windowing system (e.g., X, *Windows*™) helps make tools more portable.

▶ Changes to the user interaction design independent of code generation

In many tools, once it has generated code for the user interface, the interface can no longer be changed without generating completely new code. Some tools, however, do allow an interface developer to make changes to the interface, and then the tool automatically generates new code just for the changed portions.

▶ Runtime performance of the interface produced by the tool

Some tools produce output that is compiled, while others produce output that is interpreted. The choice of compiled versus interpreted output can greatly affect the performance of an interface at runtime. A compiled interface almost always has faster performance than interpreted code, which is notoriously slow. A tool should produce output that has a satisfactory runtime speed. Otherwise, the usability of the interface can be severely affected. Maybe the best choice is a tool that produces code that can be translated both ways—interpreted for fast turn-around during development and compiled for fast performance in versions that are deployed.

▶ Cost, documentation, and customer support

Cost of these tools, as mentioned, can range from free to many tens of thousands of dollars. Most tools, however, are in the few-hundred-dollar price range. As with all software packages, documentation for tools varies drastically, in both its length and its quality. The only way you can assess documentation quality is through your hands-on use of the tool and its materials. Customer support also varies widely across tools; many of these tools are from brand-new companies that have never sold commercial software and don't have a good idea of the commitment needed to provide adequate customer support. Some new companies, though, do provide very good customer support in the form of hotlines and help desks.

11.7.2 Detailed Approach to Evaluating Tools

Because there has been so much attention focused in the past few years on how to compare and evaluate user interface development tools, we have developed a procedure that uses a standardized technique to quantitatively evaluate and compare these tools. Hundreds of requests attest to the need for it. The results of the procedure are *quantifiable criteria* for systematically and consistently evaluating and comparing user interface development tools. Following is an overview of this procedure, with representative results from a tool comparison done with the first version of the procedure (Hix & Schulman, 1991). A second, greatly extended version has been developed but has not yet been validated, so it is not discussed here.

The procedure revolves around hands-on use of all tools to be evaluated and the completion of a 58-page form-based checklist. The general procedure is shown in Figure 11.1.

The form-based checklist is a matrix of three dimensions:

- *Functionality* dimension—This indicates what the tool can do—that is, what interaction styles, techniques, and features can be produced by the tool.
- *Usability* dimension—This indicates how well the user of the tool can get the tool to perform its possible functions, in terms of ease of use and human performance.
- *Specification/implementation techniques* dimension—This indicates the techniques an interface developer must use in the tool to produce an individual function.

An important point must be emphasized here: This procedure evaluates tools, *not* tool products (i.e., interfaces). Several requests have come from people who thought this was for evaluating interfaces themselves. While it could certainly be adapted to that purpose, that is not its intention, and it is not offered as a means for evaluating interfaces.

The *functionality dimension* is organized into three sections. The major categories and some of the subcategories of each of these sections are briefly presented here:

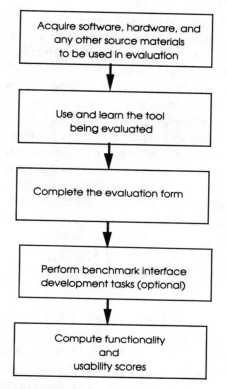

Figure 11.1. Procedure for tool evaluation. From Hix & Schulman, Human-Computer Interface Development Tools: A Methodology for Their Evaluation, *Communications of the ACM*, pp. 74–87.

- *Types of interfaces* a tool supports
  * Interaction styles (e.g., menus, forms, windows, multimedia)
  * Features of interfaces (e.g., graphics, animation, transitions, audio, video)
  * Hardware devices (input and output devices)
- *Types of support* provided for the general process of interface development (e.g., rapid prototyping, methodology, formative evaluation data collection and analysis, database management system)
- *General characteristics* of a tool (e.g., integration, reusability, extensibility, modifiability)

Each subcategory is further decomposed into items, as appropriate (e.g., 15 types of menus, 20 input devices, and 9 rapid prototyping items)

The *usability dimension* of a tool's evaluation is measured by two methods. First, *subjective evaluation* measures ease of use for each of the three sections of the functionality dimension. Only for each function the tool can produce, the evaluator indicates on the form whether it was difficult, adequate, or easy to use the tool to produce that function. These levels are indicated by a frowning face, a bland face, and a smiling face, respectively. To reduce individual evaluators' interpretation of the terms difficult, adequate, and easy, each face usability icon is defined in some detail. Second, *objective evaluation* measures human performance with a tool; an evaluator uses the tool to perform benchmark interface development tasks that are appropriate for the intended development environment in which the tool will be used. Typically, an evaluator should perform the same benchmark tasks with each tool, if the functionality of each permits.

The *specification/implementation techniques dimension* includes direct manipulation, coding in a textual language, and other techniques such as tabular manipulation, form-filling, and rule-based definitions.

Because the procedure produces quantifiable results (numbers), calculations must be performed once the evaluation form is completed. This can be done either manually or using an electronic spreadsheet. Numeric results include

- *Functionality ratings*—These indicate the number of interface functions the tool supports. These are calculated as the percentage of the total number of functions on the form that are possible with a tool.
- *Usability ratings*—These indicate the ease of use with which possible functions can be produced with the tool. These are calculated considering only those functions that are possible with the tool. The tool evaluator chooses from the three-value scale (consisting of a frowning face, a bland face, and a smiling face, for indicating low, moderate, and high usability, respectively). Then by assigning a 1 for each frowning face selected, a 2 for each bland face, and a 3 for each smiling face, the average rating earned by a tool is expressed as the percentage of the highest possible usability rating.
- *Specification/implementation technique ratings*—These indicate the degree to which a technique is used in the tool for producing possible functions. These are calculated as the percentage of use of a specific technique relative to all possible techniques.

We wanted to determine whether this procedure is a good instrument for evaluating interface development tools. In particular, it is important that the procedure provide *reliable* results; that is, if you use the form, and two other people also use the form to evaluate the same tool, the results that all three of you get should be statistically similar. Otherwise, the results are due to chance, rather than reliability of the procedure across different tool evaluators. In order to determine whether the procedure is indeed reliable, we evaluated three tools as part of an empirical study to assess the first version of the evaluation form (Hix & Schulman, 1991). The three tools evaluated were

- Bricklin's *Demo*™ (version 1)
- *HyperCard*™ (version 1.2.1)
- SmethersBarnes *Prototyper*™ (version 1)

These tools were chosen because they support the development of different application types, and therefore would be expected to have different functionality and usability. Demo™, for example, is IBM-compatible and is useful primarily for developing sequential, non-direct manipulation interfaces. Prototyper™ runs on the Macintosh™ and is specifically for developing Macintosh™-style interfaces. Hypercard™, while not specifically an interface development tool, is ubiquitous and has a fair number of interface development features.

In the first stage of the empirical study, six participants trained themselves on each of two tools, so that, in a fully counterbalanced design, four people were evaluating each tool. It took an average of 6 to 10 hours for a participant to learn each tool. In the second stage, a few baseline tasks were administered to all participants, to perform using each of the tools they had learned, to ensure a common minimum level of expertise of each person with each of the two tools they had learned. In the third stage, all participants completed the evaluation form for each of their tools, which took about three hours per tool.

The mean summary results, calculated as a percentage, of functionality and usability ratings for the three sections of the evaluated version of the form are shown in Table 11.1.

The interpretation of these values is, for example, that HyperCard™ produces 70% of all types of interfaces listed on the form, with a usability rating of 87% for those types.

The procedure also produces more detailed numbers for each of these three sections. For example, Table 11.2 shows mean summary results, again as a percentage, of functionality and usability for the first section listed in Table 11.1, the types of interfaces the tools can produce.

Interpretation here is again simple: There are 14 kinds of menus listed on the form; Demo™ can produce 82% of them, and 73% of the 12 types of forms, with a usability of 78% and 76%, respectively. Therefore, Demo™ might be said to have good functionality and good usability for menus and forms. Demo's™ support of different kinds of hardware, however, is not very good.

We drew two kinds of conclusions from the empirical reliability study: conclusions about the tools themselves, and conclusions about the procedure. Regarding

TABLE 11.1. MEAN SUMMARY RESULTS (%) OF FUNCTIONALITY AND USABILITY RATINGS FOR ALL THREE SECTIONS OF THE EVALUATION FORM

	Demo		Hypercard		Prototyper	
	Functionality	Usability	Functionality	Usability	Functionality	Usability
Types of interfaces	52	82	70	87	46	93
Types of support	56	65	76	82	38	74
General characteristics	28	61	50	83	31	75

From Hix & Schulman, Human-Computer Interface Development Tools: A Methodology for Their Evaluation, *Communications of the ACM*, pp. 74–87.

TABLE 11.2. TYPES OF INTERACTION STYLES AND FEATURES THE TOOLS CAN PRODUCE: MEAN SUMMARY RESULTS (%) OF FUNCTIONALITY AND USABILITY RATINGS

	No. of Items	Demo		Hypercard		Prototyper	
		Functionality	Usability	Functionality	Usability	Functionality	Usability
Interaction styles							
Menus	14	82	78	84	82	66	93
Forms	12	73	76	90	97	54	93
Typed input strings	4	19	100	69	68	19	100
Windows	3	59	92	75	81	83	91
Features of interfaces	27	46	71	84	92	37	84
Hardware devices							
Input devices	17	18	89	20	99	12	100
Output devices	7	71	78	64	85	53	92

From Hix & Schulman, Human-Computer Interface Development Tools: A Methodology for Their Evaluation, *Communications of the ACM*, pp. 74–87.

the tools themselves, based on the numeric results, HyperCard™ has significantly higher functionality for types of interaction styles and features a tool can produce than Demo™ or Prototyper™. This was reasonable because HyperCard™ is a more general-purpose tool. Prototyper™ is more usable in producing various types of interaction styles and features; again this was reasonable because Prototyper™ runs on a Macintosh™ and might therefore be expected to be easier to use. HyperCard™ also runs on a Macintosh™, of course, but its greater functionality may actually interfere with, and therefore lower, its usability. HyperCard™ provides more types of support, followed by Demo™ and then Prototyper™, and HyperCard™ has higher usability for those types of support.

While the results about the tools were inherently interesting and were presented here to give you some feeling for how the evaluation procedure is used, results about the reliability of the evaluation procedure were actually of more interest in this empirical study because that had been its purpose in the first place. Across-evaluator results were surprisingly similar. A statistic (Cronbach's alpha) that is a measure of internal consistency was used to determine whether the procedure was reliable. Some investigation showed that the differences in reliability were from interpretation of glossary definitions and the expertise level of different evaluators. In particular, despite the inclusion of a glossary to help reduce individual interpretation of items on the form, there were still differences of opinion about what a particular term meant. Also, when some functions were not explicitly or easily possible, some evaluators used intuition and creativity to produce that feature in a sometimes obscure manner. The checklist on which the evaluation procedure is based guides an evaluator in evaluating tools but can also narrow the set of functions evaluated for a tool. That is, because the checklist is so lengthy, an evaluator is not likely to think of anything else that is not on the checklist as a possible tool feature that might need to be considered.

In summary, the numeric ratings from this procedure provide reliable numbers as guidelines for evaluating and comparing tools but do not give absolute answers. It is important not to misconstrue the procedure's focus on quantitative results. Summary ratings, such as those shown here, are only high-level results; details of the form must usually be examined to determine where the summary numbers came from, and to help in making any final decisions. This evaluation procedure provides data to be used in decision making, but those data do not mandate final decisions. However, results of reliability testing showed that two or more evaluators, using this form and procedure, would be expected to get very similar results for evaluating the same tool, making it a reliable instrument for evaluating user interface development tools and ultimately providing useful data to be used in their selection.

REFERENCES

Hix, D. & Schulman, R. S. (1991). Human–Computer Interface Development Tools: A Methodology for Their Evaluation. *Communications of the ACM, 34*(3), 74–87.

Myers, B. A. (1993). State of the Art in User Interface Software Tools. In H. R. Hartson & D. Hix (Ed.), *Advances in Human–Computer Interaction*, Vol. 2 (pp. 11–28). Norwood, NJ: Ablex.

Smith, D. C., Irby, C., Kimball, R., Verplank, W., & Harslem, E. (1982). Designing the Star User Interface. *BYTE, 7*(4), 242–282.

≡ 12

Making It Work:
Ensuring Usability
in Your Development
Environment

12.1   WHAT HAS BEEN COVERED IN THIS BOOK?

"I've been taught to interface to databases, to interface to networks, to interface software to hardware, and to interface software to software—but I've never been taught to interface to the user!" This comment from an interface developer drives home the dramatic need for education in the trenches on how to develop an interface with high usability. That has been precisely the goal for this book; it has presented material about the *product*—the user interface itself—and the *process*—the methodology, life cycle, and techniques by which an interaction design should be developed in order to ensure that it has high usability.

In particular, it has presented a representative overview of human factors material about the product, including

- General user interaction *guidelines* and how to produce a customized style guide for your project
- *Interaction styles* and guidelines about when to use each of them in a design

For the process, this book went into much more depth about major activities in developing an interaction design, including

- An iterative, *evaluation-centered star life cycle* for user interaction development, and its relationship to software engineering
- A *behavioral, user-centered representation technique*, the UAN, for writing down the design of a direct manipulation interface
- *Usability specifications* as a metric for quantitatively establishing usability goals for an interaction design, and as a technique for controlling the iterative life cycle
- *Rapid prototyping* as an approach to getting users to try out an interaction design early in its development, while there is still time to make changes
- *Formative evaluation* of an interaction design, early and continually throughout its development, having representative users performing representative tasks, and applying cost/importance and other analyses to determine which modifications will have the greatest effect on improved usability of an interaction design

Finally, the book concluded with an overview of

- *User interface development tools*, and a quantitative approach to their evaluation and comparison

In sum, we have addressed consideration for design of the content of quality interfaces, and how to provide an environment and process within which quality interfaces can be developed. Having completed this material, you should now be able to develop a more usable human–computer interface by

- Using human factors guidelines and behavioral representation techniques for interaction design
- Establishing usability specifications for an interaction design and testing the design against them as it evolves
- Participating in prototyping, formative evaluation, and iterative refinement of an interaction design
- Understanding user interface development tools

12.2   BUT I CAN'T POSSIBLY DO ALL THIS

Perhaps at this point, having worked your way through the material in each chapter and having dutifully performed the exercises, you're thinking, "I really like these ideas, but I don't know where to begin. There's just too much new stuff to try to do." Or as someone once said at the end of a three-day class, "I know just enough now to be dangerous!" You're certainly not alone if you're feeling this way. This final chapter should help you get started with putting these ideas to work in your user interface development environment.

First, your biggest challenge may be not technical at all, but will probably be *selling all these new-fangled ideas to management!* After all, *you* can do anything that *management* wants! This selling requires workable techniques to convince managers that they should let you try these ideas out. They are surely familiar with software engineering principles and paradigms and probably even encourage and/or enforce their use. Managers also may have heard a few user interface development buzzwords, such as "user-centered design," or "iterative refinement," or "rapid prototyping." What they probably don't realize, however, is that, by necessity, the user interaction development process is not at all linear but is highly and continually iterative. This, in turn, changes just about everything managers hold dear, including scheduling, control, organizational roles, territoriality, project management, communication, test facilities, and tools.

The material presented in this book is, in fact, the basis for controllability, accountability, and quantitative methods that are so important, and rightfully so, to managers. If you were around in the days when structured programming and software engineering were emerging as the accepted approaches to software development, you will remember that there was the inevitable opposition to it, largely because people claimed there wasn't time to do all those things that software engineering espoused. Today, the same argument about why proper engineering of user interfaces can't be done is bearing less and less weight as people realize there's not time *not* to do the activities that it incorporates. Remember the old saying: "There's never time to do it right, but always time to do it over."

As mentioned in Chapter 1, managers may not be aware that there is a problem with user interfaces. They may, in fact, view these techniques as a solution to a nonexistent problem. You've surely heard comments about how well the product is selling, or how the users aren't complaining about it, or how it incorporates the latest new gee-whiz interaction style or device. These comments can be mistaken for indicators that the product's user interface is good. This cannot possibly be the case, though; look at all the software that has sold millions of copies, despite some really horrible user interfaces. It is important to remember the "personware" factor and to realize that more and more successful interfaces are being developed using the techniques presented here because these techniques have been shown to work. The field of user interfaces is highly volatile, a constantly moving target. This means that, as Lewis Carroll wrote in *Alice in Wonderland*, "You have to keep running just to stay in the same place!"

12.3   SO WHERE DO I BEGIN?

OK, so you're convinced you want to try these new ideas, but you're not quite sure where or how to start. Throughout, this book has included hints on how to make all this work in your user interface development environment. This chapter pulls together, in one place, several important pragmatic suggestions.

The single most important suggestion, already made at various points throughout the book, is the following:

▶ Start small.

Choose an interface development project that is small enough so that you won't be overwhelmed from the beginning as you apply these new techniques. If you are working on only one very large interface project, choose some reasonable portion of it. Select, for example, a smallish subsystem of your large project, or a few of its most important functions and features. The interface project (or part of the project) you choose should be one that has some visibility, but that is not extremely high risk. Expect some rough spots in the beginning, and warn your managers of this. Tell them exactly what you intend to try and hope to accomplish the first time or two you try out this new approach, and within what time frame.

▶ Produce only a few usability specifications the first time you try them.

Along the lines of starting small, the first time you try to develop and monitor usability specifications, do just a few of them, say two based on objective measures and one based on subjective measures, just as you did in the exercise in Chapter 8. Developing reasonable usability specifications comes only from practice. You can best learn how to produce them by making an educated guess at a few, and then seeing how your observed results compare to the specifications you've set. Don't try to do too many for an interface until you've got a feeling for them. If you try to produce and monitor too many usability specifications before you are comfortable with them, you will become overwhelmed and will probably abandon any reasonable use of them. Show management the specifications, and show them the results of using them.

▶ Prototype and evaluate only a core set of functions the first few times you attempt to do formative evaluation.

If the initial prototype you develop tries to encompass too much of the interaction design, you will probably spend too much time developing it, and you will become overwhelmed if you attempt to evaluate all parts of it. For your first few prototypes and subsequent formative evaluation cycles, incorporate a core set of functions, those functions without which a user cannot perform useful work with the system being developed. Keeping the prototype small will allow you to keep the formative evaluation process manageable, until you become more knowledgeable and confident with it. Later prototypes can, and of course should, include much more of the system functionality.

▶ Find someone with whom you can apprentice.

If possible, as you are getting started, find a user interaction developer, in your organization or elsewhere, with whom you can work closely to find out what that person does. Just following an expert around for a while can give you a great deal of confidence when you start to try some of the user interaction development activities on your own. It's especially important for you to sit in on design sessions and observe usability evaluation sessions with users. In a small company, it may be hard to find a knowledgeable person with whom you can apprentice; you may be the resident expert! In most large companies, however, you should be able to find someone with whom you can work for a while.

▶ Begin building a user interface development team of appropriately skilled people.

Get at least one person on the development team who is skilled (or trainable) in user interaction development. Maybe this person is you! If it is not possible, for whatever reason, to get a full-time person, at least get a part-time (at the very minimum, a half-time) person. Give that person a title—user interface engineer or usability engineer or interaction developer or usability specialist, for example. Give the person primary responsibility for design, evaluation, and iterative refinement of the user interface. Also give that person the authority to carry out the responsibilities of the job; don't just give lip service, never once intending to listen to what the person says. Later, as the importance of this role becomes more recognized and appreciated within your organization, you can add other people to your emerging user interface development team.

▶ Get a commitment from development team members to try these new ideas.

Those members of the team who are not responsible for developing the user interface should be made aware of what those who are responsible for it will be doing, and why. Get at least some level of commitment from these noninterface people for the ideas you'll be trying out, so they will know what to expect. You want them on your side, even if a bit skeptically, rather than wondering what you're doing and why on earth you're doing it.

▶ Get training for development team members.

Get appropriate training about details of these new techniques and tools for members of the development team, especially those who are being given responsibility for the user interaction development. Even those who are not directly involved in user interface development can benefit from some formal training because—especially if they are software engineers—these ideas will be dramatically different from those they espouse. Having all members of the team with a common baseline of knowledge in these techniques is helpful in making it all work. There are many individuals and groups who will provide such training in-house, if you have enough people to warrant this, or you can send people to one of the commercial organizations that provides user interaction development training.

▶ Set up a usability lab.

Find an enclosed (or enclosable) corner, a broom closet, a vacant office, some space somewhere, and make it your official usability lab. This single activity, along with getting a user interface specialist on the development team, can have a huge impact on attitude toward these new ideas. Put a big, bold sign on the door. People will wonder what's going on in there, and they will start asking questions about what a usability lab is, and what it is to be used for. This will begin raising awareness about the increasing importance of usability in your project and organization—good PR! Get in the minimal equipment recommended in Chapter 10 (on setting up a usability lab), and then—starting small—use it to do some formative evaluations of your evolving user interaction design.

▶ Do some kind of observations of users with a prototype of the interaction design.

If you can't get management to agree to let you try all these ideas at once, get them, at a minimum, to let you either go off-site or bring in one or two participants (whichever is most appropriate for your situation), for a short period of time—two hours, half a day, a day. Informally observe people using the system, and give management a short report on your observations. Include in your report the expected impact of making changes to the interaction design based on your observations.

▶ Have developers and managers watch at least one participant from an evaluation session.

Often, developers, even after training, and managers, even after realizing the need for usability, are still reluctant to try the development process presented in this book. One of the best ways to convince both developers and managers that evaluation with users is critical to ensuring usability in your interface is to have them observe some participants. Once you get your usability lab set up, this is easy to do. Schedule a specific time for them come to the lab and watch at least one participant during an evaluation session. If you have a video hookup or a one-way mirror with which they can observe from a different room than where the participant is working, that is best for the participant. If you only have one room, let the observer sit in the room, make them *promise* to be *quiet*, and explain up front to the participant that there is an extra observer in the room. If a developer or manager simply will not come and watch a participant live during an evaluation session, show that person a few short, carefully selected video clips of some sessions. This will go a long way toward convincing skeptics about the payback of these techniques.

▶ Get consulting help when needed, especially during start-up.

By having an expert around while you try these activities the first time or two, you will learn a great deal more about how to do them (and how not to do them), and you will gain skills and confidence that will allow you to continue with subsequent activities yourself. There are two sources of consultants that you can tap. If your organization is large enough, there are probably already people somewhere in it whom you can bring in to help you get started (or, as already suggested, with whom you can apprentice). If not, if you are breaking entirely new ground in your organization by trying these ideas, or if your organization is fairly small, then you may want an outside consultant to help you get started. While this may sound like an expensive proposition, remember what Red Adair, the famous Texas oil-well firefighter said when someone confronted him about his costs for putting out oil-well fires: "If you think the experts are expensive, wait until you bring in the amateurs!"

▶ Generate a success story, no matter how small.

Often, when developers are asked, "What will it take for you to get approval to begin trying some of these new ideas?" they respond, "Failure!" To convince people that these ideas will work, start by showing them failure when the right process is *not* used for developing the user interaction design. Set up some version of the system that is in pretty bad shape, usability-wise, in your usability lab. Make a five-minute videotape of a user having a really terrible time trying to use the interface. Using the techniques presented in this book, revise the interaction design, or at least the worst part of it. Then make another five-minute videotape of a user (the same one is probably better, but a different one would be effective, too) using the revised design to perform the same tasks as in the first videotape. Presumably, of course, the user will love—or at least like and be able to use—the revised design. Show the two video clips to managers, and explain to them the process that got you from the first version to the second one. If your video clips are different enough, they will make the point for you, and dramatically. What managers will usually want to know after such a presentation is, "Why didn't we start ensuring usability with this process before now?" This success story—demonstrating the effectiveness of the process in action—will do more to help sell these ideas than anything else you can do.

▶ If you don't feel comfortable trying a complete cycle the first time, try some parts of a full iteration.

We strongly agree that, as Nielsen (1992) said, "Anything is better than nothing." People often fear they won't be successful the first time they try these techniques. These techniques are so effective that you almost can't lose. Any data you collect from even a short session with a single user is invaluable input that you can use to make improvements in the usability of the interface. Don't be afraid to try these techniques; you will quickly become comfortable with them.

▶ Start a regularly scheduled brown-bag user interface lunch bunch.

Either within your project, or your organization, or your community, start a regular get-together for people interested in user interface development. This kind of a support group can have many purposes, from simply being a forum for commiserating about how bad user interfaces are, or how difficult they are to develop; to serving as a critique group for your or others' emerging interaction designs; to getting advice on some particular development activity; to being an educational forum for presenting and sharing relevant papers, showing videotapes of interest, and so on. Most important, it raises awareness of the attention being paid to the user interface. Publicize it widely, on electronic bulletin boards and any other communication medium you have available. Begin by meeting once a month, then meet more often if interest and attendance warrant it. Instead, perhaps, subgroups with interest in some specific topic(s) may want to meet more than once a month. Many places that have tried this idea have been amazed at how quickly their group has grown and how popular and effective it can be.

▶ Start a small internal newsletter and/or electronic bulletin board specifically related to human–computer interaction and usability.

A nice spin-off to the brown-bag lunch idea is a small newsletter to serve as another forum for exchanging ideas. This newsletter can be published either on paper or electronically (or both). In it, you can talk about actual evaluation sessions, suggest readings from new articles and books, give conference reports, relate success stories—essentially the same kinds of things that you discuss during the brown-bag lunch groups. An internal electronic bulletin board is an excellent medium for exchanging information, asking questions, posting answers, making suggestions, and so on. This kind of communication will greatly increase the visibility of human–computer interaction and usability in your organization.

▶ Encourage attendance at conferences related to human–computer interaction.

The largest annual conference on HCI is the Computer–Human Interaction (CHI, pronounced like the Greek letter χ) Conference on Human Factors in Computing Systems. Its attendance has steadily increased every year since the first one was held in Gaithersburg, Maryland, in 1982. CHI has a variety of activities, including the standard fare of paper presentations, panels, and poster sessions. It also has special interest group (SIG) meetings; impromptu birds-of-a-feather sessions; book exhibits; demonstrations of tools and other applications by both research and commercial groups; and exhibits of unusual, often futuristic, user interface technology. It is probably the single best place to get a large dose of HCI-related work. In addition, the annual User Interface Software and Technology Symposium, or UIST, is a much smaller, single-track forum for exchanging state-of-the-art ideas and results. The Human Factors Society Conference also has many sessions dedicated to user interface presentations. HCI International, Interact, and other conferences also abound.

▶ Get management commitment.

Again, this is your most important nontechnical challenge. First, lay out your usability evaluation plan, at least roughly. Then, have a one-on-one meeting with some key upper-level manager, and convince that person to let you try your plan. If you're prepared and keep the plan pretty simple, chances are very good that you'll get the support you want. Ask this manager to call a meeting to discuss the plan with the development team. Hint: Let the manager run the meeting, as if it's all the manager's idea. If this doesn't work, you run the meeting, but have the manager there to support you.

▶ Focus on the *process*, not just on the product.

Focus on the process of ensuring a usable interface and on the activities that help you accomplish this.

12.4   WHERE SHOULD RESPONSIBILITY FOR ENSURING USABILITY RESIDE?

Applying the appropriate techniques for the process of user interaction development raises the question of where responsibility for ensuring usability should reside in an organization. There are at least three different approaches to this: a team approach, a distributed approach, and a retooling approach.

Typically, a *team approach* is preferable. This gives the development group more ownership of their final product and gives a more integrated approach to development. A somewhat new concept—*cross-functional teams*—espouses inclusion of members with various skills—programming, user interaction design, systems analysis, formative evaluation, documentation, and so on—on a development team. Most team members will participate in more than one activity of the team; that is, they will participate across several functions of the team. So, for example, a programmer may do some user interaction design, and a systems analyst may help with software design.

In one successful instantiation of the team approach, the entire development team was located in close physical proximity with each other. The team consisted of one or more software engineers, user interaction developers, marketing people, graphic artists, human factors engineers, technical writers, and trainers. The usability lab was in the center of the physical space, with team members' offices located around the lab. Some of the most interesting team interaction occurred when software engineers began attending usability evaluation sessions. At first, only one or two attended; as development progressed, there literally was standing room only in the control room of the lab. In fact, all team members were told when usability test sessions were scheduled, and many attended regularly. Everyone was anxious to see how users would respond to the newest cycle of changes to the interface.

In a *distributed approach,* a user interaction developer may serve on several development teams, moving from team to team at appropriate times in the development process. This approach is probably the least desirable of the three because it tends to fragment the process and can stretch the user interaction developer too thin. For example, one human factors engineer was assigned to rotate among 11 different projects with a total of 248 software engineers! This, of course, is an extreme case—so much so that the human factors engineer was relatively ineffective on any of the 11 projects. In a more reasonable situation, say one user interaction developer working with three or four small to medium projects, this person can have an impact on usability of the interface.

In addition to fragmentation, another problem with the distributed approach is a lack of team ownership of the product. Also, the approach is reminiscent of the "priest with a parachute" paradigm mentioned in Chapter 1: The user interaction developer drops in every so often and attempts to make a contribution, but because the interaction developer is not a full-time member of the team, this person may have less respect and therefore less responsibility and authority.

There are a couple of situations in which the distributed approach can have an impact. If there is little or no hope of getting a full-time user interaction developer on a team, then someone even part-time is better than no one at all. Some organizations single out usability evaluation as one activity in the development process that can be effectively performed by a group specializing in usability evaluation, rather than by members of the development team. This usability evaluation group is a group whose service is distributed to development teams throughout an organization.

A *retooling approach* is a sort of combination of the other two approaches and might be a better alternative than the distributed approach when there is no hope of getting a full-time user interaction developer on a team. In this grow-your-own approach, (at least) one person on the development team retools by learning the appropriate skills and taking on responsibility for usability of the team's product. This usability advocate is often a software engineer because there typically are more of them than any other role on a development team. Then, a user interaction developer can interact, as in the distributed approach, across several teams and/or projects, each with its own usability advocate.

The usability advocate, under the guidance of the expert developer, performs many of the activities in the interaction development process, rather than having the user interaction developer trying to do all activities for all the teams with which they both are interacting. As in the distributed approach, the user interaction developer is a consultant to these teams and projects, working with them only part of the time. Now, however, the user interaction developer has the usability advocate with whom to interact, and the advocate has the support of the rest of the team.

There are a couple of cautions in using the retooling approach. First, a little knowledge of the user interaction development process can be dangerous. Usability advocates can quickly get carried away before they fully understand the process. They need to be patient and rely quite heavily on the advice and guidance of the expert user interaction developer consulting with their project, especially in the beginning. Second, if managers see the retooling approach working, they may use it as an excuse to say, "OK, the usability advocate is enough. We don't need specially trained user interaction developers on our team." However, it is often the case that the advocate will, in fact, be instrumental in convincing managers that a full-time user interaction developer is indeed needed in order to ensure usability in the interface. In sum, it is better to have a usability advocate than no one at all on a team, or than a totally fragmented user interaction developer working across too many teams.

12.5   DEVELOPING A PLAN TO ENSURE USABILITY

Even after these suggestions on where to begin, you may still ask, "But *where* do I begin?" To give you some specific guidance in producing a usability plan for your development efforts, we offer the following list of activities, in approximate chronological order, which you will need to consider. It is important to note that this chronological order is very loose because, in fact, many of the listed activities will be performed more than once when you revisit them during various cycles of iteration in the development process.

It is also important to note that this list is neither exhaustive nor detailed. It is just a checklist for guidance to help you remember all the different activities you might consider when formulating your usability plan. It can also help with scheduling for your project, by laying out many of the needed activities for you; then you can decide how to allocate your time among them.

Early Activities

- Perform needs analysis
- Determine user classes
- Interview representatives of user classes
- Develop written user profiles
- Perform a functional analysis
- Develop hierarchical user task structure, based on task analysis
- Extract a delimited set of core tasks from a complete task analysis

Design Activities

- Develop a customized style guide
- Develop a conceptual design
- Develop a detailed design

Usability Specification Activities

- Establish usability specifications
- Define appropriate corresponding benchmark tasks
- Produce appropriate corresponding questionnaires

Prototyping Activities

- Develop pencil-and-paper prototypes to test the conceptual design
- Develop interactive prototypes to test the conceptual design
- Develop pencil-and-paper prototypes to test the design details
- Develop interactive prototypes to test the design details

Formative Evaluation Activities

- Develop the experiment
- Select appropriate participants
- Develop other tasks, as needed, for test sessions
- Establish the protocol and procedures for test sessions
- Pilot test everything in the lab (or the field)
- Conduct evaluation sessions
- Collect data
- Analyze quantitative data
- Analyze qualitative data

Redesign Activities

- Determine changes to be made in the design
- Implement changes in the design

Iteration Activities

- Repeat any and all of the preceding activities until the usability specifications are met

12.6   PARTING WORDS

Like just about everything else in the 1980s, developers of interactive systems seemed to concentrate on producing the greatest possible functionality, making their systems bigger, but unfortunately not necessarily better, at least for their users. That decade of functionality often left the user in the dust; at times, all the nifty functions and features, bells and whistles available in many software packages actually obscured the basic tasks a user wished to accomplish. Now, in the 1990s, we are observing, along with an economic and political refocusing, a refocusing of interactive system developers toward users. This is happening, at least in part, because time-tested and well-understood techniques are finally available that allow developers to ensure usability in their interfaces. Those techniques are what have been presented in this book. The 1990s are emerging as the decade of usability and accessibility.

There is a great deal of both art and science in user interaction development. Both are needed to produce an effective, usable interface. *Art* is needed, to encourage creativity and innovation in interfaces. *Science* is needed, to give structure and organization to an otherwise seemingly open-loop, endless process. Until recently, there has been a great deal of hand-waving, and too little science applied to the design and evaluation of user interfaces. The guidelines, methods, techniques, and tools presented in this book provide the foundation for making development of a user interface a much more scientific process. This incredible "machine that changed the world" with its powers to compute can perhaps now have an even more dramatic impact, as developers learn how to make it communicate more effectively by ensuring usability of the user interface.

REFERENCE

Nielsen, J. (1992). Finding Usability Problems Through Heuristic Evaluation. *Proceedings of CHI Conference on Human Factors in Computing Systems*, New York: ACM, 373–380.

Index